Sensor-Based Human Activity Recognition

Sensor-Based Human Activity Recognition

Guest Editor

Kimiaki Shirahama

MDPI

Basel • Beijing • Wuhan • Barcelona • Belgrade • Novi Sad • Cluj • Manchester

Guest Editor
Kimiaki Shirahama
Department of Information Systems
Design
Doshisha University
Kyoto
Japan

Editorial Office
MDPI AG
Grosspeteranlage 5
4052 Basel, Switzerland

This is a reprint of the Special Issue, published open access by the journal *Sensors* (ISSN 1424-8220), freely accessible at: https://www.mdpi.com/journal/sensors/special_issues/2VW3F3Z9V0.

For citation purposes, cite each article independently as indicated on the article page online and as indicated below:

Lastname, A.A.; Lastname, B.B. Article Title. *Journal Name* **Year**, *Volume Number*, Page Range.

ISBN 978-3-7258-7072-1 (Hbk)
ISBN 978-3-7258-7073-8 (PDF)
https://doi.org/10.3390/books978-3-7258-7073-8

Contents

About the Editor

Kimiaki Shirahama

Kimiaki Shirahama is a professor at the Department of Information Systems Design, Doshisha University, Japan. He is leading Co-Creation Informatics Laboratory (CCILAB). His research focuses on the application of artificial intelligence to multimedia data analysis. In particular, his research interests include multimedia data processing, machine learning, data mining, and sensor-based human activity recognition. His recent research projects span large-scale video retrieval, extensions of large language models for video captioning and stock prediction, applications of diffusion models to visual feature space analysis and imputation of missing modality data, and human–AI coordination based on reinforcement learning. In 2012, 2023, and 2024, Prof. Shirahama's team achieved the top performances at the Semantic Indexing (SIN) lite task, the Medical Instructional Question Generation (MIQG) task, and the Query-Focused Instructional Step Captioning (QFISC) task, respectively, at the NIST-sponsored TREC Video Retrieval Evaluation (TRECVID).

sensors

MDPI

Article

DaRA Dataset: Combining Wearable Sensors, Location Tracking, and Process Knowledge for Enhanced Human Activity and Human Context Recognition in Warehousing

Friedrich Niemann [1,2,*], Fernando Moya Rueda [3], Moh'd Khier Al Kfari [4], Nilah Ravi Nair [1,2], Dustin Schauten [3], Veronika Kretschmer [5], Stefan Lüdtke [4] and Alice Kirchheim [1,2,5]

1 Chair of Material Handling and Warehousing, TU Dortmund University, LogistikCampus, Joseph-von-Fraunhofer-Str. 2-4, 44227 Dortmund, Germany; nilah.nair@tu-dortmund.de (N.R.N.); alice.kirchheim@tu-dortmund.de (A.K.)
2 Lamarr Institute for Machine Learning and Artificial Intelligence, 44227 Dortmund, Germany
3 MotionMiners GmbH, 44227 Dortmund, Germany; fernando.moya@motionminers.com (F.M.R.); dustin.schauten@motionminers.com (D.S.)
4 Institute for Visual and Analytic Computing, University of Rostock, 18055 Rostock, Germany; mohd.kfari@uni-rostock.de (M.K.A.K.); stefan.luedtke@uni-rostock.de (S.L.)
5 Fraunhofer Institute for Material Flow and Logistics IML, 44227 Dortmund, Germany; veronika.kretschmer@iml.fraunhofer.de
* Correspondence: friedrich.niemann@tu-dortmund.de

Abstract

Understanding human movement in industrial environments requires more than simple step counts—it demands contextual information to interpret activities and enhance workflows. Key factors such as location and process context are essential. However, research on context-sensitive human activity recognition is limited by the lack of publicly available datasets that include both human movement and contextual labels. Our work introduces the DaRA dataset to address this research gap. DaRA comprises over 109 h of video footage, including 32 h from wearable first-person cameras and 77 h from fixed third-person cameras. In a laboratory environment replicating a realistic warehouse, scenarios such as order picking, packaging, unpacking, and storage were captured. The movements of 18 subjects were captured using inertial measurement units, Bluetooth devices for indoor localization, wearable first-person cameras, and fixed third-person cameras. DaRA offers detailed annotations with 12 class categories and 207 class labels covering human movements and contextual information such as process steps and locations. A total of 15 annotators and 8 revisers contributed over 1572 h in annotation and 361 h in revision. High label quality is reflected in Light's Kappa values ranging from 78.27% to 99.88%. Therefore, DaRA provides a robust, multimodal foundation for human activity and context recognition in industrial settings.

Keywords: dataset; logistics; wearable; inertial measurement unit; Bluetooth; video; third-person view; first-person view; human activity recognition; human context recognition

1. Introduction

Human activity recognition (HAR) from wearable sensor data is a valuable tool in areas such as sports performance analysis, rehabilitation support or smart homes [1]. Beyond everyday and health-related scenarios, sensor-based HAR is highly relevant in industry. In particular, intralogistics environments present a strong use case, with workers performing tasks such as picking, transporting, packing, unpacking, and storing goods. Here, HAR can serve as a foundation for identifying inefficiencies in workflows, optimizing warehouse layouts, and improving worker ergonomics [2].

The dominant approach to HAR involves mapping sensor signals to activities of interest using machine learning models, such as convolutional neural networks (CNNs) [3,4]. These models rely on well-annotated training datasets. Over the past few years, several datasets targeting manual work in intralogistics have been published, including OpenPack [5,6] and AndyData-lab-onePerson [7,8]. While these datasets have enabled initial progress, their activities are usually restricted to predefined lists of discrete activity classes. In practice, however, many industrial tasks cannot be sufficiently described by a single activity label. Depending on the research or application goal, additional layers of information may be required; e.g., coarse semantic definitions of activities called *attributes* [9] can be used to refer to body postures and sub-activities of both hands, as in the LARa dataset [10], or contextual information, as in the CAARL dataset [11].

The authors of [12] describe activities as entities that take place within a context but can also exist independently of it. Based on this understanding, we distinguish between human movements as the foundation of HAR (e.g., walking, grasping, sitting, bending) and context, which is not strictly required for HAR but can serve as additional information to understand the human movement—human context recognition (HCR). Context includes, among other things, information about the location, time, process, identity, and conditions of subjects and information about the physical environment [13,14]. **Context information** can be categorized into the following:

- **Sensor data**, for example, positional data of subjects and objects;
- **Class labels**, including the location of a subject and its tools, the subject's process steps, or an order ID;
- **Knowledge**, such as order composition or an ideal process flow.

Existing datasets do not fully capture these aspects. Additionally, these datasets are based on simplified, controlled conditions, limiting their applicability to realistic warehouse operations. This lack of detailed, context-rich data hinders progress toward context-sensitive HAR and HCR in industrial settings.

To address this gap, we present the **DaRA** (**D**ata Fusion for **a**dvanced **R**esearch in industrial **A**pplications) dataset [15], a novel multimodal dataset for HAR and HCR in intralogistics. DaRA was recorded in a laboratory environment replicating a realistic warehouse, using multiple sensors. It features a distinctive hierarchical annotation scheme with 12 class categories and 207 class labels, covering not only human movements but also contextual information such as location and process stage. This level of detail and quality makes DaRA a unique contribution to the field. An overview of the DaRA dataset is provided in Table 1, and its positioning within the taxonomy of HAR datasets is shown in Figure A1.

https://doi.org/10.3390/s26020739

Table 1. Overview of the DaRA dataset (BPMN = Business Process Model and Notation, IMUs = Inertial Measurement Units).

General	Download DaRA Dataset	[15]
	Recording Environment	semi-controlled laboratory (Section 3.1.1)
	Scenario	warehousing: order picking, packaging, unpacking, storage (Section 3.1.2)
		BPMN (Section 3.3.2)
	Dataset Size	31:55:26 h of recording time (Section 3.3.3)
	Data Availability/Usage	Section 3.6
Sensor (Section 3.1.3)	Action Cameras Fixed Cameras IMUs Beacons	1 camera per subject, 29.97 fps, 32 h 6 cameras, 29.97 fps, 77 h 6 IMUs per subject (2 sets), 100 Hz 57 beacons, 10 Hz
Subjects (Section 3.2)	Number Age Weight Height	18 (4 female, 14 male) 21 to 67 years (avg. 37.4 years) 62 to 103 kg (avg. 81.1 kg) 160 to 187 cm (avg. 175.8 cm)
Annotation	Class Categories (Section 3.4)	12 categories with human movements and context
	Class Labels (Section 3.4)	207 labels, 68,174 label representations
	Annotation (Section 3.5.2)	1572 h manual annotated by 15 domain experts and trained internal annotators
	Revision (Section 3.5.3)	361 h manual revision by 8 experts and automated plausibility checks
	Label Quality (Section 4.1)	Light's Kappa from 78.27% to 99.88% depending on the class category

2. Related Work

The DaRA is a rich dataset for HAR in logistic applications, composed of time-series recordings from Inertial Measurement Units (IMUs), Bluetooth Low Energy (BLE), and videos; it also contains detailed annotations for processes, activities, locations, and movements. This dataset will be relevant for time-series-based HAR, video-based HAR, localization using BLE and process predictions. For justifying and describing DaRA's characteristics, we dive into HAR methods in logistics environments, HAR and context and HAR datasets.

2.1. HAR and Context

HAR can significantly benefit from integrating contextual information, enhancing performance and robustness by leveraging additional data sources that provide insight into the environment or task structure. For example, high-level process states can be used to inform HAR models, improving their ability to distinguish between visually or kinematically similar activities that occur in different contexts [16]. Similarly, location data and information about objects being handled (e.g., picking cart, item, computer) contribute valuable semantic context that refines the outcomes of activity recognition [11]. First-person view approaches for detecting and classifying objects enable more accurate recognition of object-related activities [17].

The authors in [9,18] highlight the importance of semantic attribute annotations for HAR, which support transfer learning and context-aware behavior modeling. Attribute-based activity representations, introduced from computer vision, enable zero-shot learning

https://doi.org/10.3390/s26020739

and class generalization, with approaches using uncertainty sampling and evolutionary algorithms achieving performance comparable to or better than traditional class-based methods [19].

Symbolic HAR methods offer an additional way for incorporating context. They represent human activities and their dependencies using symbolic structures, such as rules, graphs, or ontologies. For instance, some systems model the causal structure of activities with precondition-effect rules. This means certain actions can only happen when specific object states or locations are present [20–22]. Contextual information can be integrated into the observation model of these methods, which links sensor input to system states.

2.2. HAR Method in Production and Logistics

Production and logistics have human-centered processes, thereby requiring consideration of HAR models that help gain insights into human movements and the ergonomics of individuals. For example, measuring the proportion of different activities during work has been used for optimization tasks such as reducing walking distances or minimizing waiting times for order picking and warehouse processes [9,13,23,24]. Another example is recognizing worker movements, such as bending or carrying heavy items repeatedly, which is beneficial for ergonomic assessment of the worker's day. Through HAR, such repetitions of these activities can be identified and used to build alert systems that guide workers toward ergonomic practices. Recognition of activities is also relevant for documenting scenarios with repetitive tasks, where a register of activities is to be kept without compromising subjects' identities [25].

Companies such as MotionMiners (https://www.motionminers.com/, accessed on 18 January 2026) and ProGlove (https://proglove.com/, accessed on 18 January 2026) are already deploying HAR methods in logistics environments. These systems use wearables or handheld devices to capture worker movements and provide task-specific assistance.

2.3. HAR Datasets

The majority of publicly available HAR datasets are focused on three application domains: healthcare/rehabilitation/nursing, exercise and athletic performance, and smart homes and Ambient Assisted Living (AAL) [26]. These domains primarily encompass the recognition of the following:

- Activities of Daily Living (ADL) [27] like cooking, eating and drinking, sleep behavior, and step counting (e.g., *Daily Log* [28,29], *ILMHAR* [30,31]), *SLAM HAR* [32,33]);
- Locomotion (e.g., *RealWorld* [34,35], *UMAFall* [36,37], *HuGaDB* [38,39]);
- Gestures (e.g., *HCI gestures* [40,41], *Hand Gesture* [42,43], *LaRED* [44], *HaGRID* [45,46]);
- Dancing (e.g., *3DLife/Huawei ACM MM Grand Challenge 2011* [47,48], *HDM12 Dance* [49], *Martial Arts, Dancing and Sports (MADS) Dataset* [50,51]);
- The analysis of sports activities (e.g., *BodyAttack Fitness* [40,41], *UMONS-TAICHI* [52,53], *UCF Sports* [54,55], *Hang-Time* [56,57]);
- Fall detection, particularly in individuals with physical impairments (e.g., *UMAFall* [36,37], *Teruel-Fall (tFall)* [58,59], *SisFall* [60,61], *Fall-UP* [62,63]).

In contrast, other application domains of HAR, such as traffic and mobility, entertainment and gaming, behavioral research and psychology, robotics and human–machine interaction, as well as security and surveillance, are comparatively underrepresented in the freely available datasets. The industry domain, comprising production and logistics, has become increasingly relevant since 2017, leading to a growing number of available datasets in this field (see Table 2).

https://doi.org/10.3390/s26020739

Table 2. Overview of HAR datasets with application domains in industry (production and logistics). Note that the abbreviation *MoCap* refers to the motion capture system, *RGB* refers to colored videos, and *RGB-D* refers to colored videos along with depth information. Columns where the information is unclear or wasn't obtained are marked with a '-'. ✓ indicates that the dataset is publicly available. Reference is abbreviated as Ref. and Number as Nr.

	Dataset				Sensors		Subjects	Recording	Labels		Annotation
Name	Ref.	Year	Public	Size	Nr.	Type	Nr.	Environment	Category	Nr. and Type	
MPP Dataset	[64,65]	2025	✓	3:23 h	2	inertial	4	real-world	human–object interactions	7 activity classes	domain expert
IHAD$_v$ 1	[66]	2023	-	459,180 images	1	visual (RGB)	-	controlled	human–object interaction	12 activity classes	not mentioned
HRI30	[67,68]	2022	✓	15 GB	1	visual	11	controlled	body pose, human–object and human–robot interactions	30 actions	manually annotated
CoAx	[69,70]	2022	✓	1:58 h	1	visual (RGB-D)	6	controlled	human–object and human–robot interactions	10 action and 8 object annotations	action and object annotation
OpenPack	[5,6]	2022	✓	53.8 h	20	visual, inertial, physiological/biosensors, other	16	controlled	human-to-object interactions	11 activity classes	expert
InHARD-DT	[71,72]	2022	✓	25.8 GB	34	visual (RGB, MoCap), inertial	12	virtual	human–object and human–robot interactions	18 event/action classes	auto-labelled
HA4M	[73,74]	2022	✓	4.1 TB	1	visual (RGB, RGB-D, Infrared)	41	controlled	human–object interaction	12 actions	manual annotation
Assembly101	[75,76]	2022	✓	513 h	13	visual	53	controlled	human-to-object interactions	1380 fine-grained, 202 coarse actions	trained annotators
COVERED	[77,78]	2022	✓	860 MB	1	visual	-	real-world	postures, human–robot interactions	6 semantic segmentation classes	

https://doi.org/10.3390/s26020739

Table 2. *Cont.*

Name	Dataset Ref.	Year	Public	Size	Nr.	Sensors Type	Subjects Nr.	Recording Environment	Labels Category	Labels Nr. and Type	Annotation
CAARL	[11,79]	2021	✓	2:33 h	46	visual (RGB, MoCap), inertial	2	controlled	postures/static activities, human-to-object interaction, locomotion	8 activity classes, 19 attributes	annotation tool SARA
WGD	[80]	2021	-	-	8	visual (MoCap, RGB)	8	controlled	posture, human–object interactions	-	-
Physical Human–Robot Contact Detection	[81,82]	2021	✓	79.9 MB	2	visual (RGB-D)	-	controlled	human–robot interactions, postures	5 actions	-
ABC Bento	[83,84]	2021	✓	499 MB	20	visual (MoCap)	4	controlled	human-to-object interaction	10 labels	participants are designing methods
InHARD	[85,86]	2020	✓	51.6 GB	35	visual (MoCap, RGB)	16	semi-controlled	human–object interaction	14 low-level, 74 high-level action classes	annotation tool Anvil
LARa	[10,87–89]	2020	✓	12:6 h	54	visual (RGB, MoCap), inertial	16	controlled	postures/static activities, human–object interaction, locomotion	8 activity classes, 19 attributes	annotation tool SARA
MECCANO	[90,91]	2020	✓	10.5 MB	1	visual	20	controlled	human–object interaction	61 action classes with verb and object/s and bounding box annotations	manual
IKEA ASM	[92,93]	2020	✓	35:26 h	3	visual (RGB, RGB-D)	48	controlled	human–object interaction	33 verb-object	Amazon Turk manual annotators

https://doi.org/10.3390/s26020739

Table 2. *Cont.*

Name	Dataset Ref.	Year	Public	Size	Sensors Nr.	Sensors Type	Subjects Nr.	Recording Environment	Category	Labels Nr. and Type	Annotation
AndyData-lab-onePerson	[7,8]	2019	✓	5 h	34	visual (MoCap, RGB), inertial, tactile/force	13	controlled	postures/static activities, human–object interaction	6 general, 5 detailed posture, 8 action	annotation tool Anvil
PPG-DaLiA	[94,95]	2019	✓	36 h	2	inertial, physiological/biosensors	15	semi-controlled	postures/static activities, ADL, sports	9 activity labels	protocol-defined
HAD-AW	[96,97]	2018	✓	102 MB	1	inertial	16	real-world	ADL, sports	8 ADLs consisting of 31 motion primitives	not explicitly mentioned
Nath et al.	[98]	2018	-	40 min	2	inertial	2	semi-controlled, real-world	human–object interaction	5 activity labels	manually
ExtraSensory Dataset	[99,100]	2017	✓	5000 h	1	inertial, positioning, acoustic, environmental, other (phone state)	60	real-world	ADL	116 original labels, 51 cleaned labels	by the user
Skoda Mini Checkpoint	[40,101]	2008	✓	–	20	inertial	1	controlled	human–object interaction	10 gesture, 70 instances of each gesture	experimenters

https://doi.org/10.3390/s26020739

Table 2 presents a brief survey of datasets for industrial settings since 2008. References for the datasets and dataset website links are provided where available. The year of publication, the public availability status, the dataset size, the number and types of sensors used, and the number of subjects who participated in the recording process are noted. Depending on how each dataset creator described it, the dataset size is presented as hours of recordings, as the memory utilized by the dataset, or, in the case of IHADv, as the number of images. Sensor types can be visual, such as MoCap, RGB, and RGB-D sensors, or non-visual, such as inertial, biosensors, and tactile sensors. The number of sensors refers to the devices placed on the human or in the environment. In MoCap, the number of sensors refers to the number of cameras used during recording. Four categories of recording environments were identified, namely, real-world, semi-controlled, controlled, and virtual. Controlled environments refer to laboratory settings, while semi-controlled environments can be a sensor setup within a real-world scene. In the unique case of InHARD-DT [71], subjects' movements were recorded during their interactions with the virtual reality scene. This category provides insight into the fluidity and realness of movement performed by the individuals. Next, the label category, number, and annotation type are addressed. Label category is based on whether the labels focus on posture, human–object interactions, human–robot interactions, ADLs, or sports. In the *label number and type* column, the availability of coarse labels is noted where available. For instance, one can provide broad activity labels, such as walking, running, and holding a box, or finer labels, such as using the left hand, the right hand, or a small item in hand. The final column, *Annotation*, refers to who or how the activities were labeled in the dataset. It could be domain expert annotation, manual annotation with required subjects, auto-labeling by the subject performing the activity, or no annotation effort, as the activities are conducted in a protocol-defined manner.

The table shows that there has been an increase in human–object and human–robot interactions, whereas the initial datasets focus on human posture in industrial contexts [13]. Each dataset is unique in its sensor selection, number of subjects, recorded human movement information, and activity class labels. Only four datasets have more than 40 subjects. Similarly, only four datasets are based on real-world environments. The most interesting part of the table is the *Labels* categories. It can be noted that most datasets focus solely on activity classes. Very few works have focused on presenting coarse actions or semantic information. Even fewer have included contextual information.

Though these datasets broadly cover industrial movements, they do not include all possible movements within the industrial context. For instance, the movements included in packaging differ from those in order picking, and the movements in car assembly differ from those in Activities of Daily Living. From Table 2, we see that a few datasets, such as IKEA ASM [93] and Skoda Mini Checkpoint [101], focus on assembly movements, while few others, such as Physical Human–Robot Contact Detection [81] and COVERED [77], focus on human–robot collaboration scenarios that are of interest in the future of industrial settings. Datasets such as OpenPack [5], LARa [10], and CAARL [79] specifically focus on logistics scenarios such as packaging and order picking. The movements included in these datasets are closest to those presented in DaRA. While LARa and CAARL were recorded with a focus on MoCap and IMU sensors, OpenPack includes IMU, blood volume pulse, electrodermal activity, LiDAR, and depth image sensors. Further, OpenPack focuses solely on the packaging scenario and doesn't include order picking, whereas LARa and CAARL include both, with order picking given priority. While OpenPack, LARa, and CAARL have coarse labels, the label types differ across them. LARa and CAARL have an action-class and attribute-label structure. This means that the action class standing has an attribute representation that denotes whether the standing action is still or with small-step motions, whether the item is in the left, right, or both hands, and the size of the item. However, in

https://doi.org/10.3390/s26020739

OpenPack, the annotation is used on the operation performed and its sub-action classes. Thus, the close box operation has the subclasses *bend flap* and *attach tape*. However, the subactions do not span the entire operation. Actions that are in between these subclasses are not always labeled.

2.4. Research Gaps

Although the number of available datasets has been steadily increasing, there remains a significant shortage of datasets that reflect realistic recording and working conditions, contain rich metadata, provide comprehensive contextual sensor data, and include annotated contextual class labels. Without contextual information, the interpretation of recognized activities, the description of workflows, the identification of errors, and the derivation of optimization measures are severely limited or even impossible, which undermines the primary objective of HAR and HCR in the industrial domain.

Inconsistencies in labeling, inadequate dataset documentation, and restricted data accessibility further undermine comparability, generalization, and reproducibility, ultimately limiting practical applicability. The movements or activity annotation labels in industrial datasets available are specific to the task focused upon; for example, in Assembly 101 [76] (see Table 2), the coarse labels were *attach track* or *attach cabin*, while the fine labels were *picked up the chassis* or *screw track with a hand*. These labels are difficult to transfer to different scenarios, even when the action performed is similar. Consequently, more datasets addressing human motion in various industrial settings are of interest. In [80,97,102], the movements were made for the respective annotation labels. Therefore, motion continuity could be missing unless the dataset is focused on recording continuous activities in the scenario. Although repeating the same activity is intended to simplify the annotation process and ensure balanced activity class recordings, this practice is detrimental to motion variability.

Consequently, DaRA has continuous movements, where the subjects performing the activities are oblivious to the annotation labels, and, thereby, annotators of the DaRA dataset had the excruciating task of identifying transitions from one activity to another while labeling. This dataset further facilitates the study of learning jitter in annotation labels and how to address transitions in a movement. With the detailed annotation label and contextual data available, it is possible to extend the annotation label into detailed textual data, which can later be used to annotate movements with similar characteristics.

3. DaRA Dataset

This industrial dataset, focused on logistics activities of order picking and packaging in a semi-controlled laboratory environment, was created following the checklist in [103]. The dataset description follows the approach proposed by [104]. To ensure compliance with the FAIR principles [105], the data was made easily **f**indable and **a**ccessible on Zenodo, **i**nteroperable, and **r**eusable with the availability of metadata in this paper and in the documentation on Zenodo.

This section presents the results of the dataset creation process and the specifications of the dataset **DaRA** [15]; see Figure 1. First, the experimental setup is described, including the laboratory environment, scenarios, and sensors used. Next, the selection of subjects is explained, followed by a detailed description of the data collection process. Subsequently, the 12 different class categories are introduced and assigned to their respective class labels. This is followed by an explanation of the annotation and revision process.

Figure 1. Logo of the DaRA dataset. At the core of the dataset and the logo is the human at work, manipulating and transporting objects in warehouses.

The dataset quality is evaluated based on annotation consistency, device data loss rate, and a use case, i.e., solving HAR for DaRA's main and sub-activities. Finally, we provide guidance on how to use the dataset effectively. We provide a Python script (version 1) [106] that allows users to customize the annotation results to extract precise information required for their specific use case.

3.1. Experimental Setup

The following sections describe the laboratory where the recordings took place, the eight logistics scenarios, and the three types of sensors used.

3.1.1. Introduction to the Laboratory Picking Lab

The experimental setup was established in the Picking Lab at the Fraunhofer Institute for Material Flow and Logistics IML (https://www.iml.fraunhofer.de/en/fields_of_activity/material-flow-systems/intralogistics_and_it_planning/services/Picking_Lab.html, accessed on 18 January 2026). The Picking Lab is a research infrastructure designed for application-oriented logistics research [107]. It focuses on key questions such as process optimization, logistical information technology (IT), human–technology interaction, and ergonomics [108]. The lab replicates a small-scale order picking warehouse (see Figure 2) and is specifically designed to evaluate technologies and processes in the context of conventional order picking systems based on the person-to-goods principle. This environment allows the investigation of both technological and procedural aspects of order fulfilment. It can be considered semi-controlled because it presents a realistic warehouse that replicates essential technical and logistical characteristics of an authentic warehouse within a controlled laboratory environment.

The standardized environment consists of eight rack complexes across five aisles, complemented by an open area in front of the rack storage system (see Figure 3). This configuration enables the implementation of realistic scenarios for typical intralogistics applications, including e-commerce, small-parts picking, and handling bulky or hanging goods.

A wide range of items is available for handling:

- Small items (from 0.4 g), such as screws, locknuts, washers, or bits;
- Medium items (approximately 50 to 800 g), such as softshell jackets, ties, gloves, hoodies, bags, shirts, or notebooks;
- Large items (up to 5149 g), such as palm soil, axes, and hacksaws.

The item master data, including dimensions, weight, designation, storage location, item photographs, and customer orders, are documented and accessible on Zenodo (see *Documentation.pdf* file).

The items are stored in compartments, such as small load carriers, open-fronted storage bins, without bins, cartons, hanging rails with clothes hangers, or flow channels, according to their characteristics. Electronic rack labels are used for identification. The Picking Lab is equipped with a cloud-based warehouse management system (WMS) that interfaces with the IT systems of the picking technologies.

https://doi.org/10.3390/s26020739

Figure 2. Picking Lab at the Fraunhofer Institute for Material Flow and Logistics (IML) in Dortmund, Germany. The photo shows eight numbered industrial rack complexes. The rack complex 1 stores small items in open-fronted storage bins. Complexes 2 and 3 hold hanging goods and loose items without bins. Complex 4 features flow channels for unboxed items and those in cardboard boxes. Complex 5 contains medium-sized flat goods, while complex 6 mainly stores medium-sized to bulky flat goods in green and blue open-fronted storage bins. Bulky and heavy items are located primarily in complexes 7 and 8.

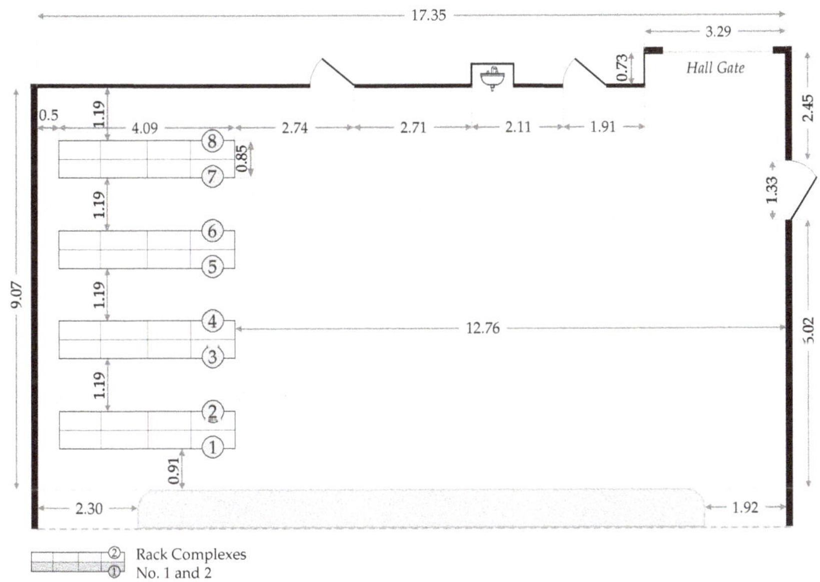

Figure 3. Floor plan of the Picking Lab, showing the eight rack complexes and the open area in front of the racks used for workflow simulation. All measurements are given in meters.

3.1.2. Logistics Scenarios

Laboratory Layout and Scenario Integration

The open area of the Picking Lab was divided into distinct work zones. Including the *Aisle Path* within the rack storage system, the lab comprises nine main areas (see Figure 4). Additionally, the *Aisle Path*, *Cross Aisle Path*, and *Path* were subdivided into further zones to cover detailed process steps.

https://doi.org/10.3390/s26020739

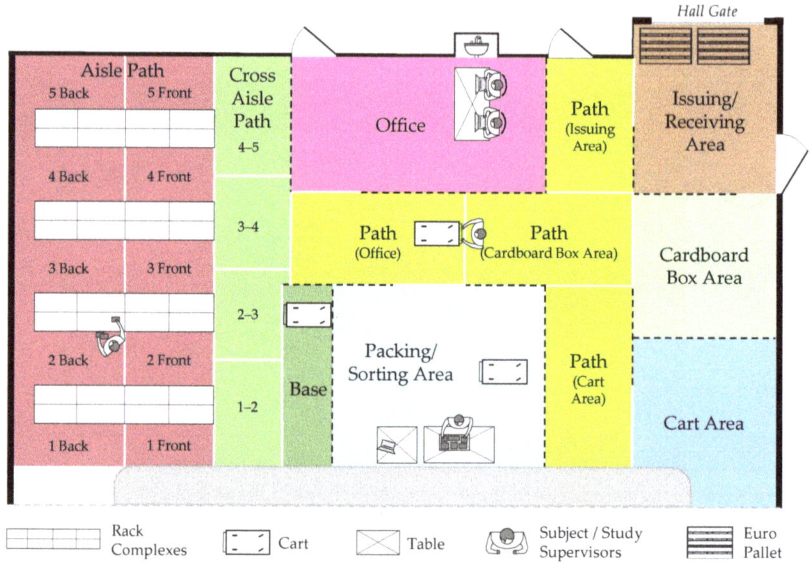

Figure 4. Floor plan of the Picking Lab. The entire setup is color-coded into nine main areas. The colors correspond to the annotation tool SARA annotation tool's coding scheme [88,109]. The dashed black lines represent physical boundaries formed by barrier stands with belt straps, while the solid white lines indicate conceptual boundaries marked by tape on the floor.

Realistic Material Flow Integration

In contrast to the isolated processes typically represented in state-of-the-art datasets, this study implemented a holistic, realistic warehouse-specific material flow. During each recording session, three subjects simultaneously traversed the entire material flow, as illustrated in Figure 4. Supervisors acted as warehouse managers, located primarily in the *Office*, where they assigned orders and managed information technology, accepted returns upon order completion, and assisted subjects when needed. The experimental setup is depicted in Figure 5.

Figure 5. Panorama view of the warehouse setup. The photo was taken in the *Packing/Sorting Area* (light blue area in Figure 4) behind the packing table, with a view towards the *Office* (pink area in Figure 4). Within the office, the study supervisor is seated at a desk, from which subjects receive their assignments. Behind the supervisor, to the right from the photo's perspective, is the *Issuing/Receiving Area* by the black hall gate. The boxes in front of it indicate the *Cardboard Box Area*. The *Cart Area* is situated further ahead, where three picking carts are located. These areas are connected by a ⊣ shaped path. On the left side of the photograph, the *Base*, *Cross Aisle Paths*, and the Picking Lab with its eight rack complexes and five *Aisle Paths* are visible.

https://doi.org/10.3390/s26020739

Overview of Scenarios

A total of eight scenarios were implemented. They differ in terms of the high-level process (retrieval vs. storage), the IT used, customer orders, picking strategies, and intentional errors in the picking lists. Scenarios 1–3 and 7 focused on retrieval, while scenarios 4–6 and 8 focused on storage. As in a real warehouse, the process steps in the scenarios were predefined, but the movements required to perform them were not prescribed to the subjects, allowing for realistic motion.

Retrieval (Scenarios 1–3)

Retrieval scenarios started with order preparation. Subjects received their picking orders and assigned information technologies in the *Office* area. They proceeded via the *Path* to the *Cart Area* to select a picking cart, then collected empty cardboard boxes in the *Cardboard Box Area*.

Picking began with transporting the cart to the *Base*, where it remained during the picking process. Items were put into cardboard boxes on the cart, reflecting a Pick & Pack approach where items are picked directly into shipping-ready boxes.

The picking strategy followed a single-order picking principle: each picking task corresponded exactly to one customer order. This straightforward, order-oriented approach did not require further sorting or consolidation. Information relevant to order fulfillment, such as item identifiers, required quantities, and storage locations, was provided to the picker through different forms of guidance and confirmation media. In this paper, these means of information provision are collectively referred to as *information technologies* (Figure 6):

1. Scenario 1: Paper list with pen.
2. Scenario 2: Portable Data Terminal (PDT).
3. Scenario 3: Paper list with glove scanner.

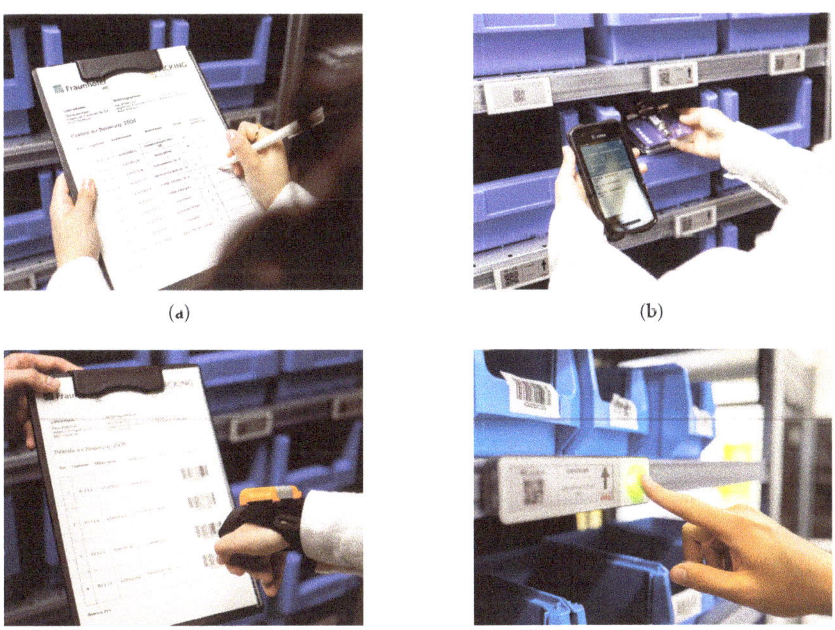

Figure 6. Information technology for guiding the picker: (**a**) picking list with pen, (**b**) portable data terminal, (**c**) picking list with glove scanner, (**d**) Pick-by-Light signal.

https://doi.org/10.3390/s26020739

Subjects moved between their carts in the *Base* and the respective item positions within the *Aisle Path*, following a return-aisle strategy, where aisles were entered and exited at the same end repeatedly. For scenarios 1–3, subjects were instructed to enter each aisle separately for each position of the order, without processing multiple positions simultaneously.

In scenarios 2 and 3, a *pick-by-light* system guided subjects, using optical signals on rack complexes and storage compartments to the correct items. While the light indicated the picking location, the number of items to be picked was displayed on either the list or the PDT.

Once all items for an order were picked and placed into the boxes on the cart, the cart was transported to the *Packaging Area*, where packaging materials (e.g., bubble wrap, shipping labels, delivery notes, box cutters, and tape) were provided. After packaging, orders were finalized by transporting the boxes to the *Issuing/Receiving Area*, where they were placed on pallets. Finally, subjects returned their IT (picking list, pen, portable data terminal, glove scanner) at the *Office*.

Each subject repeated this retrieval process three times, handling different customer orders (order IDs: *2904*, *2905*, *2906*) and employing different information technologies in each iteration.

Intentional Errors in Picking Lists

To reflect realistic warehouse processes, the scenarios intentionally included disruptive elements. Planned errors included incorrect storage locations on picking lists (scenario 1), quantity discrepancies (scenario 3), inappropriate box sizes, waiting times due to limited packaging stations, and missing materials, such as plastic bags, which had to be retrieved from the *Office*. Additionally, unplanned errors occurred, such as device handling mistakes or quantity and type errors during picking or storage.

Storage (Scenarios 4–6)

Following the retrieval runs, storage processes were conducted in scenarios 4–6. These began with order acceptance in the *Office* and goods receipt in the *Issuing/Receiving Area*. At this stage, previously completed retrieval orders (processed three times each) were placed on pallets.

Each subject processed one storage order three times. After transportation to the *Packaging/Sorting Area*, boxes were unpacked, and items were sorted for storage. Storage involved placing items into the rack storage system, guided exclusively by paper lists with pens.

Upon completing storage, subjects finalized their orders by returning empty boxes to the *Cardboard Box Area*, their lists and pens to the *Office*, and the carts to the *Cart Area*.

Multi-Order Picking (Scenarios 7–8)

Scenarios 7 (retrieval) and 8 (storage) followed the same structure as the previous scenarios but introduced multi-order picking. Two customer orders (*2904* and *2905*) were processed in parallel within a single picking batch. Items were directly assigned to the corresponding customer's cardboard box, leveraging higher picking density to reduce average travel time per order.

Subjects were free to determine their route strategies and were allowed to process multiple order lines with different items simultaneously. Additionally, these scenarios were conducted without any disruptions or errors in the picking lists—representing a "perfect run". In scenarios 7 and 8, only one subject worked in the laboratory to circumvent waiting times. All eight scenarios are summarized in Table 3.

https://doi.org/10.3390/s26020739

Table 3. Specification of the eight recorded scenarios. An 'X' denotes that the criterion is fulfilled.

		Scenario							
		1	2	3	4	5	6	7	8
High-Level Processes	Retrieval (picking and packing)	X	X	X				X	
	Storage (unpacking and storing)				X	X	X		X
Picking Strategies	Single-order picking (serial)	X	X	X	X	X	X		
	Multi-order picking (parallel)							X	X
Information Technologies	Picking list and pen	X			X	X	X	X	X
	Portable data terminal		X						
	Picking list and glove scanner			X					
Customer Order	2904	X			X			X	X
	2905		X			X		X	X
	2906			X			X		
Errors in Picking List	With intentional errors	X		X					
	Without intentional errors		X		X	X	X	X	X

3.1.3. Sensor Configuration

The logistics scenarios were recorded using action cameras, fixed cameras, wearable devices with IMUs and BLE Received Signal Strength Indicator (RSSI) sensors, and Beacons (see Figure 7). Additionally, a cloud-based warehouse management system from Logistics Reply (https://www.reply.com/, accessed on 18 January 2026) logged the picking activities using a PDT.

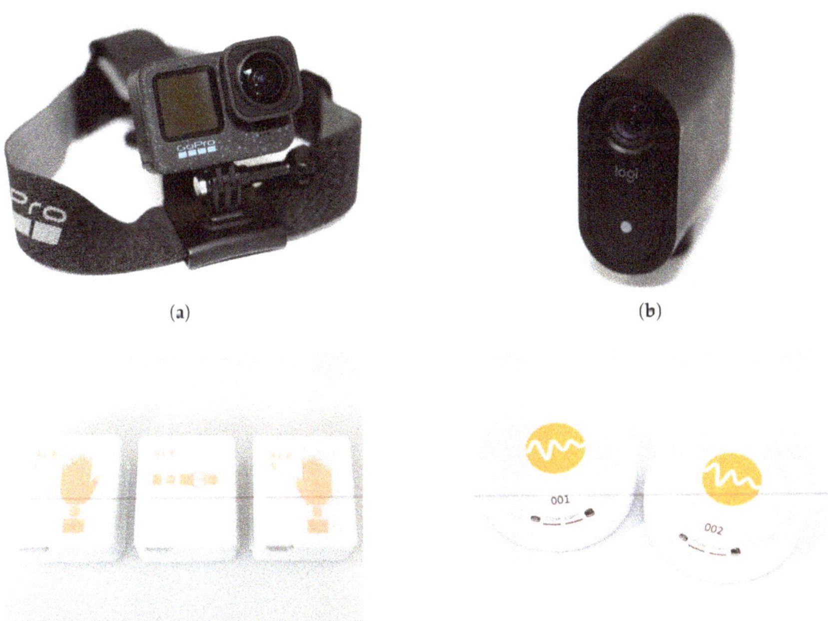

(**a**) (**b**) (**c**) (**d**)

Figure 7. Sensors used to capture movements of the subjects and picking carts: (**a**) GoPro 12 action camera with ultra-wide-angle digital lens and head strap, (**b**) Mevo camera from Logitech without tripod, (**c**) one wearable set from MotionMiners with IMU and BLE sensors in each of the three devices, (**d**) first two beacons from MotionMiners.

https://doi.org/10.3390/s26020739

Action Cameras

Each subject was equipped with a GoPro Hero 12 action camera (https://gopro.com/, accessed on 18 January 2026) for first-person view (FPV). The camera was attached to the forehead and pointed slightly downwards to capture not only the subjects' field of vision but also the movements of their arms and legs. Due to individual adjustments, the viewing angles varied slightly.

The ultra-wide-angle digital lens with a field of view of up to 177° allowed the largest possible recording field to be covered (see Figure 8a–c). The FPV videos were used for documentation, annotation, and revision.

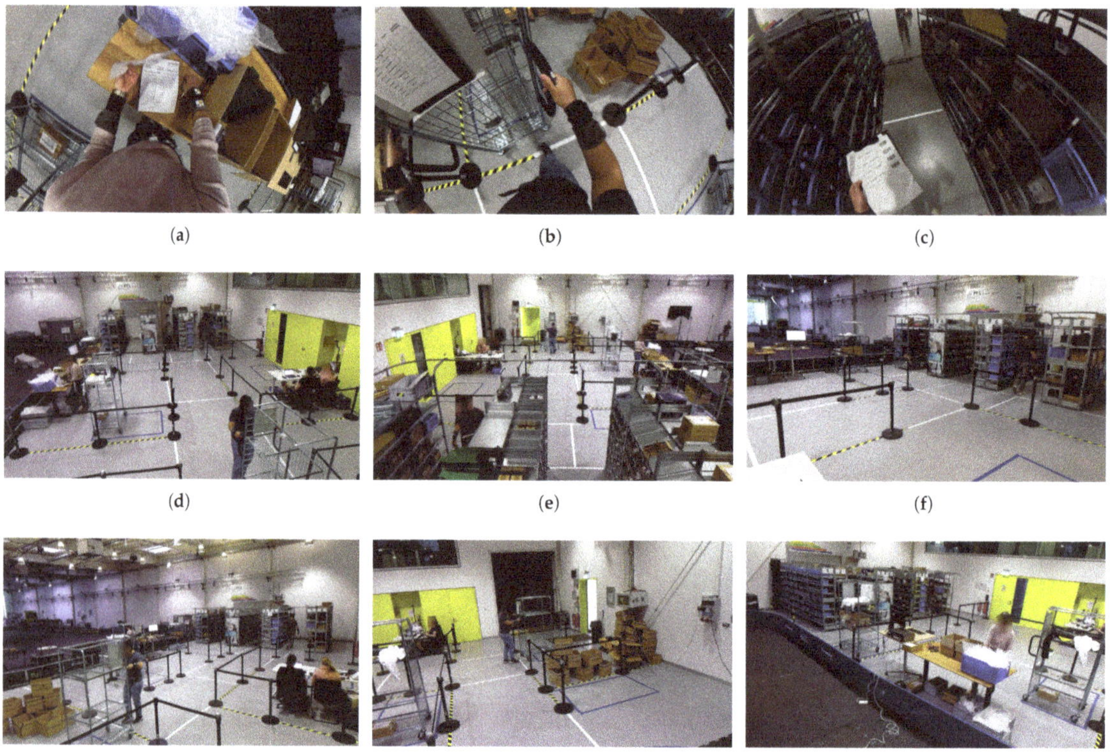

(a) (b) (c) (d) (e) (f) (g) (h) (i)

Figure 8. The images show the synchronized perspectives of all nine cameras at frame 31,171 in recording session 5. (**a**–**c**) display the first-person views of the subjects captured by action cameras: (**a**) Subject S13 is located in the *Packaging/Sorting Area*, (**b**) Subject S14 is on the *Path* in front of the *Cardboard Box Area*, and (**c**) Subject S15 is located in the front of *Aisle Path* 4. (**d**–**i**) show the six fixed cameras, numbered according to the dataset. (**d**) Fixed Camera 1: Main camera for annotation placed in *Cardboard Box Area*, directed towards the aisles and Fixed Camera 2. (**e**) Fixed Camera 2: Positioned in *Aisle* 3, facing Fixed Camera 1. (**f**) Fixed Camera 3: Located in the *Office*. (**g**) Fixed Camera 4: Placed in the goods *Issuing/Receiving Area*. (**h**) Fixed Camera 5: Facing the goods *Issuing/Receiving Area* and the hall gate. (**i**) Fixed Camera 6: Oriented towards the *Packaging/Sorting Area* and *Aisle* 1. The position of the fixed cameras is also shown in Figure 9 of the floor plan.

Mounting the camera on the forehead proved to be the optimal solution for comprehensive field-of-view coverage and an annotation-friendly perspective, especially compared to mounting it on the shoulder or chest. Nevertheless, some limitations in use occurred during the recordings. Some subjects found the mounting pressure uncomfortable, and the

https://doi.org/10.3390/s26020739

camera was unstable on those with straight hair. This occasionally required the subjects to readjust the camera during recording. Subject S01, in particular, frequently corrected the camera position at the beginning as the camera had slipped.

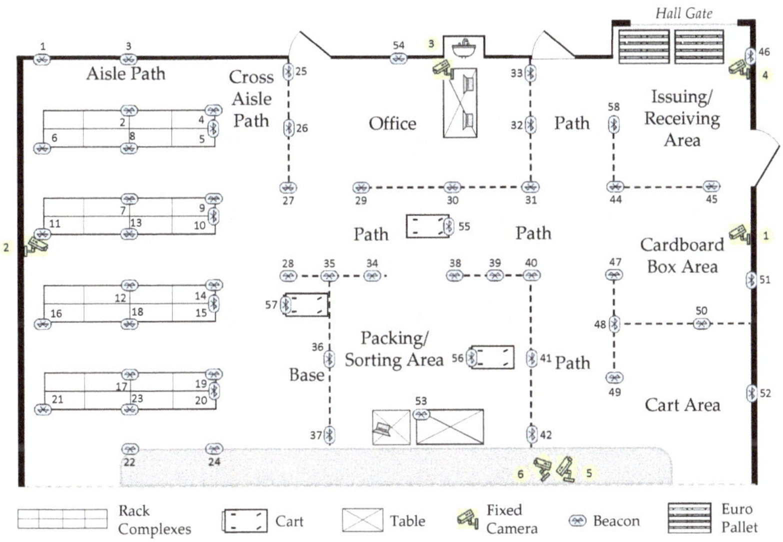

Figure 9. Floor plan of the Picking Lab: positions of the six fixed cameras (green) and the 57 beacons (blue). Beacons 1–42, 44–54 and 58 are stationary, while beacons 55–57 are dynamic and attached to the picking carts. (Beacon 43 was defective, so it was not used).

The recording was made at 29.97 fps and was interrupted only during a battery change during the session. The battery change resulted in black sequences in the action camera videos.

Fixed Cameras

In addition to the action cameras, six permanently installed Mevo cameras from Logitech (https://mevo.com/, accessed on 18 January 2026) were utilized to capture the entire test field. These cameras enabled a third-person view (TPV) of the subjects (see Figure 8d–i). The TPV videos were also used for annotation and revision. In particular, fixed camera 1 (see Figure 8d) provided a comprehensive overview and served as the primary stream for annotation, alongside the FPV videos from the action camera. The recordings were also made at 29.97 fps and ran uninterrupted throughout the entire session, ensuring complete documentation.

Wearable Devices with IMUs and BLE RSSI sensors

The subjects' movements were recorded using wearable sensor sets comprising three MotionMiners devices. Every device is equipped with a three-axial IMU and a BLE sensor. The three devices were attached to both wrists and to the front of the torso with a belt. Pictograms on the devices ensured correct placement to minimize attachment errors (see Figure 7c).

Each subject wore two of these sets to mitigate sensor failure and enable analysis of data quality. Throughout the entire recording session, the wearable devices remained securely attached to the subjects and were not adjusted by the study supervisors. The IMUs comprise linear acceleration and angular momentum sensors operating at a sampling rate

https://doi.org/10.3390/s26020739

of 100 Hz. The Bluetooth sensor measured the RSSI for all received beacon-emitter signals at a sampling rate of 10 Hz.

All sensor data are stored on the sensors during recording and are transferred upon recording completion. This approach eliminated potential disruptions from wireless data transmission and ensured a robust, interference-free data collection process without requiring intervention.

Beacon Emitters

To track the subjects' positions, 54 Bluetooth beacons were placed evenly across the Picking Lab (see Figure 9). The beacons were placed at heights ranging from 0.7 to 1.3 m on various structures, including racks, walls, a table, and barrier stands. Additionally, a beacon was placed on each picking cart at a height of 0.9 m to enable its position to be tracked when a subject was using it.

A notable challenge in position tracking arises from the varying environmental conditions. In the *Aisles* between the racks, Bluetooth signals are physically shielded by the metal racks and stored items. This results in stronger signal attenuation, which simplifies local positioning because signals can be clearly assigned to specific areas. In contrast, Bluetooth signals propagate more evenly in open areas such as the *Office*, the *Base*, and the *Packaging/-Sorting Area*. This uniform signal distribution complicates region-based tracking, making it harder to distinguish between areas and increasing the likelihood of misassignments. The tracking was achieved by a proprietary machine learning algorithm. An initial calibration for each region helps account for differences in propagation.

3.2. Subjects

A total of 18 subjects participated in the data collection (see Figure 10). The selection process aimed to ensure a realistic representation of the working population in the German warehouse sector. Therefore, individuals aged up to 67 years were considered, as the statutory retirement age in Germany for those born after 1964 is 67 years. Ultimately, the sample included subjects aged 21 to 67 years, with a broad age distribution spanning individuals in their 20 s, 30 s, 40 s, 50 s, and 60 s.

According to a study by the Bundesvereinigung Logistik e.V. (BVL) from 2019, the proportion of women in the logistics, transport, and traffic sector is approximately 23%. The highest proportions of women are found in logistics-related service providers (23%) and warehousing (30%). Based on this percentage, a sample of 18 subjects would be expected to include approximately 4.14 to 5.4 women. Accordingly, five women were recruited for the study. However, in the end, only four women (22.22%) and 14 men (77.78%) participated in the study.

To ensure a diverse sample in terms of movement patterns, behaviors, and technological competence, additional demographic and physical attributes were considered. The subjects' heights ranged from 160 cm to 187 cm, while their weights varied between 62 kg and 103 kg (see Table 4). Moreover, multiple native languages were represented, including Bengali, German, English, Greek, and Turkish. The inclusion of linguistic diversity was intentional, as warehouse environments frequently employ workers with diverse language backgrounds.

https://doi.org/10.3390/s26020739

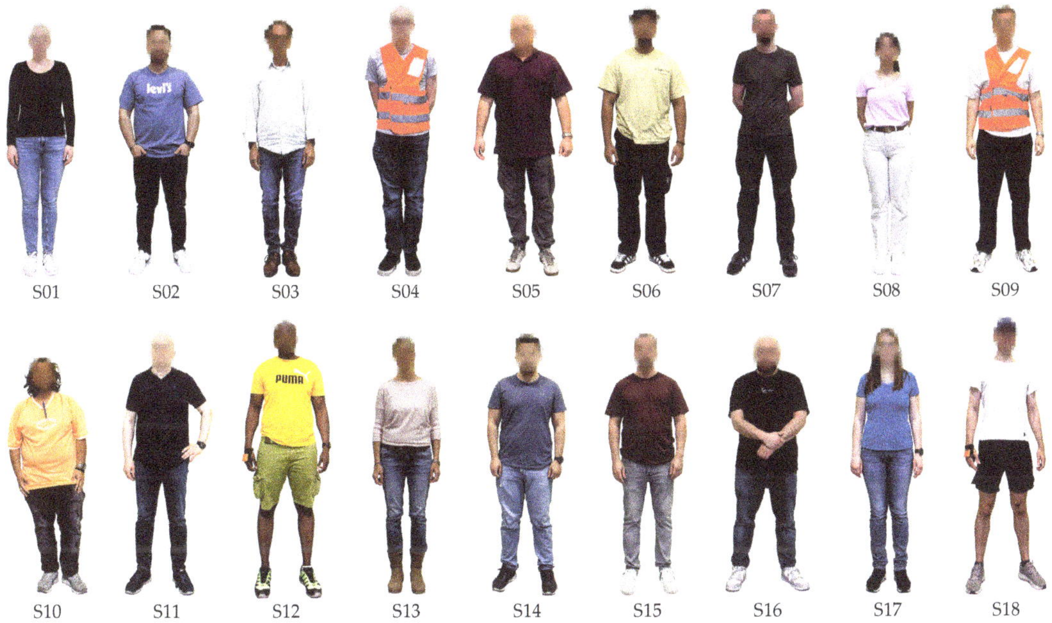

Figure 10. The 18 subjects of the dataset. In each recording session, three subjects took part simultaneously. To easily distinguish the subjects within a session, they wore upperwear or vests of different colors. For instance, in session 5, subjects S13, S14, and S15 wore a pink, a blue, and a red top, respectively (video footage from session 5, see Figure 8).

Table 4. Subject specifications. All data were collected via a digital survey (subject questionnaire) completed independently by subjects.

ID	Sex [F/M]	Age [years]	Weight [kg]	Height [cm]	Handedness [L/R]	Employment Status	Experience [from 1 = Extensive to 6 = None]		
							Order Picking	Packaging	Similar Studies
S01	F	32	68	171	R	Student	2	3	6
S02	M	27	76	167	R	Student	3	6	6
S03	M	64	69	171	R	Employee	6	5	5
S04	M	31	85	183	L	Employee	5	4	6
S05	M	67	100	177	R	Retiree	6	3	6
S06	M	24	82	178	R	Student	4	6	6
S07	M	41	70	180	R	Employee	6	5	6
S08	F	29	62	163	R	Student	6	6	6
S09	M	21	85	180	R	Student	6	6	6
S10	M	28	85	160	R	Student	3	3	6
S11	M	59	85	178	R	Employee	3	2	6
S12	M	43	103	186	R	Job seeker	6	6	4
S13	F	52	66	175	R	Employee	5	4	6
S14	M	32	80	176	R	Employee	6	5	5
S15	M	43	88	177	R	Employee	6	5	6
S16	M	29	100	175	R	Student	6	3	6
S17	F	25	75	180	R	Employee	6	5	6
S18	M	26	80	187	R	Student	6	6	6
Min.		21	62	160					
Avg.		37.4	81.1	175.8					
Max.		67	103	187					

https://doi.org/10.3390/s26020739

The sample included one left-handed subject. Considering that the average proportion of left-handed individuals in the general population is 10.6% [110], a slightly higher representation would have been desirable, indicating a minor sampling bias.

Subjects were not explicitly selected based on prior warehouse experience. However, seven subjects had prior experience in order picking, while 12 subjects had experience in packaging, gained through apprenticeships, internships, or part-time jobs. One of these subjects (S01) had full-time work experience as an industrial clerk. Additionally, three subjects had previously participated in a similar study (LARa dataset [10]). All 18 subjects had a University Entrance Qualification and either held a university degree or were in the process of obtaining one at the time of the study. The potential influence of educational background on movement patterns and behaviors was not explicitly analyzed in this study, as its impact was assumed to be negligible.

3.3. Data Recording

The data recording process is divided into three distinct phases. First, preliminary trial runs are conducted. Second, the recording process is conducted in accordance with the scenarios defined in Section 3.1.2. Third, the results of the recording are analyzed in terms of their scope and subject-specific conspicuities.

3.3.1. Preliminaries

Several days prior to data recording, subjects completed an online questionnaire and received detailed study information, along with the informed consent form. The *Subject Information and Consent Form* is part of the dataset available on Zenodo. On the day of data recording, the subjects had the opportunity to clarify any open questions with the study coordinator.

Before the actual recording, all three subjects in a session completed a trial run. During this phase, they were introduced to three information technologies (picking list, glove scanner, and PDT) and the complete order picking process. For training purposes, they processed three picking orders, each consisting of three order lines (different items). This trial run was solely intended for familiarization with the processes and technologies and was not recorded. Afterward, subjects were equipped with IMUs and an action camera, marking the start of data recording.

3.3.2. Recording Process

To guarantee a natural movement flow and authentic behavior of the subjects, the study supervisors were available to answer questions after the trial run, but provided minimal instructions.

At the commencement of each session, subjects performed up to three synchronization movements in the *Office*. These included the convergence of the extended arms above the head, the convergence of the extended arms in front of the chest, and the execution of a jump. These movements were subsequently utilized for synchronizing video data with the wearable sensor data.

Retrieval: Following the synchronization, the retrieval process was initiated. Each subject was tasked with working through scenarios 1–3 (see Figure 11 and Section 3.1.2). The paper-based picking lists were available in sufficient quantities, ensuring no delays when retrieving a new order. Conversely, only one PDT and one glove scanner were available, which occasionally led to waiting times in the office as subjects had to wait until others had completed their picking and returned the hardware. Due to the shared use of the PDT and the glove scanner, scenarios 2 and 3 were never conducted in parallel, resulting in variations in the sequence of the first three scenarios across subjects. The sequence of all scenarios is available in the documentation file on Zenodo.

https://doi.org/10.3390/s26020739

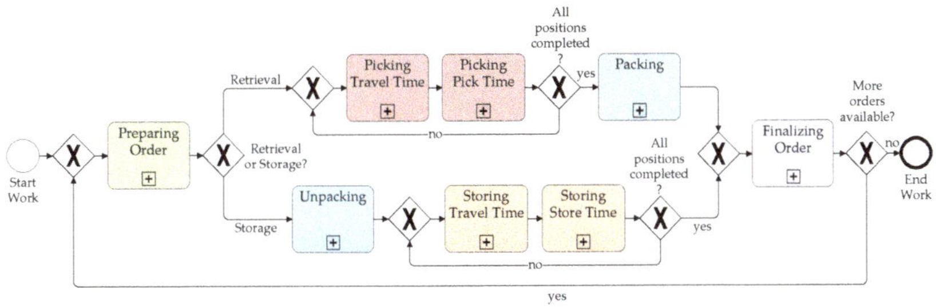

Figure 11. Idealized Business Process Model and Notation (BPMN) of the high-level processes *Retrieval* (upper path) and *Storage* (lower path) with its mid-level processes.

Storage: Following the completion of the initial three retrieval scenarios, each of the three different customer orders (ID 2904, 2905, 2906) was available three times in the *Issuing/Receiving Area*. Each subject was then assigned a customer order, which they unpacked and stored three times (see Figure 11).

In four of the six sessions, one subject (S01, S04, S09, and S14) simultaneously retrieved two orders (scenario 7) and subsequently stored them again (scenario 8).

After each session, subjects performed up to three synchronization movements again.

The workflows of the high-level processes *Retrieval* and *Storage*, as described and illustrated in Figure 11, represent an idealized model. During data collection, occasional deviations occurred. A more detailed visualization of the mid-level processes from Figure 11 is provided in Appendix A.

3.3.3. Recording Results

The data collection took place over three days, with six sessions (two per day). In each session, three subjects participated simultaneously in the Picking Lab (see Table 5). In total, data from 18 subjects were recorded over 31:55:26 h (hh:mm:ss). The individual recording durations varied between 01:20:41 and 02:35:11 h, depending on factors such as processing speed, technological competence, performed scenarios, unintended errors, waiting time, habituation effect, and fatigue.

Processing Speed: The durations indicate a moderate age-related increase in the time required. Subjects in the older age group (≥50 years) required up to approximately 35% more time than the youngest subjects (≤30 years). Although without prior experience, Subject S14 (32 years) demonstrated a significantly higher processing speed compared to the average. Across all scenarios, S14 completed tasks faster than the group mean: 36% faster in scenario 1, 23% faster in scenario 2, and 17% faster in scenario 3. In scenarios 1 and 2, S14 not only achieved the fastest completion times but also executed the tasks without picking errors. The two slowest subjects, S15 and S12, were 43 years old at the time of data recording. Weight shows a slight positive relationship with processing time, whereas height and gender appear to have no relevant influence.

Technological competence: Subject S14 demonstrated strong performance in operating the PDT in scenario 2. Despite having no prior experience with the device, S14 adapted quickly and performed significantly better than most subjects. In contrast, subject S11 encountered considerable difficulties in using the PDT, requiring 00:34:10 h to complete scenario 2, 63% slower than the average. Due to time constraints, S11 was unable to proceed with scenario 3.

https://doi.org/10.3390/s26020739

Table 5. Subject assignment. Scope of participation in the *Scenarios*, *Other* and *Total*.

ID	Recording Session	Scope of the Scenarios 1–8 [hh:mm:ss]								Other	Total
		Retrieval (Scenario 1–3)			Storage (Scenario 4–6)			Perfect Run			
		1	2	3	4	5	6	7	8		
S01	1	00:18:15	00:19:20	00:18:39	-	-	00:15:51	00:23:42	00:14:34	00:10:59	02:01:19
S02	1	00:19:43	00:16:36	00:22:16	-	00:23:56	-	-	-	00:15:43	01:38:14
S03	1	00:24:41	00:25:07	00:09:34	00:27:04	-	-	-	-	00:03:11	01:29:37
S04	2	00:16:22	00:16:09	00:17:57	-	00:32:17	-	00:26:00	00:14:28	00:13:17	02:16:30
S05	2	00:25:47	00:20:05	00:19:11	-	-	00:26:36	-	-	00:08:42	01:40:22
S06	2	00:22:08	00:16:45	00:17:27	00:25:27	-	-	-	-	00:02:29	01:24:16
S07	3	00:20:13	00:23:38	00:16:16	-	00:26:40	-	-	-	00:15:16	01:42:02
S08	3	00:19:47	00:20:10	00:15:49	-	-	00:21:29	-	-	00:03:57	01:21:11
S09	3	00:18:18	00:16:33	00:18:05	00:27:40	-	-	00:23:47	00:15:57	00:05:03	02:05:24
S10	4	00:25:18	00:24:02	00:21:07	-	-	00:26:50	-	-	00:13:37	01:50:54
S11	4	00:17:13	00:34:10	-	00:33:30	-	-	-	-	00:08:20	01:33:13
S12	4	00:24:24	00:26:29	00:28:18	-	00:31:17	-	-	-	00:10:33	02:01:00
S13	5	00:22:28	00:19:11	00:20:07	-	-	00:24:08	-	-	00:02:59	01:28:53
S14	5	00:13:27	00:16:07	00:15:44	00:28:18	-	-	00:26:57	00:19:23	00:35:15	02:35:11
S15	5	00:27:55	00:24:44	00:25:14	-	00:29:57	-	-	-	00:07:26	01:55:17
S16	6	00:23:11	00:17:25	00:20:22	-	-	00:20:17	-	-	00:16:24	01:37:38
S17	6	00:18:42	00:19:59	00:15:45	00:24:08	-	-	-	-	00:02:08	01:20:41
S18	6	00:20:02	00:20:53	00:20:56	-	00:37:01	-	-	-	00:14:51	01:53:43
Min.		00:13:27	00:16:07	00:09:34	00:24:08	00:23:56	00:15:51	00:23:42	00:14:28	00:02:08	**01:20:41**
Avg.		00:21:00	00:20:58	00:18:59	00:27:41	00:30:11	00:22:32	00:25:06	00:16:05	00:10:34	**01:46:25**
Max.		00:27:55	00:34:10	00:28:18	00:33:30	00:37:01	00:26:50	00:26:57	00:19:23	00:35:15	**02:35:11**
Sum		**06:17:54**	**06:17:22**	**05:22:46**	**02:46:07**	**03:01:08**	**02:15:11**	**01:40:26**	**01:04:21**	**03:10:10**	**31:55:26**

Performed scenarios: It was planned that each subject would go through retrieval scenarios 1 to 3, as well as a storage task from scenario 4, 5, or 6. Four of the eighteen subjects additionally completed the storage and retrieval scenarios 7 and 8, resulting in longer overall recording durations for these subjects.

Unintended errors: Certain subjects made unintended errors that affected their processing times. For instance, S03 and S11 overlooked the second and/or third pages of the picking list, resulting in incomplete picking and packing. This resulted in shortened processing times for S03 in scenario 3 (00:09:34 h) and S11 in scenario 1 (00:17:13 h).

Waiting time: The category *Other* (see Table 5) accounts for waiting times between scenarios, as well as preparatory and follow-up activities at the beginning and end of each recording session. During the packing process, subjects were instructed to wait whenever another subject was still active in the packing area. They also had to wait if the required IT was being used by someone else. This resulted in intentionally induced waiting times of up to several minutes (e.g., subject S14 with 00:35:15 h).

Habituation effect: After the initial execution of the scenarios, a habituation effect was observed. Subjects' workflows appeared smoother, and the time required for similar, recurring tasks decreased in both storage and retrieval processes. In scenario 8, subjects required approximately 60% less time for storage compared to their previous scenarios 4–6. Although the execution time for retrieval increased by about 24% (from scenarios 1–2 to scenario 7), the number of positions to be picked and packed simultaneously doubled, indicating an adaptation to increased task complexity.

Fatigue: During data recording, some subjects exhibited signs of fatigue, which were reflected in their scenario completion times. While subject S14 recorded the fastest times in scenarios 1–3, a noticeable decline in performance was observed in scenarios 7 and 8. Compared to the other subjects, S14 was the slowest in both cases, requiring 22% more time than the next slowest subject in scenario 8. These findings suggest that fatigue may

https://doi.org/10.3390/s26020739

have resulted from extended recording sessions due to waiting times and the high work pace maintained during the initial scenarios.

3.4. Class Categories and Class Labels

Prior to annotation, 12 class categories (CC01–CC12) were defined to describe the execution of the scenarios. These categories are divided into human movements and contextual information. An overview of the class categories and class labels is provided in Table 6. Detailed label descriptions and examples are available in the documentation file on Zenodo.

The first five categories capture human movements, ranging from the *Main Activity* (CC01) to four *Sub-Activities* (*Legs*, *Torso*, *Left Hand*, and *Right Hand*). *Sub-Activities* can be regarded as semantic descriptions of a *Main Activity* but also exist independently. In the literature, such semantic descriptions are commonly referred to as attributes, detailed postures, current actions, or atomic actions [111].

Table 6. Class categories and class labels (M = Human Movement, C = Context, an 'X' denotes that the criterion is fulfilled).

<table>
<tr><th colspan="3">Class Categories [CC]</th><th>M</th><th>C</th><th colspan="2">Class Labels [CL]</th></tr>
<tr><th>Icon</th><th>ID</th><th>Name</th><th></th><th></th><th>Nr.</th><th>List</th></tr>
<tr><td></td><td>CC01</td><td>Main Activity</td><td>X</td><td></td><td>15</td><td>CL001 | Synchronization; CL002 | Confirming with Pen; CL003 | Confirming with Screen; CL004 | Confirming with Button; CL005 | Scanning; CL006 | Pulling Cart; CL007 | Pushing Cart; CL008 | Handling Upwards; CL009 | Handling Centered; CL010 | Handling Downwards; CL011 | Walking; CL012 | Standing; CL013 | Sitting; CL014 | Another Main Activity; CL015 | Main Activity Unknown</td></tr>
<tr><td></td><td>CC02</td><td>Sub-Activity–Legs</td><td>X</td><td></td><td>8</td><td>CL016 | Gait Cycle; CL017 | Step; CL018 | Standing Still; CL019 | Sitting; CL020 | Squat; CL021 | Lunges; CL022 | Another Leg Activity; CL023 | Leg Activity Unknown</td></tr>
<tr><td></td><td>CC03</td><td>Sub-Activity–Torso</td><td>X</td><td></td><td>6</td><td>CL024 | No Bending; CL025 | Slightly Bending; CL026 | Strongly Bending; CL027 | Torso Rotation; CL028 | Another Torso Activity; CL029 | Torso Activity Unknown</td></tr>
<tr><td></td><td>CC04</td><td>Sub-Activity–Left Hand</td><td>X</td><td></td><td>35</td><td>Primary Position: CL030 | Upwards; CL031 | Centered; CL032 | Downwards; CL033 | Position Unknown
Type of Movement: CL034 | Reaching, Grasping, Moving, Positioning and Releasing; CL035 | Manipulating; CL036 | Holding; CL037 | No Movement; CL038 | Another Movement; CL039 | Movement Unknown
Object: CL040 | No Object; CL041 | Large Item; CL042 | Medium Item; CL043 | Small Item; CL044 | Tool; CL045 | Cart; CL046 | Load Carrier; CL047 | Cardboard Box; CL048 | On Body; CL049 | Another Logistic Object; CL050 | No Logistic Object; CL051 | Object Unknown
Tool: CL052 | Portable Data Terminal; CL053 | Glove Scanner; CL054 | Plastic Bag; CL055 | Picking List; CL056 | Pen; CL057 | Button; CL058 | Computer; CL059 | Bubble Wrap; CL060 | Tape Dispenser; CL061 | Knife; CL062 | Shipping/Return Label; CL063 | Elastic Band; CL064 | Another Tool</td></tr>
<tr><td></td><td>CC05</td><td>Sub-Activity–Right Hand</td><td>X</td><td></td><td>35</td><td>Primary Position: CL065 | Upwards; CL066 | Centered; CL067 | Downwards; CL068 | Position Unknown
Type of Movement: CL069 | Reaching, Grasping, Moving, Positioning and Releasing; CL070 | Manipulating; CL071 | Holding; CL072 | No Movement; CL073 | Another Movement; CL074 | Movement Unknown
Object: CL075 | No Object; CL076 | Large Item; CL077 | Medium Item; CL078 | Small Item; CL079 | Tool; CL080 | Cart; CL081 | Load Carrier; CL082 | Cardboard Box; CL083 | On Body; CL084 | Another Logistic Object; CL085 | No Logistic Object; CL086 | Object Unknown
Tool: CL087 | Portable Data Terminal, CL088 | Glove Scanner; CL089 | Plastic Bag; CL090 | Picking List; CL091 | Pen; CL092 | Button; CL093 | Computer; CL094 | Bubble Wrap; CL095 | Tape Dispenser; CL096 | Knife; CL097 | Shipping/Return Label; CL098 | Elastic Band; CL099 | Another Tool</td></tr>
<tr><td></td><td>CC06</td><td>Order</td><td></td><td>X</td><td>5</td><td>CL100 | 2904; CL101 | 2905; CL102 | 2906; CL103 | No Order; CL104 | Order Unknown</td></tr>
<tr><td>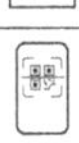</td><td>CC07</td><td>Information Technology</td><td></td><td>X</td><td>5</td><td>CL105 | List and Pen; CL106 | List and Glove Scanner; CL107 | Portable Data Terminal; CL108 | No Information Technology; CL109 | Information Technology Unknown</td></tr>
<tr><td>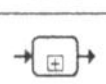</td><td>CC08</td><td>High-Level Process</td><td></td><td>X</td><td>4</td><td>CL110 | Retrieval; CL111 | Storage; CL112 | Another High-Level Process; CL113 | High-Level Process Unknown</td></tr>
<tr><td>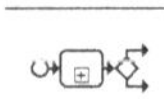</td><td>CC09</td><td>Mid-Level Process</td><td></td><td>X</td><td>10</td><td>CL114 | Preparing Order; CL115 | Picking–Travel Time; CL116 | Picking–Pick Time; CL117 | Unpacking; CL118 | Packing; CL119 | Storing–Travel Time; CL120 | Storing–Store Time, CL121 | Finalizing Order; CL122 | Another Mid-Level Process; CL123 | Mid-Level Process Unknown</td></tr>
</table>

https://doi.org/10.3390/s26020739

Table 6. *Cont.*

Class Categories [CC] Icon	ID	Name	M	C	Class Labels [CL] Nr.	List
	CC10	Low-Level Process		X	31	CL124 | Collecting Order and Hardware; CL125 | Collecting Cart; CL126 | Collecting Empty Cardboard Boxes; CL127 | Collecting Packed Cardboard Boxes; CL128 | Transporting a Cart to the Base; CL129 | Transporting to the Packaging/Sorting Area; CL130 | Handing Over Packed Cardboard Boxes; CL131 | Returning Empty Cardboard Boxes; CL132 | Returning Cart; CL133 | Returning Hardware; CL134 | Waiting; CL135 | Reporting and Clarifying the Incident; CL136 | Removing Cardboard Box/Item from the Cart; CL137 | Moving to the Next Position; CL138 | Placing Items on a Rack; CL139 | Retrieving Items; CL140 | Moving to a Cart; CL141 | Placing Cardboard Box/Item on a Table; CL142 | Opening Cardboard Box; CL143 | Disposing of Filling Material or Shipping Label; CL144 | Sorting; CL145 | Filling Cardboard Box with Filling Material; CL146 | Printing Shipping Label and Return Slip; CL147 | Preparing or Adding Return Label; CL148 | Attaching Shipping Label; CL149 | Removing Elastic Band; CL150 | Sealing Cardboard Box; CL151 | Placing Cardboard Box/Item in a Cart; CL152 | Tying Elastic Band Around Cardboard; CL153 | Another Low-Level Process; CL154 | Low-Level Process Unknown
	CC11	Location–Human		X	26	**Main Area:** CL155 | Office; CL156 | Cart Area; CL157 | Cardboard Box Area; CL158 | Base; CL159 | Packing/Sorting Area; CL160 | Issuing/Receiving Area; CL161 | Path; CL162 | Cross Aisle Path; CL163 | Aisle Path **Path:** CL164 | Path (Office); CL165 | Path (Cardboard Box Area); CL166 | Path (Cart Area); CL167 | Path (Issuing Area) **Cross Aisle Path:** CL168 | 1–2; CL169 | 2–3; CL170 | 3–4; CL171 | 4–5 **Aisle Path:** CL172 | 1; CL173 | 2; CL174 | 3; CL175 | 4; CL176 | 5; CL177 | Front; CL178 | Back **Other:** CL179 | Another Location; CL180 | Location Unknown
	CC12	Location–Cart		X	27	**Main Area:** CL181 | Transition between Areas; CL182 | Office; CL183 | Cart Area; CL184 | Cardboard Box Area; CL185 | Base; CL186 | Packing/Sorting Area; CL187 | Issuing/Receiving Area; CL188 | Path; CL189 | Cross Aisle Path; CL190 | Aisle Path **Path:** CL191 | Path (Office); CL192 | Path (Cardboard Box Area); CL193 | Path (Cart Area); CL194 | Path (Issuing Area) **Cross Aisle Path:** CL195 | 1–2; CL196 | 2–3; CL197 | 3–4; CL198 | 4–5 **Aisle Path:** CL199 | 1; CL200 | 2; CL201 | 3; CL202 | 4; CL203 | 5; CL204 | Front; CL205 | Back **Other:** CL206 | Another Location; CL207 | Location Unknown

Categories CC06–CC12 capture contextual information, which refers to complementary information that places an activity within its content-related, procedural, and spatial frames. This includes the customer *Order* (CC06), the use of *Information Technology* (CC07), the embedding of the activity in *Processes* (CC08–CC10), and the *Location* of the subject (CC11) or the picking cart (CC12).

Certain categories are organized hierarchically. *Sub-Activity–Left Hand* and *Sub-Activity–Right Hand* are subdivided into *Primary Position*, *Type of Movement*, *Object*, and *Tool*, while *Locations* is subdivided into *Main Area*, *Path*, *Cross Aisle Path*, *Aisle Path*, and *Other*.

Depending on the category, between four and 35 class labels were defined, yielding a total of 207 distinct labels. When all categories are combined, annotation and revision result in 68,174 unique label representations. A total of 3,444,327 frames were annotated and revised for each of the 12 class categories. The label *Unknown*, used when annotators were unsure, was largely resolved during review and remains in only 0–0.07% of cases. It does not occur in CC06–CC09, CC11, or CC12 and appears in less than 0.01% (CC10) to 0.07% (CC05) of the remaining classes.

Figure 12 illustrates the complexity of the annotation process and the resulting label representations. The example depicts the order picking process for two positions (order lines), each comprising the route from the base to the item, retrieval of the item from a rack, scanning the barcodes of the storage compartment and the item, confirmation of the retrieval, transportation of the item back to the base, and placement on the picking cart.

In the first frames of Figure 12, the picker begins processing the first position by walking along the cross aisle to the next position in the third aisle path, holding a portable data terminal in the right hand, with the left hand inactive, performing the retrieval process (order 2905) during the travel time phase, while the cart remains at the base.

https://doi.org/10.3390/s26020739

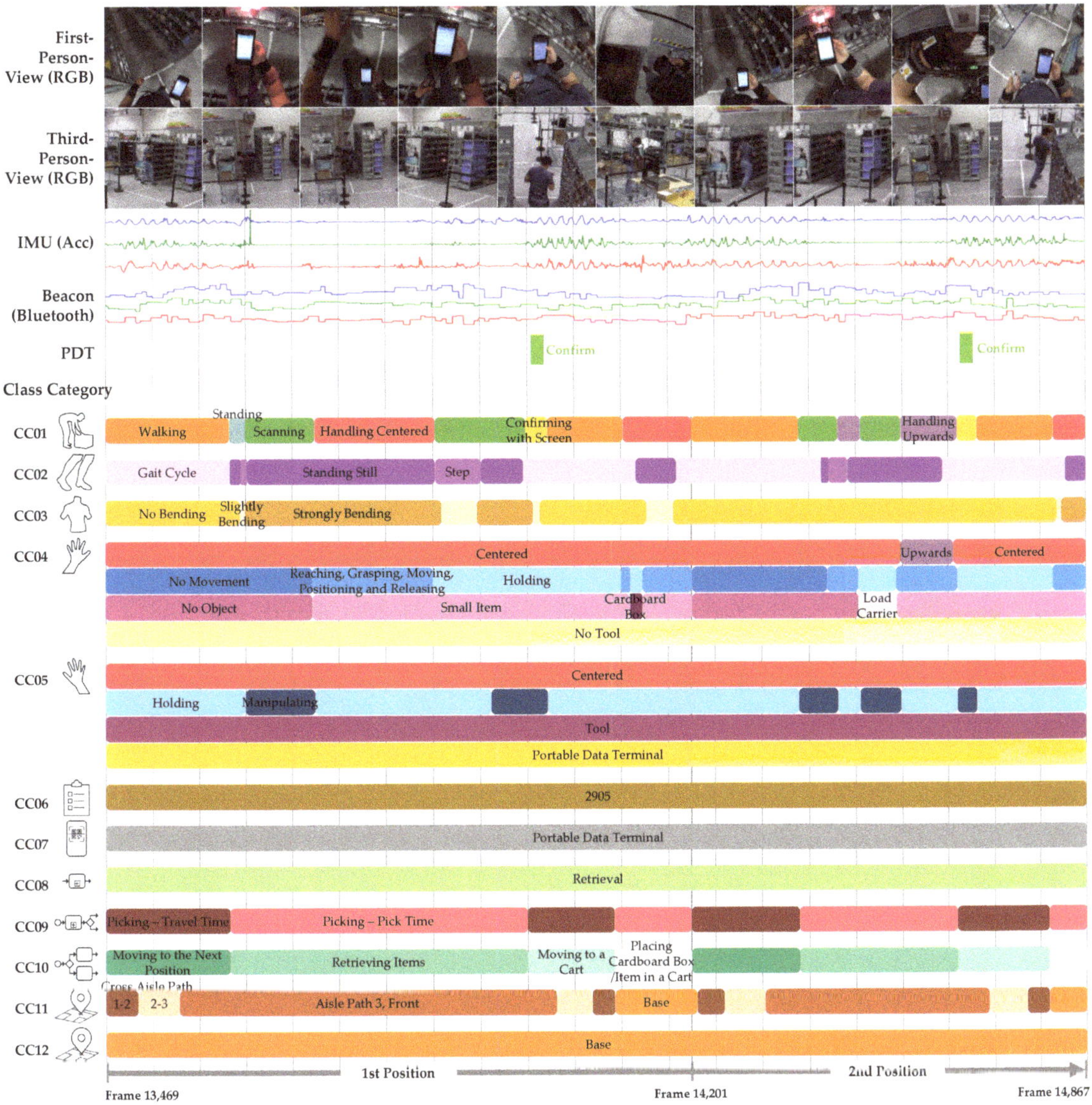

Figure 12. Example sequence from the DaRA dataset (duration: 1398 frames ≈ 46.6 s) showing two order picking positions performed by subject S14 during the scenario 2 of the recording session 5. The first four layers display sensor data, including cropped first-person views and examples from five of the six third-person RGB camera views, energy of the inertial recordings from the MotionMiners IMU set 44-C (blue = right wrist, green = belt, red = left wrist), and RSSI from the same device set connecting to the beacon number 13 (position of beacon see Figure 9). The fifth layer shows two pick confirmations transmitted by PDT and stored in the WMS. The subsequent layers depict the 12 class categories with their revised labels, where one label of some categories (e.g., *CC06 Order*; see Table 6) spans the entire sequence, while others (e.g., *CC02 Sub-Activity - Legs*) contain multiple annotation segments with different labels. (The style of this figure is based on [6]). A video of this sequence is available on YouTube (https://youtu.be/qU0XvKY20SE, accessed on 18 January 2026).

Upon reaching the rack, the subject stands and searches for the correct compartment, checking the display for the quantity to be retrieved. The *Strongly Bending* motion then begins as the subject scans the storage location code. The onset of the bending movement is clearly visible in the torso IMU data (green) as a distinct peak (see Figure 12). Additional motion segments and their corresponding labels can also be visually identified in the IMU signals—for instance, those belonging to class CC02. Segments of the *Gait Cycle* are characterized by rhythmic oscillations in the torso IMU data (green), whereas the signal amplitude becomes more erratic and decreases noticeably during *Standing Still* and *Step* phases.

3.5. Annotation and Revision

The following sections describe the methodology, procedure, and time effort involved in annotation and revision.

3.5.1. Annotation Methodology

After video export and synchronization, annotation and subsequent revision—following the *silver standard with more-experienced revisers* as described in [112]—were conducted using the SARA tool [88,109]. The labels are annotated segment-wise in time, meaning that label segments were defined with flexible durations based on the natural onsets and offsets of movements. The commencement and cessation of these segments, in addition to the selection of labels, are determined by the annotator's perspective.

Regarding label exclusivity, either a single label or a multi-label was applied, depending on the class category. With a single label, exactly one label was assigned to each time interval, as in class categories CC01, CC02, CC07, CC08, CC09, and CC10 (for class categories, see Table 6). In contrast, in the multi-label category, either multiple labels were allowed (CC03, CC06, CC11, CC12) or required (CC04, CC05).

All labels were assigned as hard labels, i.e., with unambiguous allocation (e.g., 100% *Walking* in CC01 or 100% *No Bending* in CC03; see the example in Figure 12).

3.5.2. Annotation Sessions

The dataset was manually annotated by 15 domain experts and by trained internal annotators. Each annotator received instructions and an annotation guideline (see the *Documentation.pdf* file) and performed test annotations (see [113]) to ensure the label quality. Subsequently, annotators were assigned specific subjects, and each recording was annotated in full by exactly one annotator per class category (single-annotator labeling).

Annotation was performed either individually or jointly, depending on the class category (see Table 6). *Main Activity* (CC01) and *Locations* (CC11–CC12) were annotated separately, while CC06–CC08 and CC09–CC10 were annotated jointly. A sequential annotation strategy was applied to reduce effort and minimize errors, particularly for less experienced annotators.

To further increase consistency, we integrated dependency rules into the tool as CSV files that specify all valid label combinations within and across categories. Once this dependency file is imported, the annotator is prevented from selecting any invalid combinations. For example, *Walking* and *Standing* cannot co-occur in *Main Activity*. Similarly, *Sub-Activities* (CC02–CC05) were annotated with reference to the previously assigned *Main Activity*, ensuring segment alignment. In this way, annotators of *Sub-Activities* simultaneously acted as revisers of *Main Activity*.

3.5.3. Annotation Revision

Following the annotation, both manual and automated revision of the annotated labels were conducted. During manual revision, each annotated file (e.g., *Location–Human* class category for subject S05; see Figure 13) was imported into SARA Tools with the video files, thereby enabling synchronized playback of both the videos and the labels. Each file

https://doi.org/10.3390/s26020739

was revised once (except files from *Main Activity*) by one of the eight revisers. In cases of a mislabeled or misplaced segment, new labels were assigned, or the start and end boundaries of segments were adjusted.

The *Main Activity*, unlike the other class categories, was revised not separately but in parallel with the annotation of the *Sub-Activities* CC02–CC05. For this purpose, the already annotated class labels of the Main Activity were extended by the class labels of CC02. The goal was to preserve the existing Main Activity segments, as they are conceptually closely related to the Sub-Activities. During the annotation of CC02, the annotator examined the Main Activity and manually corrected it when necessary. Due to the use of dependencies, the incorrectly annotated Main Activity labels had to be adjusted to assign the CC02 class labels. For example, it was not possible to annotate *CL016 | Gait Cycle* if *CL012 | Standing* was already assigned within the same segment. This procedure was repeated analogously for CC03 through CC05, with the revised Main Activity labels carried forward continuously.

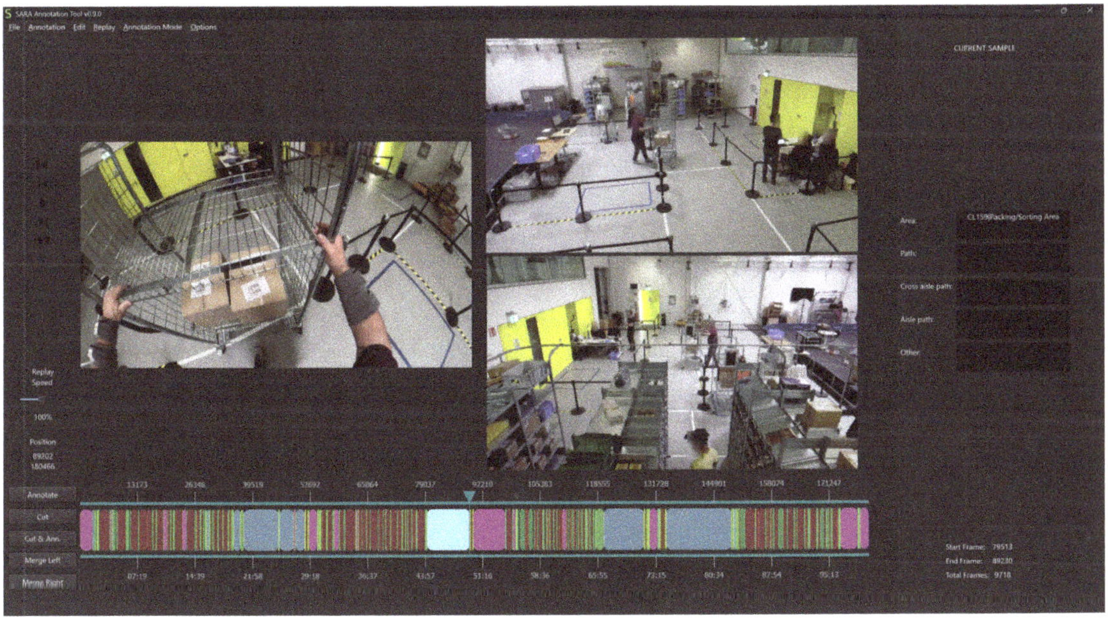

Figure 13. Screenshot from the tool SARA [88,109], displaying the fully annotated and revised recording (180,466 frames) of the *Location–Human* class category for subject S05 wearing a purple shirt during session 2. On the left, the FPV from the action camera is shown, while the right side displays the TPV from fixed cameras 1 and 2. To the right of the videos, the annotator assigned the label *Packaging/Sorting Area*, which was verified by the reviser. The lower color gradient represents the set segments. Each of the 564 segments corresponds to a new area, with the segment width indicating the duration the subject remained in that area. The colors align with the floor plan coding scheme (see Figure 4). The displayed frame (89,202) captures the subject in the *Packaging/Sorting Area* (light blue), just as they are about to leave it and enter the *Path* (lime green).

In addition, automated plausibility checks were applied to identify frames with an excessive or insufficient number of labels (the number varies depending on the class category), as well as mutually exclusive label sequences either within a single class category (e.g., in the class category *Location*, the label *Aisle Path* cannot directly follow *Cart Area* because other areas are in between) or across multiple categories.

https://doi.org/10.3390/s26020739

3.5.4. Time Effort

For all class categories, the annotation required 1572 person-hours (PH), and the revision amounted to 361 PH (see Table 7). The time requirements refer exclusively to the main annotation and revision. They do not include time spent on annotator training, test annotations, or correcting errors identified through automated checks. The effort varied significantly across class categories. In the case of annotation, the average labeling effort for a one-minute video ranged from 6 sec (*Order, Information Technology*, and *High-Level Process*) to over 12 min (*Sub-Activity–Left Hand*).

Table 7. Effort for annotating and revising 3,444,327 frames of video footage (31:55:26 hh:mm:ss) from S01–S18 for every CC. The ratio indicates the average time required to annotate or revise one minute of video footage, calculated as the total annotation or revision time divided by 31:55:26 hh:mm:ss.

	Class Category	**Annotation**		**Revision**	
		Total	**Ratio**	**Total**	**Ratio**
			[hh:mm:ss]		
CC01	Main Activity	172:35:30	0:05:24	–	–
CC02	Sub-Activity–Legs	278:44:27	0:08:44	68:12:31	0:02:08
CC03	Sub-Activity–Torso	108:12:37	0:03:23	76:13:01	0:02:23
CC04	Sub-Activity–Left Hand	384:24:34	0:12:02	71:15:00	0:02:14
CC05	Sub-Activity–Right Hand	378:12:41	0:11:51	73:46:51	0:02:19
CC06 CC07 CC08	Order Information Technology High-Level Process	3:13:20	0:00:06	1:01:40	0:00:02
CC09 CC10	Mid-Level Process Low-Level Process	129:15:32	0:04:03	39:20:41	0:01:14
CC11	Location–Human	92:08:38	0:02:53	22:51:42	0:00:43
CC12	Location–Cart	25:19:00	0:00:48	8:30:55	0:00:16
Total	**All Categories**	**1572:06:19**	**0:49:15**	**361:12:21**	**0:11:19**

3.6. *Available Data and Dataset Utilization*

The DaRA dataset, available through the Zenodo repository [15], supports a broad spectrum of research applications such as human activity recognition, human context recognition, indoor localization, process mining, and process recognition.

The dataset comprises both **sensor data** and **revised annotations** for three sensor modalities: camera (29.97 fps), IMU (100 Hz), and BLE (10 Hz). Within each recording session, the three FPV and six TPV camera streams are temporally synchronized, i.e., they start simultaneously but may differ in overall duration depending on the speed at which the recording session is completed. In total, the FPV camera recordings comprise 31:55:26 h (see Table 5) and the TPV camera recordings amount to 77:18:24 h. Video annotations were synchronized with the wearable sets (IMU and Beacon) based on defined synchronization movements. The **Python script** (version 1) used to perform the synchronization is available on GitHub [106]. Further details are provided in the *Documentation.pdf* file. In total, the dataset contains 1056 revised annotation files, including the following:

- A total of 216 annotations for the synchronized cameras (18 subjects × 12 class categories);
- A total of 420 annotations each for the IMU data and the Beacon data ([18 subjects × 2 wearable sets—one faulty wearable set from subject S10] × 12 class categories).

The **WMS data** (available in CSV format) includes picking confirmations recorded via the PDT. All timestamps are synchronized with the video data and the corresponding annotation files.

Class label configuration files, called **scheme files** (available in JSON format), enable the import, visualization, and editing of annotations in conjunction with the video recordings within the SARA annotation tool [88,109]. A dedicated scheme file is provided for each class category, defining the corresponding annotation structure.

The accompanying **documentation file** (PDF format) provides further information on the dataset. It includes an annotation guideline, detailed descriptions of all 12 class categories and their 207 class labels, and the master item data, containing information on storage location, physical dimensions, and weight. Furthermore, the documentation features item photographs, the three customer orders, and information about the sensor placement, synchronization, and sequence, as well as the start and end of the scenarios.

Finally, a **Python script** for **preprocessing** (ZIP archive) is provided to enable customized modification of the annotation files [106]. The script supports interactive selection of class categories, with optional filtering of *Unknown* and/or *Other* labels. It decomposes structured classes by splitting *Location—Human/Cart* into Main and Sub locations, and *Left/Right Hand* into *Primary Position*, *Type of Movement*, *Object*, and *Tool*. It can also construct compact *input* and *output* combination columns for downstream analysis. The processed results are exported as synchronized per-subject CSV files.

4. Evaluation—Dataset Quality

The overall quality of the dataset is determined by the consistency of the labels after annotation and revision, the quality of the acquired sensor data, and the application of the labels and sensor data for HAR.

4.1. Annotation and Revision Quality

The annotators were required to conduct test annotations for each class category they annotated or revised. For the class categories CC06–CC08, the entire recording of subject S09 was test-annotated. For the other categories, excerpts of over five minutes from subjects S04, S05, and S06 were test-annotated. The revisers had to revise the test annotations for their respective class categories. The test video recordings, along with all test annotations and revisions, have been published as an additional dataset on Zenodo [113].

To assess annotation quality as well as the revised datasets, we used Cohen's κ [114] for exactly two annotators and Light's κ [115] for more than two annotators, the latter being the mean of all pairwise Cohen's κ values. Overall agreement was summarized as macro-κ, defined as the unweighted average of per-label κ. Because extremely rare labels in the test annotations can yield unstable κ estimates (e.g., if only one annotator marked 10 frames in the test annotation as *Sitting* while others did not), we pre-specified a filtered macro-κ that includes only labels with sufficient support (≥0.5% of frames and ≥30 positive frames).

After revision, we observed high average macro Light's κ across categories, ranging from 78.27% (CC02, *Sub-Activity—Legs*) to 99.88% (CC06, *Order*) (see Table 8). According to common benchmarks [116–118], this corresponds to *substantial* to *almost perfect* agreement. We also found a clear difference between human movement categories (CC01–CC05; 78.27–81.61%) and context categories (CC06–CC12; 90.95–99.88%). A similar pattern is already visible in the unrevised test annotations. Overall, these findings indicate that context segments were easier and more consistently labeled than human movements.

Significant enhancements from the annotation to the revision, for example, in CC02 (*Sub-Activity—Legs*; from 60.99% to 78.27%), in CC03 (*Sub-Activity—Torso*; from 40.83% to 81.61%) and CC10 (*Low-Level Process*; from 73.25% to 90.95%), are partly attributable

https://doi.org/10.3390/s26020739

to the use of *Another* and *Unknown* labels during annotation whenever an unambiguous assignment seemed infeasible. During revision, such segments were typically reassigned to more specific labels, thereby substantially increasing agreement.

Table 8. Strength of agreement over annotations and revisions divided by class categories. As the labels of classes CC04 and CC05 are semantically equivalent, test annotation was performed exclusively for *Sub-Activity–Left Hand* (CC04). It is evident that the label definitions are equivalent; therefore, the resulting Light's kappa value can be directly applied to the *Sub-Activity–Right Hand* (CC05).

ID	Class Category Name	Cohen's/Light's Kappa [%] Annotation	Revision
CC01	Main Activity	75.77	80.59
CC02	Sub-Activity–Legs	60.99	78.27
CC03	Sub-Activity–Torso	40.83	81.61
CC04 CC05	Sub-Activity–Left Hand Sub-Activity–Right Hand	71.32	78.35
CC06	Order	95.44	99.88
CC07	Information Technology	95.20	99.86
CC08	High-Level Process	94.53	99.85
CC09	Mid-Level Process	89.63	98.63
CC10	Low-Level Process	73.25	90.95
CC11	Location–Human	88.54	98.04
CC12	Location–Cart	92.47	98.16

4.2. Sensor Data Quality

The recordings from all six fixed cameras are synchronized and corrected across all six sessions. Correcting here means adding blank frames to keep all the videos synchronized for annotation purposes. Due to a battery change, the cameras did not record the same material. However, synchronization and data integrity are unaffected. All nine video streams from the action and fixed cameras were automatically synchronized and then manually verified and corrected as needed. The synchronization of the videos for each session was verified using several sections with rapid movements by the subjects, such as gait cycle, and white markings on the floor. Any residual temporal offsets are minimal, on the order of zero to three frames. An illustrative example is shown in Figure 8, where a one-frame offset is visible: in (b) the foot remains on the line, whereas in (h) it has moved slightly behind it.

The MotionMiners devices record IMU data and RSSI from all the beacons in the layout. Each device set per subject comprises three devices (right arm, left arm, and torso) and records a three-dimensional accelerometer, a three-dimensional gyroscope, and RSSI readings from all beacons spread across the layout. The RSSI signals are used for indoor localization by means of a fingerprinting method, where a region is represented by statistical features from the RSSI signals from the three devices for a specific period of time. Localization is carried out by distance classification.

The MotionMiners devices guarantee the recording of IMU data with no data loss at a sampling rate of 100 Hz, as they record the data and transfer it upon completion. Still, when devices are damaged, complete recordings are lost—MotionMiners seeks to reduce such cases. One of the two device sets of test subject S10 recorded incorrectly and is therefore not included in the dataset.

https://doi.org/10.3390/s26020739

4.3. Quality of Revised Annotations and Sensors Combined—Deploying DaRA for HAR

We trained a tCNN-IMU, similar to [4,10], using the IMU data as a HAR baseline. This serves as a high-quality example showing that the data and annotations can, in principle, be used to train AI methods. The tCNN-IMU processes sequence segments with a feature map input of size $[T, 18]$, where T is the sequence length and 18 is the number of sequence channels, corresponding to $[x, y, z]$ accelerometer and gyroscope measurements from the three devices. The sequence segments are extracted following a sliding-window approach with a window size of $T = 150$, step size of $s = 25$ (16.7% overlapping). The tCNN-IMU computes either an activity class $\boldsymbol{k}$ or a binary-attribute representation $\boldsymbol{a}$. An attribute representation is a combination of sub-activity labels (short activities or limb movements) $\boldsymbol{a} \in \mathbb{B}$, creating a sort of semantic description of an activity. Each attribute indicates whether a specific sub-activity is present during the activity. Following [4], input sequences are normalized per sensor channel to the range of $[0, 1]$. Additionally, a Gaussian noise with parameters $[\mu = 0, \sigma = 0.01]$ is added.

Following the training procedures from [3,42], the IMU data is divided into three sets: training, validation, and testing. The training set comprises recordings from subjects $[S02, S03, S04, S06, S07, S08, S10, S11, S12, S13, S15, S16]$. The validation and testing sets are composed of recordings from $[S01, S05, S18]$ and $[S09, S14, S17]$, respectively. An early stopping approach is followed using the validation set. This set is also used to find appropriate training hyperparameters. Recordings with labels *Synchronization*, *Another Main Activity*, and *Main Activity Unknown* are not considered for training. The architecture is trained using batch gradient descent with RMSProp, with an RMS decay of 0.9, a learning rate of 1×10^{-4}, and a batch size of 400. Moreover, Dropout was applied to the first and second fully connected layers. The tCNN-IMU is trained using a softmax layer to predict activity classes directly with Cross-Entropy Loss, or a Sigmoid layer to predict an attribute representation with Binary-Cross-Entropy Loss.

Tables 9 and 10 present the performance of the method solving HAR on the DaRA IMU dataset using the softmax layer and sigmoid layer. Precision is computed as $P = \frac{TP}{TP+FP}$. Recall is computed as $R = \frac{TP}{TP+FN}$. Having TP, FP, and FN as the true positives, false positives, and false negatives. The weighted F1 is calculated as $wF1 = \sum_i^C 2 \times \frac{n_i}{N} \times \frac{P_i \times R_i}{P_i + R_i}$, with n_i being the number of window samples of class $C_i \in C$. *Confirm with Pen*, *Walking* and *Standing* activities show the best performances. These results align with [4,9], which show that using attribute predictions for HAR improves classification performance. However, these are preliminary results, as the DaRA datasets include multiple annotation levels, HAR and process predictions using HMMs, transformers, or LSTMs should be considered.

Table 9. Recall [%] and precision [%] of human activity recognition (HAR) with predicting the activity classes using Softmax on the DaRA IMU dataset.

Main Activity	Metric	
	Recall	**Precision**
Confirm with Pen	91.18	3.05
Confirm with Screen	0.00	0.00
Confirm with Button	57.50	4.01
Scan	18.97	7.42
Pull	78.16	66.89
Push	74.21	90.38
Handling Upwards	54.17	61.39
Handling Centered	71.99	84.23
Handling Downwards	66.45	54.37
Walking	80.00	75.36
Standing	81.88	67.83

https://doi.org/10.3390/s26020739

Table 10. The overall accuracy [%] and wF1 [%] of HAR using Softmax for predicting activities k and Sigmoid for predicting an attribute vector $\boldsymbol{a}$ on the IMU of the DaRA dataset. An attribute representation $\boldsymbol{a}$ is a combination of sub-activity labels with $\boldsymbol{a} \in \mathbb{B}$, creating a sort of semantic description of an activity.

Metric	Softmax	Attributes
Acc [%]	72.12	74.62
wF1 [%]	70.40	73.70

Table 11 shows the confusion matrix from the activity class predictions using the tCNN-IMU with the softmax layer. The three *confirm* activities show poor performance, i.e., low precision with very high false positives. These activities are very difficult because they have a shorter duration than others, e.g., with fewer samples. Besides, these activities are not carried out by all the subjects. *Scan* tends to be predicted as *Handling Center*, which are semantically similar.

Table 11. Confusion matrix from the class predictions using tCNN-IMU with the softmax layer.

Main Activity	Confusion Matrix										
	Confirm with			Scan	Pull	Push	Handling			Walk.	Stand.
	Pen	Screen	Button				Up.	Cen.	Down.		
Confirm with Pen	124	0	0	32	7	43	1948	1623	83	121	87
Confirm with Screen	0	0	5	0	1	12	45	367	42	106	107
Confirm with Button	0	0	46	3	0	3	161	609	167	155	2
Scan	0	63	1	291	6	9	340	1924	534	156	600
Pull	0	0	0	0	2347	775	6	374	3	3	1
Push	0	0	0	0	249	6276	0	411	0	3	5
Handling Upwards	11	1	12	191	19	58	7899	4513	14	119	29
Handling Centered	1	26	4	502	319	883	3251	64,222	2079	3157	1805
Handling Down.	0	1	1	51	0	2	63	4858	6711	467	190
Walking	0	0	6	2	15	303	155	5398	62	20,004	598
Standing	0	0	5	462	40	93	714	4906	404	714	15,473

We primarily experimented with IMU data for human activity recognition (HAR) using main activity labels and sub-activity labels with an existing method, namely tCNN-IMU [4,10]. This initial evaluation of DaRA provides a baseline for HAR. Process prediction, localization using BLE RSSI, and the combination of multiple devices and label types are to be carried out as part of future work. As part of future work, we aim to experiment with the relationship between activities and location using low- and mid-level processes, using learning methods such as LSTMs, Transformers, and HMMs. This experimentation is based on the strong relation between repetitive activities, location areas, and structured processes within logistics tasks.

5. Discussion and Future Works

5.1. Discussion

This paper introduced the DaRA dataset, a novel multimodal dataset for HAR and HCR in intralogistics. It includes multiple sensors and extensive class labels that describe both human movements and context, allowing activities to be characterized in terms of content, procedure, and spatial setting.

The DaRA dataset helps address key research gaps in HAR and HCR. First, there is a lack of datasets specifically designed for industrial domains. Second, existing datasets often lack contextual sensor data or labels, which are essential for a comprehensive un-

https://doi.org/10.3390/s26020739

derstanding of activities. Finally, DaRA offers rich metadata that are rarely available in comparable datasets.

The dataset provides high-quality annotations and detailed sensor data. Limitations arise from the recording environment and subject characteristics. The semi-controlled lab setting enables realistic movements but does not fully reflect real-world warehouse processes, and only selected intralogistics processes and technologies are covered. Furthermore, women are underrepresented among subjects, and the subjects were not professional warehouse workers.

A trained neural network achieved an F1 score of over 73.70% for activity recognition, demonstrating successful classification of human movements. The next logical step is to advance HCR, where context may be derived from both sensor data and classified activities.

5.2. Future Works

The created DaRA dataset can be used for the well-established field of HAR as well as for HCR. HCR encompasses indoor localization and, in particular, the still underexplored and increasingly relevant research area of process recognition. For a comprehensive optimization of workflows in a warehouse environment, it is not sufficient to know solely *what* a person is doing (main and sub-activity); it is equally important to determine *where* (location) and, most importantly, *within which process step* this activity is being performed. In this way, recognized activities can be embedded into a semantically meaningful and human-interpretable context.

Furthermore, the dataset offers substantial potential for logistics simulations, motion prediction, policy learning in robotics [119,120], multi-view integration, the detection and identification of logistics objects, and studies on RGB-based person and action recognition. Although multimodal data have been shown to yield superior predictive performance in neural networks compared to unimodal approaches, DaRA deliberately pursues the objective of enabling robust recognition using as few information sources and sensor types as possible in industrial settings. Consequently, a unimodal design was adopted in this work to produce a lightweight neural network architecture that operates reliably with reduced GPU resources. Nevertheless, future experiments incorporating multimodal data are desirable to systematically evaluate the trade-off between additional sensor modalities and potential gains in predictive performance.

Based on the provided labels for the recordings, further studies can be conducted on temporal jitter in motion annotations and on the derivation of textual annotations. Future versions of DaRA are also intended to provide skeletal information extracted from RGB videos, thereby facilitating policy learning in robotics and supporting simulation-based research.

Author Contributions: Conceptualization, F.N. and S.L.; methodology, F.N., F.M.R. and S.L.; validation, F.N., F.M.R. and S.L.; software, F.M.R. and M.K.A.K.; formal analysis, F.N., F.M.R. and M.K.A.K.; investigation, F.N., F.M.R. and N.R.N.; resources, V.K., F.N., F.M.R., S.L. and A.K.; data curation, F.N., D.S., F.M.R. and S.L.; writing—original draft preparation, F.N., F.M.R., M.K.A.K., N.R.N. and S.L.; writing—review and editing, F.N., F.M.R., M.K.A.K., N.R.N., V.K., D.S.; visualization, F.N.; supervision, S.L. and A.K.; project administration, F.N.; funding acquisition, F.N. and S.L. All authors have read and agreed to the published version of the manuscript.

Funding: This project is supported by the Federal Ministry for Economic Affairs and Climate Action (BMWK) on the basis of a decision by the German Bundestag (Funding Code: KK5072230MA3, KK5110002MA3, KK5526202MA3) and the Federal Ministry of Research, Technology and Space of Germany and the state of North Rhine-Westphalia as part of the Lamarr Institute for Machine Learning and Artificial Intelligence.

https://doi.org/10.3390/s26020739

Institutional Review Board Statement: The study was approved by the Joint Ethics Committee of Faculties 9, 11–17 of TU Dortmund University (GEKTUDO2024-02, 15 April 2024).

Informed Consent Statement: Informed consent was obtained from all subjects involved in the study. Written informed consent has been obtained from the subjects to publish this paper and the dataset.

Data Availability Statement: The dataset described and used in this work is freely available on Zenodo: [15].

Acknowledgments: The authors sincerely thank everyone who contributed to the recordings, annotations, revisions, and figure creation. Special appreciation goes to the Fraunhofer Institute for Material Flow and Logistics (IML) for providing access to their Picking Lab for data recording. We would also like to thank Sebastian Beierle (Chair of Material Handling and Warehousing) for providing the photographs in Figures 2, 6 and 7, and Markus Heinzelmann (Chair of Material Handling and Warehousing) for creating the icons used in Table 6 and Figure 12, as well as the DaRA logo in Figure 1.

Conflicts of Interest: Authors Fernando Moya Rueda and Dustin Schauten were employed by the company MotionMiners GmbH. The remaining authors declare that the research was conducted in the absence of any commercial or financial relationships that could be construed as a potential conflict of interest.

Abbreviations

The following abbreviations are used in this manuscript:

ADL	Activities of Daily Living
BLE	Bluetooth Low Energy
BPMN	Business Process Model and Notation
CAARL	Context-Aware Activity Recognition in Logistics
CC	Class Category
CL	Class Label
CNN	Convolutional Neural Network
DaRA	Data Fusion for advanced Research in industrial Applications
FN	False Negative
FP	False Positive
fps	Frame per Second
FPV	First-Person View
HAR	Human Activity Recognition
HCR	Human Context Recognition
HMM	Hidden Markov Model
Hz	Herz
ID	Identification
IMU	Inertial Measurement Unit
IT	Information Technology
LARa	Logistic Activity Recognition Challenge
LSTM	Long Short-Term Memory
MoCap	Motion Capture
Nr.	Number
P	Precision
PDT	Portable Data Terminal
PH	Person-Hours
R	Recall
RGB	Red–Green–Blue (refering to colored video)
RGB-D	Red–Green–Blue and Depth (refering to colored video with depth information)
RSSI	Received Signal Strength Indicator

TN	True Negative
tcnn	Temporal Convolutional Neural Network
TP	True Positive
TPV	Third-Person View
WMS	Warehouse Management System

Appendix A

Categories	Realization Options	
HAR Application Domains	healthcare / rehabilitation / nursing	exercise and athletic performance
	traffic and mobility	smart homes and AAL
	entertainment and gaming	behavioral research / psychology
	robotics/human-machine interaction	industry (production / logistics)
	security and surveillance	other
Recording Environments	controlled	semi-controlled
	real-world	
Scenarios	scripted	free-living
	hybrid	
Sensor Types	inertial sensors	visual sensors
	physiological/biosensors	acoustic sensors
	environmental sensors	positioning sensors
	tactile and force sensors	other
Label Categories	postures / static activities	locomotion
	gestures / fine-motor activities	human-to-object interaction
	activities of daily living (ADL)	sports
	composite / high-level activities	health events
	environmental / procedural context	behavior
Label Time Structure	frame-wise labeling	segment-wise labeling
	window-based labeling	
Exclusivity of the Labels	single-label	multi-label
Label Hierarchy	flat labels	hierarchical labels
Label Certainty / Uncertainty	hard labels	probabilistic labels
	confidence-annotated labels	
Annotation Methods	manual	fully automatic
	semi-automatic	sensor fusion-based
	crowd-sourced	
Annotators	domain expert	trained internal annotator
	study subject	non-expert
Annotator Labeling	single annotator labeling	multiple annotator labeling
	consensus labeling	
Revision Methods	manual review by experts	automated plausibility checks
	comparison of multiple annotations	

Figure A1. Positioning of the DaRA dataset (green) within the taxonomy of HAR datasets.

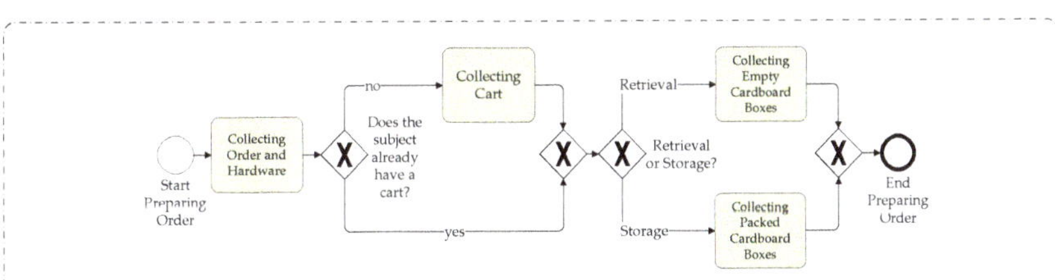

Figure A2. Idealized BPMN of the mid-level process *Preparing Order* with its low-level processes.

https://doi.org/10.3390/s26020739

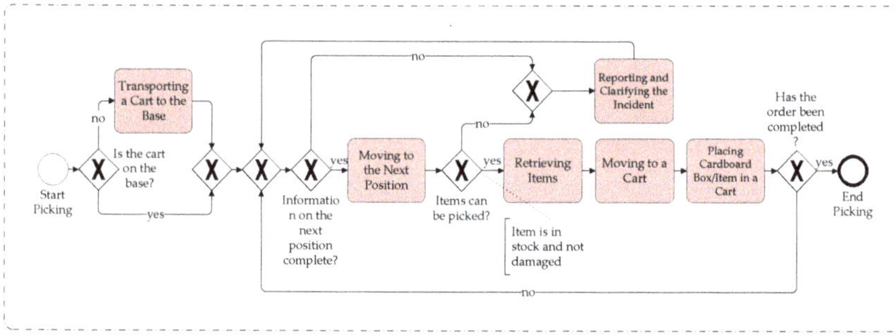

Figure A3. Idealized BPMN of the mid-level processes *Picking–Travel Time* and *Picking–Pick Time* with its low-level processes.

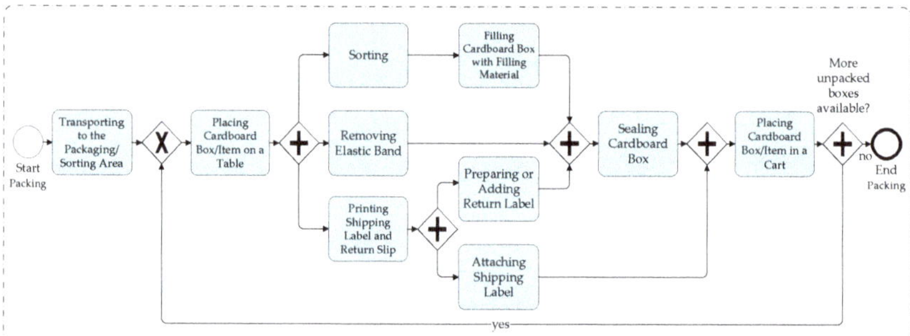

Figure A4. Idealized BPMN of the mid-level process *Packing* with its low-level processes.

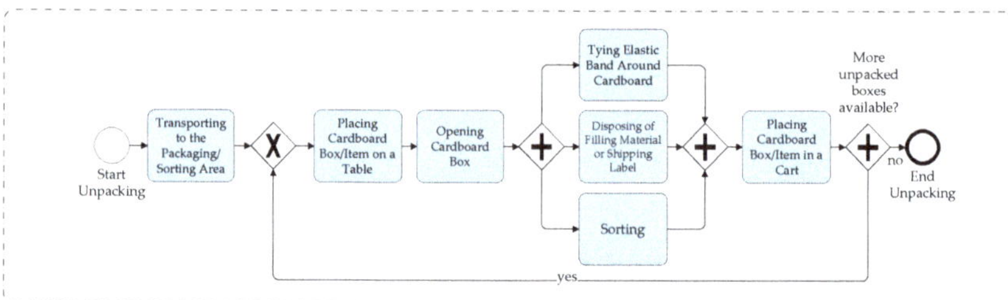

Figure A5. Idealized BPMN of the mid-level process *Unpacking* with its low-level processes.

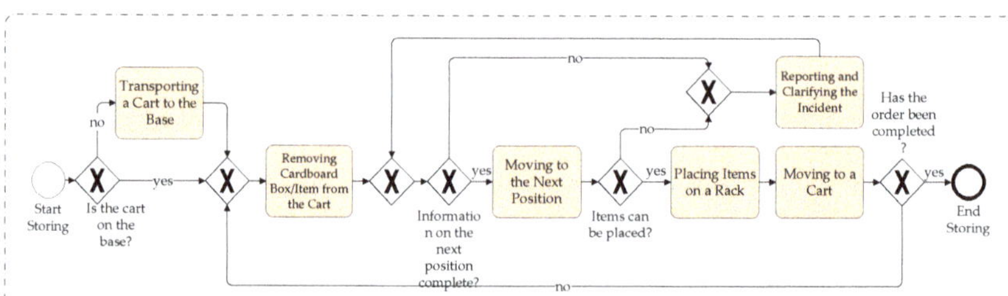

Figure A6. Idealized BPMN of the mid-level processes *Storing–Travel Time* and *Storing–Store Time* with its low-level processes.

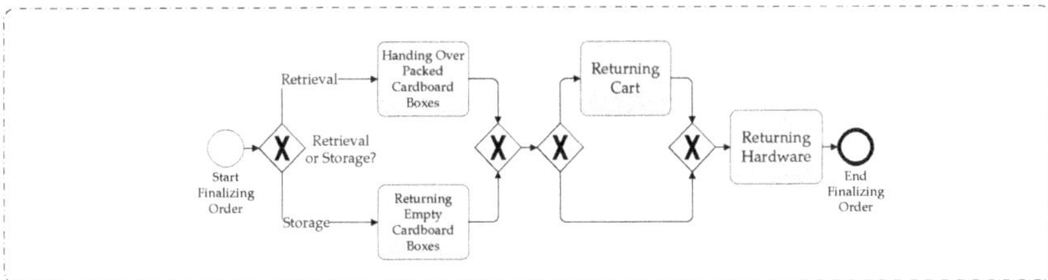

Figure A7. Idealized BPMN of the mid-level process *Finalizing Order* with its low-level processes.

References

1. Chen, K.; Zhang, D.; Yao, L.; Guo, B.; Yu, Z.; Liu, Y. Deep learning for sensor-based human activity recognition: Overview, challenges, and opportunities. *ACM Comput. Surv. CSUR* **2021**, *54*, 77.
2. Reining, C.; Niemann, F.; Moya Rueda, F.; Fink, G.A.; ten Hompel, M. Human activity recognition for production and logistics—A systematic literature review. *Information* **2019**, *10*, 245. [CrossRef]
3. Ordóñez, F.J.; Roggen, D. Deep convolutional and lstm recurrent neural networks for multimodal wearable activity recognition. *Sensors* **2016**, *16*, 115. [CrossRef] [PubMed]
4. Moya Rueda, F.; Grzeszick, R.; Fink, G.A.; Feldhorst, S.; Ten Hompel, M. Convolutional neural networks for human activity recognition using body-worn sensors. *Informatics* **2018**, *5*, 26. [CrossRef]
5. Yoshimura, N.; Morales, J.; Maekawa, T.; Hara, T. OpenPack: A Large-Scale Dataset for Recognizing Packaging Works in IoT-Enabled Logistic Environments. In Proceedings of the 2024 IEEE International Conference on Pervasive Computing and Communications (PerCom), Biarritz, France, 11–15 March 2024; pp. 90–97. [CrossRef]
6. OpenPack OpenPack Dataset. 2022. Available online: https://open-pack.github.io/ (accessed on 18 January 2026).
7. Maurice, P.; Malaisé, A.; Amiot, C.; Paris, N.; Richard, G.J.; Rochel, O.; Ivaldi, S. Human movement and ergonomics: An industry-oriented dataset for collaborative robotics. *Int. J. Robot. Res.* **2019**, *38*, 1529–1537. [CrossRef]
8. Maurice, P.; Malaisé, A.; Ivaldi, S.; Rochel, O.; Amiot, C.; Paris, N.; Richard, G.J.; Fritzsche, L. AndyData-Lab-onePerson. 2019. Available online: http://zenodo.org/record/3254403#.XmDpQahKguV (accessed on 10 October 2025).
9. Reining, C.; Schlangen, M.; Hissmann, L.; ten Hompel, M.; Moya, F.; Fink, G.A. Attribute representation for human activity recognition of manual order picking activities. In Proceedings of the 5th international Workshop on Sensor-Based Activity Recognition and Interaction, Berlin, Germany, 20–21 September 2018; pp. 1–10.
10. Niemann, F.; Reining, C.; Moya Rueda, F.; Nair, N.R.; Steffens, J.A.; Fink, G.A.; Ten Hompel, M. LARa: Creating a Dataset for Human Activity Recognition in Logistics Using Semantic Attributes. *Sensors* **2020**, *20*, 4083. [CrossRef]
11. Niemann, F.; Lüdtke, S.; Bartelt, C.; Ten Hompel, M. Context-Aware Human Activity Recognition in Industrial Processes. *Sensors* **2021**, *22*, 134. [CrossRef] [PubMed]
12. Dourish, P. What we talk about when we talk about context. *Pers. Ubiquitous Comput.* **2004**, *8*, 19–30. [CrossRef]
13. Bordel, B.; Alcarria, R.; Robles, T. Recognizing human activities in Industry 4.0 scenarios through an analysis-modeling-recognition algorithm and context labels. *Integr. Comput.-Aided Eng.* **2021**, *29*, 83–103. [CrossRef]
14. Schmidt, A.; Beigl, M.; Gellersen, H.W. There is more to context than location. *Comput. Graph.* **1999**, *23*, 893–901. [CrossRef]
15. Niemann, F.; Rueda, F.M., Nair, N.R.; Orth, A.; Kfari, M.K.A.; Frichert, M.; Abdulaal, A.; Abu Seer, M.; Almatalka, H.; Asskar, H.; et al. Data Fusion for advanced Research in industrial Applications (DaRA)—A Multi-Sensor, Multi-Level Annotated Dataset for Human Activity and Human Context Recognition in Warehousing. 2026. Available online: https://zenodo.org/records/10468175 (accessed on 18 January 2026).
16. Lüdtke, S.; Rueda, F.M.; Ahmed, W.; Fink, G.A.; Kirste, T. Human Activity Recognition using Attribute-Based Neural Networks and Context Information. *arXiv* **2021**, arXiv:2111.04564. [CrossRef]
17. Diete, A.; Sztyler, T.; Weiland, L.; Stuckenschmidt, H. Recognizing grabbing actions from inertial and video sensor data in a warehouse scenario. *Procedia Comput. Sci.* **2017**, *110*, 16–23. [CrossRef]
18. Moya Rueda, F.; Fink, G.A. Learning Attribute Representation for Human Activity Recognition. In Proceedings of the 2018 24th International Conference on Pattern Recognition (ICPR), Beijing, China, 20–24 August 2018; pp. 523–528. [CrossRef]
19. Cheng, H.T.; Sun, F.T.; Griss, M.; Davis, P.; Li, J.; You, D. Nuactiv: Recognizing unseen new activities using semantic attribute-based learning. In Proceedings of the 11th Annual International Conference on Mobile Systems, Applications, and Services, Taipei, Taiwan, 25–28 June 2013; pp. 361–374.
20. Riboni, D.; Sztyler, T.; Civitarese, G.; Stuckenschmidt, H. Unsupervised recognition of interleaved activities of daily living through ontological and probabilistic reasoning. In Proceedings of the 2016 ACM International Joint Conference on Pervasive and Ubiquitous Computing, Heidelberg, Germany, 12–16 September 2016; pp. 1–12.

https://doi.org/10.3390/s26020739

21. Krüger, F.; Nyolt, M.; Yordanova, K.; Hein, A.; Kirste, T. Computational state space models for activity and intention recognition. A feasibility study. *PLoS ONE* **2014**, *9*, e109381. [CrossRef]
22. Rueda, F.M.; Lüdtke, S.; Schröder, M.; Yordanova, K.; Kirste, T.; Fink, G.A. Combining symbolic reasoning and deep learning for human activity recognition. In Proceedings of the 2019 IEEE International Conference on Pervasive Computing and Communications Workshops (PerCom Workshops), Kyoto, Japan, 11–15 March 2019; pp. 22–27.
23. Dönnebrink, R.; Moya Rueda, F.; Grzeszick, R.; Stach, M. Miss-placement Prediction of Multiple On-body Devices for Human Activity Recognition. In Proceedings of the 8th International Workshop on Sensor-Based Activity Recognition and Artificial Intelligence, iWOAR '23, Lübeck, Germany, 21–22 September 2023. [CrossRef]
24. Bassani, G.; Avizzano, C.A.; Filippeschi, A. Deep Learning Algorithms for Human Activity Recognition in Manual Material Handling Tasks. *Sensors* **2025**, *25*, 6705. [CrossRef]
25. Kaczmarek, S.; Fiedler, M.; Bongers, A.; Wibbeling, S.; Grzeszick, R. Dataset and Methods for Recognizing Care Activities. In Proceedings of the 7th International Workshop on Sensor-Based Activity Recognition and Artificial Intelligence, iWOAR '22, Rostock, Germany, 19–20 September 2022. [CrossRef]
26. Al Farid, F.; Bari, A.; Miah, A.S.M.; Mansor, S.; Uddin, J.; Kumaresan, S.P. A Structured and Methodological Review on Multi-View Human Activity Recognition for Ambient Assisted Living. *J. Imaging* **2025**, *11*, 182. [CrossRef]
27. Pabón, J.; Gómez, D.; Cerón, J.D.; Salazar-Cabrera, R.; López, D.M.; Blobel, B. A Comprehensive Dataset for Activity of Daily Living (ADL) Research Compiled by Unifying and Processing Multiple Data Sources. *J. Pers. Med.* **2025**, *15*, 210. [CrossRef]
28. Sztyler, T.; Carmona, J.; Völker, J.; Stuckenschmidt, H. Self-tracking Reloaded: Applying Process Mining to Personalized Health Care from Labeled Sensor Data. In *Transactions on Petri Nets and Other Models of Concurrency XI*; Koutny, M., Desel, J., Kleijn, J., Eds.; Series Title: Lecture Notes in Computer Science; Springer: Berlin/Heidelberg, Germany, 2016; Volume 9930, pp. 160–180. [CrossRef]
29. Pires, I.; Garcia, N.M. *Raw Dataset with Accelerometer, Gyroscope, Magnetometer, Location and Environment Data for Activities Without Motion*; Mendeley Data: Aveiro, Portugal, 2022; Volume 3. [CrossRef]
30. Cerón, J. Jesusceron/DataPreProcess, 2021. Original-Date: 2020-01-14T15:03:34Z. Available online: https://github.com/jesusceron/DataPreProcess (accessed on 18 January 2026).
31. Ceron, J.D.; Kluge, F.; Küderle, A.; Eskofier, B.M.; López, D.M. Simultaneous Indoor Pedestrian Localization and House Mapping Based on Inertial Measurement Unit and Bluetooth Low-Energy Beacon Data. *Sensors* **2020**, *20*, 4742. [CrossRef] [PubMed]
32. Cerón, J. Jesusceron/SLAM_HAR_IL, 2023. Original-Date: 2022-02-01T21:40:27Z. Available online: https://github.com/jesusceron/SLAM_HAR_IL (accessed on 18 January 2026).
33. Ceron, J.D.; López, D.M.; Kluge, F.; Eskofier, B.M. Framework for Simultaneous Indoor Localization, Mapping, and Human Activity Recognition in Ambient Assisted Living Scenarios. *Sensors* **2022**, *22*, 3364. [CrossRef]
34. Sztyler, T. Human Activity Recognition. Available online: https://www.uni-mannheim.de/dws/research/projects/activity-recognition/dataset/dataset-realworld/ (accessed on 10 October 2025).
35. Sztyler, T.; Baur, H. On-Body Localization of Wearable Devices: An Investigation of Position-Aware Activity Recognition. Available online: http://publications.wim.uni-mannheim.de/informatik/lski/Sztyler2016Localization.pdf (accessed on 20 March 2025).
36. Casilari, E.; Santoyo-Ramón, A.J. UMAFall: Fall Detection Dataset (Universidad de Malaga). Available online: http://figshare.com/articles/UMA_ADL_FALL_Dataset_zip/4214283 (accessed on 10 October 2025).
37. Casilari, E.; Santoyo-Ramón, J.A.; Cano-García, J.M. UMAFall: A Multisensor Dataset for the Research on Automatic Fall Detection. *Procedia Comput. Sci.* **2017**, *110*, 32–39. [CrossRef]
38. Chereshnev, R.; Kertész-Farkas, A. Romanchereshnev/HuGaDB. Available online: http://github.com/romanchereshnev/HuGaDB (accessed on 10 October 2025).
39. Chereshnev, R.; Kertész-Farkas, A. HuGaDB: Human Gait Database for Activity Recognition from Wearable Inertial Sensor Networks. In *Analysis of Images, Social Networks and Texts*; Van Der Aalst, W.M., Ignatov, D.I., Khachay, M., Kuznetsov, S.O., Lempitsky, V., Lomazova, I.A., Loukachevitch, N., Napoli, A., Panchenko, A., Pardalos, P.M., et al., Eds.; Series Title: Lecture Notes in Computer Science; Springer International Publishing: Cham, Switzerland, 2018; Volume 10716, pp. 131–141. [CrossRef]
40. Wiki Datasets. wiki:dataset [Human Activity Recognition Datasets]. Available online: http://har-dataset.org/doku.php?id=wiki:dataset (accessed on 18 January 2026).
41. Forster, K.; Roggen, D.; Troster, G. Unsupervised Classifier Self-Calibration through Repeated Context Occurences: Is there Robustness against Sensor Displacement to Gain? In Proceedings of the 2009 International Symposium on Wearable Computers, Linz, Austria, 4–7 September 2009; pp. 77–84. [CrossRef]
42. Bulling, A.; Blanke, U.; Schiele, B. A tutorial on human activity recognition using body-worn inertial sensors. *ACM Comput. Surv.* **2014**, *46*, 33. [CrossRef]
43. Bulling, A.; Blanke, U.; Schiele, B. Andreas-Bulling/ActRecTut. Available online: http://github.com/andreas-bulling/ActRecTut (accessed on 10 October 2025).

44. Hsiao, Y.S.; Sanchez-Riera, J.; Lim, T.; Hua, K.L.; Cheng, W.H. LaRED: A large RGB-D extensible hand gesture dataset. In Proceedings of the 5th ACM Multimedia Systems Conference, Singapore, 19–21 March 2014; pp. 53–58. [CrossRef]
45. HaGRID HaGRID—HAnd Gesture Recognition Image Dataset. Available online: https://github.com/hukenovs/hagrid?tab=readme-ov-file (accessed on 18 January 2026).
46. Kapitanov, A.; Kvanchiani, K.; Nagaev, A.; Kraynov, R.; Makhliarchuk, A. HaGRID–HAnd Gesture Recognition Image Dataset. *arXiv* **2022**, arXiv:2206.08219. [CrossRef]
47. Essid, S.; Lin, X.; Gowing, M.; Kordelas, G.; Aksay, A.; Kelly, P.; Fillon, T.; Zhang, Q.; Dielmann, A.; Kitanovski, V.; et al. 3DLife ACM MM Grand Challenge 2011–Realistic Interaction in Online Virtual Environments. Available online: http://perso.telecom-paristech.fr/essid/3dlife-gc-11/ (accessed on 10 October 2025).
48. Essid, S.; Lin, X.; Gowing, M.; Kordelas, G.; Aksay, A.; Kelly, P.; Fillon, T.; Zhang, Q.; Dielmann, A.; Kitanovski, V.; et al. A multi-modal dance corpus for research into interaction between humans in virtual environments. *J. Multimodal User Interfaces* **2012**, *7*, 157–170. [CrossRef]
49. Vögele, A.; Krüger, B. HDM12 Dance–Documentation on a Data Base of Tango Motion Capture. Available online: https://cg.cs.uni-bonn.de/publication/voegele-2016-hdm12 (accessed on 18 January 2026).
50. Zhang, W.; Liu, Z.; Zhou, L.; Leung, H.; Chan, A.B. Martial Arts, Dancing and Sports dataset: A challenging stereo and multi-view dataset for 3D human pose estimation. *Image Vis. Comput.* **2017**, *61*, 22–39. [CrossRef]
51. Zhang, W.; Liu, Z.; Zhou, L.; Leung, H.; Chan, A.B. Martial Arts, Dancing and Sports Dataset | VISAL. Available online: http://visal.cs.cityu.edu.hk/research/mads/ (accessed on 10 October 2025).
52. Tits, M.; Laraba, S.; Caulier, E.; Tilmanne, J.; Dutoit, T. UMONS-TAICHI. Available online: http://github.com/numediart/UMONS-TAICHI (accessed on 10 October 2025).
53. Tits, M.; Laraba, S.; Caulier, E.; Tilmanne, J.; Dutoit, T. UMONS-TAICHI: A multimodal motion capture dataset of expertise in Taijiquan gestures. *Data Brief* **2018**, *19*, 1214–1221. [CrossRef]
54. CRCV | Center for Research in Computer Vision at the University of Central Florida. Available online: https://www.crcv.ucf.edu/data/UCF_Sports_Action.php (accessed on 18 January 2026).
55. Rodriguez, M.D.; Ahmed, J.; Shah, M. Action MACH a spatio-temporal Maximum Average Correlation Height filter for action recognition. In Proceedings of the 2008 IEEE Conference on Computer Vision and Pattern Recognition, Anchorage, AK, USA, 23–28 June 2008; pp. 1–8. [CrossRef]
56. Hoelzemann, A.; Romero, J.L.; Bock, M.; Van Laerhoven, K.; Lv, Q. Hang-Time HAR: A Benchmark Dataset for Basketball Activity Recognition Using Wrist-Worn Inertial Sensors. Available online: https://zenodo.org/record/7920485 (accessed on 18 January 2026).
57. Hoelzemann, A.; Romero, J.L.; Bock, M.; Van Laerhoven, K.; Lv, Q. Hang-Time HAR: A Benchmark Dataset for Basketball Activity Recognition Using Wrist-Worn Inertial Sensors. *Sensors* **2023**, *23*, 5879. [CrossRef] [PubMed]
58. Medrano, C.; Igual, R.; Plaza, I.; Castro, M. Fall ADL Data | EduQTech. Available online: https://www.unizar.es/ (accessed on 10 October 2025).
59. Medrano, C.; Igual, R.; Plaza, I.; Castro, M. Detecting Falls as Novelties in Acceleration Patterns Acquired with Smartphones. *PLoS ONE* **2014**, *9*, e94811. [CrossRef] [PubMed]
60. Sucerquia, A.; López, J.D.; Vargas-Bonilla, J.F. SisFall | SISTEMIC. Available online: https://www.kaggle.com/datasets/nvnikhil0001/sis-fall-original-dataset (accessed on 10 October 2025).
61. Sucerquia, A.; López, J.; Vargas-Bonilla, J. SisFall: A Fall and Movement Dataset. *Sensors* **2017**, *17*, 198. [CrossRef]
62. Martinez-Villaseñor, L.; Ponce, H.; Brieva, J.; Moya-Albor, E.; Núñez Martínez, J.; Peñafort Asturiano, C. HAR-UP. Available online: http://sites.google.com/up.edu.mx/har-up/ (accessed on 10 October 2025).
63. Martínez-Villaseñor, L.; Ponce, H.; Brieva, J.; Moya-Albor, E.; Núñez-Martínez, J.; Peñafort-Asturiano, C. UP-Fall Detection Dataset: A Multimodal Approach. *Sensors* **2019**, *19*, 1988. [CrossRef]
64. Forkan, A.; Jayaraman, P.P.; Antonmeryl, C.; Montori, F.; Banerjee, A.; Fizza, K.; Georgakopoulos, D. Internet of Things Dataset for Human Operator Activity Recognition in Industrial Environment. In Proceedings of the 34th ACM International Conference on Information and Knowledge Management, Seoul, Republic of Korea, 10–14 November 2025; pp. 6356–6360.
65. Forkan, A.; Jayaraman, P.P.; Antonmeryl, C.; Montori, F.; Banerjee, A.; Fizza, K.; Georgakopoulos, D. A Dataset for Assessing Worker Activities in Industrial Settings. Available online: https://digitalinnovationlab.github.io/mppdataset (accessed on 18 January 2026).
66. Sturm, F.; Hergenroether, E.; Reinhardt, J.; Vojnovikj, P.S.; Siegel, M. Challenges of the creation of a dataset for vision based human hand action recognition in industrial assembly. In *Proceedings of the Science and Information Conference, Chengdu, China, 25–27 August 2023*; Springer: Berlin/Heidelberg, Germany, 2023; pp. 1079–1098.
67. Iodice, F.; De Momi, E.; Ajoudani, A. Hri30: An action recognition dataset for industrial human-robot interaction. In Proceedings of the 2022 26th International Conference on Pattern Recognition (ICPR), Montreal, QC, Canada, 21–25 August 2022; pp. 4941–4947.

68. Iodice, F.; Momi, E.D.; Ajoudani, A. HRI30: An Action Recognition Dataset for Industrial Human-Robot Interaction. 2022. Available online: https://zenodo.org/records/5833411 (accessed on 18 January 2026).
69. Lagamtzis, D.; Schmidt, F.; Seyler, J.R.; Dang, T. Coax: Collaborative action dataset for human motion forecasting in an industrial workspace. In Proceedings of the ICAART (3), Online, 3–5 February 2022; pp. 98–105.
70. Lagamtzis, D.; Schmidt, F.; Seyler, J.; Dang, T. CoAx–Collaborative Action Dataset. Available online: https://dlgmtzs.github.io/dataset-coax/ (accessed on 18 January 2026).
71. Dallel, M.; Havard, V.; Dupuis, Y.; Baudry, D. Digital twin of an industrial workstation: A novel method of an auto-labeled data generator using virtual reality for human action recognition in the context of human–robot collaboration. *Eng. Appl. Artif. Intell.* **2023**, *118*, 105655. [CrossRef]
72. Dallel, M.; Havard, V.; Baudry, D.; Savatier, X. InHARD-DT–Industrial Human Action Recognition Dataset–Digital Twin. 2022. Available online: https://zenodo.org/records/7644247 (accessed on 18 January 2026).
73. Cicirelli, G.; Marani, R.; Romeo, L.; Domínguez, M.G.; Heras, J.; Perri, A.G.; D'Orazio, T. The HA4M dataset: Multi-Modal Monitoring of an assembly task for Human Action recognition in Manufacturing. *Sci. Data* **2022**, *9*, 745. [CrossRef]
74. Cicirelli, G.; Marani, R.; Romeo, L.; Domínguez, M.G.; Heras, J.; Perri, A.G.; D'Orazio, T. Human Action Multi-Modal Monitoring in Manufacturing (HA4M) Dataset. Available online: https://baltig.cnr.it/ISP/ha4m (accessed on 18 January 2026).
75. Sener, F.; Chatterjee, D.; Shelepov, D.; He, K.; Singhania, D.; Wang, R.; Yao, A. Assembly101: A Large-Scale Multi-View Video Dataset for Understanding Procedural Activities. *arXiv* **2022**, arXiv:2203.14712. [CrossRef]
76. Assembly101. Assembly101: A Large-Scale Multi-View Video Dataset for Understanding Procedural Activities. Available online: https://assembly-101.github.io/ (accessed on 18 January 2026).
77. Munasinghe, C.; Amin, F.M.; Scaramuzza, D.; van de Venn, H.W. Covered, collaborative robot environment dataset for 3d semantic segmentation. In Proceedings of the 2022 IEEE 27th International Conference on Emerging Technologies and Factory Automation (ETFA), Stuttgart, Germany, 6–9 September 2022; pp. 1–4.
78. Munasinghe, C.; Amin, F.M.; Scaramuzza, D.; van de Venn, H.W. COVERED, CollabOratiVE Robot Environment Dataset for 3D Semantic Segmentation. Available online: https://github.com/Fatemeh-MA/COVERED (accessed on 18 January 2026).
79. Niemann, F.; Bas, H.; Steffens, J.A.; Nair, N.R.; ten Hompel, M. Context-Aware Activity Recognition in Logistics (CAARL)—A optical marker-based Motion Capture Dataset. 2021. Available online: https://zenodo.org/records/5680951 (accessed on 18 January 2026).
80. Tamantini, C.; Cordella, F.; Lauretti, C.; Zollo, L. The WGD—A dataset of assembly line working gestures for ergonomic analysis and work-related injuries prevention. *Sensors* **2021**, *21*, 7600. [CrossRef]
81. Mohammadi Amin, F.; Rezayati, M.; van de Venn, H.W.; Karimpour, H. A mixed-perception approach for safe human–robot collaboration in industrial automation. *Sensors* **2020**, *20*, 6347. [CrossRef]
82. Rezayati, M.; van de Venn, H.W. Physical Human-Robot Contact Detection. Available online: https://data.mendeley.com/datasets/ctw2256phb/2 (accessed on 18 January 2026).
83. Alia, S.S.; Adachi, K.; Nahid, N.; Kaneko, H.; Lago, P.; Inoue, S. Bento Packaging Activity Recognition Challenge. 2021. Available online: https://abc-research.github.io/bento2021/data/ (accessed on 18 January 2026).
84. Alia, S.S.; Adachi, K.; Nahid, N.; Kaneko, H.; Lago, P.; Inoue, S. Bento Packaging Activity Recognition Challenge, IEEE DataPort. 2021. Available online: https://ieee-dataport.org/competitions/bento-packaging-activity-recognition-challenge (accessed on 18 January 2026).
85. Dallel, M.; Havard, V.; Baudry, D.; Savatier, X. InHARD–Industrial Human Action Recognition Dataset in the Context of Industrial Collaborative Robotics. Available online: https://zenodo.org/records/4003541 (accessed on 18 January 2026).
86. Dallel, M.; Havard, V.; Baudry, D.; Savatier, X. InHARD–Industrial Human Action Recognition Dataset in the Context of Industrial Collaborative Robotics. In Proceedings of the 2020 IEEE International Conference on Human-Machine Systems (ICHMS), Rome, Italy, 7–9 September 2020; pp. 1–6. [CrossRef]
87. Niemann, F.; Reining, C.; Moya Rueda, F.; Bas, H.; Altermann, E.; Nair, N.R.; Steffens, J.A.; Fink, G.A.; ten Hompel, M. Logistic Activity Recognition Challenge (LARa Version 02)—A Motion Capture and Inertial Measurement Dataset. 2022. Available online: https://zenodo.org/records/5761276 (accessed on 18 January 2026).
88. Niemann, F.; Reining, C.; Moya Rueda, F.; Nair, N.R.; Oberdiek, P.; Bas, H.; Spiekermann, R.; Altermann, E.; Steffens, J.A.; Fink, G.A.; et al. Logistic Activity Recognition Challenge (LARa Version 03)—A Motion Capture and Inertial Measurement Dataset. 2023. Available online: https://zenodo.org/records/8189341 (accessed on 18 January 2026).
89. Niemann, F.; Reining, C.; Moya Rueda, F.; Nair, N.R.; Steffens, J.A.; Fink, G.A.; ten Hompel, M. Logistic Activity Recognition Challenge (LARa)—A Motion Capture and Inertial Measurement Dataset. 2020. Available online: https://zenodo.org/records/3862782 (accessed on 18 January 2026).
90. Ragusa, F.; Furnari, A.; Livatino, S.; Farinella, G.M. The meccano dataset: Understanding human-object interactions from egocentric videos in an industrial-like domain. In Proceedings of the IEEE/CVF Winter Conference on Applications of Computer Vision, Virtual, 5–9 January 2021; pp. 1569–1578.

https://doi.org/10.3390/s26020739

91. Ragusa, F.; Furnari, A.; Livatino, S.; Farinella, G.M. The Meccano Dataset: Understanding Human-Object Interactions from Egocentric Videos in an Industrial-like Domain. 2021. Available online: https://iplab.dmi.unict.it/MECCANO/ (accessed on 18 January 2026).
92. Ben-Shabat, Y.; Yu, X.; Saleh, F.; Campbell, D.; Rodriguez-Opazo, C.; Li, H.; Gould, S. The IKEA ASM dataset: Understanding people assembling furniture through actions, objects and pose. In Proceedings of the IEEE/CVF Winter Conference on Applications of Computer Vision, Virtual, 5–9 January 2021; pp. 847–859.
93. Ben-Shabat, Y.; Yu, X.; Saleh, F.; Campbell, D.; Rodriguez-Opazo, C.; Li, H.; Gould, S. The IKEA ASM Dataset: Understanding People Assembling Furniture through Actions, Objects and Pose. 2020. Available online: https://ikeaasm.github.io/ (accessed on 18 January 2026).
94. Attila Reiss, I.I. PPG-DaLiA, 2019. UCI Machine Learning Repository. Available online: https://archive.ics.uci.edu/dataset/495/ppg+dalia (accessed on 18 January 2026).
95. Reiss, A.; Indlekofer, I.; Schmidt, P.; Van Laerhoven, K. Deep PPG: Large-Scale Heart Rate Estimation with Convolutional Neural Networks. *Sensors* **2019**, *19*, 3079. [CrossRef]
96. Ashry, S.; Elbasiony, R.; Gomaa, W. An LSTM-based Descriptor for Human Activities Recognition using IMU Sensors. In Proceedings of the 15th International Conference on Informatics in Control, Automation and Robotics, Porto, Portugal, 29–31 July 2018; pp. 494–501. [CrossRef]
97. Mohammed, S.; Gomaa, W. HAD-AW Data-Set Benchmark for Human Activity Recognition Using Apple Watch. 2018. Available online: http://www.researchgate.net/publication/324136132_HAD-AW_Data-set_Benchmark_For_Human_Activity_Recognition_Using_Apple_Watch (accessed on 10 October 2025).
98. Nath, N.D.; Chaspari, T.; Behzadan, A.H. Automated ergonomic risk monitoring using body-mounted sensors and machine learning. *Adv. Eng. Inform.* **2018**, *38*, 514–526. [CrossRef]
99. Vaizman, Y.; Ellis, K.; Lanckriet, G. Recognizing Detailed Human Context in the Wild from Smartphones and Smartwatches. *IEEE Pervasive Comput.* **2017**, *16*, 62–74. [CrossRef]
100. ExtraSensory. The ExtraSensory Dataset. Available online: http://extrasensory.ucsd.edu/ (accessed on 18 January 2026).
101. Zappi, P.; Lombriser, C.; Stiefmeier, T.; Farella, E.; Roggen, D.; Benini, L.; Tröster, G. Activity Recognition from On-Body Sensors: Accuracy-Power Trade-Off by Dynamic Sensor Selection. In *Wireless Sensor Networks*; Verdone, R., Ed.; Series Title: Lecture Notes in Computer Science; Springer: Berlin/Heidelberg, Germany, 2008; Volume 4913, pp. 17–33. [CrossRef]
102. Kwapisz, J.R.; Weiss, G.M.; Moore, S.A. WISDM Lab: Dataset. Available online: http://www.cis.fordham.edu/wisdm/dataset.php (accessed on 10 October 2025).
103. Niemann, F.; Rueda, F.M.; Al Kfari, M.K.; Nair, N.R.; Lüdtke, S.; Kirchheim, A. Towards Standardized Dataset Creation for Human Activity Recognition: Framework, Taxonomy, Checklist, and Best Practices. In *Annotation of Real-World Data for Artificial Intelligence Systems*; Tonkin, E.L., Tourte, G.J.L., Yordanova, K., Eds.; Series Title: Communications in Computer and Information Science; Springer Nature: Cham, Switzerland, 2026; Volume 2706, pp. 74–93. [CrossRef]
104. Gebru, T.; Morgenstern, J.; Vecchione, B.; Vaughan, J.W.; Wallach, H.; Iii, H.D.; Crawford, K. Datasheets for datasets. *Commun. ACM* **2021**, *64*, 86–92. [CrossRef]
105. Wilkinson, M.D.; Dumontier, M.; Aalbersberg, I.J.; Appleton, G.; Axton, M.; Baak, A.; Blomberg, N.; Boiten, J.W.; Da Silva Santos, L.B.; Bourne, P.E.; et al. The FAIR Guiding Principles for scientific data management and stewardship. *Sci. Data* **2016**, *3*, 160018. [CrossRef]
106. Rueda, F.M.; Al Kfari, M.K. Data4Sim, 2025. Version 1. Available online: https://github.com/wilfer9008/Data4Sim (accessed on 18 January 2026).
107. Elke, L.; Braun, C.; Krooß, A.; Wings, L.M.; Niemann, F.; Kretschmer, V. Bewegungsdaten als Planungsgrundlage. *Logist. J. Proc.* **2024**, *20*, 1–10. [CrossRef]
108. Wings, L.M.; Mazur, E.; Kretschmer, V. Light it Up! Integrationsleitfaden von Pick-by-Light für die Kommissionierung. 2024. Available online: https://publica.fraunhofer.de/entities/publication/13b962a2-5130-4436-aa0d-f28e5f5e00ce (accessed on 18 January 2026).
109. Moya Rueda, F.; Ravi Nair, N.; Spiekermann, R.; Altermann, E.; Oberdiek, P.; Reining, C.; Fink, G.A. Retrieval-Based Annotation for Multi-Channel Time Series Data of Human Activities. In *Annotation of Real-World Data for Artificial Intelligence Systems*; Tonkin, E.L., Tourte, G.J.L., Yordanova, K., Eds.; Series Title: Communications in Computer and Information Science; Springer Nature: Cham, Switzerland, 2026; Volume 2706, pp. 53–73. [CrossRef]
110. Papadatou-Pastou, M.; Ntolka, E.; Schmitz, J.; Martin, M.; Munafò, M.R.; Ocklenburg, S.; Paracchini, S. Human handedness: A meta-analysis. *Psychol. Bull.* **2020**, *146*, 481–524. [CrossRef]
111. Aggarwal, J.; Ryoo, M. Human activity analysis: A review. *ACM Comput. Surv.* **2011**, *43*, 16. [CrossRef]

https://doi.org/10.3390/s26020739

112. Tran, H.; Potter, V.; Mazzucchelli, U.; John, D.; Intille, S. Towards Practical, Best Practice Video Annotation to Support Human Activity Recognition. In *Annotation of Real-World Data for Artificial Intelligence Systems*; Tonkin, E.L., Tourte, G.J.L., Yordanova, K., Eds.; Series Title: Communications in Computer and Information Science; Springer Nature: Cham, Switzerland, 2026; Volume 2706, pp. 94–118. [CrossRef]
113. Niemann, F.; Rueda, F.M.; Nair, N.R.; Orth, A.; Kfari, M.K.A.; Frichert, M.; Abdulaal, A.; Abu Seer, M.; Almatalka, H.; Asskar, H.; et al. Test Annotations for Quality Evaluation of the DaRA Dataset—Annotated and Revised Video Data with Activity and Context Labels. 2026. Available online: https://zenodo.org/records/15118022 (accessed on 18 January 2026).
114. Cohen, J. A Coefficient of Agreement for Nominal Scales. *Educ. Psychol. Meas.* **1960**, *20*, 37–46. [CrossRef]
115. Light, R.J. Measures of response agreement for qualitative data: Some generalizations and alternatives. *Psychol. Bull.* **1971**, *76*, 365–377. [CrossRef]
116. Landis, J.R.; Koch, G.G. The Measurement of Observer Agreement for Categorical Data. *Biometrics* **1977**, *33*, 159. [CrossRef]
117. Monserud, R.A.; Leemans, R. Comparing global vegetation maps with the Kappa statistic. *Ecol. Model.* **1992**, *62*, 275–293. [CrossRef]
118. Fleiss, J.L.; Levin, B.; Paik, M.C. *Statistical Methods for Rates and Proportions*, 1st ed.; Wiley Series in Probability and Statistics; Wiley: Hoboken, NJ, USA, 2003. [CrossRef]
119. Zhong, R.; Hu, B.; Liu, Z.; Qin, Q.; Feng, Y.; Wang, X.V.; Wang, L.; Tan, J. A two-stage framework for learning human-to-robot object handover policy from 4D spatiotemporal flow. *Robot. Comput.-Integr. Manuf.* **2026**, *98*, 103171. [CrossRef]
120. Castellani, C.; Turco, E.; Bo, V.; Malvezzi, M.; Prattichizzo, D.; Costante, G.; Pozzi, M. Soft Human-Robot Handover Using a Vision-Based Pipeline. *IEEE Robot. Autom. Lett.* **2025**, *10*, 891–898. [CrossRef]

https://doi.org/10.3390/s26020739

sensors

MDPI

Article

Towards User-Generalizable Wearable-Sensor-Based Human Activity Recognition: A Multi-Task Contrastive Learning Approach

Pengyu Guo [1] and Masaya Nakayama [2,*]

1 Department of Electronic Engineering and Information Systems, The University of Tokyo, Tokyo 113-8654, Japan; kaku-houu@g.ecc.u-tokyo.ac.jp
2 Information Technology Center, The University of Tokyo, Tokyo 113-8654, Japan
* Correspondence: nakayama@nc.u-tokyo.ac.jp

Abstract

Human Activity Recognition (HAR) using wearable sensors has shown great potential for personalized health management and ubiquitous computing. However, existing deep learning-based HAR models often suffer from poor user-level generalization, which limits their deployment in real-world scenarios. In this work, we propose a novel multi-task contrastive learning framework that jointly optimizes activity classification and supervised contrastive objectives to enhance generalization across unseen users. By leveraging both activity and user labels to construct semantically meaningful contrastive pairs, our method improves representation learning while maintaining user-agnostic inference at test time. We evaluate the proposed framework on three public HAR datasets using cross-user splits, achieving comparable results to both supervised and self-supervised baselines. Extensive ablation studies further confirm the effectiveness of our design choices, including multi-task training and the integration of user-aware contrastive supervision. These results highlight the potential of our approach for building more generalizable and scalable HAR systems.

Keywords: Human Activity Recognition (HAR); user-generalization; contrastive learning; multi-task learning; wearable sensor; supervised contrastive learning

1. Introduction

Human Activity Recognition (HAR) is a general task that aims to recognize human activities based on various types of signals, such as images/videos, wireless signals, and wearable sensors. It plays a crucial role in a wide range of applications that directly impact health, safety, efficiency, and overall quality of life.

With the rapid development of the global economy and digital technology, the concept of "active health" has gained increasing attention. This approach emphasizes long-term, continuous, and dynamic tracking of individuals' behaviors throughout the entire life cycle. It aims to assess an individual's status, behavioral trends, and developmental trajectory, empowering users to proactively adjust their lifestyles and promote healthy behaviors [1]. HAR, particularly when applied to daily activity monitoring, plays a central role in this context by helping users understand and manage their physical routines, ultimately facilitating personalized health management.

Among various HAR modalities, wearable sensor-based HAR is especially promising. Compared to vision-based methods [2], it is less intrusive and less affected by environmental variations. Compared to wireless signal-based methods [3], it benefits from a "one device per user" configuration, which avoids inter-user interference and mitigates the need to retrain models in different environments. Furthermore, with the rapid advancement and increasing ubiquity of the Internet of Things (IoT), wearable HAR has received widespread attention. The sensor manufacturing industry has matured significantly, making standardized hardware more affordable and accessible. These trends make wearable sensor-based HAR a low-cost and scalable solution for large-scale deployment.

In recent years, deep learning-based HAR systems have achieved promising results by extracting rich temporal and spatial features from sensor data. However, a key challenge remains: user generalization.

Most existing methods assume that the training and test data are drawn from the same distribution [4–8], which limits their ability to generalize to unseen users.

In real-world applications, sensor signals often vary significantly across individuals due to differences in body shape, movement patterns, sensor placement, and personal habits [9,10]. Consequently, models trained on a fixed user group often fail to generalize to new users—this phenomenon is commonly known as the user generalization problem.

To address this challenge, it is essential to learn user-invariant representations that capture the semantic essence of activities while minimizing user-specific variations. Prior works have explored personalized HAR frameworks [11–16], typically adopting a two-stage approach: pre-training on a general dataset followed by fine-tuning on data from the target user. While effective, these methods suffer from two major limitations: (1) collecting data from each new user increases deployment costs, and (2) the two-stage training pipeline adds complexity and computational overhead.

In parallel, several studies have aimed to improve user generalization directly during training by learning domain-invariant representations [10,17,18]. These methods often introduce regularization terms, domain alignment losses, or adversarial objectives to reduce inter-user variability. Although they achieve promising zero-shot performance, such methods usually rely on indirect modeling of user differences and require assumptions such as known domain boundaries or sufficient domain diversity. Moreover, the resulting training pipelines can be complex and sensitive to hyperparameter tuning. In contrast, we take a more direct approach by explicitly leveraging available user labels during training. By formulating a multi-task objective that combines activity classification and supervised contrastive learning based on user and activity labels, our method encourages the model to learn user-invariant yet task-discriminative representations. This strategy avoids domain-specific assumptions and enables efficient generalization to unseen users without requiring per-user adaptation.

In summary, we propose a single-stage learning framework that integrates supervised classification and supervised contrastive learning in a unified multi-task setup. This design enables the model to learn robust and transferable activity representations that generalize well to unseen users, without relying on any user-specific fine-tuning.

The main contributions of this work are summarized as follows:

- We propose a novel multi-task supervised contrastive learning framework for user-generalizable wearable HAR. By jointly leveraging activity and user labels during training, the framework explicitly promotes user-invariant yet activity-discriminative representations, allowing the model to perform user-independent inference without any per-user calibration.
- We introduce a unified single-stage optimization strategy that integrates supervised classification and contrastive objectives into one cohesive learning process. This design avoids the objective misalignment and complexity commonly seen in two-stage pipelines, providing a simple and effective approach for improving user-level generalization.

This paper is organized as follows. Section 2 reviews related work on human activity recognition (HAR) using wearable sensors, outlining recent advances and challenges. Section 3 describes our proposed framework, including its motivation, overall architecture, and key components. Section 4 presents the experimental setup, datasets, and results to evaluate the effectiveness of our approach, including comparisons with baseline methods and ablation studies. Section 5 provides an in-depth analysis of the results and discusses comparisons with related methods and ablation studies. Finally, Section 6 concludes the paper.

2. Related Work

2.1. Wearable Sensor-Based HAR Model

Sensor-based HAR aims to recognize human activities using various wearable sensors [18]. The wearable sensor-based approach plays an important role in this field due to its advantages in popularity, computational efficiency, and privacy protection, with wearable sensors serving as the main interfaces [19]. Therefore, we focus on the wearable sensor-based approach in this work.

Early practical HAR systems demonstrated the feasibility of recognizing daily activities using body-worn or smartphone sensors in real-world environments. For example, Bao and Intille [20] and Ravi et al. [21] deployed multi-sensor systems to collect data from subjects performing everyday tasks, while Kwapisz et al. [22] validated activity recognition using smartphone accelerometers in unconstrained settings. Subsequent studies such as Weiss et al. [23] further evaluated wearable devices in realistic usage scenarios, providing important insights into device placement and user variability. These works laid the foundation for later HAR research.

In recent years, researchers have proposed various HAR models based on wearable sensors to achieve robust and accurate performance, including feature engineering combined with deep learning models [24] or traditional machine learning models [25], as well as purely deep learning-based approaches [4–8,26–29].

2.2. Contrastive Learning for HAR

Contrastive learning aims to learn discriminative feature representations by contrasting positive and negative sample pairs. Most existing frameworks follow a two-stage pipeline: pre-training with a pretext task and fine-tuning on labeled data. In self-supervised settings, the encoder is trained on unlabeled data and then frozen during fine-tuning, making it especially useful when labeled data are limited.

Owing to this advantage, contrastive learning has been widely adopted in wearable sensor-based human activity recognition (HAR). Haresamudram et al. [30] introduced Contrastive Predictive Coding (CPC) to HAR, leveraging future timestep prediction to encode temporal dependencies. Their self-supervised approach improved performance in low-label regimes and enhanced robustness for transitional activities. Chen et al. [31] proposed SimCLR, which generated two augmented views per sample and trains a Siamese encoder using the NT-Xent loss. Tang et al. [32] applied SimCLR to wearable HAR using a TPN [33] backbone, while Khaertdinov et al. [34] proposed CSSHAR by combining SimCLR with a CNN-Transformer encoder.

A well-known limitation of self-supervised contrastive learning is the presence of false negative pairs. To mitigate this issue, Wang et al. [35] proposed ClusterCLHAR, which employed clustering to reduce false negatives. However, due to the unsupervised nature of clustering, this issue cannot be fully resolved. Alternatively, Prannay et al. [36] introduced Supervised Contrastive Learning (SupCon), where label information was used during pre-training to construct more semantically consistent positive and negative pairs, thereby providing stronger inductive biases.

2.3. Personalization and User Generalization Approaches

Despite the success of deep learning in wearable HAR, a persistent challenge remains: the user-dependency problem—models trained on specific users often fail to generalize to unseen individuals due to differences in gait, movement patterns, and sensor placement. Recent studies have explored two main directions to address this issue: personalization and user generalization.

2.3.1. Personalized Approaches

Personalization-based methods adapt models to individual users. CrossHAR [11] learned a shared latent space and applied user-aware recalibration with limited labeled data. Distributed online learning [12] has shown promise for personalized adaptation in streaming IoT scenarios. Saha et al. [13] proposed a lightweight one-dimensional convolutional neural network (CNN), and transfer learning was used to fine-tune the network model using real-time perceived data. On-device training on a smartphone was used for model fine-tuning, enabling the HAR system to achieve personalized customization without compromising privacy or increasing computational costs. Pixi et al. [14] proposed a hybrid framework that combined offline representation learning with on-device classifier adaptation. To address privacy concerns, recent works have explored implicit personalization. IPL-JPDA [15] leveraged pseudo-labeling and multimodal sensing for cross-user adaptation without target labels. Additionally, FedHAR [16] enabled decentralized semi-supervised personalization via prototype-based memory updates and consistency regularization.

While personalized HAR methods effectively handle user heterogeneity, they typically involve two-stage pipelines and require data from target users, raising concerns about privacy and data quality. Although federated and pseudo-labeling approaches offer privacy-preserving alternatives, the lack of reliable target user data remains a key bottleneck for real-world deployment.

2.3.2. User Generalization

Generalization-based methods aim to learn user-invariant representations without relying on target user data. GILE [17] employed variational inference and an independent excitation mechanism to disentangle latent spaces and achieve zero-shot generalization. CCIL [10] was a concept-level regularization strategy that ensured consistency across activity classes by aligning both feature and logit spaces. AFFAR [18] learned domain-invariant and domain-specific features and adaptively fused information from multiple source domains. While effective, these methods often require complex training pipelines or strong assumptions about domain shifts.

While generalization-based methods achieved good zero-shot performance without relying on target user data, their effectiveness often depends on complex regularization objectives and the availability of diverse source domains. These requirements can limit scalability or robustness when applied to real-world scenarios with limited domain variability or resource constraints. In contrast, our approach directly leverages user and activity labels through a multi-task contrastive learning framework, providing a simpler and more interpretable training process while enhancing generalization through explicit semantic alignment. This design offers a viable alternative to complex domain generalization procedures, especially when user labels are available during training.

3. Methodology

3.1. Problem Setup

The high-level motivation for improving user-level generalization has been introduced in Section 1. Here, we provide the technical rationale and formal problem setup that guide the design of our multi-task supervised contrastive framework.

Given a labeled dataset

$$\mathcal{D} = \{(x_i, y_{act,i}, y_{user,i})\}_{i=1}^{N},$$

where each sample is annotated with both an activity label y_{act} and a user label y_{user}, our objective is to learn an encoder $F_\theta(\cdot)$ that produces a representation supporting two properties: (1) accurate activity classification via a downstream classifier $G_\varphi(\cdot)$, and (2) robust generalization to unseen users.

Optimizing the first property is straightforward through supervised learning. However, relying solely on the classification loss does not explicitly enforce user-invariant structure in the representation space. To address this limitation, we incorporate a supervised contrastive learning objective that encourages samples sharing the same activity label to cluster together while pushing apart samples from different activities. Formally, this regularizes F_θ to produce representations that emphasize activity semantics while reducing user-specific variations.

We adopt a multi-task learning (MTL) formulation to jointly optimize the classification and contrastive objectives. MTL enables the encoder to benefit from complementary supervision signals and improves representation robustness across users. Instead of a two-stage pre-training and fine-tuning pipeline, we employ a single-stage joint optimization strategy. This avoids potential objective misalignment between pretext and downstream tasks and simplifies the training process by allowing both objectives to guide representation learning simultaneously.

In summary, the problem setup requires learning activity-discriminative yet user-invariant representations from data annotated with both activity and user labels. Within this formulation, our multi-task supervised contrastive framework provides a unified optimization process in which the classification and contrastive objectives jointly guide the encoder to capture activity semantics while suppressing user-specific variations [37]. This enables the resulting representations to generalize effectively to users unseen during training, without requiring any user-specific adaptation.

3.2. Multi-Task Contrastive Learning Framework

An overview of the proposed framework is shown in Figure 1.

As illustrated, during the training phase, data augmentations are applied to generate two distinct views for each input sample. These augmented views are processed by a shared encoder $F_\theta(\cdot)$ to obtain feature representations f_{cl}. In parallel, the raw input data are also passed through the same encoder to produce f_{raw}.

The features f_{cl} are then fed into a projection head $H_\phi(\cdot)$ to compute the contrastive loss L_{CL}, whereas f_{raw} is passed to a classification head $G_\varphi(\cdot)$ to compute the classification loss L_{CE}.

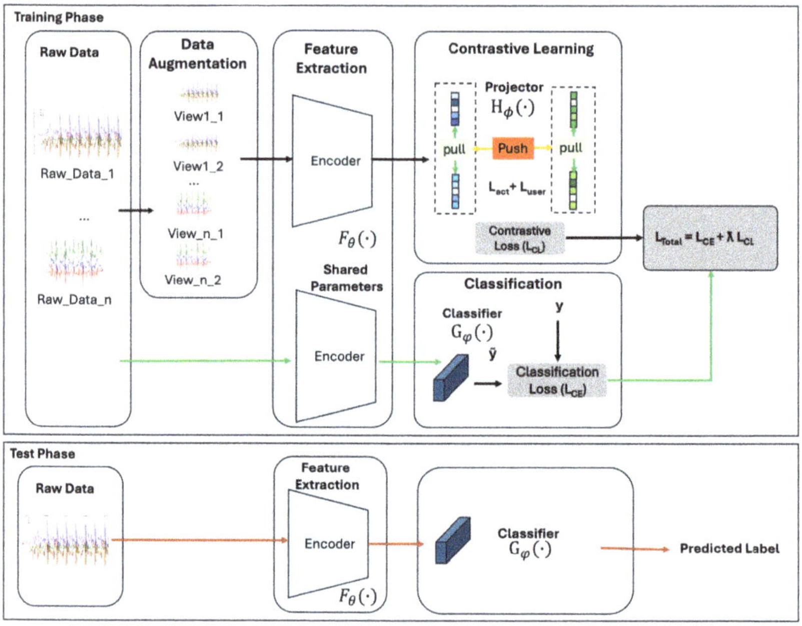

Figure 1. Overview of the proposed Multi-Task Contrastive Learning Framework for User-Generalizable HAR.

3.2.1. Model Architecture

Figure 2 illustrates the overall model architecture used in this work.

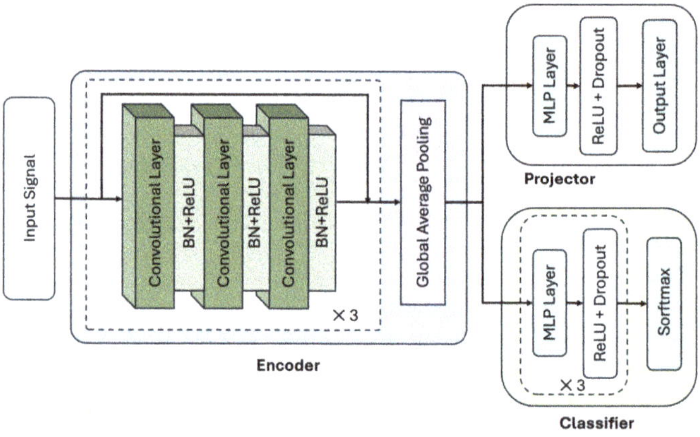

Figure 2. Model architecture. The encoder consists of residual blocks with convolutional layers, followed by global average pooling. The projector and classifier are built from MLP layers with non-linear activations and dropout.

To support deployment on wearable devices, where computational resources and battery life are often constrained, we design our framework around a lightweight neural network for efficient feature extraction. In this work, we adopt ResNet [38] as the backbone encoder owing to its strong representational capability and computational efficiency.

As shown in Figure 2, the encoder consists of three stacked residual blocks, each containing three convolutional layers with batch normalization and ReLU activation. A global average pooling layer is applied after the residual blocks to aggregate temporal features into a fixed-length representation. Unless otherwise specified, we follow the original ResNet configuration reported by Wang Z. et al. [38], with only the input and output dimensions adapted to fit each dataset.

It is worth noting that the focus of this work is not on the specific architecture of the encoder. Our framework is model-agnostic and can be flexibly adapted to other backbone networks.

The projection head $H_\phi(\cdot)$ is used exclusively during training for contrastive learning. It projects high-dimensional encoder outputs into a lower-dimensional latent space, serving as an information bottleneck to prevent contrastive signals from directly influencing the encoder. We adopt a non-linear projector composed of one hidden MLP layer with ReLU activation and dropout. The hidden layer size is selected based on the characteristics of each dataset.

The classification head $G_\varphi(\cdot)$ consists of three fully connected MLP layers, each followed by ReLU activation and dropout. The final output layer maps the features to activity logits for classification.

3.2.2. Activity Classification Task

The activity classification task serves as the primary task of our framework. Its goal is to predict the activity label corresponding to a given sensor input. During both training and inference, raw data segments are directly processed by the encoder $F_\theta(\cdot)$ to extract semantic features. These features are then passed to the classification head $G_\varphi(\cdot)$ to produce the predicted class logits.

Let $\mathbf{x}_{\text{raw}}$ denote the raw input sample, and let $y \in \{0, \ldots, C-1\}$ be the corresponding ground-truth activity label, where C is the total number of activity classes. The predicted probability distribution over the classes is obtained via the softmax output of the classifier:

$$\hat{y} = \text{softmax}(G_\varphi(F_\theta(\mathbf{x}_{\text{raw}}))). \tag{1}$$

The classification objective is optimized using the standard cross-entropy loss:

$$\mathcal{L}_{\text{CE}} = -\sum_{c=0}^{C-1} y_c \cdot \log(\hat{y}_c), \tag{2}$$

where $\hat{y}_c$ is the predicted probability of class c, and y_c is a binary indicator that equals 1 if the true label corresponds to class c, and 0 otherwise.

In our multi task framework, this classification loss $\mathcal{L}_{\text{CE}}$ supervises both the encoder F_θ and the classifier G_φ, guiding the model to learn features that are discriminative for activity recognition. During inference, only this classification branch is used to predict activity labels from unseen raw inputs, without relying on augmented views or the projection head.

3.2.3. Contrastive Learning Task

To enhance the generalization ability of the model across different users, we introduce a supervised contrastive learning (SupCon) task as an auxiliary objective during training.

Contrastive learning typically involves four stages: (1) data augmentation, (2) feature extraction, (3) projection and optimization, and (4) fine-tuning with labeled data. In our framework, the contrastive task is incorporated into a multi-task training paradigm, where it shares the encoder with the classification task and is optimized jointly in a single-stage process.

(a) Data Augmentation. Each input sample is augmented twice to produce two distinct views, which are then fed into the encoder $F_\theta(\cdot)$ followed by the projection head $H_\phi(\cdot)$, yielding normalized embeddings for contrastive learning.

We adopt a set of simple yet effective augmentations tailored for time-series data [34]. Given a collection of augmentation operators $\mathcal{A} = \{a_1, a_2, ..., a_n\}$, each operator is applied to the input signal with a fixed probability p. To ensure that every instance is transformed, jittering is applied as a base augmentation (i.e., $p = 1$). The augmentation methods used include:

- Jittering: Adds Gaussian noise to the signal.
- Scaling: Multiplies the signal by a random scalar drawn from a normal distribution.
- Channel Shuffle: Randomly permutes the channels of multivariate time-series data.
- Rotation: Randomly inverts the sign of the signal values.
- Permutation: Divides the signal into segments and permutes their order.

(b) Projection Head. The projection head $H_\phi(\cdot)$ maps the encoder output to a lower-dimensional latent space where the contrastive loss is applied. This component acts as an information bottleneck, ensuring that contrastive supervision does not directly interfere with the encoder's activity-discriminative space.

To stabilize contrastive learning and enable meaningful similarity comparisons, we apply ℓ_2-normalization to the projected features. Specifically, the output $\mathbf{z}_i$ of the projection head is normalized as follows:

$$\mathbf{z}_i = \frac{H_\phi(f_i)}{\|H_\phi(f_i)\|_2}, \tag{3}$$

where f_i denotes the encoder output for the i-th input sample, and $\|\cdot\|_2$ represents the Euclidean norm. This operation projects all feature vectors onto the unit hypersphere, ensuring unit length.

Such normalization is essential in contrastive learning frameworks such as SimCLR [32] and SupCon [36], where similarity is computed via the dot product (cosine similarity). Without normalization, the model may exploit feature magnitudes rather than directions to minimize the loss, leading to unstable training or representation collapse. Moreover, this step enhances the robustness of the learned representations, particularly under small batch sizes or high-temperature settings in the contrastive loss.

(c) Positive and Negative Sampling. The construction of positive and negative sample pairs is crucial for the effectiveness of contrastive learning. We adopt a hard negative sampling strategy tailored to the user generalization challenge. Specifically, given the projected embedding $\mathbf{z}_i$ of the i-th view and its corresponding activity label y_i, we define:

- Positive pairs: samples with the same activity label across different users.
- Negative pairs: samples with different activity labels but from the same user.

This design encourages the model to learn activity-discriminative yet user-invariant features by forcing it to ignore user-specific variations that are not semantically meaningful.

Figure 3 illustrates how our method differs from traditional SimCLR or activity-only supervised contrastive learning in the construction of positive and negative pairs. By mining hard negatives from the same user but different activities, our approach encourages the model to suppress subject-specific biases and learn user-invariant features more effectively.

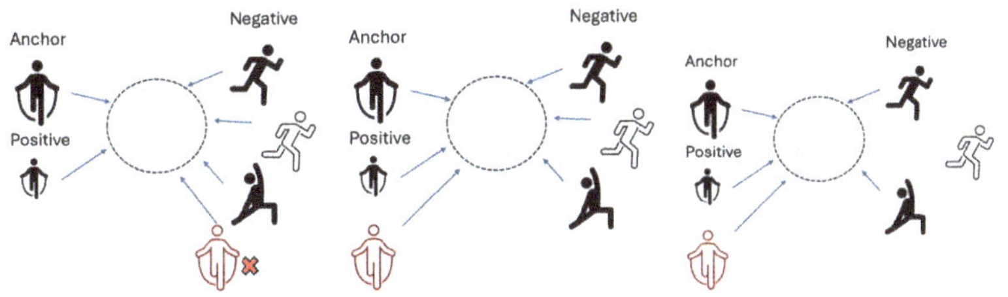

(**a**) SimCLR Sampling (**b**) Activity-only Sampling (**c**) Our Proposal

Figure 3. Comparison of positive and negative pair construction strategies.

(d) Contrastive Loss. We adopt the supervised contrastive loss (SupCon) [36], defined as:

$$\mathcal{L}_{\mathrm{CL}} = \sum_{i \in \mathcal{I}} \frac{-1}{|\mathcal{P}(i)|} \sum_{p \in \mathcal{P}(i)} \log \frac{\exp(\mathbf{z}_i \cdot \mathbf{z}_p / \tau)}{\sum_{a \in \mathcal{A}(i)} \exp(\mathbf{z}_i \cdot \mathbf{z}_a / \tau)}, \tag{4}$$

where τ is a temperature hyperparameter, $\mathcal{I}$ is the index set of all anchors in the batch, $\mathcal{P}(i)$ is the set of positives for anchor i, and $\mathcal{A}(i)$ includes all positives and negatives except i itself. The similarity is measured using the dot product between the projected embeddings.

(e) Training and Inference. The contrastive loss is applied only during training and backpropagates through the encoder and projection head. It is discarded during inference. Nevertheless, it serves as a strong regularizer that improves the robustness and transferability of the learned features, thereby enhancing user-level generalization in the classification task.

3.2.4. Loss and Optimization

The total loss is defined as a weighted combination of the two objectives:

$$\mathcal{L}_{\mathrm{total}} = \mathcal{L}_{\mathrm{CE}} + \lambda \cdot \mathcal{L}_{\mathrm{CL}}, \tag{5}$$

where $\lambda \in [0, 1]$ controls the trade-off between the main and auxiliary tasks.

During optimization, the model parameters are updated as follows:

$$\begin{cases} \theta \leftarrow \theta - \alpha \left(\dfrac{\partial \mathcal{L}_{\mathrm{CE}}}{\partial \theta} + \lambda \dfrac{\partial \mathcal{L}_{\mathrm{CL}}}{\partial \theta} \right), \\ \varphi \leftarrow \varphi - \alpha \left(\dfrac{\partial \mathcal{L}_{\mathrm{CE}}}{\partial \varphi} \right), \end{cases} \tag{6}$$

where α denotes the learning rate. In our training scheme, the classification loss $\mathcal{L}_{\mathrm{CE}}$ updates both the encoder $F_\theta(\cdot)$ and the classifier $G_\varphi(\cdot)$, while the contrastive loss $\mathcal{L}_{\mathrm{CL}}$ updates only the encoder.

During testing, the raw data are directly fed into the encoder to extract features, which are then passed through the classifier to obtain the predicted activity labels.

3.3. *Evaluation Metrics*

We adopt the macro-averaged F1 score as the primary evaluation metric. It is defined as:

$$\mathrm{F1} = \frac{2}{C} \sum_{c=0}^{C-1} \frac{p_c \cdot r_c}{p_c + r_c}, \tag{7}$$

where C denotes the total number of activity classes, and p_c and r_c represent the precision and recall for class c, respectively.

Macro-averaging treats all classes equally by computing the unweighted mean across classes, which makes it more robust to class imbalance—a common issue in human activity recognition datasets.

4. Experiments

4.1. Dataset and Preprocessing

We evaluated our framework on three public datasets that are widely used as benchmarks in this field. These datasets include diverse participants, activities, and sensor configurations, providing standardized benchmarks for evaluating user-level generalization and ensuring fair comparison across studies. Table 1 summarizes the basic information of the dataset.

4.1.1. MobiAct [39]

The MobiAct dataset, published in 2016, was collected using a smartphone. It includes data from 66 participants aged between 20 and 47 years, who performed 16 types of activities: 4 types of falls and 12 types of Activities of Daily Living (ADLs). The recorded signals include acceleration (x, y, z axes), angular velocity (x, y, z axes), and orientation (azimuth, pitch, roll). The acceleration data range is ± 2 g.

The dataset contains a total of 3199 samples, comprising 767 falls and 2432 ADLs, sampled at 200 Hz. In this study, data from 11 types of ADLs are used for experiments: standing (STD), walking (WAL), jogging (JOG), jumping (JUM), going upstairs (STU), going downstairs (STN), sitting (SIT), standing up from a chair (CHU), sitting down on a chair (SCH), stepping into a car (CSI), and stepping out of a car (CSO). The lying data are excluded because they were recorded as part of the falling process and therefore do not represent independent ADL activities.

4.1.2. UCI HAR [40]

The UCI HAR dataset, published in 2013, contains data collected from 30 participants aged between 19 and 48 years. The data were recorded using a smartphone worn on the waist. This dataset focuses on six types of ADLs: walking, walking upstairs, walking downstairs, sitting, standing, and lying.

The dataset comprises 10,299 samples, each lasting 2.56 s and sampled at 50 Hz.

4.1.3. USC-HAD [41]

The USC-HAD dataset, published in 2012, contains data collected from 14 participants aged between 21 and 49 years. The data were recorded using an Inertial Measurement Unit (IMU) worn on the right hip. This dataset includes 12 types of ADLs: walking forward, walking left, walking right, walking upstairs, walking downstairs, running forward, jumping, sitting, standing, sleeping, taking the elevator up, and taking the elevator down.

The dataset comprises 840 samples, each sampled at 100 Hz.

Table 1. Datasets.

Dataset	Classes	Frequency	Sensors	Subject
MobiAct [39]	11	200 Hz	A, G, O	66
UCI HAR [40]	6	50 Hz	A, G	30
USC-HAD [41]	12	100 Hz	A, G	14

A: Accelerometer; G: Gyroscope; O: Orientation (ignored).

To facilitate comparison and data processing, we downsampled all datasets to 50 Hz in the experiments and divided the data into 1 s windows with a 50% overlap. We downsampled the datasets to 50 Hz for two main reasons: (1) Standardization and comparability: A 50 Hz sampling rate is a common and well-established practice in the HAR literature. This standardization allows for consistent window sizes in terms of time duration. (2) Signal characteristics: According to the Nyquist theorem, a 50 Hz sampling rate is sufficient to capture all signal dynamics up to 25 Hz. For human-scale activities (e.g., walking, running, jumping), most discriminative information lies in low-frequency bands, typically well below 10–15 Hz [42]. Downsampling to 50 Hz can reduce computational amount without losing the core kinematic patterns required for accurate activity classification. Unless otherwise stated, datasets are split by users. For each dataset, we allocated 20% of users' data as the validation set and 20% as the test set, with the remaining 60% used for training.

4.2. Implementation Details

In this work, we use the AdamW [43] optimizer. For each dataset, the training hyperparameters were fine-tuned, as detailed in Table 2. All experiments were implemented in PyTorch 2.7.1 on a local workstation equipped with an Apple M3 Pro GPU (Apple Inc., Cupertino, CA, USA) running macOS Sonoma 14.3. The backbone configuration follows the original ResNet configuration reported by Wang, Z et al. [38] unless otherwise specified.

Table 2. Training settings.

Dataset	α	Projection Size	Batch Size	τ	Epochs (*ES*)	λ
MobiAct	0.0003	256	256	0.1	200 (30)	0.2
UCI HAR	0.0003	256	256	0.1	100 (30)	0.4
USC-HAD	0.0001	256	256	0.1	200 (30)	0.3

α: learning rate. τ: temperature. *ES*: Early Stopping Patience. λ: Auxiliary weight.

4.3. Main Results

To comprehensively evaluate the effectiveness of our proposed method, we compare it against a wide range of baseline approaches spanning multiple learning paradigms:

- Supervised Baselines: Traditional HAR models trained in a fully supervised manner, leveraging various backbone architectures such as the hybrid CNN-Transformer-BiLSTM (CTBL) [27], and the convolutional autoencoder (CAE) [28], DeepConvLSTM [29], CNN-Transformer (Sup. CSSHAR) [34].
- Self-Supervised Learning Baselines: Contrastive or predictive representation learning approaches trained in two stages. This group includes Contrastive Predictive Coding (CPC) [30], CSSHAR [34], and ClusterCL-HAR [35]
- Personalized Baselines: Approaches tailored for personalized HAR through user-specific fine-tuning or model adaptation. Representative methods include ProtoHAR [44] and FedHAR [16].
- User-Generalization Baselines: Methods explicitly designed to enhance user-level generalization and mitigate subject-domain shifts in wearable sensor-based HAR. This category includes GILE [17], CCIL [10], AFFAR [18], and Multi-task SSL [33].

Together, these baselines cover a diverse spectrum of learning strategies—from traditional supervised models to advanced self-supervised frameworks—and provide a solid foundation for evaluating the generalization performance of our method across users and datasets.

We performed three independent user-disjoint validation runs. The results are summarized in Table 3.

Table 3. Macro-F1 Score (%) on Three HAR Datasets (Ave. ± STD.).

Type	Method	MobiAct	UCI-HAR	USC-HAD
Sup.	DeepConvLSTM [29]	82.40 ± 1.82	82.64 ± 0.86	67.14 ± 2.56
	Sup. CSSHAR [34]	82.97 ± 1.10	**93.73 ± 1.02**	59.53 ± 1.06
	CTBL [27]	78.66 ± 5.30	92.72 ± 1.48	69.11 ± 4.29
	CAE [28]	78.75 ± 1.76	79.82 ± 0.97	49.88 ± 1.87
SSL	CSSHAR [34]	80.22 ± 1.02	90.51 ± 0.60	60.57 ± 1.92
	CPC [30]	81.54 ± 1.30	82.08 ± 1.04	52.31 ± 1.95
	ClusterCLHAR * [35]	-	92.12	58.85
Pers.	ProtoHAR * [44]	-	-	71.71
	FedHAR * [16]	-	79.34	-
Gen.	Multi-task SSL [33]	76.40 ± 1.59	82.30 ± 1.36	49.83 ± 3.58
	GILE * [17]	-	88.17	-
	CCIL * [10]	-	-	57.5
	AFFAR * [18]	-	-	72.58
Ours	**MultiSupConHAR**	**85.93 ± 1.23**	91.07 ± 2.09	**76.84 ± 1.09**

*: Official results reported in original paper. Bold numbers indicate the best performance on each dataset.

Table 3 presents the macro-F1 scores of our proposed method and a range of baseline methods on three benchmark HAR datasets: MobiAct, UCI-HAR, and USC-HAD. As shown, our method MultiSupConHAR achieves the best performance on MobiAct (85.93% ± 1.23%) and USC-HAD (76.84% ± 1.09%), and ranks second on UCI-HAR (91.07% ± 2.09%), slightly behind supervised CSSHAR (93.73% ± 1.02%), which employs a CNN-Transformer backbone, and CTBL (92.72% ± 1.48%), which employs a CNN-Transformer-BiLSTM backbone.

Compared with standard supervised baselines such as DeepConvLSTM and CTBL, our method shows significant improvements, especially on the USC-HAD dataset, with gaining ranging from 9.99% to 16.57% improvement. On USC-HAD, our method outperforms all other methods, including personalized and generalized HAR approaches, demonstrating strong generalization capability across subjects.

Moreover, MultiHAR also achieves consistently better performance than contrastive self-supervised methods such as CSSHAR, Multi-task SSL, CPC, CAE, and ClusterCLHAR, indicating the benefit of combining contrastive learning with supervised classification in a multi-task framework.

We also report the model size, FLOPs, and memory usage in Table 4. Tables 5–7 present the test classification reports of our method on the three datasets.

Table 4. Model Size, FLOPs, and Memory.

Method	Metric	MobiAct	UCI HAR	USC-HAD
DeepConvLSTM	Model size	458.00 k	458.00 k	458.00 k
	FLOPs (Inference)	53.20 M	53.20 M	53.20 M
	Memory (Inference)	2.35 M	2.35 M	2.35 M
CSSHAR	Model size (parameters)	9.30 M	5.40 M	6.60 M
	FLOPs (Inference)	823.70 M	491.44 M	614.75 M
	Memory (Inference)	48.40 M	26.98 M	31.59 M
MultiSupConHAR	Model size (parameters)	565.60 k	566.00 k	566.40 k
	FLOPs (Inference)	48.50 M	48.50 M	48.50 M
	Memory (Inference)	2.20 MB	2.20 MB	2.20 MB

Table 5. Classification Report on UCI HAR (%).

Class	Precision	Recall	F1 Score	Support
Walking	99.48	80.00	88.68	950
Walking upstairs	81.28	99.16	89.33	950
Walking Downstairs	100.0	92.02	95.85	890
Sitting	86.65	91.06	88.80	962
Standing	88.67	88.09	88.38	1075
Laying	99.43	100.0	99.71	1045
Accuracy			91.77	5872
Macro Avg	92.58	91.72	91.79	5872
Weighted Avg	92.52	91.77	91.80	5872

Table 6. Classification Report on MobiAct (%).

Class	Precision	Recall	F1 Score	Support
Standing	94.19	99.27	96.66	6445
Walking	99.38	88.82	93.80	5964
Jogging	95.34	94.00	94.67	1718
Jumping	99.77	99.88	99.83	1736
Stairs up	70.84	87.42	78.26	906
Stairs down	68.23	90.45	77.78	838
Stand to sit	91.18	72.37	80.69	257
Sitting	91.94	95.13	93.51	863
Sit to stand	80.00	70.33	74.85	91
Car-step in	80.71	70.10	75.03	388
Car-step out	77.41	60.61	67.99	424
Accuracy			94.49	25,116
Macro Avg	84.75	84.03	84.01	25,116
Weighted Avg	94.60	94.49	94.44	25,116

Table 7. Classification Report on UCS-HAD (%).

Class	Precision	Recall	F1 Score	Support
Walking Forward	69.90	89.80	78.64	2054
Walking Left	88.67	67.65	76.75	1354
Walking Right	90.85	76.57	83.10	1354
Walking Upstairs	94.51	83.38	88.60	1342
Walking Downstairs	96.59	82.26	88.85	1274
Running Forward	91.12	94.64	92.85	672
Jumping Up	100.0	98.50	99.24	666
Sitting	89.77	79.33	84.23	1350
Standing	50.25	85.60	63.33	1160
Sleeping	100.0	100.0	100.0	1960
Elevator Up	37.08	34.99	36.00	886
Elevator Down	47.53	30.68	37.29	942
Accuracy			79.13	14,996
Macro Avg	79.69	76.96	77.41	14,996
Weighted Avg	81.08	79.13	79.17	14,996

4.4. Ablation Study

To gain deeper insights into the effectiveness of the proposed multi-task contrastive learning framework, we conduct a series of ablation studies under the LOSO (Leave-One-Subject-Out) evaluation setting. These experiments are designed to disentangle the contributions of individual design components and provide empirical justification for each design choice.

Specifically, we examine the following aspects:

- Effectiveness of Multi-Task Training: We compare three settings—supervised classification only (primary task), supervised contrastive learning followed by downstream classification (auxiliary task only), and our joint multi-task training approach.
- Contrastive Learning Strategies: We investigate different strategies for constructing positive and negative pairs, including with/without user labels, with/without activity labels, and compare two-stage versus single-stage training schemes.
- Auxiliary Task Weight(λ): We vary the weight of the contrastive loss in the total loss function, testing $\lambda \in \{0.1, \ldots, 0.9\}$ to observe its influence on model performance.
- Hyperparameter Sensitivity: We study the impact of key hyperparameters, including batch size, the presence of a projection head, and the hidden dimensionality of the projection head.

These ablation analyses aim to address the following research questions:

1. Does joint multi-task training yield better HAR classification performance than training on individual tasks alone?
2. How should positive and negative pairs be constructed? Is incorporating user identity during training beneficial?
3. Is the proposed single-stage multi-task approach more effective than a two-stage contrastive pre-training followed by fine-tuning?
4. How sensitive is model performance to the choice of contrastive loss weight (λ)?
5. Are the selected hyperparameters (e.g., batch size, projection head) optimal for both performance and generalization?

All experiments in this section use the same ResNet backbone.

4.4.1. Effectiveness of Multi-Task Training

To evaluate the effectiveness of combining classification and contrastive learning in a multi-task framework, we compare the following variants:

- Supervised Classification Only (Primary Task Only): The model is trained solely with the cross-entropy loss for activity classification.
- SupCon Only (Act + User): A two-stage training approach in which the model is first trained using the supervised contrastive loss with both activity and user labels. The encoder is then frozen, and a classifier is fine-tuned on the fully labeled dataset.
- MultiSupConHAR (SupCon Act + User): Our proposed method, where the model is trained end-to-end by jointly optimizing the classification loss and the supervised contrastive loss.

This comparison allows us to evaluate whether multi-task training provides a synergistic advantage over single-objective approaches.

The results are summarized in Table 8.

Table 8. Macro-Average F1 Score (%) of Different Tasks.

Task	MobiAct	UCI HAR	US-HAD
Supervised Only	75.13	89.71	71.35
SupCon (Act + User)	82.81	92.22	67.14
MultiSupConHAR	**86.01**	**93.16**	**77.13**

Bold numbers indicate the best performance on each dataset.

Table 8 presents the macro-averaged F1 scores of different training paradigms on the three HAR datasets. Our proposed multi-task framework consistently outperforms both the supervised-only model and the two-stage SupCon model across all datasets.

Specifically, the proposed method achieves 86.01% on MobiAct, 93.16% on UCI-HAR, and 77.13% on USC-HAD. Compared with the supervised-only baseline, the performance improvements are 10.88%, 3.45%, and 5.78%, respectively. When compared with the SupCon-only variant, our method also yields consistent gains of 3.20%, 0.94%, and 9.99% on the three datasets.

These results demonstrate that jointly optimizing the classification and contrastive objectives within a unified training framework leads to superior performance compared with using either objective alone.

4.4.2. Contrastive Strategy Analysis

To examine the impact of different contrastive learning strategies on user-level generalization, we compare several variants based on how positive and negative pairs are constructed, and whether contrastive learning is applied in a two-stage or multi-task manner. Specifically, we consider the following settings:

- SimCLR (Two-stage): Self-supervised contrastive learning based solely on data augmentations, without using any labels. The construction of positive and negative pairs follows Figure 3a. The encoder is then frozen, and a classifier is fine-tuned on the fully labeled dataset. The contrastive loss is computed using the XNent loss Formulation (8) [34].
- SupCon (Act Only, Two-stage): Supervised contrastive learning using only activity labels to construct positive and negative pairs (Figure 3b). The encoder is then frozen, and a classifier is fine-tuned on the fully labeled dataset.
- SupCon (Act + User, Two-stage): A stricter version of SupCon, in which both activity and user labels must match to form positive and negative pairs (Figure 3c).
- Multi-task + SimCLR: A joint training approach where SimCLR-based self-supervised contrastive learning is used as an auxiliary task alongside activity classification (Figure 3a). The contrastive loss is computed using the XNent loss Formulation (8) [34].
- Multi-task + SupCon (Act Only): Joint training with SupCon using activity labels (Figure 3c).

$$\mathcal{L}_{\text{XNent}} = \sum_{i=1}^{N} \log \frac{\exp(\mathbf{z}_i \cdot \mathbf{z}_p / \tau)}{\sum_{j \in \mathcal{A}(i)} \exp(\mathbf{z}_i \cdot \mathbf{z}_j / \tau)} \tag{8}$$

This comparison aims to address the following questions.

- Does leveraging label information in contrastive learning improve downstream HAR performance?
- Does incorporating both user and activity identities into positive sampling help the model learn more user-invariant features?
- Do multi-task learning variants outperform their two-stage counterparts across different strategies?

For the self-supervised contrastive learning settings, we followed dataset-specific hyperparameter configurations as reported in previous studies [34,45]. Specifically, during the pre-training stage, we used a learning rate of 0.0001 for MobiAct and UCI-HAR, and 0.00001 for USC-HAD. During the fine-tuning stage, a fixed learning rate of 0.0001 was used for all datasets. All other hyperparameters were kept consistent with those used in the MultiSupConHAR setting.

In the two-stage training pipeline, the encoder was frozen during the fine-tuning stage, and only the classifier was trained. All self-supervised models were pre-trained for 200 epochs and subsequently fine-tuned for another 100 epochs.

The results are presented in Table 9.

Table 9. Macro-Average F1 Score (%) of Different Contrastive Strategies.

Method	MobiAct	UCI HAR	USC-HAD
Supervised	82.81	92.22	67.14
SimCLR	72.28	81.35	56.94
SupCon (Act Only)	78.22	89.24	71.56
SupCon (Act + User)	75.13	89.71	71.35
Multi-task (SimCLR)	80.44	91.83	73.73
Multi-task (SupCon Act Only)	82.38	92.69	74.36
MultiSupConHAR	**86.01**	**93.16**	**77.13**

Bold numbers indicate the best performance on each dataset.

As shown in Table 9, our proposed method outperforms all contrastive learning strategies across the three datasets.

Among the baselines, supervised contrastive learning using activity labels (SupCon Act Only) performs better than the self-supervised SimCLR approach in both two-stage and multi-task settings. The multi-task variants (SimCLR or SupCon) consistently outperform their corresponding two-stage counterparts. Furthermore, the combination of activity and user label supervision (Act + User) under multi-task training yields the best overall results.

4.4.3. Auxiliary Task Weight Analysis

We further investigate the impact of the loss balancing weight λ, which controls the contribution of the contrastive objective within the multi-task training framework. We vary λ from 0.1 to 0.9 and report the macro-F1 scores on the three datasets, as shown in Figure 4.

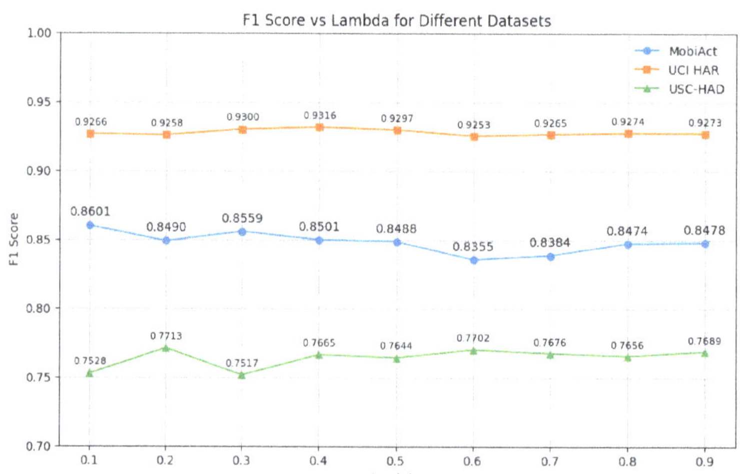

Figure 4. Effect of contrastive loss weight λ on model performance (F1 score) across different datasets.

Overall, we observe that incorporating the contrastive loss ($\lambda > 0$) consistently improves performance compared with purely supervised learning across all datasets. For MobiAct, the best performance is achieved at $\lambda = 0.1$, while USC-HAD performs best at $\lambda = 0.2$. In contrast, UCI-HAR exhibits relatively stable performance across a wider range of λ values, with the highest score observed at $\lambda = 0.4$.

These results suggest that the optimal value of λ may vary depending on dataset characteristics. Datasets with higher inter-class similarity or more diverse activity types (such as MobiAct and USC-HAD) appear to be more sensitive to the choice of λ, requiring a careful balance between the main classification and auxiliary contrastive objectives. In general, setting λ to a value below 0.5 yields better performance, indicating that a moderate contrastive loss weight is sufficient to enhance representation learning without overwhelming the primary classification task.

Interestingly, performance degrades slightly when λ is too large (e.g., 0.6–0.7 on MobiAct), possibly due to the overemphasis on the auxiliary task. These findings indicate that careful tuning of λ is beneficial, and that incorporating contrastive learning as an auxiliary task with a moderate weight enhances cross-user generalization without compromising classification performance.

4.4.4. Hyperparameter Analysis

We further investigate the sensitivity of our model to several key hyperparameters within the contrastive learning framework. Specifically, we evaluate the effects of batch size, the presence or absence of a projection head, and the hidden dimensionality of the projection head. These factors are known to influence the learning dynamics and the quality of the learned representations in contrastive learning [46]. All experiments were conducted under the multi-task training setup with SupCon (Act + User) on the three datasets, while keeping all other settings fixed.

(a) Batch Size. We evaluated the effect of batch size on model performance by varying it across {64, 128, 256, 512, 1024}. The results, shown in Figure 5, indicate that moderate batch sizes generally lead to better performance across all datasets.

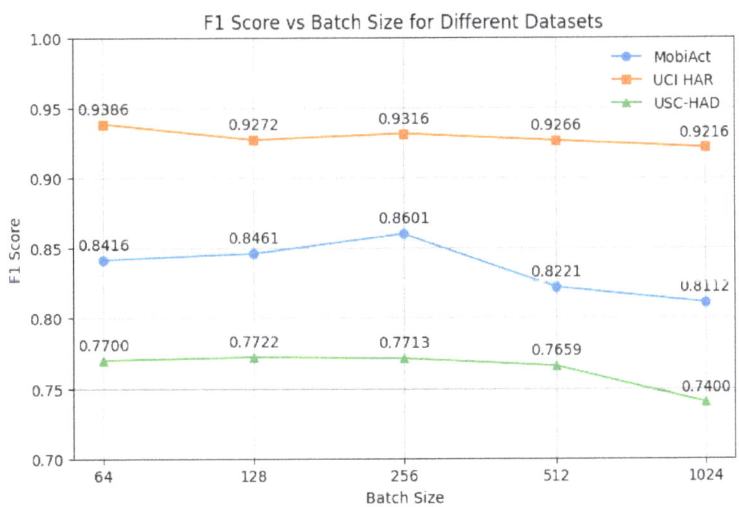

Figure 5. Effect of batch size on F1 score across three datasets.

On the MobiAct dataset, performance peaks at a batch size of 256 with a macro-F1 score of 86.01%, while larger batch sizes (e.g., 512 and 1024) result in noticeable degradation. A similar trend is observed on USC-HAD, where performance decreases significantly from 77.13% at a batch size of 256 to 74.00% at a batch size of 1024. In contrast, UCI-HAR appears relatively less sensitive to the batch size, although a slight decline in performance is observed as the batch size increases.

(b) Projection Head. To assess the impact of the projection head in the contrastive learning task, we compare model performance with and without a two-layer MLP projection head placed before the contrastive loss. As shown in Figure 6, incorporating a projection head consistently improves the F1 score across all datasets. The most significant improvement is observed on the MobiAct dataset, where the F1 score increases from 78.87% to 86.01%. Smaller but consistent gains are also observed on UCI-HAR and USC-HAD.

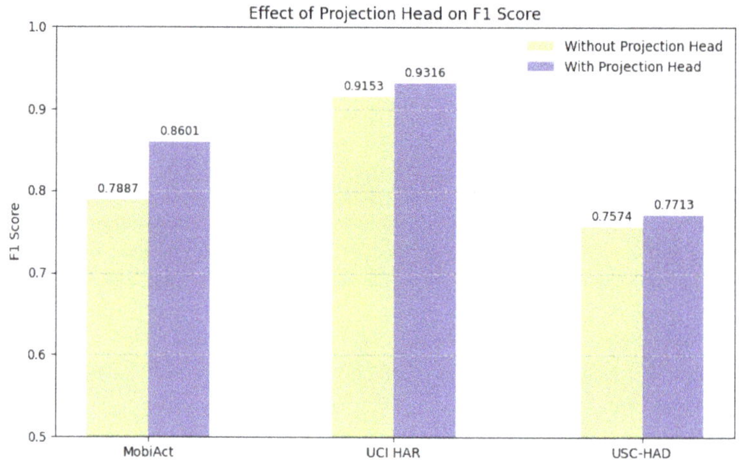

Figure 6. Effect of projection head on F1 score across three datasets.

We further examine the effect of the hidden dimension size in the projection head. As shown in Figure 7, we evaluate hidden dimensions of {64, 128, 256, 512, 1024}. The results indicate that a moderate hidden size (256) yields the best performance across all datasets.

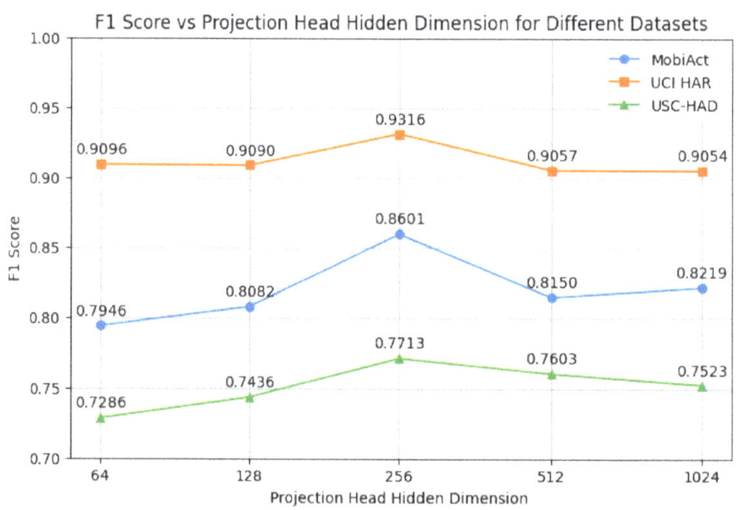

Figure 7. Effect of hidden dimension size in the projection head on F1 score.

5. Discussion

As demonstrated in the previous section, our method—MultiSupConHAR—achieved performance comparable to the baselines, demonstrating its effectiveness in enhancing user generalization in HAR.

5.1. Main Results and Comparisons

Our proposed method outperforms most baseline models across the three HAR datasets and achieves the best overall performance. Although its performance is slightly lower than that of Sup. CSSHAR and CTBL on the UCI-HAR dataset, the results demonstrate that introducing supervised contrastive learning effectively enhances user generalization. Furthermore, as shown in Table 4, although our method has a slightly larger number of parameters compared to the classic DeepConvLSTM baseline, it has lower Flops and memory usage during inference because it does not use recurrent structures such as LSTM.

Compared with self-supervised contrastive learning methods, our approach not only achieves higher accuracy but also eliminates the need for a two-stage training process. This design reduces training costs and mitigates the potential risk of objective mismatch between the pre-training and fine-tuning stages. For instance, CSSHAR [34] adoptd a SimCLR-based framework with a CNN–Transformer encoder. Its model complexity is relatively high (9.3 M, 5.4 M, and 6.6 M parameters on the three datasets), whereas our method uses a ResNet encoder with only 481K parameters, resulting in significantly lower computational and energy demands—making it more suitable for edge-device deployment. Other methods, such as CPC [30] and ClusterCLHAR [35], also involved two-stage training. CPC (Contrastive Predictive Coding) learned temporal dependencies by predicting future latent representations from past context vectors. ClusterCLHAR performed clustering-based instance discrimination during pre-training. Both methods were designed to leverage unlabeled data by pre-training on unannotated signals and subsequently fine-tuning on labeled data. While this strategy helps alleviate label scarcity, it does not improve cross-user generalization under fully supervised settings.

We also compared our method with personalization-based approaches such as ProtoHAR [44] and FedHAR [16], which employed federated learning to build user-specific models. Both methods first trained a general model and then fine-tuned personalized models on client devices. This design effectively addresses privacy concerns by keeping user data local. However, they still require new user data to be collected and labeled, followed by local re-training—again, a two stage process. In contrast, our method achieves better performance within a single-stage pipeline without requiring per-user re-training.

Existing approaches to user generalization in HAR can be broadly categorized into three directions:

1. Self-supervised pretraining (e.g., Multi-task SSL [33]) learns transformation-aware representations through auxiliary tasks. While effective for representation learning, these methods typically rely on separate pretraining and fine-tuning stages, which limits task-level integration.
2. Domain disentanglement methods (e.g., GILE [17]) aim to separate domain-invariant and domain-specific features through probabilistic modeling. These approaches enable zero-shot transfer but involve complex, sampling-based training procedures.
3. Alignment-based strategies(e.g., CCIL [10], AFFHAR [18]) introduce explicit mechanisms (e.g., concept matrices, domain alignment losses) to enforce consistency across users or domains. Although these methods encourage generalization, they add extra training components and regularization overhead.

Our method offers an alternative perspective by unifying classification and supervised contrastive learning within a multi-task setting. This formulation leverages both activity and user labels to directly guide representation learning, without relying on external alignment modules or multi-stage training.

This design enables end-to-end optimization and promotes stable training dynamics. Moreover, the encoder remains compact (only 481K parameters), making it well-suited for deployment on resource-constrained devices. As demonstrated by our experiments, the proposed approach achieves competitive user-level generalization while maintaining a simple and modular architecture.

Overall, the framework provides a balanced integration of task-driven supervision and contrastive learning, offering a practical pathway toward generalizable HAR under real-world constraints.

5.2. Ablation Study Discussion

Our proposed method is built upon two key design choices. First, we introduce contrastive learning as an auxiliary task and jointly optimize it with the primary classification task in an end-to-end manner. Second, we adopt a supervised contrastive loss that utilizes both activity and user labels to construct positive and negative pairs, enabling user-aware representation learning.

As shown in Table 8, the multi-task setting outperforms individual single-task settings, validating the effectiveness of our joint optimization strategy.

As shown in Table 9, our proposed multi-task method consistently outperforms all contrastive learning variants across the three datasets. We highlight several key observations:

1. Supervised contrastive learning (SupCon) achieves higher performance than self-supervised contrastive learning (SimCLR), indicating that label supervision is beneficial for wearable HAR tasks.
2. Multi-task variants consistently outperform their two-stage counterparts, highlighting the advantages of end-to-end joint training in balancing generalization and optimization stability.
3. Interestingly, while incorporating both activity and user labels (Act + User) into the contrastive learning process improves performance in the multi-task setting, we observe limited or no improvement in the two-stage setting. This difference may arise from how the two paradigms utilize supervision signals during optimization.

In the two-stage setting, the encoder is pre-trained solely using the contrastive loss, independent of the downstream classification objective. Although user labels are used to guide the sampling of positive and negative pairs, the learned representations are not explicitly aligned with the classification task. As a result, the semantic structure induced by user supervision may not transfer effectively to the downstream task and may even interfere with fine-tuning due to objective misalignment.

By contrast, the multi-task setting jointly optimizes both contrastive and classification losses. This end-to-end formulation ensures that user-level supervision is integrated in a way that remains compatible with the classification objective. The contrastive loss shapes the feature space by introducing user-level discrimination, while the classification loss anchors the representations around activity semantics. We hypothesize that this synergy improves hard negative mining and leads to more transferable representations across users.

Moreover, joint training reduces the risk of representation drift between the pre-training and fine-tuning stages—a common issue in two-stage pipelines where the learned contrastive space is decoupled from the final task objective.

These findings support our design choice: integrating activity- and user-aware contrastive learning into a multi-task framework offers a favorable trade-off between user generalization and learning stability.

Figure 4 illustrates the impact of the contrastive loss weight λ on model performance.

The optimal value of λ varies across datasets. Datasets with higher inter-class similarity or a larger number of activities (e.g., MobiAct and USC-HAD) appear more sensitive to λ, requiring careful calibration to balance the main classification and auxiliary contrastive objectives.

Overall, setting $\lambda < 0.5$ yields better performance, suggesting that a moderate contrastive loss weight is sufficient to enhance feature learning without overwhelming the primary classification task. In contrast, performance slightly degrades when λ is too large (e.g., 0.6–0.7 on MobiAct), possibly due to an overemphasis on the auxiliary objective. These results confirm the importance of tuning λ to achieve robust and generalizable performance.

We further investigate the effects of batch size, the presence of a projection head, and the hidden dimensionality of the projection head. The corresponding results are shown in Figures 5–7.

- Batch Size: Consistent with prior studies [46], excessively large batch sizes can reduce gradient diversity and introduce optimization instability. We select a batch size of 256 to balance computational efficiency and model performance.
- Projection Head: The inclusion of a projection head improves performance, aligning with previous findings in contrastive learning [32]. The projection head serves as a representation bottleneck, decoupling the contrastive space from the classification space and thereby enhancing generalization.
- Hidden Dimension: Using overly small (e.g., 64) or large (e.g., 1024) hidden dimensions leads to performance degradation. This suggests that under-parameterization limits representational capacity, while over-parameterization may cause overfitting or training instability. A moderate hidden dimension (e.g., 256) provides the best trade-off.

These ablation results comprehensively validate each component of our framework and highlight the robustness and generalizability of our multi-task contrastive learning approach for user-level HAR.

Figure 8 shows the confusion matrices of our model on the UCI HAR, MobiAct, and USC-HAD datasets. Overall, the model achieves a high diagonal advantage on all datasets, indicating that most activities are correctly identified. However, some systematic misclassifications are still observed.

For the UCI HAR dataset, the main confusion occurs between "walking" and "walking upstairs," and between "sitting" and "standing." These activities have similar dynamic patterns or transitional postures, leading to overlapping temporal features in the sensor space.

In the MobiAct dataset, although there are many activity categories, most categories are accurately distinguished. However, transitional actions such as "standing to sitting/sitting in a chair" and "sitting to standing (chair raised)" exhibit significant confusion (e.g., mutual misclassification rates of approximately 15–25%), reflecting the challenge of identifying short-term transitional states with subtle kinematic differences. Significant confusion also occurs between "standing" and "car step-in/car step-out." Short-term transitional states also exist between these actions.

For the USC-HAD model, errors primarily occur in walking-related activities (e.g., walking forward, left, and right), due to the similar periodic motion patterns of these activities. Furthermore, elevator movements (going up and down) are frequently confused with standing, likely because these movements involve smaller amplitude of body motion or because data such as acceleration and angular velocity during the uniform motion phase of an elevator ride are consistent with the standing state.

These observations suggest that while the proposed model captures discriminative representations of most activities, further improvement may require temporal context modeling or explicit transition state enhancement to better distinguish between fine and low-motor activities.

Figures 9–11 shows the t-SNE visualization of representations on the UCI HAR, MobiAct, and USC-HAD datasets of our proposal and supervised ResNet.

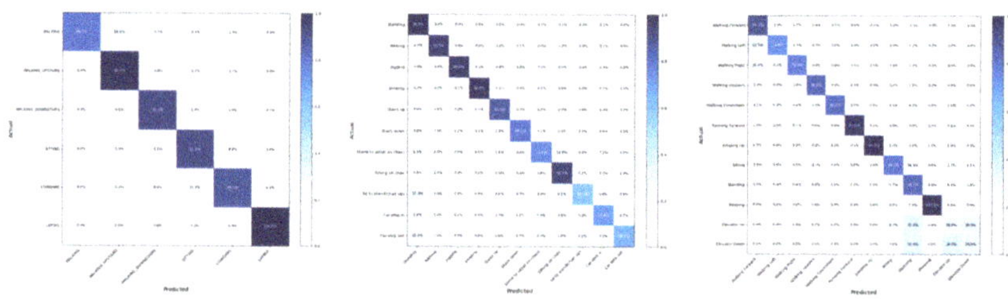

(**a**) UCI HAR (**b**) MobiAct (**c**) USC-HAD

Figure 8. Comfusion Matrix.

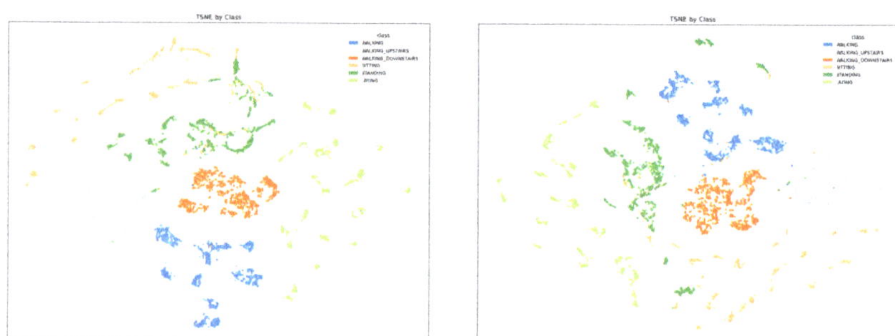

(**a**) MultiSupConHAR (**b**) Supervised ResNet

Figure 9. t-SNE visualization of representations (UCI HAR).

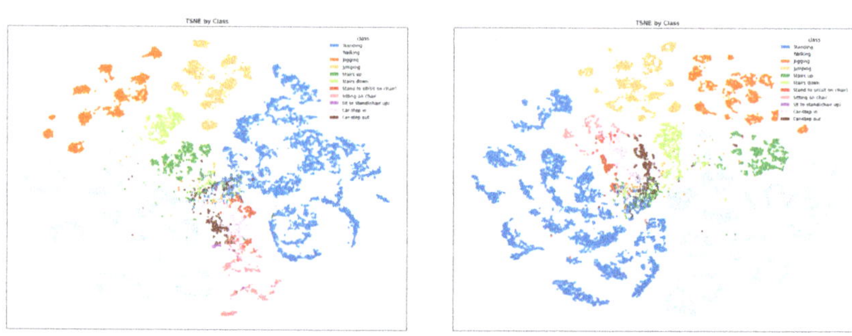

(**a**) MultiSupConHAR (**b**) Supervised ResNet

Figure 10. t-SNE visualization of representations (MobiAct).

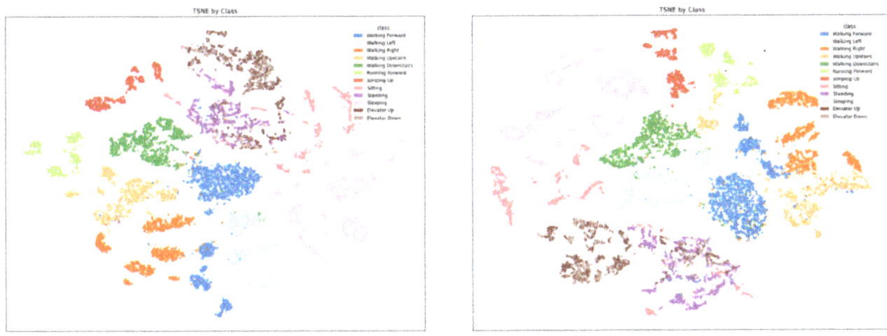

(**a**) MultiSupConHAR (**b**) Supervised ResNet

Figure 11. t-SNE visualization of representations (USC-HAD).

6. Conclusions and Future Work

This study presented a multi-task contrastive learning framework for user-generalizable human activity recognition (HAR) using wearable sensor data. By jointly optimizing supervised classification and contrastive objectives with both activity and user labels, the proposed method effectively enhances feature representations without requiring user-specific adaptation. Extensive cross-user evaluations on three public datasets verified its effectiveness and robustness, outperforming baseline and state-of-the-art methods on MobiAct and USC-HAD, and achieving comparable results on UCI HAR. The ablation analyses further confirmed the benefits of joint training, supervised contrastive loss, and task-aware pair construction.

At the same time, the findings of this work highlight several directions for further research.

First, since the framework relies on fully labeled data for both activity and user identities, future studies could explore semi-supervised and self-supervised extensions—such as pseudo-labeling, contrastive pretraining, or weak supervision—to reduce annotation requirements.

Second, validation was limited to public datasets. Additional in-the-wild deployment and long-term evaluation would provide stronger evidence of robustness to variations in sensor placement and user lifestyle.

Finally, the present framework mainly targets cross-user generalization; integrating complementary strategies such as domain adaptation, meta-learning, or adversarial data generation may enable broader cross-domain and cross-device transferability.

Moreover, insights from recent computer vision research—such as multiview attention networks with random interpolation–based augmentation [47], content–style contrastive frameworks for domain generalization [48], and weakly supervised adversarial segmentation approaches [49] could inspire future extensions of sensor-based HAR towards more robust and adaptive models.

Overall, the proposed framework provides methodological contributions and outlines a potential direction for developing scalable and label-efficient user-generalizable HAR systems.

Author Contributions: Conceptualization, P.G.; methodology, P.G.; software, P.G.; validation, P.G.; formal analysis, P.G.; data curation, P.G.; writing—original draft preparation, P.G.; writing—review and editing, M.N.; visualization, P.G.; supervision, M.N.; project administration, P.G.; All authors have read and agreed to the published version of the manuscript.

Funding: This research received no external funding.

Institutional Review Board Statement: Not applicable.

Informed Consent Statement: Not applicable.

Data Availability Statement: In this study, we used three publicly available datasets—MobiAct, UCI HAR, and USC-HAD—which can be accessed online. MobiAct—https://bmi.hmu.gr/the-mobifall-and-mobiact-datasets-2/. Accessed on 1 October 2022. USC-HAD—https://sipi.usc.edu/had/. Accessed on 1 October 2022. UCI HAR—https://github.com/arijitiiest/UCI-Human-Activity-Recognition?tab=readme-ov-file. Accessed on 1 October 2022. Model checkpoints can be provided upon reasonable request for research purposes.

Acknowledgments: We thank all researchers who published the public datasets UCI HAR, MobiAct, and USC-HAD. We thank all participants in these projects.

Conflicts of Interest: The authors declare no conflicts of interest.

References

1. Zhou, Z.; Jin, D.; He, J.; Zhou, S.; Wu, J.; Wang, S.; Zhang, Y.; Feng, T. Digital Health Platform for Improving the Effect of the Active Health Management of Chronic Diseases in the Community: Mixed Methods Exploratory Study. *J. Med. Internet Res.* **2024**, *26*, e50959. [CrossRef]
2. Sun, Z.; Ke, Q.; Rahmani, H.; Bennamoun, M.; Wang, G.; Liu, J. Human Action Recognition From Various Data Modalities: A Review. *IEEE Trans. Pattern Anal. Mach. Intell.* **2023**, *45*, 3200–3225. [CrossRef]
3. Kobir, M.I.; Machado, P.; Lotfi, A.; Haider, D.; Ihianle, I.K. Enhancing Multi-User Activity Recognition in an Indoor Environment with Augmented Wi-Fi Channel State Information and Transformer Architectures. *Sensors* **2025**, *25*, 3955. [CrossRef]
4. Gupta, S. Deep Learning Based Human Activity Recognition (HAR) Using Wearable Sensor Data. *Int. J. Inf. Manag. Data Insights* **2021**, *1*, 100046. [CrossRef]
5. Huang, W.; Zhang, L.; Wu, H.; Min, F.; Song, A. Channel-Equalization-HAR: A Light-Weight Convolutional Neural Network for Wearable Sensor Based Human Activity Recognition. *IEEE Trans. Mob. Comput.* **2023**, *22*, 5064–5077. [CrossRef]
6. Han, C.; Zhang, L.; Tang, Y.; Huang, W.; Min, F.; He, J. Human Activity Recognition Using Wearable Sensors by Heterogeneous Convolutional Neural Networks. *Expert Syst. Appl.* **2022**, *198*, 116764. [CrossRef]
7. Huang, W.; Zhang, L.; Gao, W.; Min, F.; He, J. Shallow Convolutional Neural Networks for Human Activity Recognition Using Wearable Sensors. *IEEE Trans. Instrum. Meas.* **2021**, *70*, 2510811. [CrossRef]
8. Tang, Y.; Zhang, L.; Min, F.; He, J. Multiscale Deep Feature Learning for Human Activity Recognition Using Wearable Sensors. *IEEE Trans. Ind. Electron.* **2023**, *70*, 2106–2116. [CrossRef]
9. Chowdhury, R.R.; Kapila, R.; Panse, A.; Zhang, X.; Teng, D.; Kulkarni, R.; Hong, D.; Gupta, R.K.; Shang, J. ZeroHAR: Sensor Context Augments Zero-Shot Wearable Action Recognition. In Proceedings of the AAAI Conference on Artificial Intelligence, Philadelphia, PA, USA, 25 February–7 March 2025; Volume 39, pp. 16046–16054. [CrossRef]
10. Xiong, D.; Wang, S.; Zhang, L.; Huang, W.; Han, C. Generalizable Sensor-Based Activity Recognition via Categorical Concept Invariant Learning. In Proceedings of the AAAI Conference on Artificial Intelligence, Philadelphia, PA, USA, 25 February–7 March 2025; Volume 39, pp. 923–931. [CrossRef]
11. Hong, Z.; Li, Z.; Zhong, S.; Lyu, W.; Wang, H.; Ding, Y.; He, T.; Zhang, D. CrossHAR: Generalizing Cross-Dataset Human Activity Recognition via Hierarchical Self-Supervised Pretraining. *Proc. ACM Interact. Mob. Wearable Ubiquitous Technol.* **2024**, *8*, 64. [CrossRef]
12. Bianchi, V.; Bassoli, M.; Lombardo, G.; Fornacciari, P.; Mordonini, M.; De Munari, I. IoT Wearable Sensor and Deep Learning: An Integrated Approach for Personalized Human Activity Recognition in a Smart Home Environment. *IEEE Internet Things J.* **2019**, *6*, 8553–8562. [CrossRef]
13. Saha, B.; Samanta, R.; Roy, R.B.; Chakraborty, C.; Ghosh, S.K. Personalized Human Activity Recognition: Real-Time On-Device Training and Inference. *IEEE Consum. Electron. Mag.* **2025**, *14*, 84–89. [CrossRef]
14. Kang, P.; Moosmann, J.; Liu, M.; Zhou, B.; Magno, M.; Lukowicz, P.; Bian, S. Bridging Generalization and Personalization in Wearable Human Activity Recognition via On-Device Few-Shot Learning. *arXiv* **2025**, arXiv:2508.15413. Available online: https://arxiv.org/abs/2508.15413 (accessed on 15 September 2025).
15. Fu, Z.; He, X.; Wang, E.; Huo, J.; Huang, J.; Wu, D. Personalized Human Activity Recognition Based on Integrated Wearable Sensor and Transfer Learning. *Sensors* **2021**, *21*, 885. [CrossRef]
16. Yu, H.; Zhang, W.; Li, Z.; Chen, Y.; Liu, J.; Song, A. FedHAR: Semi-Supervised Online Learning for Personalized Federated Human Activity Recognition. *IEEE Trans. Mob. Comput.* **2023**, *22*, 3318–3332. [CrossRef]
17. Qian, H.; Pan, S.J.; Miao, C. Latent Independent Excitation for Generalizable Sensor-Based Cross-Person Activity Recognition. In Proceedings of the AAAI Conference on Artificial Intelligence, Virtual Event, 2–9 February 2021; Volume 35, pp. 11921–11929. [CrossRef]

18. Qin, X.; Wang, J.; Chen, Y.; Lu, W.; Jiang, X. Domain Generalization for Activity Recognition via Adaptive Feature Fusion. *ACM Trans. Intell. Syst. Technol.* **2023**, *14*, 9. [CrossRef]
19. Chen, L.; Hoey, J.; Nugent, C.D.; Cook, D.J.; Yu, Z. Sensor-Based Activity Recognition. *IEEE Trans. Syst. Man Cybern. C Appl. Rev.* **2012**, *42*, 790–808. [CrossRef]
20. Bao, L.; Intille, S.S. Activity Recognition from User-Annotated Acceleration Data. In *Pervasive Computing*; Ferscha, A., Mattern, F., Eds.; Lecture Notes in Computer Science; Springer: Berlin/Heidelberg, Germany, 2004; Volume 3001, pp. 1–17.
21. Ravi, N.; Dandekar, N.; Mysore, P.; Littman, M. Activity Recognition from Accelerometer Data. In Proceedings of the Seventeenth Conference on Innovative Applications of Artificial Intelligence, Pittsburgh, PA, USA, 9–13 July 2005; pp. 1541–1546.
22. Kwapisz, J.R.; Weiss, G.M.; Moore, S.A. Activity Recognition Using Cell Phone Accelerometers. *SIGKDD Explor. Newsl.* **2010**, *12*, 74–82. [CrossRef]
23. Weiss, G.M.; Timko, J.L.; Gallagher, C.M.; Yoneda, K.; Schreiber, A.J. Smartwatch-Based Activity Recognition: A Machine Learning Approach. In Proceedings of the 2016 IEEE-EMBS International Conference on Biomedical and Health Informatics (BHI), Las Vegas, NV, USA, 24–27 February 2016; pp. 426–429.
24. Hassan, M.M.; Gumaei, A.; Aloi, G.; Fortino, G.; Zhou, M. A Smartphone-Enabled Fall Detection Framework for Elderly People in Connected Home Healthcare. *IEEE Netw.* **2019**, *33*, 58–63. [CrossRef]
25. Chen, J.; Sun, Y.; Sun, S. Improving Human Activity Recognition Performance by Data Fusion and Feature Engineering. *Sensors* **2021**, *21*, 692. [CrossRef]
26. Guo, P.; Nakayama, M. Transformer-Based Human Activity Recognition Using Wearable Sensors for Health Monitoring. In Proceedings of the 9th International Conference on Biomedical Engineering and Applications (ICBEA), Seoul, Republic of Korea, 27 February–2 March 2025; pp. 68–72.
27. Guo, P.; Nakayama, M. CNN-Transformer-Bi-LSTM: A Hybrid Deep Learning Framework for Wearable Sensor-Based Human Activity Recognition. In Proceedings of the 8th International Conference on Signal Processing and Machine Learning (SPML), Hohhot, China, 15–17 July 2025; pp. 10–15.
28. Haresamudram, H.; Anderson, D.V.; Plötz, T. On the Role of Features in Human Activity Recognition. In Proceedings of the ACM International Symposium on Wearable Computers (ISWC), London, UK, 9–13 September 2019; pp. 78–88.
29. Ordóñez, F.J.; Roggen, D. Deep Convolutional and LSTM Recurrent Neural Networks for Multimodal Wearable Activity Recognition. *Sensors* **2016**, *16*, 115. [CrossRef]
30. Haresamudram, H.; Essa, I.; Plötz, T. Contrastive Predictive Coding for Human Activity Recognition. *Proc. ACM Interact. Mob. Wearable Ubiquitous Technol.* **2021**, *5*, 65. [CrossRef]
31. Chen, T.; Kornblith, S.; Norouzi, M.; Hinton, G. A Simple Framework for Contrastive Learning of Visual Representations. In Proceedings of the 37th International Conference on Machine Learning (ICML), Virtual Event, 13–18 July 2020; Volume 119, pp. 1597–1607.
32. Tang, C.I.; Perez-Pozuelo, I.; Spathis, D.; Mascolo, C. Exploring Contrastive Learning in Human Activity Recognition for Healthcare. *arXiv* **2020**, arXiv:2011.11542. Available online: https://arxiv.org/abs/2011.11542 (accessed on 15 September 2025).
33. Saeed, A.; Ozcelebi, T.; Lukkien, J. Multi-Task Self-Supervised Learning for Human Activity Detection. *Proc. ACM Interact. Mob. Wearable Ubiquitous Technol.* **2019**, **3**, 61. [CrossRef]
34. Khaertdinov, B.; Ghaleb, E.; Asteriadis, S. Contrastive Self-Supervised Learning for Sensor Based Human Activity Recognition. In Proceedings of the IEEE International Joint Conference on Biometrics (IJCB), Shenzhen, China, 4–7 August 2021; pp. 1–8.
35. Wang, J.; Zhu, T.; Chen, L.L.; Ning, H.; Wan, Y. Negative Selection by Clustering for Contrastive Learning in Human Activity Recognition. *IEEE Internet Things J.* **2023**, *10*, 10833–10844. [CrossRef]
36. Khosla, P.; Teterwak, P.; Wang, C.; Sarna, A.; Tian, Y.; Isola, P.; Maschinot, A.; Liu, C.; Krishnan, D. Supervised Contrastive Learning. In Proceedings of the 34th International Conference on Neural Information Processing Systems (NeurIPS), Vancouver, BC, Canada, 6–12 December 2020; pp. 18661–18673.
37. Caruana, R. Multitask Learning. *Mach. Learn.* **1997**, *28*, 41–75. [CrossRef]
38. Wang, Z.; Yan, W.; Oates, T. Time Series Classification from Scratch with Deep Neural Networks: A Strong Baseline. In Proceedings of the International Joint Conference on Neural Networks (IJCNN), Anchorage, AK, USA, 14–19 May 2017; pp. 1578–1585. [CrossRef]
39. Chatzaki, C.; Pediaditis, M.; Vavoulas, G.; Tsiknakis, M. Human Daily Activity and Fall Recognition Using a Smartphone's Acceleration Sensor. In *Information and Communication Technologies for Ageing Well and e-Health*; Springer: Cham, Switzerland, 2017; Volume 736, pp. 100–118.
40. Anguita, D.; Ghio, A.; Oneto, L.; Parra, X.; Reyes-Ortiz, J.L. A Public Domain Dataset for Human Activity Recognition Using Smartphones. In Proceedings of the European Symposium on Artificial Neural Networks (ESANN), Bruges, Belgium, 24–26 April 2013.

41. Zhang, M.; Sawchuk, A.A. USC-HAD: A Daily Activity Dataset for Ubiquitous Activity Recognition Using Wearable Sensors. In Proceedings of the ACM International Joint Conference on Ubiquitous Computing (UbiComp), Pittsburgh, PA, USA, 5–8 September 2012.
42. Twomey, N.; Diethe, T.; Fafoutis, X.; Elsts, A.; McConville, R.; Flach, P.; Craddock, I. A Comprehensive Study of Activity Recognition Using Accelerometers. *Informatics* **2018**, *5*, 27. [CrossRef]
43. Loshchilov, I.; Hutter, F. Decoupled weight decay regularization. *arXiv* **2017**, arXiv:1711.05101. [CrossRef]
44. Cheng, D.; Zhang, L.; Bu, C.; Wang, X.; Wu, H.; Song, A. ProtoHAR: Prototype Guided Personalized Federated Learning for Human Activity Recognition. *IEEE J. Biomed. Health Inform.* **2023**, *27*, 3900–3911. [CrossRef] [PubMed]
45. Chen, X.; Zhou, X.; Sun, M.; Wang, H. Temporal Contrastive Learning for Sensor-Based Human Activity Recognition: A Self-Supervised Approach. *IEEE Sens. J.* **2025**, *25*, 1839–1850. [CrossRef]
46. Qian, H.; Tian, T.; Miao, C. What Makes Good Contrastive Learning on Small-Scale Wearable-Based Tasks? *arXiv* **2022**, arXiv:2202.05998. [CrossRef].
47. Li, P.; Tao, H.; Zhou, H.; Zhou, P.; Deng, Y. Enhanced Multiview Attention Network with Random Interpolation Resize for Few-Shot Surface Defect Detection. *Multimed. Syst.* **2025**, *31*, 36. [CrossRef]
48. Wang, Z.; Tao, H.; Zhou, H.; Deng, Y.; Zhou, P. A Content-Style Control Network with Style Contrastive Learning for Underwater Image Enhancement. *Multimed. Syst.* **2025**, *31*, 60. [CrossRef]
49. Apedo, Y.; Tao, H. A Weakly Supervised Pavement Crack Segmentation Based on Adversarial Learning and Transformers. *Multimed. Syst.* **2025**, *31*, 266. [CrossRef]

sensors

MDPI

Article

Personalized Smart Home Automation Using Machine Learning: Predicting User Activities

Mark M. Gad [1], Walaa Gad [2], Tamer Abdelkader [3] and Kshirasagar Naik [4,*]

[1] Media Engineering and Technology (MET) Department, German University in Cairo, Cairo 11835, Egypt; magedmark50@gmail.com
[2] Faculty of Computer and Information Sciences, Ain Shams University, Cairo 11566, Egypt; walaagad@cis.asu.edu.eg
[3] Faculty of Computer Science and Engineering, Galala University, Suez 435611, Egypt; tamer.abdelkader@gu.edu.eg
[4] Department of Electrical and Computer Engineering, University of Waterloo, Waterloo, ON N2L 3G1, Canada
* Correspondence: snaik@uwaterloo.ca

Abstract

A personalized framework for smart home automation is introduced, utilizing machine learning to predict user activities and allow for the context-aware control of living spaces. Predicting user activities, such as 'Watch_TV', 'Sleep', 'Work_On_Computer', and 'Cook_Dinner', is essential for improving occupant comfort, optimizing energy consumption, and offering proactive support in smart home settings. The Edge Light Human Activity Recognition Predictor, or EL-HARP, is the main prediction model used in this framework to predict user behavior. The system combines open-source software for real-time sensing, facial recognition, and appliance control with affordable hardware, including the Raspberry Pi 5, ESP32-CAM, Tuya smart switches, NFC (Near Field Communication), and ultrasonic sensors. In order to predict daily user activities, three gradient-boosting models—XGBoost, CatBoost, and LightGBM (Gradient Boosting Models)—are trained for each household using engineered features and past behaviour patterns. Using extended temporal features, LightGBM in particular achieves strong predictive performance within EL-HARP. The framework is optimized for edge deployment with efficient training, regularization, and class imbalance handling. A fully functional prototype demonstrates real-time performance and adaptability to individual behavior patterns. This work contributes a scalable, privacy-preserving, and user-centric approach to intelligent home automation.

Keywords: smart home automation; machine learning; human activity recognition; edge computing; intelligent environments; gradient boosting models; personalization; context-aware systems

1. Introduction

Smart home automation uses sensor networks and signal processing to create adaptive environments that engage with human behavior intelligently. As a means of improving user comfort, efficiency, and safety, modern systems do not just aim at automating routine activities but also to learn and predict the user's behavior proactively. Machine learning-based approaches are increasingly being utilized within domestic technology to monitor, anticipate, and react to everyday human activity in real time. This allows for more discriminating energy management, security, and care-at-home services.

Conventional automation platforms are often limited by static rules, fixed schedules, or user-programmed scenes. These systems are useful in straightforward situations; however, they are not adaptable enough to handle behavioral variability and customization. Furthermore, system design and data processing become even more complex when heterogeneous devices—from cameras and motion sensors to smart switches and voice assistants—are integrated. These difficulties call for learning-based systems that can recognize patterns in behavior and make adjustments on their own.

In smart environments, machine learning—especially supervised learning—has become a popular method for predicting and identifying activity. Even though deep learning models—like convolutional neural networks (CNNs) and long short-term memory (LSTM) networks—have shown encouraging results, they frequently call for large amounts of labeled data and significant processing power. Furthermore, deep neural networks' inability to be interpreted poses problems for applications that must be safe and user-facing. In contrast, gradient boosting decision tree (GBDT) ensembles—such as XGBoost, CatBoost, and LightGBM—offer strong predictive performance, interpretable outputs [1], and efficient training on structured tabular data. These characteristics make GBDT models particularly suitable for smart home sensor data, where time-series information is often presented in fixed-length sequences and categorical formats [2].

Enhancing prediction accuracy necessitates time-aware feature engineering. Without the need for intricate recurrent architectures, models can learn user routines through temporal indicators such as time of day, day of the week, rolling activity statistics, and historical trends. Furthermore, it has been demonstrated that user-level personalization, in which distinct models are trained for each resident, enhances generalization and system responsiveness.

The main goal of this work is to build a system that is able to predict each unique user's future behavior to enable personalized automation in residential settings. This system can proactively automate devices, optimize energy consumption, and enhance comfort and safety by precisely predicting human activities, such as cooking, sleeping, or leaving the house. The ability to precisely predict human activities, such as leaving the home or going to sleep, can directly enhance energy management beyond simple automation. By anticipating future behavior, the system can proactively limit the use of unnecessary appliances, optimize climate control schedules, and cut off any unused power to devices that are about to become idle. This proactive approach ensures that resources are not wasted, leading to significant reductions in overall power consumption and contributing to a more sustainable and cost-effective smart home environment. Instead of reacting to static schedules or direct user input, the suggested framework learns from past activity patterns and contextual cues to predict needs and carry out control decisions automatically. The core prediction model EL-HARP is deployed within this framework to perform these activity forecasts. This predictive capability allows a seamless orchestration of appliances, lighting, and environmental controls in a way that adapts to each resident's habits and lifestyle.

In addition to developing a machine learning-based prediction pipeline, this work also aims to introduce a functional smart home system design that demonstrates a practical method for collecting behavioral data in real residential settings. The CASAS dataset [3] is employed for model training and evaluation; however, the system architecture includes physical sensor deployments such as facial recognition modules, NFC tags, ultrasonic presence sensors, and smart switches—to emulate realistic residential scenarios. These components collectively form a prototype environment capable of recording, labeling, and responding to user activities, thereby laying the foundation for future datasets based on real-time, in-home deployments.

During the development of the proposed smart home activity prediction framework, several key challenges were encountered:

1. Sensor noise and class imbalance in the CASAS dataset affected learning reliability. Several activity classes exhibited sparse and inconsistent representation, while others included overlapping or ambiguous sensor patterns. Labels such as "Other Activity" and "Entertain Guests" were found to be frequent sources of noise and were excluded through targeted preprocessing [4].
2. Imbalanced class distributions can lead to high overall accuracy but poor accuracy for underrepresented classes. This discrepancy is particularly evident when comparing accuracy with the weighted F1-score, revealing skewed recognition performance across different activity types.
3. Computational constraints prevented the use of many state-of-the-art deep learning architectures. Real-time deployment on edge hardware such as the Raspberry Pi 5 requires lightweight and interpretable models, necessitating trade-offs between model complexity and performance [2].
4. Label ambiguity and activity overlap have also been recognized as significant challenges during model training. Sensor events triggered by activities such as "Relaxing" and "Watching TV" often exhibited high similarity, hindering clear class separation. These issues have been previously reported in the literature [4], and their effects were observed during both data preprocessing and evaluation.

To address these challenges, the EL-HARP framework was designed as a modular, edge-deployable system for personalized activity prediction and automation. Raw sensor streams are first ingested via a temporal feature-extraction pipeline that denoises events, computes instantaneous, rolling, and historical embeddings, and assembles fixed-length input sequences. These sequences are then fed into per-user gradient-boosted tree ensembles (XGBoost, CatBoost, LightGBM) to produce real-time activity forecasts. EL-HARP orchestrates all components data preprocessing, on-device inference, automation logic, and interactive labeling within Docker containers running on a Raspberry Pi 5. Performance was measured in terms of prediction accuracy, weighted F1-score, and inference latency on the edge. A fully functional prototype demonstrated EL-HARP's ability to generalize across heterogeneous sensor inputs, maintain sub-100 ms response times, and continuously adapt to user behavior via incremental, voice-driven retraining.

The primary contributions of this work are summarized as follows:

- A comprehensive, modular smart home automation framework is proposed, integrating real-time sensing and actuation with personalized prediction of a wide range of user activities, including Watch_TV, Sleep, Leave_Home, Cook_Dinner, and Personal_Hygiene.
- A novel time-aware feature engineering strategy is developed, combining temporal signals and historical behavior patterns to enhance the accuracy and interpretability of activity prediction models. This strategy, applied to gradient-boosting models (XGBoost, CatBoost, LightGBM), achieves particularly strong predictive performance with LightGBM.
- The proposed framework and prediction approach demonstrate practical and efficient deployment on constrained edge devices, enabling a privacy-preserving and adaptive smart home solution designed for real-world environments.

The remainder of this paper is organized as follows: Section 2 provides an overview of related work in smart home automation and activity prediction. Section 3 details the proposed EL-HARP framework, including its architecture, hardware components, and software integrations. Section 4 elaborates on the data-processing pipeline, feature engineering strategies, and the machine learning models employed for activity prediction. Section 5 presents the experimental setup, discusses the evaluation methodology, and analyzes the performance results. Finally, Section 6 concludes the paper with a summary of key findings and outlines directions for future work.

2. Related Work

Smart home automation has advanced significantly recently, leveraging development in machine learning techniques and high-performance edge computing platforms and continuously developing human activity recognition (HAR) datasets to analyze and predict the user activities and optimize resource utilization. This section will go through recent contributions across HAR datasets, edge computing platforms, and machine learning techniques used in this field.

2.1. Datasets for Smart Home Automation

Annotated, high-quality datasets are pivotal for human activity recognition research. The following are recent notable datasets that are frequently used.

- MuRAL [5]: MuRAL, the a multi-resident ambient sensor dataset with natural language annotations, was first made available in 2025. It consists of more than 21 h of multi-user sensor data gathered from 21 smart-home sessions. Research on multi-resident activity recognition and natural language comprehension is facilitated via the dataset's inclusion of resident identities, high-level activity labels, and fine-grained natural language descriptions. However, since it is a newly released dataset, it lacks established benchmarks in the literature and has seen limited adoption in studies, which may pose challenges for comparative evaluation and generalizability.
- CASAS-SMART consists of a sizable, long-term collection of ambient sensor data from actual homes and is a popular public resource for human activity recognition (HAR) research. Time-stamped events from basic, non-intrusive sensors, such as motion and door sensors, which are discreetly installed to monitor daily activities, are the main source of data for the dataset. Researchers can train and assess machine learning models to infer human actions from sensor patterns by labeling this raw data stream with particular activities. The dataset is not only used for creating predictive HAR models but also for creating anomaly detection and ambient assisted living systems, where spotting departures from typical behavior can be crucial for keeping an eye on wellbeing and health.
- Smart Meter Dataset [6] includes power readings for several different households. It is employed in hybrid transformer–RNN architectures that prioritize highly accurate and privacy-aware activity forecasting and recognition.
- Opportunity Dataset is employed to identify human activity through the use of ambient and wearable sensors. It contains sensor-rich recordings with numerous annotated activities, which are frequently used for sequence modeling in deep learning research.

2.2. Edge Computing Platforms

Deploying machine learning models within home environments necessitates efficient, low-power hardware solutions, such as the following.

- Home Assistant Appliances [7]: Zigbee, Thread, and Matter protocols are supported via devices such as Home Assistant Yellow and Green, which provide integrated solutions. Although they support a wide range of protocols and are easy to use, their onboard AI processing power is limited.

- NVIDIA Jetson Platforms [8]: For deep learning tasks, offer GPU acceleration that is appropriate for computationally demanding applications. Although they are more expensive and use more power, they provide excellent AI performance and scalability.
- Raspberry Pi (RPi) Systems [2] are used as direct-sensor central controllers that facilitate data storage, automation, and remote control at the network edge. Although they are flexible and reasonably priced, their processing power is constrained for intricate models.

2.3. Machine Learning for Energy Management and Optimization

Beyond activity recognition, machine learning is a cornerstone for optimizing power consumption and integrating renewable energy sources in smart homes. This field leverages predictive and control-based methods to create more efficient and sustainable systems.

2.3.1. Prediction of Power Generation

To effectively manage energy from renewable sources, the accurate forecasting of power generation is essential. Recurrent Neural Networks (RNNs) and their advanced variants, such as Long Short-Term Memory (LSTM) networks, are particularly well suited to this task. These models excel at processing and learning from sequential data, making them ideal for predicting solar power output based on historical time-series data of weather, temperature, and cloud cover. By providing precise forecasts, these models enable energy management systems to make informed decisions about when to store energy, consume it, or sell it back to the grid.

2.3.2. Reinforcement Learning for Control

For dynamic energy management, Reinforcement Learning (RL) and Deep Reinforcement Learning (DRL) offer a powerful framework. In this approach, an intelligent agent learns to make optimal control decisions by interacting with the smart home environment to maximize a long-term reward, such as minimizing energy costs or enhancing occupant comfort. Research in this area includes using RL for modulating specific systems like heat pumps and photovoltaic systems [9] and for managing demand response using historical data [10]. More advanced models, like multi-agent reinforcement learning, are also being explored [11].

- Optimal Power Scheduling: DRL has been used to create automated systems that manage demand response. For instance, in "An optimal power scheduling method for demand response in home energy management system" [12], a system learns to shift the operation of appliances to off-peak hours to reduce electricity bills.
- Autonomous Control: More advanced methods, such as Actor-Critic learning, enable agents to manage complex systems like HVAC and battery storage simultaneously. The paper "Autonomous Price-aware Energy Management System in Smart Homes via Actor-Critic Learning with Predictive Capabilities" [13] proposes a system that uses DRL to make real-time decisions based on electricity prices and predicted energy needs, balancing cost and comfort.
- Electric Vehicle (EV) Charging: The optimization of EV charging is a critical application. Researchers have used DRL to develop "effective charging planning" [14] strategies that minimize charging time. Similarly, a Continuous Deep Deterministic Policy Gradient (CDDPG)-based approach has been introduced for precise and continuous control of EV charging to manage grid load and reduce costs [15].

These applications highlight the shift from reactive to proactive and predictive energy management, positioning machine learning as a core component of future smart home systems.

2.4. Machine Learning Techniques

Recent developments in smart-home human activity recognition use a wide range of machine learning techniques, from edge-optimized architectures and techniques robust to incomplete data to self-supervised learning approaches. Every one of these approaches offers advantages and disadvantages that affect accuracy, resource usage, and deployment suitability. A selection of important studies is highlighted below. Non-intrusive techniques using ambient sensors like Wi-Fi signals and cameras are gaining prominence [16,17].

Additionally, new sensing techniques are always being investigated; for instance, thermal imaging combined with Internet of Things devices has proven useful for identifying activity in homes [18]. In a related study, Lin et al. (2023) [19] explored a suite of machine learning algorithms, including gradient boosting, to infer user activities directly from heterogeneous IoT device network traffic, demonstrating the viability of a non-intrusive and privacy-preserving approach based on network flow patterns.

Ali et al. (2025) [20] introduced an Innovative IoT and Edge Intelligence Framework for monitoring senior citizens by employing anomaly detection from sensor data from non-wearable devices. This system, which was created especially for edge deployment, is a good contender for real-time home health monitoring because it obtained 82.36% Precision and 86.03% F1 Score on the CASAS TM029 dataset.

Feng et al. (2024) [21] suggested a centralised Intensive Care Unit (ICU) Command Centre Architecture that can use Transformer models and attention mechanisms to fuse medical data, including smart home sensors. The suggested masked modeling technique can be applied to HAR settings where missing sensor events are common, even though the original study concentrated on critical care applications. Their architecture achieved F1 scores of 85.0% on the CASAS Aruba and 64.0% on the CASAS Milan datasets, demonstrating strong robustness to incomplete inputs.

Chen et al. (2024) [22] incorporated Self-Supervised Learning with Self-Attention, efficiently utilizing unlabeled data to lessen reliance on manual annotation. Their method demonstrated strength in pretraining but limitations under minimally labeled conditions, achieving 85.63% F1 (Aruba-1) and 59.74% (Milan).

Srivatsa & Plötz (2024) [23] employed Graph Neural Networks to simulate the interactions of smart home sensors. The technique records intricate spatial–temporal patterns by converting sensor events into graph representations. Across several CASAS datasets, F1 scores varied from 78.3% to 88.7%.

Fiori et al. (2025) [24] presented GNN-XAR (Graph Neural Network-Explainable Activity Recognition), an explainable GNN framework that is tailored for HAR. With an average accuracy of 86.5% on the CASAS Milan and Aruba datasets, it highlights model transparency through the use of attention-based graph modelling.

Zhou et al. (2022) [25] created TinyHAR, a small deep learning model designed for deployment on the edge. Its practical utility is demonstrated by the fact that it maintains high performance up to 89.0% accuracy across various HAR datasets while reducing the model size by >90% when compared to baselines.

Khan et al. (2022) [26] put into practice a Hybrid Deep Learning Model for HAR in smart homes that combines CNN and Bi-LSTM layers. Both temporal and spatial features are successfully captured through the dual architecture. Despite its strength, it requires more computing power than non-deep models. On the CASAS dataset, its accuracy was 89.0%.

Khan et al. (2025) [27] introduced a Multimodal Temporal Transformer for HAR, which focuses on fusing features from diverse sensors to capture complex temporal dependencies. This deep learning approach offers a powerful alternative to traditional methods but is computationally expensive and less suited for real-time edge deployment.

Dao et al. (2025) [28] proposed RFAR, a real-time system for firefighter activity recognition using wearable accelerometers. While achieving a very high accuracy of 97.35% on the UCI HAR dataset, this approach is limited to a specific application and relies on wearable, single-modality sensors, which differs from the multi-sensor ambient environment of smart homes.

Yang et al. (2025) [29] presented a privacy-preserving HAR method by fusing Inertial and High-resolution Acoustic Data. This work highlights the importance of data fusion and privacy, though its deep learning fusion model is more complex than a GBDT approach.

Li et al. (2023) [30] developed an approach for HAR based on Multi-environment Sensor Data. Their deep learning model, HENN-MSD, achieved a state-of-the-art accuracy of 96.57% on the CASAS dataset, showcasing the performance potential of complex deep architectures for activity generalization.

Furthermore, deep unified models combining convolutional neural networks with edge computing have been applied for tasks like face recognition [31], while ensemble boosting methods like XGBoost have been shown to improve the consistency of accuracy in various classification tasks [32]. More recent work explores few-shot learning with MLLMs and visual reinforcement learning to advance HAR [33]. An overview is given in Table 1.

Table 1. Summary of representative machine learning techniques for smart home HAR.

Study (Year)	Dataset(s)	Method	Key Advantage	Reported Performance
Ali et al. (2025) [20]	CASAS TM029	IoT Edge Framework	Real-time elderly monitoring on edge devices	86.03% (F1)
Feng et al. (2024) [21]	CASAS Aruba/Milan	Masked Modeling (Transformer)	Robust to missing sensor events	85.0% (Aruba F1), 64.0% (Milan F1)
Chen et al. (2024) [22]	CASAS Aruba/Milan	SSL + Self-Attention	Reduces reliance on labeled data	85.63% (F1)
Srivatsa & Plötz (2024) [23]	CASAS (Multiple)	Graph Neural Networks	Captures spatial-temporal structure	78.3–88.7% (F1)
Fiori et al. (2025) [24]	CASAS Milan/Aruba	GNN-XAR	Interpretable GNN with attention graphs	86.5% (Accuracy)
Zhou et al. (2022) [25]	Multiple HAR Datasets	TinyHAR (Edge DL)	Lightweight design for microcontrollers	89.0% (Accuracy)
Khan et al. (2022) [26]	CASAS Dataset	CNN + Bi-LSTM Hybrid	Strong spatio-temporal feature modeling	89.0% (Accuracy)
Dao et al. (2025) [28]	UCI HAR	RFAR (Wearable System)	Real-time, high accuracy on wearable data	97.35% (Accuracy)
Li et al. (2023) [30]	CASAS	Deep Learning (HENN-MSD)	High accuracy on multi-environment data	96.57% (Accuracy)

2.5. Open Challenges

Despite significant advancements, several challenges persist, as follows.

- Personalization vs. Privacy: Balancing model accuracy with user data privacy, especially in multi-resident scenarios. The use of tailored small language models on edge devices is a promising approach to this issue [34], as is the use of machine learning to detect cyber attacks [35]. Generative AI could also be used to simplify the user-centric setup of these systems [36].
- Generalization: Ensuring models perform well across diverse home environments and sensor configurations. This includes the challenge of continuous adaptation and continual learning to avoid forgetting past knowledge [37].

- Edge Constraints: developing models that operate efficiently on resource-constrained edge devices.
- Robustness: handling sensor noise, missing data, and unpredictable user behaviors.

Future studies should concentrate on creating interpretable, lightweight models that can learn customized routines while protecting user privacy and performing well on edge devices. In this regard, EL-HARP is presented as a portable, interpretable model created especially for effective, private activity prediction in smart home settings with limited resources.

3. Methodology

This section outlines EL-HARP, a unified framework for personalized activity recognition and automation in smart homes. It integrates a real-world IoT prototype with on-device machine learning tailored for edge deployment. EL-HARP encompasses the full sensing-to-action pipeline—real-time data collection, temporal feature extraction, and a lightweight, adaptive gradient-boosted ensemble—running entirely on embedded hardware. The system refines its behavior through incremental learning and user feedback, ensuring continuous personalization and responsiveness without relying on cloud services.

The end-to-end framework comprises the following components:

1. A physical smart home prototype integrating commodity sensors and embedded controllers;
2. Five real-time functional blocks supporting live activity detection and automation;
3. A structured logging subsystem for collecting appliance and behavior patterns;
4. A full data processing pipeline encompassing filtering, feature extraction, and temporal encoding;
5. Gradient boosting–based activity classification and continuous retraining at the edge.

The system is designed to operate entirely offline, support user-specific routines, and evolve over time based on in-home feedback. All inference and learning are performed on-device, preserving privacy and enabling personalized automation without relying on centralized servers.

Figure 1 provides a visual summary of this architecture. The top section shows the physical sensing modules connected to a Raspberry Pi 5 controller, while the middle layer outlines the five main functional components of the system. These include presence detection, room transition handling, activity prediction with confirmation, combo-based learning, and activity end detection.

Outputs from these components are written to structured files (`activity_log.txt`, `combos.json`, and `voice transcripts`), which feed into a multi-stage processing pipeline. The data undergoes filtering, feature engineering, and sequence generation before being used to retrain the underlying machine learning model. The bottom segment of the diagram highlights the continuous loop: data collected from live operation directly informs model updates and redeployment—closing the loop between sensing, inference, and learning.

Together, these components validate that personalized smart home intelligence can be realized with embedded, privacy-preserving systems that evolve over time without central cloud reliance.

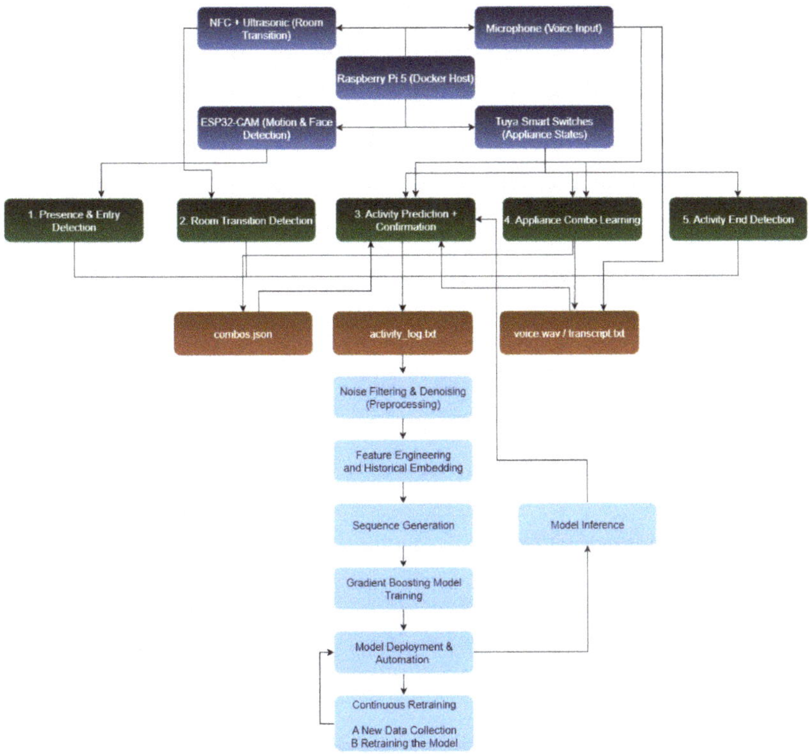

Figure 1. System architecture of the EL-HARP framework, showing the hardware interface, five real-time control functions, structured logging, and the downstream learning pipeline.

3.1. Hardware and System Architecture

The smart home prototype is built around a Raspberry Pi 5 (8 GB) that hosts all core services in Docker containers. Five types of sensors and devices connect to the Pi to capture user presence, location, and appliance usage:

- ESP32-CAM Modules: Mounted at each entrance, they provide motion-triggered video streaming. Video frames are forwarded to the Pi for OpenCV-based face detection and recognition.
- NFC Readers + Ultrasonic Sensors: Installed at door thresholds to detect room-to-room transitions. NFC tags carried by residents identify the user, while the ultrasonic sensor confirms directional movement.
- Tuya-Compatible Smart Switches: Deployed on major appliances (lights, TV, kettle). Their on/off states are polled via Home Assistant to infer ongoing activities.
- Microphone: Captures short voice responses during user confirmation or when labeling unknown appliance combinations. Audio is stored temporarily and passed to a local Whisper engine.
- Raspberry Pi 5: Serves as the central controller, running:
  - OpenCV Container: For face recognition.
  - Home Assistant Container: For device polling and state management.
  - Node-RED Container: For orchestrating logic flows.
  - Whisper Container: For offline voice transcription.
  - Inference Engine Container: Hosting the EL-HARP LightGBM model.

All devices communicate locally over the home network; no data is transmitted externally. Figure 2 illustrates this layered architecture.

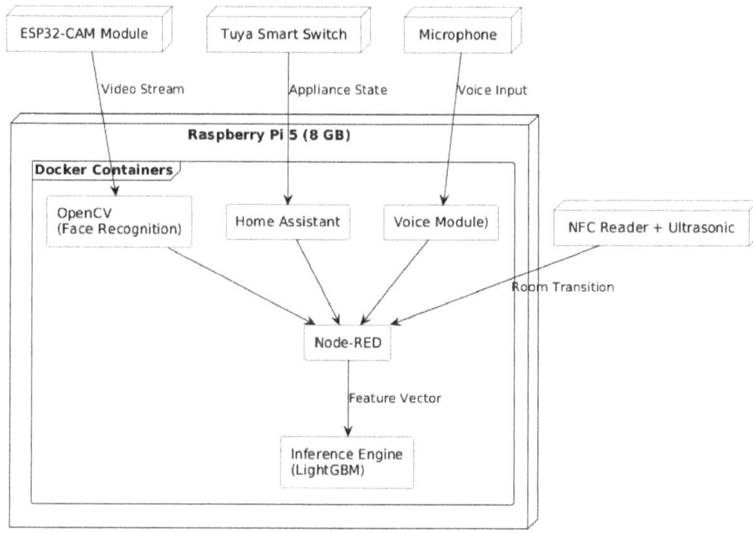

Figure 2. Hardware and system architecture of the smart home prototype: sensing modules feed into Dockerized services on Raspberry Pi 5, which in turn manage control logic, logging, and model inference.

3.2. Real-Time Functional Blocks

Five real-time subsystems run on the Raspberry Pi within Node-RED to detect presence, track location, predict activities, learn new appliance combinations, and detect activity end. All subsystems log events in the format:

$$\text{Timestamp, Person, Room, Activity, Value}$$

where Value is either 'on' (start) or 'off' (end).

1. Presence and Entry Detection

Triggered through ESP32-CAM motion, face recognition assigns a user ID to an entry room. Presence is logged immediately, as outlined in Algorithm 1.

Algorithm 1 onUserDetected

Require: *userId*, *timestamp*
Ensure: An activity log entry is created and the user's context is updated.
1: $room \leftarrow$ ENTRY_ROOM
2: **if** *userId* not in *userCtx* **then**
3: initialize $userCtx[userId]$
4: **end if**
5: $userCtx[userId].currentRoom \leftarrow room$
6: $userCtx[userId].currentActivity \leftarrow$ null
7: logActivity(*timestamp*, *userId*, *room*, "presence", "on")

2. Room Transition Detection

Each NFC scan toggles between two rooms defined for that reader. The transition process is outlined in Algorithm 2.

Algorithm 2 onRoomScan (with NFC toggle)

```
Require: userId, tagId, timestamp
Ensure: A room transition is logged and the user's current room is updated.
(roomA, roomB) ← lookupTagRooms(tagId)
lastRoom ← userCtx[userId].currentRoom
if lastRoom = roomA then
    room ← roomB
else if lastRoom = roomB then
    room ← roomA
else
    room ← roomA {default on first scan}
end if
userCtx[userId].currentRoom ← room
logActivity(timestamp, userId, room, "transition", "on")
```

3. Activity Prediction and Automation (with Confirmation)

Upon each room entry, features are built and passed to the EL-HARP model. The predicted activity is confirmed via voice; on affirmation, automation executes and the activity start is logged. This process is summarized in Algorithm 3.

Algorithm 3 onRoomEnter (with user confirmation)

```
Require: userId, timestamp
Ensure: An activity is logged and the user's activity context is updated, or a pending
    configuration is saved for learning.
ctx ← userCtx[userId]
features ← buildFeatures(ctx.currentRoom, ctx.historyVector, ctx.weightVector,
    timestamp)
activity ← runModelInference(features)
speak("Are you currently activity?")
reply ← getUserResponse()
if reply = "yes" then
    executeAutomation(userId, activity)
    logActivity(timestamp, userId, ctx.currentRoom, activity, "on")
    ctx.currentActivity.label ← activity
    ctx.currentActivity.combo ← readApplianceStates()
    ctx.currentActivity.timestamp ← timestamp
else
    ctx.pendingConfig ← readApplianceStates()
    ctx.timerCount ← 0
end if
```

4. Appliance-Combo Logging and Voice-Prompt Learning

Every 30 s, the system checks whether the current appliance state matches the pending combo. Known combos are logged immediately; unknown ones trigger a voice prompt and update the mapping. This routine is implemented in Algorithm 4.

5. Activity End Detection

If the appliance combo no longer matches the recorded combo for the active activity for over 10 s, an "off" event is logged, and the activity session is cleared. Algorithm 5 summarizes this process.

Algorithm 4 checkPersistentCombo and handleCombo

```
Require: timestamp
Ensure: An activity is logged, and a new activity-appliance combination is learned if not
    already known.
for all userId in userCtx do
  ctx ← userCtx[userId]
  combo ← readApplianceStates()
  if combo = ctx.pendingConfig then
    ctx.timerCount += 1
  else
    ctx.pendingConfig ← combo
    ctx.timerCount ← 1
  end if
  if ctx.timerCount ≥ 30 then
    if isKnownCombo(combo) then
      label ← lookupComboLabel(combo)
    else
      speak("What are you doing?")
      label ← whisperTranscribe(recordAudio())
      updateComboMap(combo, label)
    end if
    logActivity(timestamp, userId, ctx.currentRoom, label, "on")
    ctx.currentActivity ← label
  end if
end for
```

Algorithm 5 detectActivityEnd

```
Require: timestamp
Ensure: An activity-end event is logged and the user's activity context is cleared.
for all userId in userCtx do
  ctx ← userCtx[userId]
  if ctx.currentActivity ≠ null then
    currentCombo ← readApplianceStates()
    if currentCombo ≠ ctx.currentActivity.combo then
      increment disconnect timer
    else
      reset disconnect timer
    end if
    if disconnect timer ≥ 10 s then
      logActivity(timestamp, userId, ctx.currentRoom, ctx.currentActivity.label, "off")

      ctx.currentActivity ← null
    end if
  end if
end for
```

Data Storage and Services

- Activity Logs: `/home/pi/activity_log.txt`, each line 'Timestamp, Person, Room, Activity, Value'.
- Combo Mappings: `/home/pi/combos.json`, JSON maps appliance states to activities.
- Voice Files: `/tmp/voice.wav` and `/tmp/voice.wav.txt` for temporary audio/-transcription.
- Dockerized Services: OpenCV, Home Assistant, Node-RED, Whisper, and inference engine each run in isolated containers on the Pi.

In the remainder of this section, each stage is described in detail:

3.3. Data Collection

This study's data collection strategy encompasses two complementary scenarios to support both rigorous evaluation and live personalization. In the proof-of-concept evaluation, experiments are conducted on a curated subset of the publicly available CASAS Smart Home dataset. Sensor events and annotated activities from 21 independent single-resident households—each exhibiting distinct daily routines and environmental contexts—are used to validate the generalizability of the feature engineering and sequence design across diverse living scenarios. These CASAS-trained models are not deployed directly; they serve solely to demonstrate feasibility, with no cross-user transfer in the live system (Box 1 in Figure 3).

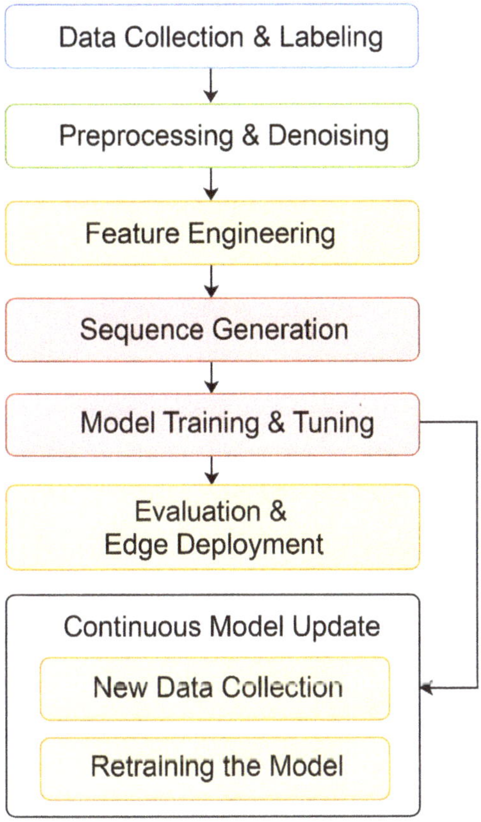

Figure 3. System workflow with continuous retraining loop.

In the real-world deployment scenario, EL-HARP operates exclusively on the resident's own data. The system initializes in a minimal "cold-start" state and continuously collects live sensor events via the Sensing Layer. Each new labeled event—whether resulting from a confirmed model prediction or from a voice-prompted annotation—is appended to the local activity log. At regular, configurable intervals (Box 7 in Figure 1), this freshly accrued data is ingested into the continuous retraining loop, enabling fully local personalization, strict privacy preservation, and adaptation to evolving routines without reliance on any external datasets.

3.4. Preprocessing and Denoising

The second step involves cleaning and standardizing the dataset. Given the nature of the CASAS dataset as a long-term, multi-user research resource, the data often contains various forms of noise—such as sensor glitches, overlapping event bursts, and infrequent or mislabeled activity classes. The preprocessing pipeline consists of three main stages:

1. Data Transformation
    - Event Pairing: Each binary sensor logs `on/off` events. Consecutive `on/off` pairs for the same sensor define an interval $(t_{\text{on}}, t_{\text{off}})$. Intervals shorter than a threshold (e.g., 2 s) are discarded to reduce spurious noise.
    - Activity Label Assignment: each valid interval is mapped to a pre-annotated CASAS activity label (e.g., Cooking, Sleeping), producing a sequence of timestamped activity intervals.
2. Label Cleaning
    - Noise-Prone Class Removal: Ambiguous or sparsely represented classes (e.g., `Other_Activity`, `Entertain_Guests`, `ENTER`) are removed entirely, as they usually represent sensor noise.
    - Null-Label Filtering: Time steps with $A_t = \texttt{NULL}$ are retained for context, but any sequence whose final label is `NULL` will be discarded in sequence generation.
3. Class Imbalance Handling:
    - After filtering, if the ratio of majority to minority classes exceeds 10:1, majority-class under-sampling is applied so that no class has more than five times the instances of the smallest class.

It is worth noting that such extensive preprocessing may not be necessary in real-world deployments. A continuously operating system like EL-HARP can enforce stricter data quality at the source (e.g., consistent sensor configuration, real-time logging). Therefore, while this pipeline standardizes historical datasets like CASAS for fair evaluation, future on-device systems may adopt more lightweight validation strategies.

3.5. Feature Engineering

At this stage, raw sensor events are transformed into structured numerical representations that capture user behavior across multiple time scales. A combination was extracted of instantaneous features (e.g., current room, time of day), short-term rolling features (e.g., room and activity trends over the past few hours), and long-term historical features (e.g., most frequent past activities across the previous 21 days with decay weighting). This layered design enables the model to learn from both immediate context and recurring daily patterns.

All preprocessing is performed on a per-person, timestamp-sorted dataframe. Categorical variables (`Room`, `Activity`) are encoded as integers, and continuous-derived quantities are standardized to zero mean and unit variance within each household. At each timestamp, the following features are computed and grouped into three categories based on their temporal scope:

1. Instantaneous Features (Current Context)

- Room ID (R_t): Encoded room identifier at time t, where $R_t \in \{0, \ldots, R-1\}$ and R is the number of unique rooms.
- Time of Day (sinusoidal encoding): The hour of the day $h_t \in \{0, \ldots, 23\}$ is converted to two cyclic features:

$$\text{time\_sin}_t = \sin\!\left(2\pi \frac{h_t}{24}\right), \quad \text{time\_cos}_t = \cos\!\left(2\pi \frac{h_t}{24}\right).$$

- Day of Week (d_t): An integer representing the weekday, where $d_t \in \{0, \ldots, 6\}$, with 0 corresponding to Monday.

2. Short-Term Rolling Features (Recent Behavior)

- Hourly Activity Count ($N_h(t)$): Total number of activity events recorded within the hour containing timestamp t, defined as follows:

$$N_h(t) = \big|\{\tau \mid \text{hour\_of\_day}(\tau) = \text{hour\_of\_day}(t), \\ \text{date}(\tau) = \text{date}(t), \text{ and } A(\tau) \neq \text{null\_activity}\}\big|.$$

- Room Entropy (H_R): A scalar indicating the diversity of room usage by the user, calculated as the Shannon entropy of room visits:

$$H_R = -\sum_{i=0}^{R-1} p_i \log p_i,$$

where p_i is the proportion of activity events occurring in room i over the entire observation period. This feature is static and computed once per user, but it provides a critical baseline for understanding short-term deviations.

- Rolling Activity Mean (3 h): The mean of encoded activity values within the 3-h trailing window ending at time t:

$$\mu_{act,3h}(t) = \frac{1}{|\mathcal{W}_t^{3h}|} \sum_{\tau \in \mathcal{W}_t^{3h}} A(\tau), \quad \text{where } \mathcal{W}_t^{3h} = \{\tau \mid t - 3\text{h} \leq \tau \leq t\}.$$

- Rolling Room Mean (6 h): The mean of encoded room ID values within the 6-h trailing window ending at time t:

$$\mu_{room,6h}(t) = \frac{1}{|\mathcal{W}_t^{6h}|} \sum_{\tau \in \mathcal{W}_t^{6h}} R(\tau), \quad \text{where } \mathcal{W}_t^{6h} = \{\tau \mid t - 6\text{h} \leq \tau \leq t\}.$$

3. Historical Features (Long-Term Routine)

To capture long-term periodic behaviors, a 21-day history embedding is constructed:

- For each day $d \in \{1, \ldots, 21\}$, the dominant activity label from a 2 h window centered around the same time of day, d days prior to t, is extracted:

$$h_t[d] = mode\{A(\tau) \mid \tau \in [t - d \text{ days} - 1\text{h},\ t - d \text{ days} + 1\text{h}]\}.$$

- A decay weight, w_d, is assigned based on the recency and weekday alignment:

$$w_d = \begin{cases} 1.8, & \text{if } d \text{ is a multiple of 7 AND } weekday(t-d) = weekday(t), \\ 1.5, & \text{if } d \text{ is a multiple of 7 (but not satisfying above condition)}, \\ \max(0.24,\ 0.96 - 0.12\,d), & \text{if } weekday(t-d) = weekday(t) \text{ (but not satisfying above conditions)}, \\ \max(0.2,\ 0.8 - 0.1\,d), & \text{otherwise.} \end{cases}$$

This yields two feature vectors per timestamp:

$$h_t = [h_t[1], \ldots, h_t[21]] \in \mathbb{Z}^{21}, \quad w_t = [w_1, \ldots, w_{21}] \in \mathbb{R}^{21}.$$

3.6. Sequence Generation

The fourth step in Figure 3 illustrates how the live sensor stream and logged events are converted into supervised learning samples of fixed length $L = 30$. Each sample consists of the following:

- $\mathbf{X}^{(i)} \in \mathbb{R}^{30\times 8}$: the most recent 30 standardized feature vectors;
- $\mathbf{h}^{(i)} \in \mathbb{Z}^{D}$: the D-day history vector ($D = 21$);
- $\mathbf{w}^{(i)} \in \mathbb{R}^{D}$: the corresponding decay weights;
- $y^{(i)} \in \mathbb{Z}$: the activity label at time i;

where any sequence with $y^{(i)} = \text{NULL}$ is discarded.

Sliding Window Extraction

For each timestamp index, $i \geq L$,

$$\mathbf{X}^{(i)} = \begin{bmatrix} \mathbf{x}_{i-L} \\ \mathbf{x}_{i-L+1} \\ \vdots \\ \mathbf{x}_{i-1} \end{bmatrix} \in \mathbb{R}^{30\times 8}, \qquad y^{(i)} = A_i.$$

Feature–History Configurations

To evaluate the influence of different feature sets on performance, three input configurations are defined:

Configuration 1: Minimal + 7-Day History **X** uses only instantaneous context (room ID, time_sin, time_cos, weekday), paired with the 7 most recent days in **h** (and their weights in **w**).

Configuration 2: Extended + 21-Day History Adds short-term rolling features (hourly activity count, room entropy) to **X** and extends **h** and **w** to 21 days.

Configuration 3: Enhanced + Rolling Statistics + 21-Day History Further includes 3 h and 6 h rolling means in **X**, retains the full 21-day history, and applies cyclic encodings for time-of-day and weekday.

Data Storage

Each complete training tuple, $\{\mathbf{X}^{(i)}, \mathbf{h}^{(i)}, \mathbf{w}^{(i)}, y^{(i)}\}$, is flattened—dropping any columns constant within that household—and appended to an on-device Hierarchical Data Format 5 (HDF5) cache. Encoded class mappings (`activity_classes`, `room_classes`) are stored alongside. This cache supports both initial training and the continuous retraining of EL-HARP directly on the Raspberry Pi.

3.7. Model Training and Tuning

This stage covers model selection, hyperparameter tuning, and the transition from proof-of-concept to live deployment.

Model Architectures

Three gradient-boosted decision tree (GBDT) ensembles were chosen for activity recognition:

- XGBoost [38]: Histogram-based tree construction, multi-class softmax objective, strong regularization.
- CatBoost [39]: Ordered boosting, native categorical handling, automatic feature combinations.
- LightGBM [40]: Gradient-based one-side sampling (GOSS), exclusive feature bundling (EFB), histogram splitting for low memory.

All models used categorical cross-entropy (multi-class log-loss) with 2% injected label noise to simulate annotation errors. Table 2 summarizes their inference speed, memory footprint, and edge suitability.

Table 2. Edge deployability characteristics of selected models.

Model	Inference Speed	Memory Footprint	Edge Suitability
XGBoost	Medium	Medium	High–Moderate (requires tuning)
CatBoost	Fast	Low	High (native categorical handling)
LightGBM	Very Fast	Very Low	Very High (optimized for embedded deployment)

Dataset Splitting

For each of the 21 single-resident households, sequences were split into 80% training, 10% validation, and 10% test. Stratification by label was applied when each class had $\geq$20 samples; otherwise, a random split was used.

Hyperparameter Optimization and Early Stopping

Several hyperparameter configurations were assessed on validation subsets from different users. The setting that consistently achieved the best performance across households was selected and used for all models. Models were trained with early stopping (patience = 100 rounds) on validation log-loss. Common settings: Subsampling and feature-fraction (or Random Subspace Method (RSM)) were both set to 0.8 across all models. Table 3 details the full hyperparameter configurations.

Table 3. Hyperparameter settings for XGBoost, CatBoost, and LightGBM.

Parameter	XGBoost	CatBoost	LightGBM
Learning rate	0.10	0.05	0.01
Depth/Leaves	6	6	15
Number of estimators/iterations	300	1000	1000
Subsample fraction	0.80	0.80	0.80
Feature-fraction/RSM	0.80	0.80	0.80
Regularization (L1/L2)	2.0/2.0	0.0/2.0	0.0/0.10
Minimum child weight/samples	5	10	50
Early stopping rounds	100	100	100

3.8. Evaluation and Edge Deployment

The final stage of the EL-HARP framework focuses on model evaluation used for maintaining system personalization over time.

Model performance is assessed per user using three complementary premises:

- Accuracy (Activity Recognition Accuracy): The percentage of correctly predicted activity labels across all test samples.
- Weighted F1-Score: A class-weighted harmonic mean of precision and recall that accounts for label imbalance.
- Confusion Matrix Analysis: A per-class visualization of prediction performance, helping to diagnose misclassification trends between similar or overlapping activities.

All metrics are computed on the test set of each household. Validation scores are calculated using the same metrics and used for early stopping during training. Formal equations and result tables are provided in Section 4.

3.9. Continuous Personalization and Edge Adaptation

To ensure long-term adaptability, EL-HARP includes an efficient retraining loop that runs entirely on the deployed edge device.

On-device inference and logging:

The trained LightGBM model and preprocessing pipeline are containerized and deployed on a Raspberry Pi 5. As live sensor events are streamed in, they are transformed into structured feature sequences and passed through the model for real-time prediction. Each instance is then appended to a persistent HDF5 log with timestamp, user ID, room, and predicted activity.

Local incremental retraining:

At scheduled intervals (e.g., weekly), the following update procedure is triggered:

- Newly logged instances are retrieved from the HDF5 cache.
- These samples are appended to the existing training set.
- The LightGBM model is warm-started, extending the existing ensemble with a limited number of trees (e.g., 50).
- Validation metrics are re-evaluated on a held-out portion of recent data.

If performance improves or remains within an acceptable tolerance range, the new model replaces the previous version. Otherwise, the update is discarded to prevent model drift.

4. Results and Performance Analysis

The evaluation of XGBoost, CatBoost, and LightGBM is conducted across three different feature setups, as defined in Section 3.7: Configuration 1 (basic feature set with 7-day history), Configuration 2 (an extended feature set with 21-day history), and Configuration 3 (augmented features incorporating rolling statistics over 21 days). The primary performance metrics reported are validation accuracy (A_{val}) and validation F1-score ($F_{1,\text{val}}$), along with user-specific test accuracy values for Configuration 3. Additionally, key metrics such as activity recognition accuracy (ARA) and F1-score are used to comprehensively evaluate model performance.

4.1. Dataset Transformation and Labeling

Smart home sensor logs are inherently noisy and heterogeneous, containing inconsistent readings, redundant signals, and ambiguous activity labels. In particular, the Single-Resident CASAS dataset [3] includes classes—Other_Activity, Entertain_Guests, and ENTER—that frequently correspond to sensor glitches or uninformative transitions. To focus on meaningful daily routines, these classes were removed from every household's raw logs, following the filtering methodology of Cook et al. [41].

4.1.1. Filtering Criteria and Class Statistics

After discarding the three noisy classes, each household's log was reduced to events with well-defined activities (e.g., Sleep, Cooking, Watch_TV, etc.). Table 4 summarizes the effect of this cleaning on a subset of the 21 households.

Table 4. Cleaning summary per household: samples before and after removal of noisy classes.

Household	Original	Cleaned	Removed
user 2	104,856	15,672	89,184
user 3	42,048	6522	35,526
user 4	121,865	28,276	93,589
user 5	46,981	9484	37,497
user 6	90,017	14,024	75,993
...	...	...	...
Total	2,731,903	428,914	2,302,989

Figure 4 compares the global class distributions before and after filtering, illustrating the removal of low-frequency, high-ambiguity labels and the relative preservation of core daily activities.

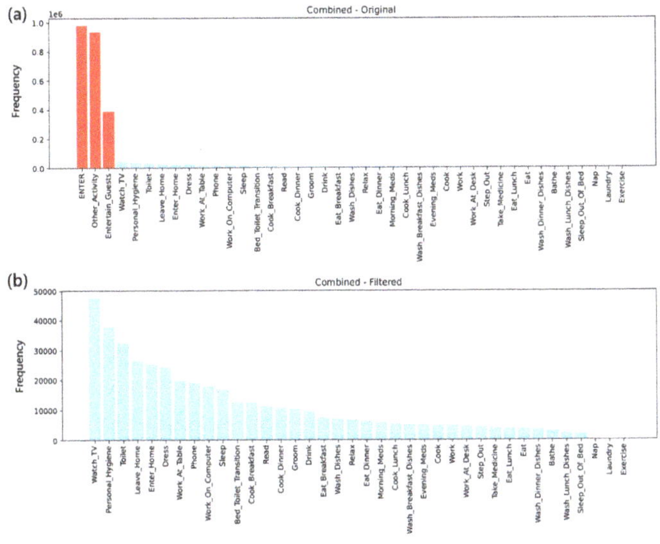

Figure 4. Global distribution of activity classes across 21 households: (**a**) before filtering, showing dominance of noise classes such as ENTER and Other Activity; (**b**) after filtering, illustrating the removal of low-frequency, high-ambiguity labels and the relative preservation of core daily activities.

4.1.2. Example: Raw vs. Cleaned Sequence

The following listings provide representative samples of the raw sensor log (before filtering and labeling) and its cleaned, structured counterpart. Figure 5 shows a representative raw sensor log collected from various IoT devices in the smart home. As seen, the log contains low-level, mixed events with redundant and unstructured entries. After preprocessing and labeling, the data is transformed into a clean, structured sequence suitable for feature extraction and modeling, as illustrated in Figure 6.

Raw Sensor Log (Before Processing)

```
2011-07-06 19:13:30.610431 D010 Ignore Ignore CLOSE Control4-Door
2011-07-06 19:13:30.615000 M0005 EntranceDoor LivingRoom ON Control4-MotionArea
2011-07-06 19:13:30.620000 ENT002 Ignore LivingRoom ON Control4-NFC
2011-07-06 19:13:34.001641 TV001 Ignore TVPower ON Control4-Device
2011-07-06 19:13:34.005550 M0007 LivingRoom TV ON Control4-MotionArea
2011-07-06 19:57:38.382270 TV001 TVPower Ignore OFF Control4-Device
2011-07-06 19:57:44.865736 M0015 Corridor Kitchen ON Control4-MotionArea
2011-07-06 19:57:44.868900 ENT002 Ignore Kitchen ON Control4-NFC
2011-07-06 19:57:46.287388 M0016 Kitchen Sink ON Control4-MotionArea
2011-07-06 19:57:46.289500 DIV001 Ignore Ignore ON Control4-WaterFlow
2011-07-06 20:01:23.650352 DIV001 WaterFlow Ignore OFF Control4-WaterFlow
2011-07-06 20:01:24.694903 D011 Ignore Ignore OPEN Control4-Door
2011-07-06 20:01:24.696200 ENT002 Ignore DiningRoom ON Control4-NFC
```

Figure 5. Fabricated raw sensor log with mixed, low-level device events.

Structured and Labeled Log (After Processing)

```
2011-07-06 19:13:30.610431,2,LivingRoom,ENTER,on
2011-07-06 19:13:34.001641,2,LivingRoom,Watch_TV,on
2011-07-06 19:57:38.382270,2,LivingRoom,Watch_TV,off
2011-07-06 19:57:44.865736,2,Kitchen,ENTER,on
2011-07-06 19:57:46.287388,2,Kitchen,Wash_Dinner_Dishes,on
2011-07-06 20:01:23.650352,2,Kitchen,Wash_Dinner_Dishes,off
2011-07-06 20:01:24.694903,2,DiningRoom,ENTER,on
2011-07-06 20:01:25.809591,2,DiningRoom,Eat_Dinner,on
2011-07-06 20:15:00.000000,2,DiningRoom,Eat_Dinner,off
2011-07-06 20:15:10.000000,2,Kitchen,ENTER,on
2011-07-06 20:15:12.000000,2,Kitchen,Prepare_Snack,on
2011-07-06 20:17:00.000000,2,Kitchen,Prepare_Snack,off
```

Figure 6. Cleaned, structured sequence ready for feature extraction and modeling.

4.1.3. Final Class Distribution per Household

After filtering, the remaining activity classes vary in frequency by household. Figure 7 shows a representative distribution for one home, demonstrating the diversity of daily routines captured post-cleaning.

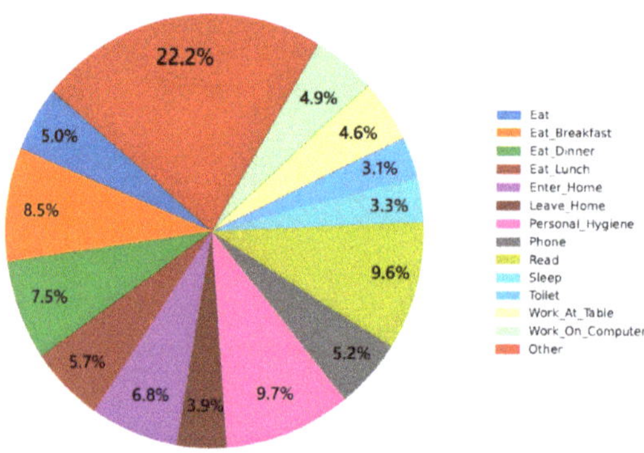

Figure 7. Activity class distribution for a representative household after filtering.

4.2. Evaluation Metrics

Key metrics include the following.

- Activity Recognition Accuracy (ARA): Proportion of correctly predicted activity segments:

$$\text{ARA} = \frac{\text{Correct Activity Segments}}{\text{Total Activity Segments}}$$

In other words, ARA is the overall accuracy of the model on the test set.

- F1-Score: The harmonic mean of precision and recall, particularly useful when activity classes are imbalanced.

$$\text{F1}_i = 2 \times \frac{\text{Precision}_i \times \text{Recall}_i}{\text{Precision}_i + \text{Recall}_i}.$$

The overall (weighted) F1-Score aggregates F1_i across all K classes by weighting each class's F1 by its support:

$$\text{F1}_\text{w} = \sum_{i=1}^{K} w_i \cdot \text{F1}_i, \quad w_i = \frac{n_i}{\sum_{j=1}^{K} n_j}.$$

4.3. Overall Validation Performance

Table 5 displays the average $\pm$ standard deviation of both A_{val} and $\text{F}_{1,\text{val}}$ across 21 users.

Table 5. Mean and standard deviation of validation accuracy and F1-score.

Model	Configuration 1		Configuration 2		Configuration 3	
	A_{val}	$F_{1,val}$	A_{val}	$F_{1,val}$	A_{val}	$F_{1,val}$
XGBoost	0.72 ± 0.05	0.73 ± 0.04	0.77 ± 0.04	0.76 ± 0.04	0.89 ± 0.03	0.89 ± 0.03
CatBoost	0.65 ± 0.06	0.64 ± 0.05	0.83 ± 0.03	0.82 ± 0.03	0.91 ± 0.02	0.91 ± 0.02
LightGBM	0.72 ± 0.05	0.72 ± 0.05	0.80 ± 0.04	0.79 ± 0.04	0.92 ± 0.02	0.92 ± 0.02

A consistent upward trend is observed from Configuration 1 to Configuration 3 across all models, with Configuration 3 yielding a 17–20 percentage point improvement in validation accuracy. LightGBM demonstrates the strongest overall performance in Configuration 3 for both metrics.

4.4. *User-Level Test Accuracy for Configuration 3*

The performance of each model on test data is further broken down across individual users under Configuration 3, as summarized in Table 6.

Table 6. User-level test accuracy statistics for Configuration 3.

Model	$\min(A_{test})$	$\max(A_{test})$	$\text{mean}(A_{test})$
XGBoost	0.764	0.937	0.887 ± 0.04
CatBoost	0.821	0.956	0.905 ± 0.03
LightGBM	0.821	0.961	0.915 ± 0.03

Among all three models, LightGBM records the highest average test accuracy of 91.5% and exhibits the lowest degree of variation across users.

4.5. *Model Generalization Behavior*

The generalization gap, denoted as $\Delta A = A_{train} - A_{val}$, reflects how well the model performance transfers from training to unseen data. Table 7 presents the mean and standard deviation of ΔA for all feature configurations.

Table 7. Average generalization gap (ΔA) for each configuration.

Model/Configuration	Configuration 1	Configuration 2	Configuration 3
XGBoost	0.24 ± 0.05	0.10 ± 0.03	0.04 ± 0.02
CatBoost	0.20 ± 0.06	0.04 ± 0.02	0.03 ± 0.02
LightGBM	0.22 ± 0.06	0.14 ± 0.04	0.03 ± 0.02

All models achieve substantial reductions in generalization gap under Configuration 3, with values falling below 0.04, reflecting improved robustness and generalization to unseen data.

4.6. *Results Interpretation*

Evaluation verifies that EL-HARP's multi-scale architectural choice—a combination of historical context, historical rolling statistics, and long-term history embeddings—the lightweight LightGBM achieves state-of-the-art performance (91.5% mean test precision). The performance matches, or surpasses even, that of deeper neural methods without compromising interpretability or efficiency. In-device trials under 100 ms with a Raspberry Pi 5 exhibit low-memory-footprint capabilities to confirm end-to-end in-device capabilities with stringent in-device data privacy. The dynamic retraining capability also retains sustained accuracy with dynamic user processes, concluding the limitation of static models in the absence of human intervention.

End-to-end containerized deployment—bundling preprocessing, feature extraction, inferencing from the model, and control logic all into modular services—enables fast deployment, easy updating, and easy interoperation with heterogeneous smart home platforms.

Collectively, all of these experiments demonstrate that EL-HARP provides a versatile, secure, and scalable home automation environment with a forward-looking orientation—with applications for energy use, elderly care, and context-dependent comfort enhancement.

5. Comparative Analysis

The optimal configuration—utilizing LightGBM combined with Configuration 3 features—demonstrates a compelling performance when compared against other distinguished smart home Human Activity Recognition (HAR) studies, as summarized in Table 8.

Table 8. Comparison with prior smart home HAR approaches.

Study	Approach	Accuracy/F1 Score
Ali et al. (2025) [20]	IoT and Edge Intelligence Framework using anomaly detection	86.03% (F1)
Feng et al. (2024) [21]	ICU Command Center with medical sensor fusion	85.0% (F1)
Chen et al. (2024) [22]	Self-Supervised Learning and Self-Attention in smart homes	85.63% (F1)
Srivatsa & Plötz (2024) [23]	Graph-based HAR using multimodal sensor GNNs	88.7% (F1)
Fiori et al. (2025) [24]	Explainable GNN-XAR on CASAS datasets	86.5% (Accuracy)
Zhou et al. (2022) [25]	TinyHAR: Lightweight deep learning for edge devices	89.0% (Accuracy)
Khan et al. (2022) [26]	Hybrid CNN-LSTM for time-sequential HAR	90.89% (Accuracy)
Dao et al. (2025) [28]	RFAR (Wearable System) for firefighter activities	97.35% (Accuracy)
Li et al. (2023) [30]	Deep Learning (HENN-MSD) for multi-environment data	96.57% (Accuracy)
This work (2025)	LightGBM + Configuration 3 Features (EL-HARP)	91.5% (Accuracy)

Relative to other HAR techniques, EL-HARP is distinctive in its proposed LightGBM model, where the best chosen Configuration 3 features achieve the 91.5% mean test accuracy.

- Ali et al. [20] achieved 86.03% (F1) using an IoT-Edge framework that focused on anomaly detection for monitoring the elderly. With more powerful general-purpose recognition capacity, EL-HARP outperforms this.
- Feng et al. [21] aimed at medical sensor fusion in an intensive care unit setting, achieving 85.0% F1, showing the domain gap where EL-HARP performs better with higher accuracies in smart home settings.
- Chen et al. [22] achieved 85.63% (F1) through the use of self-supervised learning and attention in a smart home environment. With a more straightforward architecture and superior interpretability, EL-HARP performs better than this.
- Srivatsa and Plötz [23] developed a GNN-based HAR model that produced an F1 score of 88.7%, while EL-HARP's lighter, non-deep LightGBM model produced even better accuracy.
- Fiori et al. [24] demonstrated GNN-XAR, an explainable GNN with an accuracy of 86.5% that was trained on CASAS data. With less computational overhead, EL-HARP performs five percentage points better than this.

- Zhou et al. [25] proposed TinyHAR, which achieved an accuracy of 89.0% in edge environments. While outperforming TinyHAR, EL-HARP maintains edge efficiency.
- Khan et al. [26] developed a CNN-LSTM hybrid model for HAR, which achieved an accuracy of 90.89%. With a gain of 0.61%, EL-HARP performs better than it while avoiding the complexity of deep learning.
- Dao et al. [28] achieved a high accuracy of 97.35% on the UCI HAR dataset with a real-time system for firefighter activity recognition. However, this approach relies on specific wearable sensors and a single modality, making it less generalizable and not directly comparable to HAR in a multi-sensor ambient smart home environment.
- Li et al. [30] demonstrated a state-of-the-art accuracy of 96.57% on the CASAS dataset using a complex deep learning model. While their model achieves a higher raw accuracy, its computational cost and complexity are significantly greater. In contrast, EL-HARP demonstrates that with carefully engineered features, a lightweight, non-deep model can achieve highly competitive performance, making it a more practical solution for resource-constrained edge devices.

These comparisons illustrate the efficacy of the proposed approach. Key takeaways include the following.

- Comprehensive Feature Engineering: even with non-deep models, performance is improved by incorporating temporal history, contextual windows, and rolling statistics.
- Gradient Boosting Ensembles: LightGBM is perfect for edge deployment since it achieves competitive or better accuracy than intricate deep architectures while using a lot less memory and inference time.
- Personalized Modeling: due to their ability to capture distinct activity patterns and routines, user-specific models customized for each household routinely outperform general-purpose models.

All other conditions being equal, EL-HARP utilizes the interplay of efficient modeling and robust feature building. This paper shows that less complex tree models could possibly dominate the best current deep learning architectures without compromising deployability on small smart home devices—with the use of densely-built features and special training. Smart home automation could be spread and expanded in practice as an outcome of this compromise between performance and efficiency.

6. Implications for Smart Home Automation

The empirical findings presented in Section 4 highlight several important directions for practical, personalized smart home deployment:

- Scalable Per-User Personalization: with an average test accuracy of over 90% for all households (Table 6), the findings validate that household-specific, lightweight models can facilitate reliable, context-aware automation.
- Feature Design over Architectural Complexity: the performance gains from Configuration 1 to Configuration 3 imply that meticulously designed historical and temporal features have a greater influence than more complex models.
- Resilience to Behavior Variability: the reduced generalization gap in Configuration 3 (Table 7) demonstrates that long-term behavior modeling can accommodate irregular routines and improve robustness, although short, transitional events remain challenging.
- Suitability for Edge Deployment: LightGBM supports local computation and user privacy, making it appropriate for real-time activity recognition on embedded systems like Raspberry Pi due to its small memory footprint and fast inference speed.

These findings lend support to the design approach that prioritizes effective ensemble techniques, along with strong, domain-informed feature engineering to enable adaptive, privacy-preserving automation in actual smart homes.

7. Conclusions

Here, an edge-computing-enabled, scalable, and holistic architecture, called **EL-HARP**, where HARP refers to a Human Activity Recognition framework with Advanced Robotics capabilities—Personalized sMART—has been introduced. EL-HARP offers real-time edge computing automation with lightweight gradient-boosted models in edge computing environments.

After thorough testing with the CASAS dataset, EL-HARP, under LightGBM runtime with Feature Configuration 3, attained an average test precision of 91.5%. Some of the current best algorithms fall short of this figure. These experiments attest that decision tree boosting with gradients works effectively with deeper learning algorithms with heavily contextual and temporal features but remains computationally fast in equilibrium with edge systems. In order to deal with some of the major challenges in smart home automation, such as privacy and personalization, generalization across users, low-latency edge inferencing, and incremental adaptation, EL-HARP has also been implemented over fully functional prototypes with a Raspberry Pi 5, ESP32-CAM, and Tuya-compatible sensors.

Author Contributions: Conceptualization, W.G.; Methodology, W.G. and T.A.; Software, M.M.G.; Formal analysis, M.M.G.; Investigation, W.G.; Writing—original draft, M.M.G.; Writing—review & editing, W.G., T.A. and K.N.; Supervision, T.A. and K.N.; Funding acquisition, K.N. All authors have read and agreed to the published version of the manuscript.

Funding: This research received no external funding.

Data Availability Statement: No new data were created or analyzed in this study. Data sharing is not applicable to this article.

Conflicts of Interest: The authors declare no conflicts of interest.

References

1. Zhao, G.; Wang, Y.; Wang, J. Intrusion Detection Model of Internet of Things Based on LightGBM. *IEICE Trans. Commun.* **2023**, *E106.B*, 622–634. [CrossRef]
2. Wazwaz, A.; Amin, K.; Semary, N.; Ghanem, T. Dynamic and Distributed Intelligence over Smart Devices, Internet of Things Edges, and Cloud Computing for Human Activity Recognition Using Wearable Sensors. *J. Sens. Actuator Netw.* **2024**, *13*, 5. [CrossRef]
3. Crandall, A.; Thomas, B.; Schmitter-Edgecombe, M. CASAS Smart Home Dataset-Free Living, Motion, Door, Activity Labels. 2025. Available online: https://zenodo.org/records/15708568 (accessed on 15 May 2025).
4. Singh, D.; Merdivan, E.; Kropf, J.; Holzinger, A. Class imbalance in multi-resident activity recognition: An evaluative study on explainability of deep learning approaches. *Univers. Access Inf. Soc.* **2024**, *24*, 1173–1191. [CrossRef]
5. Chen, X.; Cumin, J.; Ramparany, F.; Vaufreydaz, D. MuRAL: A Multi-Resident Ambient Sensor Dataset Annotated with Natural Language for Activities of Daily Living. *arXiv* **2025**, arXiv:2504.20505.
6. Liang, X.; Wang, H. Hybrid Transformer–RNN Architecture for Household Occupancy Detection Using Low-Resolution Smart Meter Data. In Proceedings of the 49th Annual IEEE Industrial Electronics Society Conference (IECON), Singapore, 16–19 October 2023; pp. 1–6. [CrossRef]
7. Home Assistant. Home Assistant Hardware Compatibility List: Yellow & Green Appliances. 2025. Available online: https://www.home-assistant.io/compatible/hardware/ (accessed on 15 June 2025).
8. Swaminathan, T.P.; Silver, C.; Akilan, T. Benchmarking Deep Learning Models on NVIDIA Jetson Nano for Real-Time Systems: An Empirical Investigation. *arXiv* **2024**, arXiv:2406.17749. [CrossRef]
9. Parra, D.; Møgelmose, A.; Rasmussen, C.H. A reinforcement learning approach to home energy management for modulating heat pumps and photovoltaic systems. *Appl. Energy* **2017**, *203*, 243–257.

10. Madsen, H.; Kjærgaard, M.B.; Jantzen, C.K.; Petersen, B. Batch Reinforcement Learning for Smart Home Energy Management. In Proceedings of the Twenty-Ninth AAAI Conference on Artificial Intelligence (IJCAI 2015), Austin, TX, USA, 25–30 January 2015; pp. 2572–2578.
11. Rathore, G.S.; Sharma, A.; Chauhan, S.; Kumar, P. Home Energy Management Using Multi-Agent Reinforcement Learning. *Energy* **2022**, *12*, 64–75.
12. Chen, J.; Tang, S.; Liu, Y.; Zhang, J. An optimal power scheduling method for demand response in home energy management system. *IEEE Trans. Smart Grid* **2013**, *3*, 1391–1400. [CrossRef]
13. Liu, T.; Lu, M.; Qu, M.; Song, T.; Wang, Y. Autonomous Price-aware Energy Management System in Smart Homes via Actor-Critic Learning with Predictive Capabilities. *IEEE Trans. Autom. Sci. Eng.* **2025**, *22*, 15018–15033.
14. Liu, X.; Gu, S.; Zhou, Z.; Lin, H. Effective charging planning based on deep reinforcement learning for electric vehicles. *IEEE Trans. Intell. Transp. Syst.* **2020**, *1*, 542–554. [CrossRef]
15. Zhao, W.; Song, X.; Chen, H.; Zhao, H.; Chen, P. CDDPG: A deep-reinforcement-learning-based approach for electric vehicle charging control. *IEEE Internet Things J.* **2020**, *5*, 3075–3087.
16. Ghosh, A.; Ahmed, M.F. Context-Aware Human Activity Recognition in Smart Homes: A Privacy-Preserving Approach. In Proceedings of the 2024 International Conference on Sustainable Communication Networks and Application (ICSCNA), Theni, India, 11–13 December 2024.
17. Rana, M.K.; Islam, M.M. Efficient Machine Learning for Wi-Fi CSI-based Human Activity Recognition Using Fast Monte Carlo based Feature Extraction. *Eur. Alliance Innov.* **2025**, *9*, 1–11.
18. Naik, K.; Pandit, T.; Naik, N.; Shah, P. Activity Recognition in Residential Spaces with Internet of Things Devices and Thermal Imaging. *Sensors* **2021**, *21*, 988. [CrossRef]
19. Lin, X.; Li, R.; Liu, G.; Fu, S. Exploring Machine Learning Algorithms for User Activity Inference from IoT Network Traffic. In Proceedings of the 20th IEEE International Conference on Mobile Ad Hoc and Smart Systems (MASS), Toronto, ON, Canada, 25–27 September 2023; pp. 555–564. [CrossRef]
20. Ali, A.; Montanaro, T.; Sergi, I.; Carrisi, S.; Galli, D.; Distante, C.; Patrono, L. An Innovative IoT and Edge Intelligence Framework for Monitoring Elderly People Using Anomaly Detection on Data from Non-Wearable Sensors. *Sensors* **2025**, *25*, 1735. [CrossRef]
21. Feng, W.S.; Chen, W.C.; Lin, J.Y.; Tseng, H.Y.; Chen, C.L.; Chou, C.Y.; Cho, D.Y.; Lin, Y.B. Design and Implementation of an Intensive Care Unit Command Center for Medical Data Fusion. *Sensors* **2024**, *24*, 3929. [CrossRef]
22. Chen, H.; Gouin-Vallerand, C.; Bouchard, K.; Gaboury, S.; Couture, M.; Bier, N.; Giroux, S. Enhancing Human Activity Recognition in Smart Homes with Self-Supervised Learning and Self-Attention. *Sensors* **2024**, *24*, 884. [CrossRef]
23. Srivatsa, P.; Plötz, T. Using Graphs to Perform Effective Sensor-Based Human Activity Recognition in Smart Homes. *Sensors* **2024**, *24*, 3944. [CrossRef]
24. Fiori, M.; Mor, D.; Civitarese, G.; Bettini, C. GNN-XAR: An Explainable Graph Neural Network for Smart Home Activity Recognition. In Proceedings of the 21st EAI International Conference on Mobile and Ubiquitous Systems (Mobiquitous), Oslo, Norway, 12–15 November 2024.
25. Zhou, Y.; Zhao, H.; Huang, Y.; Riedel, T.; Hefenbrock, M.; Beigl, M. TinyHAR: A Lightweight Deep Learning Model Designed for Human Activity Recognition. In Proceedings of the 2022 ACM International Symposium on Wearable Computers (ISWC '22), Cambridge, UK, 11–15 September 2022; pp. 89–93. [CrossRef]
26. Khan, I.U.; Afzal, S.; Lee, J.W. Human Activity Recognition via Hybrid Deep Learning Based Model. *Sensors* **2022**, *22*, 323. [CrossRef]
27. Khan, S.U.; Sultana, M.; Danish, S.; Gupta, D.; Alghamdi, N.S.; Woo, S.; Lee, D.G.; Ahn, S. Multimodal feature fusion for human activity recognition using human centric temporal transformer. *arXiv* **2025**, arXiv:2508.01234. [CrossRef]
28. Dao, T.H.; Le, D.D.; Do, D.H.; Nguyen, V.T. RFAR: A Real-time Firefighter Activity Recognition System Using Wearable Accelerometer. *arXiv* **2025**, arXiv:2508.05678. [CrossRef]
29. Yang, Z.; Zhang, Y.; Li, Y.; Zhu, M.; Wu, J. Fusion of Inertial and High-resolution Acoustic Data for Privacy-Preserving Human Activity Recognition. *IEEE Trans. Instrum. Meas.* **2025**, *74*, 9519320. [CrossRef]
30. Li, Y.; Hu, J.; Wang, Z.; Han, Y. Human activity recognition based on multienvironment sensor data. *Hum. Centric Comput. Inf. Sci.* **2023**, *13*, 1–15. [CrossRef]
31. Li, J.; Su, H.; Zhao, Y. Deep Unified Model for Face Recognition Based on Convolution Neural Network and Edge Computing. *IOP Conf. Ser. Mater. Sci. Eng.* **2019**, *569*, 052028. [CrossRef]
32. Bhattacharjee, D.; Khan, S. Homogenous Ensemble Boosting Approach to Improve the Consistency in the Accuracy of Text Data Classification. *Int. J. Adv. Sci. Eng. Technol. (IJASEAT)* **2025**, *13*, 38–44.
33. Chen, Z.; Zhang, J.; Zhang, Y. Few-shot Vision-based Human Activity Recognition with MLLM-based Visual Reinforcement Learning. *arXiv* **2025**, arXiv:2508.10371v1.
34. Ghorashi, V.; Ghassemi, F.; Jalaian, M. Towards Privacy-Preserving and Personalized Smart Homes via Tailored Small Language Models. *arXiv* **2025**, arXiv:2507.08878. [CrossRef]

35. Ullah, A.; Ali, T.; Zikria, Y.B.; Kim, B.S.; Kim, H.G. Using Machine Learning Techniques to Detect Cyberattacks in Smart Homes: A Survey. In Proceedings of the 2023 International Scientific Conference on Computer Science (COMSCI), Sozopol, Bulgaria, 8–20 September 2023.
36. Biswas, M.; Das, M.; Barman, H.; Kumar Dey, S. Set Up My Smart Home as I Want. *IEEE Comput. Soc.* **2025**, *57*, 65–73.
37. Ramanathan, K.K.; Singh, M.K. ConSense: Continually Sensing Human Activity with WiFi via Growing and Picking. *arXiv* **2025**, arXiv:2502.17483.
38. Chen, T.; Guestrin, C. XGBoost: A Scalable Tree Boosting System. In Proceedings of the 22nd ACM SIGKDD International Conference on Knowledge Discovery and Data Mining (KDD '16), San Francisco, CA, USA, 13–17 August 2016; ACM: New York, NY, USA, 2016; pp. 785–794. [CrossRef]
39. Dorogush, A.V.; Ershov, V.; Gulin, A. CatBoost: Gradient Boosting with Categorical Features Support. *arXiv* **2018**, arXiv:1810.11363. [CrossRef]
40. Ke, G.; Meng, Q.; Finley, T.; Wang, T.; Chen, W.; Ma, W.; Ye, Q.; Liu, T.Y. LightGBM: A Highly Efficient Gradient Boosting Decision Tree. In Proceedings of the Advances in Neural Information Processing Systems (NeurIPS), Long Beach, CA, USA, 4–9 December 2017; Volume 30, pp. 3146–3154.
41. Cook, D.J.; Schmitter-Edgecombe, M. Activity Recognition Using Hierarchical Hidden Markov Models on Streaming Sensor Data. *IEEE Trans. Syst. Man Cybern. Syst.* **2015**, *45*, 458–469. [CrossRef]

sensors

MDPI

Article

Fall Detection by Deep Learning-Based Bimodal Movement and Pose Sensing with Late Fusion

Haythem Rehouma * and Mounir Boukadoum *

Département d'informatique, Université du Québec à Montréal, Montréal, QC H2X 3Y7, Canada
* Correspondence: rehouma.haythem@courrier.uqam.ca (H.R.); boukadoum.mounir@uqam.ca (M.B.)

Abstract

The timely detection of falls among the elderly remains challenging. Single modality sensing approaches using inertial measurement units (IMUs) or vision-based monitoring systems frequently exhibit high false positives and compromised accuracy under suboptimal operating conditions. We propose a novel bimodal deep learning-based bimodal sensing framework to address the problem, by leveraging a memory-based autoencoder neural network for inertial abnormality detection and an attention-based neural network for visual pose assessment, with late fusion at the decision level. Our experimental evaluation with a custom dataset of simulated falls and routine activities, captured with waist-mounted IMUs and RGB cameras under dim lighting, shows significant performance improvement by the described bimodal late-fusion system, with an F1-score of 97.3% and, most notably, a false-positive rate of 3.6% significantly lower than the 11.3% and 8.9% with IMU-only and vision-only baselines, respectively. These results confirm the robustness of the described fall detection approach and validate its applicability to real-time fall detection under different light settings, including nighttime conditions.

Keywords: fall detection; multimodal learning; LSTM autoencoder; Transformer; IMU; pose estimation; elderly care; late fusion; nighttime monitoring

1. Introduction

Falls by the elderly remain a major public health concern due to their effect on autonomy, quality of life, and mortality [1,2], and their timely and reliable detection is essential, particularly for older adults living independently. However, distinguishing actual falls from daily activities remains challenging under realistic conditions, especially at night when visual cues are degraded by low illumination and occlusions from blankets or furniture [3–5]. The current fall detection systems rely primarily on single modality sensing using inertial measurement units (IMUs) or vision-based monitoring [1–3]. IMU-based methods, often employing simple thresholds or shallow classifiers [6–10], are inexpensive and minimally intrusive, but they lack spatial contextualization and frequently generate false alarms. Vision-based methods provide richer contextual information through background subtraction, pose estimation, and deep classifiers [11–14]. Yet, the performance of vision-based systems can degrade sharply under nocturnal conditions [5].

To obtain more accurate and reliable fall detection, multimodal sensing systems that combine information from different sensors have been increasingly explored, notably by combining inertial and vision sensors [3,15]. The sensor fusion can be performed early by combining the individual sensor outputs before further processing, with the risk of increasing noise in the processing chain, or late by having each output processed independently, and the results merged before the final decision, enabling better calibration, fault isolation, and resilience against modality-specific failures [16,17]. In this regard, decision-level fusion is more robust than early fusion, while they both endow multimodal systems with the potential of better detection performance than single modality solutions.

In this study, we propose a deep learning-based bimodal framework for fall detection that can operate at night, thanks to the integration of inertial abnormality detection by an unsupervised LSTM autoencoder [18] and pose assessment by a Transformer-based vision module [19]. By adopting decision-level fusion, the complementary strengths of IMU and vision sensing are leveraged by having the inertial cues ensure robustness when vision is impaired, and the visual cues provide spatial verification when inertial data is ambiguous.

A cohort of 16 participants was used to validate the framework, as training experiments showed the performance gains to reach a plateau at ≈12 participants as will be shown. Personalization experiments using few-shot learning also showed that at least 95% performance could be recovered with only five annotated sequences per new subject, thus mitigating inter-individual variability and addressing practical deployment needs.

Finally, RGB cameras were used for vision sensing thanks to their low cost, broad availability, and acceptability in private environments as used by our framework, since it operates by transforming the raw video frames into abstract skeletal keypoints, hence thwarting subject identification while preserving context for fall detection. Moreover, our preliminary experiments confirmed that robust performance (F1 > 96%) could be maintained with less than 5 lux illumination, thus mitigating the need for specialized sensors.

Our main contributions are as follows: (1) a decision level fused IMU–RGB architecture for nocturnal operation, (2) the combination of an unsupervised LSTM autoencoder for inertial abnormality detection and a Transformer-based vision module modeling spatiotemporal pose from 2D skeletal landmarks, (3) a few-shot personalization protocol for rapid user adaptation, (4) a systematic comparison showing the superiority of the proposed approach over unimodal and early-fusion baselines in accuracy and false alarms.

2. Related Work

2.1. Assisted Living Technologies for Fall Detection

Fall detection systems are commonly grouped into three generations [1]. The first generation relied on user-triggered alarms (e.g., wearable panic buttons) that could fail when the user is incapacitated. The second-generation introduced wearable IMUs with thresholding and classical machine learning (ML) classifiers. Today, the third-generation systems seek to combine artificial intelligence and multimodal sensing, leveraging deep neural networks to improve the detection process and context understanding.

2.2. IMU-Based Fall Detection

IMU-only approaches remain attractive for cost and privacy reasons [3,4], and they range from simple threshold-based systems [4,20] to classical ML-based classifiers such as SVM, random forests, decision trees, and k-NN [6,21–24], and deep learning models recently. For example, Zhang et al. [25] developed a dual-stream convolutional neural network with a self-attention mechanism that learns discriminative features from accelerometer and gyroscope data and assigns weights to different phases of the fall signal. The model outperformed traditional threshold-based and shallow learning approaches on public datasets, demonstrating that neural networks can enhance fall detection accuracy while remaining embeddable. However, while effective under controlled conditions, they often fail to disambiguate daily fall-like activities because of the lack of spatial confirmation, thus leading to a high false alarm rate [3]. More recent deep learning models such as unsupervised LSTM autoencoders can improve the detection robustness by sensing deviations from learned normal motion [18], but they also suffer from the lack of spatial verification.

2.3. Vision-Based Fall Detection

Vision-based methods offer a richer spatial context via silhouettes, skeletal landmarks, thermal or depth sensing, and classification thereof [5,10,11,26–28]. However, their performance is constrained in realistic settings such as low light and occlusions at night, and privacy concerns can limit their acceptance in homes [5,12].

2.4. Multimodal Approaches and Fusion Techniques

IMU and vision integration have been widely explored for potentially benefiting from complementary strengths [29,30], but the process is not trivial. As mentioned, early fusion using feature-level concatenation [31–33] brings the risk of propagating modality-specific noise and redundancy, thus reducing generalization potential [16,32]. Decision-level (late) fusion fares better in this respect, by exploiting the two modalities independently and combining their predictions at the end. Prior works combining deep outputs or video–accelerometer cues reported improved robustness, though not focusing on nocturnal operation [32,34].

2.5. Remaining Gaps and Proposed Contributions

The persisting gaps in the state of the art include (i) limited evaluation in nocturnal low-light conditions typical of bedrooms [5,12]; (ii) persistent false positives undermining trust [35]; (iii) lack of systematic multimodal integration with abnormality detection (e.g., LSTM autoencoders) [18]; and (iv) limited use of attention-based temporal modeling within multimodal pipelines [8,19]. This work addresses these gaps by introducing a bimodal IMU–RGB framework with decision-level fusion that couples an unsupervised LSTM autoencoder for inertial abnormality detection [18] with a Transformer-based vision module for pose-sequence analysis [19,36].

3. Proposed Bimodal Decision-Level Fusion Architecture

The proposed bimodal fall detection architecture consists of two distinct processing streams: (i) a vision-based stream exploiting video-based skeletal landmarks and pose evolution, and (ii) an inertial-based stream using an LSTM autoencoder for inertial abnormality detection. Both streams operate independently, and their outputs are fused by a decision-level rule for robust and reliable fall detection.

3.1. Video Processing Pipeline and Transformer-Based Fall Detection

The vision processing module begins by using MediaPipe BlazePose from Google Research [37,38] to extract 2D skeletal landmarks from the RGB video frames. BlazePose uses a detector-tracker machine leaning architecture specifically designed for real-time operation under challenging conditions, including moderate occlusions, blanket coverage and poor illumination. The two-step pose estimation pipeline proceeds as follows: (1) a lightweight detector locates a region-of-Interest (ROI) around the upper body, predicting virtual keypoints to ensure a normalized and rotation-invariant body pose region; (2) a depthwise-separable convolutional neural network regresses 33 anatomical landmark coordinates and assigns a visibility score between 0 (not visible) and 1 (fully visible) to each one of them.

At each video frame at time t, the current landmarks serve to update the ROI for the frame at $t + 1$, to allow continuous tracking without frequent full-frame detections. This tightly coupled detector–landmark interaction guarantees robust landmark estimation even under adverse conditions, including partial occlusions, low-light, and typical nighttime visual perturbations.

In this study, 2D skeletal landmarks were adopted instead of 3D, because 2D inference better satisfies the CPU-only real-time budget of the target platform and can be more robust under nocturnal low-light conditions where 3D depth-based estimation frequently fails. Furthermore, modern 2D keypoint extractors provide stable tracking and sufficient postural cues for the downstream Transformer. Future work will investigate 3D variants once illumination and computing constraints can be relaxed.

Figure 1 illustrates upright vs. prone configurations from BlazePose. The evolution of their bounding box's aspect ratio can be used to provide a coarse postural cue.

Following landmark extraction, the obtained coordinates in normalized units are converted to pixel coordinates by

$$x_i^{pixel} = x_i^{norm}.w_{frame} \text{ and } y_i^{pixel} = y_i^{norm}.h_{frame} \tag{1}$$

where w_{frame}, h_{frame} denote the frame dimensions in pixels. Then, a coarse bounding box is computed for posture estimation, with its extreme coordinates derived from the subset of the landmark points with visibility greater than a threshold (0.50 in this work):

$$x_{min} = \min_i x_i^{pixel}, \; x_{max} = \max_i x_i^{pixel} \tag{2}$$

$$y_{min} = \min_i y_i^{pixel}, \; y_{max} = \max_i y_i^{pixel} \tag{3}$$

Given the previous coordinates, the bounding box's aspect ratio ρ_f is

$$\rho_f = \frac{x_{max} - x_{min}}{y_{max} - y_{min}} \tag{4}$$

with $\rho_f > 1$ indicating a prone or horizontal posture (possible fall) and $\rho_f < 1$ indicating an upright posture. The prone states increment a fall counter with the requirement of 30 adjacent ones for fall confirmation (1 s continuity at 30 fps). This minimizes transient false alarms due to jitter or brief occlusions.

For fine-grained temporal analysis, we integrate a Transformer neural network to account for the sequential evolution of the landmarks. The Transformer model architecture includes the following:

- Input structure: The concatenated landmark coordinates as feature vectors of size 66 (33 points × 2 coordinates per point) for each of the 30 consecutive frames (1 s duration).
- Transformer Encoder: four stacked Transformer layers, each one having an 8-head self-attention mechanism to capture the complex spatiotemporal correlations and abrupt posture changes associated with falls.
- Classification Layer (Decoder): feedforward neural network to project the produced 256-dimensional embedding to a 1-dimensional output vector corresponding to "fallen" and "normal" classes via softmax probabilities.

The Transformer network is trained with manually labeled nighttime data, with 70% used for training, 15% for validation, and 15% for testing, Adam optimization (learning rate 3×10^{-4}) with cross-entropy loss [39], and early stopping to avoid overfitting.

A secondary temporal verification step aggregates the bounding box and Transformer outputs to enforce a robust fall confirmation, thus significantly reducing the likelihood of false positives due to temporary landmark occlusions or lighting fluctuations.

3.2. LSTM Autoencoder for Inertial Abnormality Detection

The inertial sensing module consists of an unsupervised abnormality detection architecture based on an LSTM autoencoder. The model is as follows:

- Encoder: Two stacked LSTM layers, each one with 128 hidden units, to compress the inertial signals (tri-axial accelerations and gyroscopic velocities) into a compact 256-dimensional latent representation.
- Decoder: A symmetric LSTM-based decoder reconstructing the original inertial sequences from the latent vectors, followed by a dense output layer (256 to 6-dimensional reconstruction).

The model training involves predominantly normal inertial data (non-fall activities), segmented into sliding windows of 60 samples with 50% overlap. Z-score normalization and band-pass filtering are used to pre-process the IMU signals for drift and noise artifact reduction as will be described in Section 4.4. The hyperparameters were optimized with validation-based grid search [40].

The reconstruction error is quantified by the Mean Squared Error (MSE) at the autoencoder's output:

$$\mathrm{MSE}(n) = \frac{1}{T}\sum_{t=1}^{T}\left\|x_n^t - \hat{x}_n^t\right\|^2,\ T = 60 \tag{5}$$

where x_n^t denotes the IMU input vector and $\hat{x}_n^t$ its corresponding reconstruction by the LSTM autoencoder. A statistical error threshold τ (e.g., 95th percentile) is used to detect abnormal motion patterns, with any reconstruction MSE exceeding τ triggering a motion abnormality alert for the associated window:

$$\text{Abnormal if } \mathrm{MSE}(n) > \tau \tag{6}$$

3.3. Decision-Level Fusion Rule

The final classification integrates the visual and inertial outputs through a decision-level fusion rule. Figure 2 depicts the runtime pipeline, showing the IMU and vision streams producing independent fall scores, each one compared to a common threshold α (0.70 used in this work), with a joint gating rule issuing the final label. More specifically, the late-fusion approach uses the vision-based fall probability $p_{fall}^{(Vision)}$ and the IMU-based abnormality score normalized into [0, 1]

$$s_{anomaly} = min\left(\frac{\mathrm{MSE}(n)}{\tau},\ 1\right) \tag{7}$$

A segment is labeled FALL when $p_{fall}^{(Vision)} > \alpha$ and $s_{anomaly} > \alpha$ (with $\alpha = 0.70$). If only one score exceeds α, the event is flagged LOW-CONFIDENCE for further verification; otherwise, the label is NORMAL.

As mentioned in Introduction, this design improves robustness against single-modality failures. For example, false positives from inertial impulses (e.g., abrupt sitting) are suppressed by visual verification, whereas vision occlusions or darkness are compensated by reliable inertial detections.

3.4. Few-Shot Personalization Protocol

To evaluate the system's adaptability to unseen users in data-scarce scenarios, we conducted a dedicated few-shot learning experiment atop the Leave-One-Subject-Out (LOSO) protocol, a variant of k-fold cross-validation [41] where each fold considers the data from a single subject. For each of the 16 participants, the model is first trained on the data from the remaining 15 subjects, yielding a subject-agnostic baseline. Subsequently, K annotated sequences from the held-out subject, $K \in \{1, 2, \ldots, 10\}$, were used to incrementally fine-tune the final fusion classifier with the inertial and visual encoders frozen. This protocol emulates post-deployment calibration under limited supervision and transfer learning from the subject-agnostic model to a new user. Next is the detailed procedure:

Let $D = \{S_1, S_2, \ldots, S_{16}\}$, where S_i is a set of time-synchronized and recorded RGB and IMU sequences for subject $i \in \{1, \ldots, 16\}$, each sequence representing labeled data over a 1 s interval (30 RGB frames at 30 fps and 60 IMU samples at 50 Hz). The sampling is class-stratified to include both fall and non-fall segments when available. Then, the following three computations are performed for each value of K:

(1) LOSO pre-training: for every subject i, a baseline model $M - i$ is trained on

$$D^{(i)}_{train} = D \setminus S_i \tag{8}$$

(2) Incremental $M - i$ fine-tuning with K sequences (few-shot). Using the held-out subject data, we uniformly sample without replacement a calibration set:

$$D^{(i,K)}_{cal} \subset S_i, \left| D^{(i,K)}_{cal} = K \right|, K \in \{1, 2, \ldots, 10\} \tag{9}$$

where K is capped to 10 to model a realistic calibration effort and because performance saturates beyond $K \approx 7$ (see Section 5.5). As mentioned, only the decision-level fusion classifier is updated (learning rate 1×10^{-4}, 50 iterations), while the IMU (LSTM) and vision (Transformer) encoders are frozen. As a result, the number of trainable parameters is less than 5 k, enabling on-device adaptation in less than 2 s on an average CPU such as Intel's I5.

(3) Evaluation and aggregation: The adapted model $M_{i,K}$ is tested on the disjoint held out set

$$D^{(i,K)}_{test} = S_i \setminus D^{(i,K)}_{cal} \tag{10}$$

For each K, we report the mean F1-score across 16 LOSO folds,

$$\overline{\mathrm{F1}(K)} = \frac{1}{16} \sum_{i=1}^{16} \mathrm{F1}\left(M_{i,K}, D^{(i,K)}_{test} \right), \tag{11}$$

and the 95% percent confidence intervals are computed across folds using Student's t with 15 degrees of freedom:

$$\overline{x} \pm t_{0.975,15} \frac{s}{\sqrt{16}} \; (with \; t_{0.975,15} \approx 2.131) \tag{12}$$

where $\overline{x}$ is the fold-wise mean, s is the sample standard deviation of the per-fold metric. The between-method differences are assessed with paired two-sided t-tests over the 16 folds (significance $p < 0.05$; here all $p < 0.001$), and the resulting $\overline{\mathrm{F1}(K)}$ curve quantifies the few-shot recovery performance as a function of K.

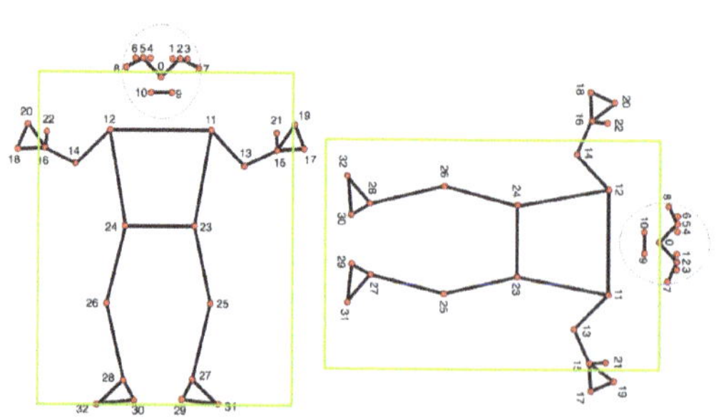

Figure 1. Skeletal MediaPipe model [42] with bounding box, showing the 33 anatomical landmark points for pose estimation: Standing up (**left**), lying down (**right**). The bounding box's aspect ratio helps detect falls.

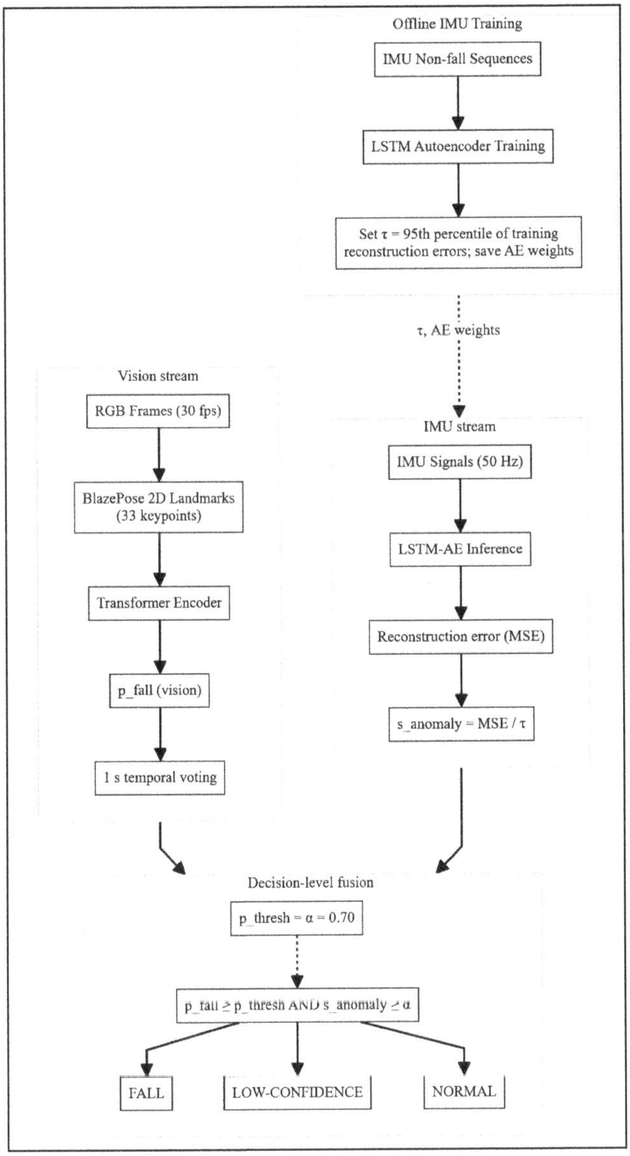

Figure 2. Proposed IMU–RGB pipeline with decision-level fusion for fall detection. Offline: the LSTM autoencoder is trained on non-fall IMU sequences and the 95th percentile of training reconstruction errors defines a threshold τ for detecting abnormal IMU sequences; the Transformer encoder is trained on vision data for binary FALL detection. *Runtime*: Vision stream: RGB video (30 fps) → BlazePose (33 2D landmarks) → Transformer inference → fall probability p_{fall} after 1 s temporal voting; IMU stream: IMU signal (50 Hz) → LSTM-AE inference → abnormality score $s_{anomaly} = MSE/\tau$ after 1 s. Decision-level fusion: FALL if $p_{fall} > p_{thresh}$ and $s_{anomaly} > \alpha$ ($p_{thresh} = \alpha = 0.70$ in this work); LOW-CONFIDENCE FALL if only one condition holds; NORMAL otherwise.

4. Experimental Setup and Dataset Description

4.1. Participants and Experimental Setup

The experimental protocol was conducted with sixteen healthy adult volunteers (eight males, eight females; mean age: 42.1 ± 4.8 years; height: 1.71 ± 0.07 m; weight: 68.9 ± 9.4 kg), none of whom reported neurological, orthopedic, or cardiovascular conditions that might affect mobility. All participants provided written informed consent in accordance with institutional ethics guidelines prior to participation.

Data acquisition was carried out in a controlled indoor environment simulating a typical nocturnal bedroom scenario. The setup included a standard single bed, pillows, blankets, a bedside table, and other common furniture items to ensure ecological realism. Ambient illumination was maintained below 5 lux to replicate realistic nighttime conditions, without the use of auxiliary lighting or infrared sources.

4.2. Data Acquisition

As Figure 3 shows, each subject wore a waist-mounted smartphone (rear waistband) secured using an adjustable elastic strap to ensure stable sensor contact. The embedded IMU (Inertial Measurement Unit) captured six-axis data: three-axis linear accelerations (±16 g) and three-axis angular velocities (±2000°/s), uniformly sampled at 50 Hz. All inertial data streams were timestamped and loosely synchronized with the RGB video stream using a local Network Time Protocol (NTP) server, achieving sufficient temporal coherence for decision-level fusion processing.

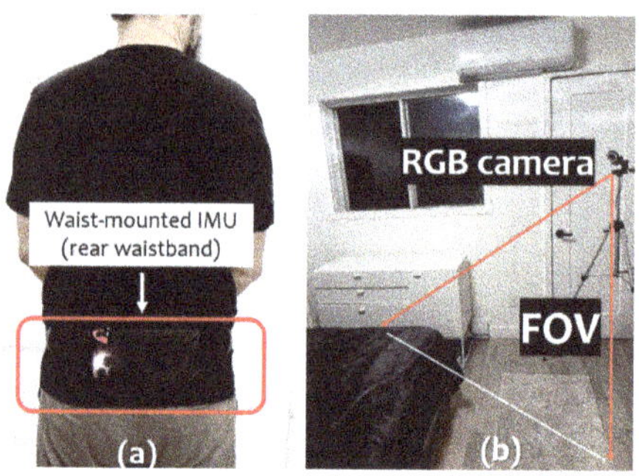

Figure 3. Experimental setup: (**a**) Waist-mounted IMU placed at the back (smartphone form factor). (**b**) RGB positioned at 1.2 m with an oblique lateral viewpoint, with the field of view (FOV) indicated in red and covering the bed area. Ambient illumination kept below 5 lux with no auxiliary IR lighting during data collection.

The RGB video data were recorded using a laterally positioned camera placed at approximately 1.2 m height to ensure a full and unobstructed view of each participant's body during all activities. The video streams were acquired at 1920 × 1080 resolution and 30 fps. The room illumination was set below 5 lux for realistic nighttime conditions.

4.3. Experimental Protocol and Data Collection

Each participant completed a total of 30 scripted trials, comprising 15 simulated falls (covering forward, backward, and lateral directions) and 15 segments of routine nocturnal activities, including lying down, rolling over in bed, sitting up, standing from a lying position, and walking within the experimental environment. Each trial lasted approximately two minutes, yielding a total of roughly one hour of data per subject. For the entire cohort of 16 participants, this resulted in 16 h of multimodal recordings. To ensure ecological validity and preserve natural behavior, participants were instructed to execute each scenario with realistic motion patterns, without rigid constraints or robotic repetitions.

As mentioned in Section 3.2, the recorded inertial signals were segmented using a sliding window approach, with 60 samples per window corresponding to approximately 1.2 s, and 50% overlap between consecutive windows to preserve temporal continuity. The concomitant video recordings were divided into sequences of 30 consecutive frames per segment (corresponding to ~1 s at 30 fps), providing temporally aligned visual input for the vision-based model components.

Leave-One-Subject-Out (LOSO) cross-validation is employed to evaluate the model's performance and to ensure robustness against inter-individual variability and to assess generalization to unseen subjects under realistic conditions.

4.4. Signal Processing and Feature Extraction

The raw IMU data underwent the following preprocessing steps:

- Z-score normalization to remove static offsets and standardize amplitude distributions across subjects.
- Filtering using a 4th-order Butterworth zero-phase digital filter with a band-pass frequency range from 0.2 Hz to 20 Hz, effectively eliminating low-frequency drift and high-frequency noise.

The resulting sequences were used as input for the IMU model in Section 3.2.

As already mentioned, the video frames were processed with MediaPipe BlazePose [38], providing real-time extraction of 33 anatomical landmarks with normalized coordinates (x, y), alongside visibility confidence scores ranging from 0 to 1. Landmarks with confidence below a threshold of 0.5 were discarded, ensuring robustness against occlusions and low illumination.

The landmarks' bounding box was computed frame-by-frame to derive posture features as detailed in Section 3.1.

4.5. Deep Learning Models

The model's architecture is described in Section 3.2 and training it was conducted on non-fall sequences, using mean squared error (MSE) loss and the Adam optimizer [39] (learning rate: 0.001, batch size: 32, 50 epochs, early stopping after 10 stagnant epochs).

The model's architecture and temporal voting are described in Section 3.1. Training was supervised with manually annotated data, using cross-entropy loss optimized by Adam (learning rate 1×10^{-4}, cosine annealing, batch size 64, 40 epochs, early stopping after 5 epochs without improvement).

4.6. Late Fusion Algorithm

The decision-level fusion rule (score computation, thresholds, and temporal vote) is formally defined in Section 3.3 and detailed in Supplementary Algorithm S3. For all experiments, a fixed threshold $\alpha = 0.70$ was used for both modalities, and a $1 - s$ temporal vote was applied on the vision stream.

4.7. Evaluation Metrics

To thoroughly evaluate the system's performance, standard metrics were used to provide a comprehensive insight into both positive event detection capability and false alarm suppression. They included the following:

$$\text{Accuracy} = \frac{\text{TP} + \text{TN}}{\text{TP} + \text{TN} + \text{FP} + \text{FN}}$$

$$\text{Precision} = \frac{\text{TP}}{\text{TP} + \text{FP}}$$

$$\text{Recall(Sensitivity)} = \frac{\text{TP}}{\text{TP} + \text{FN}}$$

$$\text{Specificity} = \frac{\text{TN}}{\text{TN} + \text{FP}}$$

$$\text{F1-Score} = 2 \times \frac{\text{Precision} \times \text{Recall}}{\text{Precision} + \text{Recall}}$$

4.8. Statistical Analysis

Comparative analyses between the proposed bimodal decision-level fusion model and the two single-modality baselines (IMU-only and vision-only) were conducted using paired-sample t-tests. A significance threshold of $p < 0.05$ was adopted to determine statistical relevance. Additionally, 95% confidence intervals were computed for the key performance metrics, precision, recall, and F1-score, to assess the statistical reliability and variability of the results across participants.

4.9. Computational Environment

All the deep learning models were implemented using PyTorch (v2.2.0; Meta Platforms Inc., Menlo Park, CA, USA). The experimental evaluations were conducted on a workstation equipped with an Intel Core i5-8265U processor (4 cores/8 threads, base 1.60 GHz, turbo up to 3.90 GHz), 8 GB of RAM, and no GPU to reflect deployment in relative resource-limited environments, hence providing an estimation of system performance for real-time applications in embedded or edge-based healthcare scenarios.

4.10. Sample-Size Adequacy via a Subject-Wise Learning Curve

To justify the cohort size, we computed a subject-wise learning curve under the LOSO protocol for sizes $m \in \{2, 4, 6, 8, 10, 12, 14, 16\}$, with the models trained on randomly selected sets of $m - 1$ training subjects and evaluated on the held-out subject, and the F1-scores averaged over all LOSO folds. Each m was repeated 10 times with different random draws, and we report the mean with 95% confidence intervals (Student's t). We define saturation as a marginal gain <0.5 percentage points when increasing from $m = 12$ to $m = 16$. Then, the obtained leaning curve allows us to assess each cohort's adequacy for training the system.

5. Results

The proposed IMU-RGB system was benchmarked against IMU-only and vision-only baselines under LOSO validation. The fusion model achieved 97.2% accuracy, 96.9% precision, 97.8% recall, 97.3% F1, 0.989 ± 0.012 AUC, and 3.6% FPR, with ≈50 ms per frame latency (~20 fps). Few-shot personalization recovered ≥95% of baseline performance with K = 5 labeled sequences. The detailed results are shown in Figures 4–6 and Table 1. Latency and few-shot results are provided in Supplementary Materials.

Table 1. Mean performance (±95% confidence intervals) under LOSO validation (N = 16). The metrics are computed per fold before averaging, with the best values shown in bold. Paired two-sided t-tests (Bimodal vs. IMU-only and Bimodal vs. Vision-only) are significant for all metrics ($p < 0.001$).

Method	Accuracy (%)	Precision (%)	Recall (%)	Specificity (%)	F1-Score (%)	FPR (%) [1]
IMU-only (LSTM)	90.3 ± 1.1%	89.6 ± 1.2%	91.7 ± 1.0%	88.7 ± 1.4%	90.6 ± 1.1%	11.3 ± 1.4%
Vision-only (Transformer)	92.9 ± 0.9%	92.2 ± 1.0%	94.0 ± 0.8%	91.1 ± 1.1%	93.1 ± 0.9%	8.9 ± 1.2%
Bimodal Late Fusion	**97.2 ± 0.6%**	**96.9 ± 0.6%**	**97.8 ± 0.5%**	**96.6 ± 0.7%**	**97.3 ± 0.6%**	**3.6 ± 0.6%**

[1] FPR = False Positive Rate.

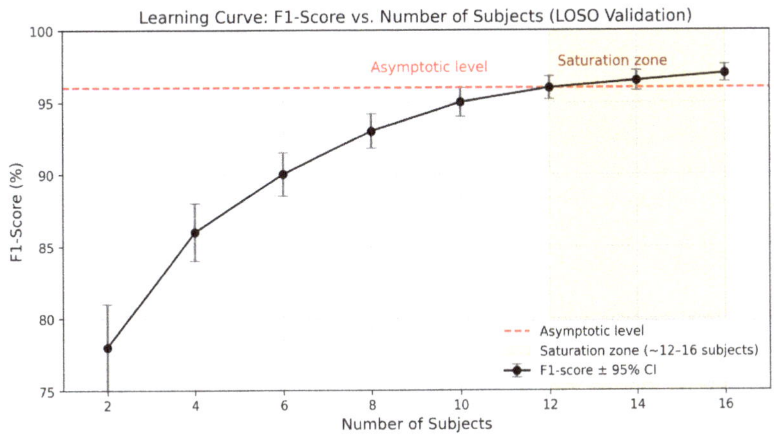

Figure 4. The red dashed line shows the estimated saturation level of the learning curve; error bars denote 95% confidence intervals. The shaded region ($n \geq 12$) marks the plateau.

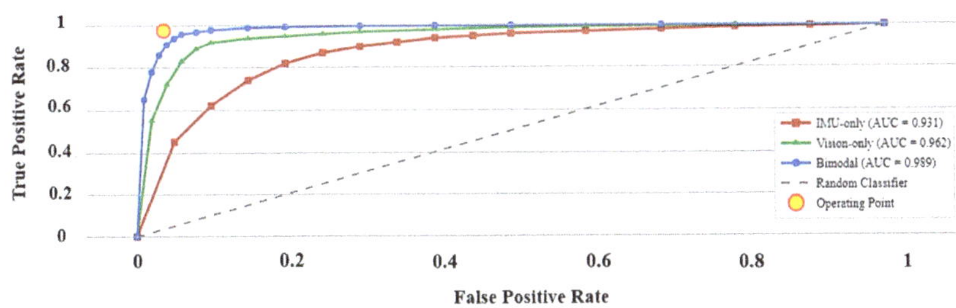

Figure 5. ROC Curves for the IMU-only LSTM auto-encoder, the vision-only Transformer, and the proposed bimodal late-fusion detector after 16 LOSO folds. The corresponding AUC means confirm the superior sensitivity–specificity trade-off of the fusion approach.

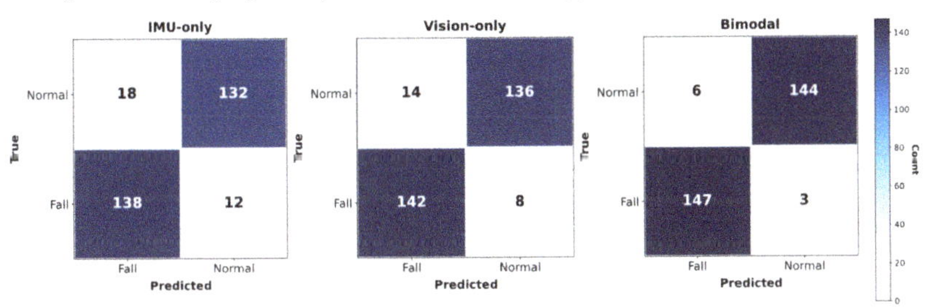

Figure 6. Typical confusion matrix over one LOSO fold ($N = 16$) for FALL versus NORMAL detections. Compared to the IMU baseline, the bimodal model reduces the false positive rate by 67% and the false negative rate by 75%, and compared to the vision baseline, those reductions are 57% and 63%, respectively.

5.1. Learning-Curve Analysis and Cohort Adequacy

Following the procedure in Section 4.10, the subject-wise learning curve in Figure 4 shows steep gains up to N = 10–12 participants before reaching a plateau at F1 = 96–97%. The red dashed line in Figure 4 marks the estimated asymptotic performance level $\hat{a}$, obtained by fitting a saturating exponential $F_1(n) = a - b\,e^{-cn}$ to the LOSO points (n = 2...16). The fitted asymptote is $\hat{a} = 96.7\%$ (95% CI: 96.2–97.2%), and this result supports our choice of N = 16 for the present study, since the corresponding performance score of 97% is consistent with this which is consistent with the obtained plateau, providing enough headroom beyond the performance knee while keeping the study practical by avoiding further participant recruitment.

5.2. Global Performance Comparison

To establish a quantitative baseline, the proposed bimodal late-fusion model was systematically benchmarked against two unimodal configurations: (i) an IMU-only abnormality detector based on an LSTM autoencoder, and (ii) a vision-only classifier based on a Transformer architecture. All models were evaluated under identical conditions using LOSO cross-validation. Table 1 presents the average performance metrics computed across the 16 LOSO folds, where each subject served once as the held-out test case. For each metric, the reported values correspond to the mean and 95% confidence interval. The bimodal architecture consistently outperformed both unimodal baselines on all metrics, achieving an accuracy of 97.2%, precision of 96.9%, recall of 97.8%, specificity of 96.6%, and an F1-score of 97.3%. These gains were statistically significant ($p < 0.001$, paired t-test), demonstrating the synergistic effect of integrating inertial and visual modalities.

5.3. Receiver-Operating Characteristics, Error Structure, and False-Alarm Control

The discriminative capacity of the proposed system was assessed along three complementary dimensions: global ROC-based performance, class-specific error structure, and false-alarm suppression. These axes jointly characterize the model's reliability under real-world deployment conditions. Figure 5 shows the obtained Receiver Operating Characteristic (ROC) curves computed across all LOSO validation folds. The proposed bimodal late-fusion system achieved an area under the curve (AUC) of 0.989 ± 0.012, markedly surpassing the vision-only Transformer (0.962 ± 0.015) and the IMU-only LSTM autoencoder (0.931 ± 0.018). These values confirm a superior trade-off between sensitivity and specificity for the bimodal system.

Confusion matrices were built to visualize the classification performance of the proposed late fusion bimodal model and two single-modal models used for comparison; Figure 6 shows an example from a single LOSO fold, leading to two key observations. First, the bimodal false positive rate is 67% lower than the IMU baseline and 57% lower than the vision baseline. Second, the false negative rate is concomitantly reduced by 75% and 63%, respectively. Using micro-averaging across all folds shows the global false-positive rate dropping from 11.3% (IMU) and 8.9% (vision) to only 3.6% under the proposed late fusion architecture. Such suppression of unnecessary alarms is critical for long-term, unobtrusive monitoring in domestic environments, where false alerts can undermine user confidence and compliance.

5.4. Computational Performance

A detailed latency decomposition is provided in the Supplementary Materials, including Table S1 and Figure S1.

5.5. Few-Shot Personalization Analysis

The subject-specific adaptation results are presented in Supplementary Materials (Figure S2), showing that $\geq$95% of baseline performance is recovered with only five labeled sequences.

6. Discussion

Under LOSO cross-validation with $N = 16$, the proposed CPU-only bimodal late-fusion framework achieved 97.2% accuracy, 97.8% recall, F1 = 97.3%, and FPR = 3.6%, while sustaining $\approx$20 fps ($\approx$50 ms per frame). Requiring agreement between modalities consistently reduced false alarms relative to unimodal baselines without sacrificing sensitivity—

essential for long-term acceptability in home monitoring. The learning-curve analysis (Section 5.1) shows performance gains saturate at F1 $\approx$ 96–97% beyond $\approx$12 subjects, supporting the adequacy of $N = 16$ for this pilot. Latency is dominated by pose-landmark extraction; Transformer/LSTM inference overheads are small and decision-level fusion is negligible, confirming feasibility for edge deployment under nocturnal conditions.

6.1. Benefits of Decision-Level Fusion over Unimodal and Early-Fusion Approaches

The IMU stream (LSTM autoencoder) is sensitive to sharp accelerometric impulses but can misclassify abrupt yet benign transitions (e.g., rapid sitting), whereas the vision stream (Transformer over 2D landmarks) captures postural context but degrades under occlusion and low light. Processing streams independently and fusing at the decision stage prevents the noise propagation typical of early fusion, reducing FPR from 11.3% (IMU-only) and 8.9% (vision only) to 3.6% while maintaining high recall (97.8%) and AUC = 0.989 $\pm$ 0.012 (Section 5.2). Under dim lighting, Li et al. [5] report 90.2% accuracy with a 12% FPR, while Feng et al. [34] achieve <2% FPR in controlled labs using depth cameras; our approach attains 97.2% accuracy with a 3.6% FPR in realistic nocturnal scenes using commodity RGB+IMU, narrowing the gap without specialized hardware.

6.2. Real-Time Execution and Latency Profile

On a modest CPU platform such as one using the Intel Core i5-8265U, the end-to-end inference time is $\approx$50.0 $\pm$ 4.7 ms per frame. The pose-landmark extraction accounts for $\approx$62% of the runtime, while the Transformer and LSTM inferences are minor contributors, and the late fusion process adds a negligible cost. If additional speed is required, optimization should prioritize the landmark extraction (input down-sampling, quantization, or lighter keypoint backbones) rather than the fusion rule. On another front, and compared with IR/depth solutions, the commodity RGB hardware typically reduces device cost by $\approx$5–10$\times$ and avoids multi-sensor calibration, while our pipeline sustains AUC = 0.989 below 5 lux illumination.

6.3. Few-Shot Learning Capabilities and Personalization

In practical deployments, all the operating points are data-driven rather than hand-tuned. The IMU abnormality gate τ is initialized as the 95th percentile of training reconstruction errors, while the vision decision threshold and the fusion gate (both 0.70) are selected via ROC analysis on validation folds. At installation, an automatic calibration routine (i) records a brief baseline of normal activity (5–10 min) to update τ for the device, and (ii) optionally performs few-shot personalization ($\leq$5 short labeled sequences) to adapt the final fusion layer to the user and site. This procedure removes per-dataset manual tuning and yields stable operating points across environments.

6.4. Communication and Alerting Pipeline (Deployment Guidance)

For real-world deployment, a reliable communication layer is required to complement the proposed on-device fall detection framework. To this end, we specify a minimal, standards-based pipeline designed for home-care integration. In this architecture, the fall detection remains fully processed locally on the device to ensure privacy, and only the event metadata is transmitted externally, with the detections conveyed as authenticated MQTT/HTTPS messages including timestamp, confidence, and modality flags. The communication stack supports acknowledgment, retry with local buffering during temporary outages, and configurable escalation channels (e.g., SMS or automated voice calls) for high-confidence events. End-to-end alert latency is targeted at below 2 s, which is consistent with healthcare monitoring requirements. To guarantee auditability and maintain IMU–camera alignment, network time synchronization (e.g., NTP) is enforced.

This communication layer thus represents a practical requirement for deployment, allowing the seamless integration into assisted-living infrastructures and providing a foundation for future large-scale validation studies.

6.5. Population Considerations: Elderly Biomechanics

Elderly falls often exhibit lower peak accelerations, slower descent or seated-collapse patterns, and kyphotic posture. These traits can damp IMU impulses and shift pose dynamics. Accordingly, the system: (a) lengthens the temporal vote when slow descent is detected, (b) slightly relaxes the IMU abnormality gate under sustained low-energy deviations, and (c) prioritizes few-shot personalization to capture user-specific kinematics. A follow-up study with older adults will quantify these adaptations.

6.6. Deployment Outlook and Cost-Efficient Scalability

The data processing is performed on a device with a default skeleton-only retention policy (2D keypoints) with zero storage of RGB frames. If the frames must be retained (e.g., for audit), face/body blurring, encryption in transit and at rest, role-based access, and short retention with explicit consent must be applied. Moreover, the camera placement uses oblique viewpoints to reduce identifiability. In any case, the privacy settings can be configurable for consistency with application site policy.

6.7. Limitations and Future Work

This study involved healthy adults (30–50 s) and simulated falls under controlled nocturnal conditions with a single lateral RGB camera and waist IMU. Real-world clutter, multi-person scenes, and true elderly falls may introduce additional variance. Future work will expand to older cohorts and longitudinal deployments, explore on-device adaptive thresholds, evaluate 3D/IR variants where lighting permits, and integrate ambient sensors (e.g., pressure mats) for further false-alarm suppression.

7. Conclusions

The proposed decision-level IMU-RGB framework achieves 97.2% accuracy, 97.8% recall, and a 3.6% false-positive rate at ~20 fps on CPU-only hardware, indicating practical readiness for nighttime home monitoring. Automatic calibration and few-shot personalization remove manual tuning and adapt to user variability, supporting real-world deployment with on-device processing and configurable privacy safeguards.

Supplementary Materials: The following supporting information can be downloaded at: https://www.mdpi.com/article/10.3390/s25196035/s1.

Author Contributions: Conceptualization, H.R. and M.B.; methodology, H.R.; software, H.R.; validation, H.R.; investigation, H.R.; resources, H.R.; data curation, H.R.; writing—original draft preparation, H.R.; writing—review and editing, M.B.; supervision, M.B.; All authors have read and agreed to the published version of the manuscript.

Funding: This research was partially funded by the NSERC, Canada.

Data Availability Statement: The original contributions presented in this study are included in the article/Supplementary Materials. Further inquiries can be directed to the corresponding authors.

Conflicts of Interest: The authors declare no conflict of interest.

References

1. Wang, X.; Ellul, J.; Azzopardi, G. Elderly Fall Detection Systems: A Literature Survey. *Front. Robot. AI* **2020**, *7*, 71. [CrossRef]
2. Iguchi, Y.; Lee, J.H.; Okamoto, S. Enhancement of Fall Detection Algorithm Using Convolutional Autoencoder and Personalized Threshold. In Proceedings of the Digest of Technical Papers—IEEE International Conference on Consumer Electronics, Las Vegas, NV, USA, 11–14 January 2021; pp. 1–4.
3. Figueiredo, I.N.; Leal, C.; Pinto, L.; Bolito, J.; Lemos, A. Exploring Smartphone Sensors for Fall Detection. *mUX J. Mob. User Exp.* **2016**, *5*, 2. [CrossRef]
4. Wang, C.T.; Liu, Z.; Chen, K.H. A Wearable Accelerometer System for Fall Detection in the Elderly. *IEEE Trans. Biomed. Eng.* **2016**, *63*, 2621–2627.
5. Li, X.Y.; Zhao, W.; Wang, R. Vision-Based Fall Detection in Low-Light Environments. In Proceedings of the IEEE ICCV Workshops, Venice, Italy, 22–29 October 2017; pp. 45–52.
6. Thompson, L.Z.; Lee, E.K.; Huang, C.M. SVM Classification of Accelerometer Data for Fall Detection. *Eng. Appl. Artif. Intell.* **2016**, *55*, 253–262.
7. Malekzadeh, M.; Clegg, R.G.; Cavallaro, A.; Haddadi, H. Mobile Sensor Data Anonymization. In Proceedings of the 2019 IEEE International Conference on Pervasive Computing and Communications (PerCom), Kyoto, Japan, 11–15 March 2019; pp. 1–10.
8. Vaswani, A.; Shazeer, N.; Parmar, N.; Uszkoreit, J.; Jones, L.; Gomez, A.N.; Kaiser, L.; Polosukhin, I. Attention Is All You Need. In Proceedings of the Advances in Neural Information Processing Systems 30 (NeurIPS 2017), Long Beach, CA, USA, 4–9 December 2017; Guyon, I., Luxburg, U.V., Bengio, S., Wallach, H., Fergus, R., Vishwanathan, S., Garnett, R., Eds.; Curran Associates, Inc.: Red Hook, NY, USA, 2017; pp. 5998–6008.
9. Wang, Y.; Yao, Q.; Kwok, J.T.; Ni, L.M. Generalizing from a Few Examples: A Survey on Few-Shot Learning. *ACM Comput. Surv.* **2020**, *53*, 63. [CrossRef]
10. Fang, H.A.; Tsai, T.; Pal, A. Pose-Based Fall Detection via Skeleton Analysis. *Pattern Recognit. Lett.* **2019**, *120*, 144–149.
11. Bian, Z.-P.; Hou, J.; Chau, L.-P.; Magnenat Thalmann, N. Fall Detection Based on Body Part Tracking Using a Depth Camera. *IEEE J. Biomed. Health Inform.* **2015**, *19*, 430–439. [CrossRef]
12. Roberts, M.C.; Varghese, P.; Guo, L. Privacy-Preserving Video Monitoring for Assisted Living. *J. Ambient. Intell. Smart Environ.* **2019**, *11*, 211–224.
13. Hochreiter, S.; Schmidhuber, J. Long Short-Term Memory. *Neural Comput.* **1997**, *9*, 1735–1780. [CrossRef]
14. Yu, X.; Feng, Z.; Wang, H.; Tang, Y.; Zhang, Y. A Novel Semi-Supervised Model for Pre-Impact Fall Detection with Limited Fall Data. *Eng. Appl. Artif. Intell.* **2024**, *132*, 108469. [CrossRef]
15. Kepski, M.; Kwolek, B. Fall Detection Using Ceiling-Mounted 3D Depth Camera. In Proceedings of the VISAPP 2014—Proceedings of the 9th International Conference on Computer Vision Theory and Applications, Lisbon, Portugal, 5–8 January 2014; pp. 423–428.
16. Zambanini, S.; Machajdik, J.; Kampel, M. Early versus Late Fusion in a Multiple Camera Network for Fall Detection. In Proceedings of the Workshop of the Austrian Association for Pattern Recognition, Vienna, Austria, 10–11 September 2010; AAPR: Vienna, Austria, 2010; pp. 1–6.
17. Baltrusaitis, T.; Ahuja, C.; Morency, L.P. Multimodal Machine Learning: A Survey and Taxonomy. *IEEE Trans. Pattern Anal. Mach. Intell.* **2019**, *41*, 423–443. [CrossRef]
18. Lachekhab, F.; Benzaoui, M.; Tadjer, S.A.; Bensmaine, A. LSTM-Autoencoder Deep Learning Model for Abnormality Detection in Electric Motor. *Energies* **2024**, *17*, 2340. [CrossRef]
19. Kibet, D.; Muthee, R.; Wafula, C.; Muriuki, G. Sudden Fall Detection of Human Body Using Transformer Model. *Sensors* **2024**, *24*, 8051. [CrossRef] [PubMed]
20. Lee, J.-S.; Tseng, H.-H. Enhanced Threshold-Based Fall Detection Using Smartphones. *IEEE Sens. J.* **2019**, *19*, 8293–8302. [CrossRef]
21. Cai, W.; Qiu, L.; Li, W.; Yu, J.; Wang, L. Practical Fall Detection Algorithm Based on AdaBoost. In Proceedings of the Proceedings of the ACM International Conference on Biomedical Signal and Image Processing, New York, NY, USA, 13–15 March 2019; pp. 1–5.
22. Lai, C.-F.; Chang, S.-Y.; Chao, H.-C. Detection of Cognitive Injured Body Region Using Multiple Triaxial Accelerometers for Elderly Falling. *IEEE Sens. J.* **2011**, *11*, 763–770. [CrossRef]
23. Balli, S.; Sagbas, E.A.; Peker, M. Human Activity Recognition from Smart Watch Sensor Data Using PCA and Random Forest. *Meas. Control* **2019**, *52*, 37–45. [CrossRef]
24. Hakim, A.; Huq, M.S.; Shanta, S.; Ibrahim, B.S. Smartphone-Based Data Mining for Fall Detection. *Procedia Comput. Sci.* **2017**, *105*, 46–51. [CrossRef]
25. Zhang, J.; Li, Z.; Liu, Y.; Li, J.; Qiu, H.; Li, M.; Hou, G.; Zhou, Z. An Effective Deep Learning Framework for Fall Detection: Model Development and Study Design. *J. Med. Internet Res.* **2024**, *26*, e56750. [CrossRef]
26. Espinosa, R.; Ponce, H.; Gutiérrez, S.; Martínez-Villaseñor, L.; Brieva, J.; Moya-Albor, E. A vision-based approach for fall detection using multiple cameras and convolutional neural networks: A case study using the UP-Fall detection dataset. *Comput. Methods Programs Biomed.* **2019**, *115*, 103520.

27. Rafferty, J.; Synnott, J.; Nugent, C.; Morrison, G.; Tamburini, E. *Fall Detection Through Thermal Vision Sensing*; Springer: Cham, Switzerland, 2016; pp. 84–90.
28. Willems, J.; Debard, G.; Vanrumste, B.; Goedemé, T. *A Video-Based Algorithm for Elderly Fall Detection*; Springer: Berlin/Heidelberg, Germany, 2009; pp. 312–315.
29. Kwolek, B.; Kepski, M. Human Fall Detection on Embedded Platform Using Depth Maps and Wireless Accelerometer. *Comput. Methods Programs Biomed.* **2014**, *117*, 489–501. [CrossRef]
30. Martínez-Villaseñor, L.; Ponce, H.; Brieva, J.; Moya-Albor, E.; Núñez-Martínez, J.; Peñafort-Asturiano, C. Up-Fall Detection Dataset: A Multimodal Approach. *Sensors* **2019**, *19*, 1988. [CrossRef]
31. Ozcan, K.; Velipasalar, S.; Varshney, P.K. Autonomous Fall Detection with Wearable Cameras by Using Relative Entropy Distance Measure. *IEEE Trans. Hum. Mach. Syst.* **2016**, *47*, 1–9. [CrossRef]
32. Castillo, J.C.; Carneiro, D.; Serrano-Cuerda, J.; Novais, P.; Fernández-Caballero, A.; Neves, J. A Multi-Modal Approach for Activity Classification and Fall Detection. *Int. J. Syst. Sci.* **2014**, *45*, 810–824. [CrossRef]
33. Shin, J.; Miah, A.S.M.; Egawa, R.; Hassan, N.; Hirooka, K.; Tomioka, Y. Multimodal Fall Detection Using Spatial-Temporal Attention and Bi-LSTM-Based Feature Fusion. *Future Internet* **2025**, *17*, 173. [CrossRef]
34. Feng, P.; Yu, M.; Naqvi, S.M.; Chambers, J.A. Deep Learning for Posture Analysis in Fall Detection. In Proceedings of the Proceedings of the IEEE Digital Signal Processing Conference, Hong Kong, China, 20–23 August 2014; pp. 12–17.
35. Cash, J.J. Alert Fatigue. *Am. J. Health-Syst. Pharm.* **2009**, *66*, 2098–2101. [CrossRef]
36. Liu, C.-L.; Lee, C.-H.; Lin, P.-M. A Fall Detection System Using K-Nearest Neighbor Classifier. *Expert. Syst. Appl.* **2010**, *37*, 7174–7181. [CrossRef]
37. Lugaresi, C.; Tang, J.; Nash, H.; McClanahan, C.; Uboweja, E.; Hays, M.; Zhang, F.; Chang, C.-L.; Yong, M.G.; Lee, J.; et al. MediaPipe: A Framework for Perceiving and Processing Reality. In Proceedings of the IEEE CVPR Workshops, Long Beach, CA, USA, 16–20 June 2019; pp. 1–9.
38. Bazarevsky, P.; Kartynnik, Y.; Grishchenko, I.; Grundmann, M. BlazePose: On-Device Real-Time Body Pose Tracking. Available online: https://arxiv.org/abs/2006.10204 (accessed on 15 June 2025).
39. Kingma, D.P.; Ba, J.L. Adam: A Method for Stochastic Optimization. In Proceedings of the 3rd International Conference on Learning Representations, San Diego, CA, USA, 7–9 May 2015.
40. Bergstra, J.; Bengio, Y. Random Search for Hyper-Parameter Optimization. *J. Mach. Learn. Res.* **2012**, *13*, 281–305.
41. Hastie, T.; Tibshirani, R.; Friedman, J. *The Elements of Statistical Learning*, 2nd ed.; Springer: New York, NY, USA, 2009; p. 27.
42. Google AI for Developers. Pose Landmark Detection Guide—MediaPipe Documentation. 2025. Available online: https://ai.google.dev/edge/mediapipe/solutions/vision/pose_landmarker#pose_landmarker_model (accessed on 20 May 2025).

sensors

MDPI

Article

Office Posture Detection Using Ceiling-Mounted Ultra-Wideband Radar and Attention-Based Modality Fusion

Wei Lu [1,2], Christopher Bird [1,3], Moid Sandhu [1,4] and David Silvera-Tawil [1,5,*]

1 Australian e-Health Research Centre, Commonwealth Scientific and Industrial Research Organisation (CSIRO), Brisbane, QLD 4029, Australia; wei.lu@csiro.au (W.L.)
2 School of Electrical Engineering and Computer Science, The University of Queensland, Brisbane, QLD 4072, Australia
3 School of Biomedical Sciences, The University of Queensland, Brisbane, QLD 4072, Australia
4 School of Computer Science, Queensland University of Technology, Brisbane, QLD 4000, Australia
5 International Centre for Future Health Systems, University of New South Wales, Sydney, NSW 2052, Australia
* Correspondence: david.silvera-tawil@csiro.au

Abstract

Prolonged sedentary behavior in office environments is a key risk factor for musculoskeletal disorders and metabolic health issues. While workplace stretching interventions can mitigate these risks, effective monitoring solutions are often limited by privacy concerns and constrained sensor placement. This study proposes a ceiling-mounted ultra-wideband (UWB) radar system for privacy-preserving classification of working and stretching postures in office settings. In this study, data were collected from ten participants in five scenarios: four posture classes (seated working, seated stretching, standing working, standing stretching), and empty environment. Distance and Doppler information extracted from the UWB radar signals was transformed into modality-specific images, which were then used as inputs to two classification models: *ConcatFusion*, a baseline model that fuses features by concatenation, and *AttnFusion*, which introduces spatial attention and convolutional feature integration. Both models were evaluated using leave-one-subject-out cross-validation. The *AttnFusion* model outperformed *ConcatFusion*, achieving a testing accuracy of 90.6% and a macro F1-score of 90.5%. These findings demonstrate the effectiveness of a ceiling-mounted UWB radar combined with attention-based modality fusion for unobtrusive office posture monitoring. The approach offers a privacy-preserving solution with potential applications in real-time ergonomic assessment and integration into workplace health and safety programs.

Keywords: ultra-wideband radar; human activity recognition; signal processing; machine learning; multimodal fusion; office ergonomics

1. Introduction

Prolonged sedentary behavior, a defining characteristic of modern office work, has been consistently linked to a range of adverse health outcomes, including musculoskeletal disorders, metabolic dysfunction, and premature mortality. Office workers typically spend approximately 65–75% of their working hours seated, often maintaining prolonged static postures that contribute to discomfort and chronic musculoskeletal pain, particularly in the neck, shoulders, and lower back [1]. In response, incorporating stretching and light activity into the workday has been shown to alleviate musculoskeletal discomfort and improve overall worker well-being. Structured workplace programs that incorporate

 https://doi.org/10.3390/s25165164

reminder-based interventions have been particularly effective in promoting compliance with recommended stretching and movement routines. For instance, reminder software has been shown to increase the frequency of stretch breaks, reduce perceived pain, and improve compliance with ergonomic health practices among computer users [2,3]. Moreover, randomized controlled studies and longitudinal workplace implementations have demonstrated that regular stretching sessions, guided by reminder software, structured group breaks, or device-assisted programs, can lead to a decrease in the prevalence of musculoskeletal disorders, particularly in the neck, shoulders, and lower back [4,5].

Recent advancements in sensing technologies have enabled a variety of systems designed to recognize sitting posture and promote office stretching, helping to mitigate risks associated with sedentary work styles. Camera-based solutions have been widely explored for workplace posture and stretch detection. Adolf et al. developed a system that utilizes a single RGB webcam and real-time pose estimation to evaluate stretching performance and provide augmented mirror feedback [6]. Similarly, Paliyawan et al. employed an RGB-D camera system to monitor skeletal posture and identify periods of prolonged sitting. This system classified motion states and offered real-time ergonomic feedback, demonstrating the feasibility of camera-based tracking for sedentary behavior monitoring [7]. In addition to camera-based methods, researchers have also investigated non-visual sensing approaches for posture monitoring in office environments. For example, Tavares et al. and Odesola et al. developed instrumented office chairs equipped with pressure mats or optical fiber arrays capable of detecting pressure distribution patterns and classifying seated postures [8,9]. Zhang et al. proposed a multimodal approach combining pressure and infrared sensors to enhance posture recognition while maintaining user privacy [10]. In a follow-up study, Zhang et al. integrated pressure and spatial temperature data to further improve classification performance [11]. While these methods provide effective posture recognition, they are subject to several limitations. Camera-based systems raise privacy concerns, are susceptible to occlusion in cluttered workspaces, and often require careful sensor placement and lighting conditions. Smart chair systems, while unobtrusive, are restricted to seated postures and cannot effectively capture dynamic stretch-related movements such as arm raises or standing stretches. Furthermore, the multimodal systems, particularly those with sensors mounted vertically on desks or walls, are limited in their ability to capture transitional or full-body stretching due to restricted fields of view and potential occlusion by furniture [9,12].

To address these limitations, we propose a ceiling-mounted ultra-wideband (UWB) radar system for office stretch detection that balances unobtrusiveness, privacy preservation, and robust posture monitoring. UWB radar is a low-power, high-resolution sensing technology that operates by emitting short-duration electromagnetic pulses and analyzing their reflections to detect the motion and position of objects in the environment. While existing UWB radar studies have primarily focused on applications such as sleep posture monitoring, fall detection, and human pose estimation, their findings demonstrate the potential of UWB radar for sensing posture-related activities. For instance, Lai et al. demonstrated that a dual UWB radar configuration can accurately classify sleep postures, showing the technology's ability to detect subtle body movements from above, even under occlusion and varying environmental conditions [13]. Similarly, Lu et al. employed a ceiling-mounted UWB radar to detect falls in cluttered indoor environments, achieving high classification accuracy through convolutional neural networks trained on distance-time waveform images, suggesting that ceiling-mounted radars can effectively capture complex full-body transitions [14]. Zhou et al. further extended the capabilities of UWB radar by demonstrating micro-Doppler-based human pose estimation, capturing limb-specific kinematic signatures without requiring direct line-of-sight [15]. Collectively, these studies demonstrate the capacity of UWB radar systems to unobtrusively monitor diverse postural behaviors, suggesting their suitability for detecting workplace stretching activities from an overhead perspective. Building on this foundation, our work introduces a ceiling-mounted UWB radar system specifically designed to classify both working and stretching activities in office environments. By leveraging both distance and Doppler signal information captured from an overhead perspective, our system differentiates five workplace scenarios: seated working, seated stretching, standing working, standing stretching, and empty environment.

The main contributions of this study are as follows:

- This study introduces a ceiling-mounted UWB radar configuration tailored for office environments. Unlike prior systems for office posture detection using desk-mounted devices [7,10–12] or chair sensors [8–12], this overhead setup offers a wide field of view and reduces potential occlusion, enabling robust monitoring of workspace postures.
- The proposed system is specifically designed to detect working and stretching postures in both seated and standing positions. By capturing these real-world office behaviors, the system enables practical monitoring to support ergonomic interventions.
- The classification model utilizes distance and Doppler information from radar signals and achieved a testing accuracy of 90.6% with leave-one-subject-out cross-validation.

2. Materials and Methods

2.1. Radar Configurations

The UWB radar used in this study is a compact monostatic UWB radar module (P440, TDSR LLC., Petersburg, VA, USA) that includes a programmable radar unit and two planar elliptical dipole antennas. Detailed specifications for the radar and antennas are provided in Tables 1 and 2. Operating as a monostatic radar, a short-duration, low-power electromagnetic pulse is emitted by the transmitting antenna, and the receiving antenna captures the reflected signals from objects in the environment. Operating in a monostatic setup, the radar system emits short-duration, low-power electromagnetic pulses via the transmitting antenna. The receiving antenna, co-located with the transmitter, captures the reflected signals from objects within the environment. The time-domain response of these reflections, with amplitude recorded as a function of propagation delay, forms a single radar frame. Each frame may include components from cross-antenna interference as well as reflections from targets located at varying distances. A typical signal frame is shown in Figure 1a. The temporal axis of a single frame, referred to as fast time, is measured in nanoseconds and corresponds to the propagation delay of the transmitted pulse, which directly relates to the distance of objects from the radar. The radar system captures one frame every 12 ms, corresponding to a frame rate of approximately 83.3 Hz. When multiple frames are acquired sequentially and aligned over time, they form a two-dimensional matrix in which the second axis, referred to as slow time, captures changes over longer durations, typically on the order of seconds. Figure 1b illustrates an example of consecutive frames acquired over a 4.8 s interval in slow time, with each frame capturing distance-related information in fast time.

Table 1. Radar specifications.

Parameter	Value
Operating band	3.1–4.8 GHz
Pulse repetition rate	10 MHz
Transmission power	~50 μW
Transfer switch isolation	~20 dB
Receive noise fatigue	~4.8 Hz

Table 2. Antenna specifications.

Parameter	Value
Polarization	Vertical
VSWR	~1.75:1
S11	~12 dB
Gain	~3 dBi
Phase response	Linear

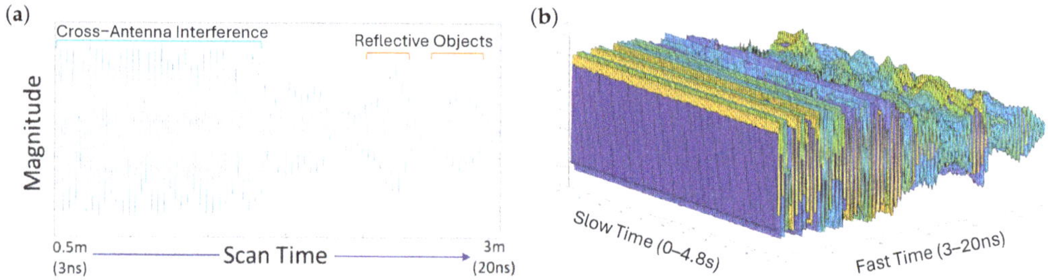

Figure 1. Examples of UWB radar signals: (**a**) a single radar frame illustrating cross-antenna interference and multiple reflected returns from surrounding objects; (**b**) consecutive radar frames collected over a 4.8 s interval. Each frame captures the reflected signal in fast time, and the frames are stacked along the slow time axis to show a longer duration.

For posture monitoring, the radar was mounted on the ceiling directly above the office worker's desk, with its antennas oriented downward to capture movement and posture within the workspace, as shown in Figure 2. The room measured 5.0 m × 5.0 m × 2.6 m (length, width, height), with the desk positioned at the center of the room. The desk height was set to 0.75 m for the sitting configuration and 1.0 m for the standing configuration. The office chair had a seat height of 0.5 m. It should be noted that the scan duration for a single frame was configured to allow a maximum path distance of 6 m (i.e., 3 m in one direction), exceeding the distance from the radar to the participant and desk setup. A laptop was connected to two monitors placed on the desk, along with a keyboard and a mouse, to simulate a typical office workstation. The radar was connected to a computer running a custom software tool designed for data acquisition.

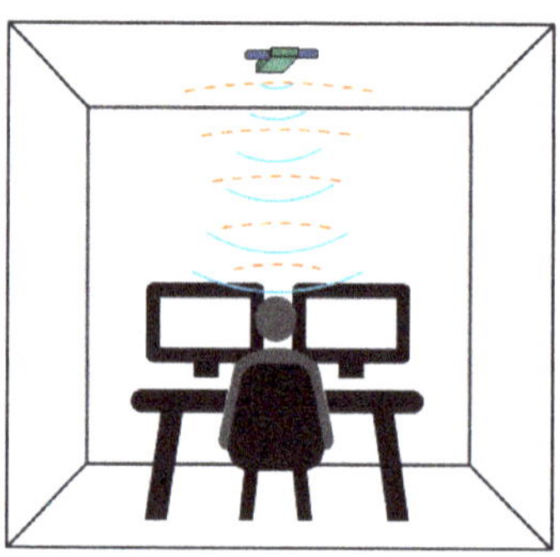

Figure 2. Setup of the ceiling-mounted UWB radar positioned above a standard office workstation. The radar is oriented downward to capture movement and posture within the workspace, accommodating both seated and standing desk configurations.

2.2. Data Collection

Posture detection using UWB radar in an office environment was formulated as a five-class classification task, using the following categories: seated working, seated stretching, standing working, standing stretching, and empty environment (i.e., when no person is present in the monitored area). These classes were selected to capture typical workplace behaviors relevant to sedentary risk assessment and ergonomic intervention [1,16].

To collect training and evaluation data for the posture classification model, a data collection trial was conducted with approval (2023_007_R) from the Health and Medical Human Research Ethics Committee of Commonwealth Scientific and Industrial Research Organisation (CSIRO). Ten adult participants (5 males and 5 females; average age 26.5 ± 7.1 years) were recruited to complete a protocol simulating office work and stretching activities. Eligibility criteria included being at least 18 years of age, able to read and speak English, and physically capable of performing light stretching and standing tasks. Individuals with pre-existing injuries or mobility restrictions were excluded from participation.

During each trial, the radar system was connected to a computer for data acquisition. A custom graphical user interface (GUI) guided participants through four posture tasks, each lasting 3 min: seated working, seated stretching, standing working, and standing stretching (Figure 3). The working tasks involved typical computer-based interactions such as typing and mouse clicking. The stretching routines were adapted from WorkSafe Victoria's ergonomic exercise guidelines, which recommend short, simple movements that can be performed without special equipment in typical office settings (e.g., shoulder rolls, pectoral stretch, and head turns) [17]. These guidelines are widely used in workplace health programs in Australia and emphasize stretches targeting the neck, shoulder, and arm areas most affected by prolonged seated or standing computer work. Illustrations of the stretching postures are provided in the Appendix A (Figure A1). Following the seated tasks, the desk was reconfigured to a standing desk to facilitate the standing activities. In addition to the four participant tasks, separate recordings were made under the "empty" condition to represent unoccupied workspace scenarios. An overview of the data collection protocol is summarized in Table 3. In total, the dataset comprised 120 min of posture data, including 12 min per participant across four postures, and 30 min of radar data under empty condition (Figure 4).

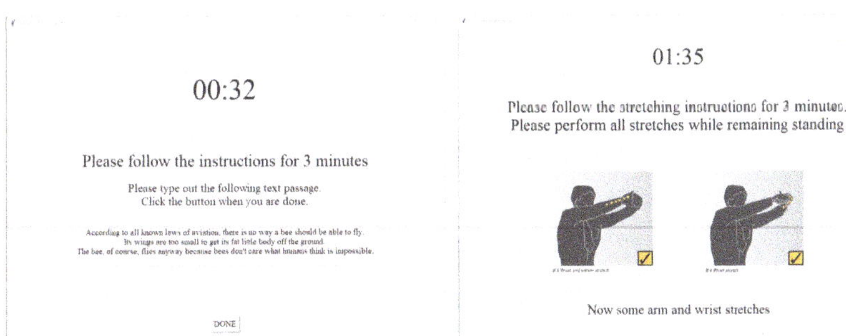

Figure 3. GUI used during data collection. The interface guided participants through a sequence of four posture tasks: seated working, seated stretching, standing working, and standing stretching, with each task lasting three minutes.

Table 3. Protocol for the data collection trial.

Class	Description
Seated working	Typing, mouse clicking, and reading while seated
Seated stretching	Stretching exercises while seated
Standing working	Typing, mouse clicking, and reading while standing
Standing stretching	Stretching exercises while standing
Empty	No person present in the workspace

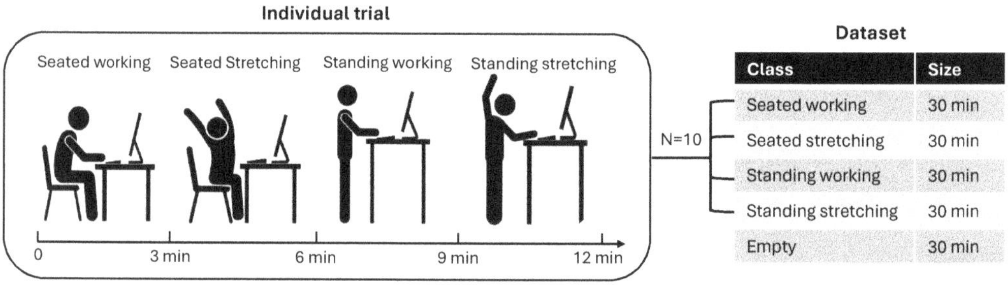

Figure 4. Overview of the data collection process. Ten participants (N = 10) were guided by a custom GUI to perform each posture class for 3 min. Additionally, 30 min of data were recorded under the "empty" condition, representing an unoccupied workspace.

2.3. *Signal Processing*

In order to characterize occupancy states and human postures, the collected radar data were processed to generate distance and Doppler images. The distance image captures the changes in spatial reflections over time, providing information about the relative position and movement of objects in the monitored area. The Doppler image captures velocity-related information by representing frequency shifts over time, reflecting the motion dynamics of observed objects.

2.3.1. Distance Image

As the first step in distance image processing, the original radar frames were augmented by sub-sampling to produce four sub-sequences of the data. Specifically, the sub-sampling was performed with a stride of four, starting from different initial frames. Let $\mathbf{X} = \{x_0, x_1, x_2, \dots, x_{N-1}\}$ denote the original radar frames collected at a frame period of 12 ms. The four sub-sequences were generated by:

$$\mathbf{X}^{(o)} = \{x_{o+4k} \mid k = 0, 1, 2, \dots\}, \quad o \in \{0, 1, 2, 3\} \tag{1}$$

Each $\mathbf{X}^{(o)}$ represents a temporally shifted version of the data with an effective frame period of 48 ms. This processing generates four sub-sequences from the same recording window. For example, the 12 min of posture data recorded per participant were sub-sampled into four temporally shifted 12 min sequences, effectively augmenting the data by four times. A distance image was constructed using 4.8 s segments from the sub-sequence, corresponding to 100 frames per image. These segments were extracted using a sliding window with 75% overlap between consecutive windows. To construct a distance image from each 4.8 s segment, every frame within the segment was first band-pass filtered along the fast time axis using a predefined infinite impulse response (IIR) filter, attenuating low-frequency background signals and high-frequency noise. The filtered signal was then processed along the slow time axis using a high-pass finite impulse response (FIR) filter, isolating areas of dynamic activity (e.g., motion due to posture changes). The resulting signal comprises 96 frames, as the first few frames were removed to eliminate edge effects from the FIR filtering. To enhance the signal's magnitude and emphasize motion-related features, an absolute value transformation was applied, followed by a low-pass IIR filter to extract the motion-related signal envelope over time. Finally, residual low-level noise was attenuated using a non-linear amplitude squashing function resembling a sigmoid function:

$$x_0 = \frac{x}{1 + 1.05^{-x+30}} \tag{2}$$

This series of operations produced distance images that represent changes in range intensity over time, capturing body movements relative to the radar. Each image has a final resolution of 96 × 288, corresponding to the number of retained slow-time frames and fast-time bins after filtering. The complete distance image generation pipeline is shown in Figure 5. In total, 26,000 distance images were extracted from the original radar data, comprising 5200 images per class across the four postures and the empty scenario.

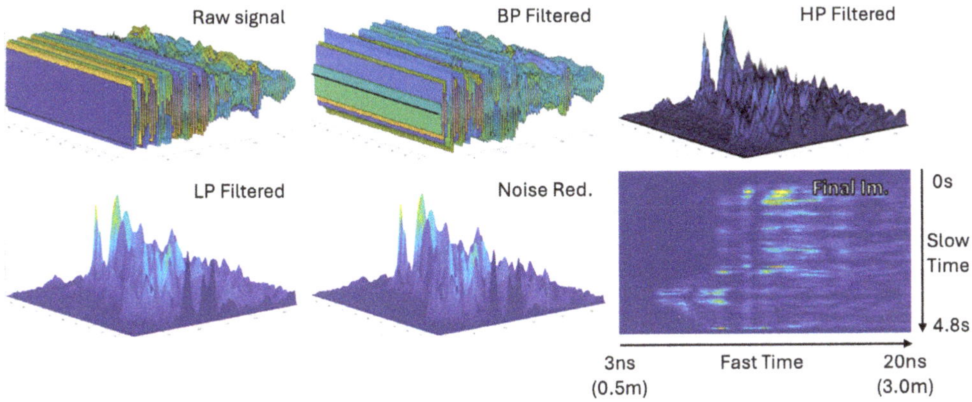

Figure 5. Step-by-step illustration of the distance image generation.

2.3.2. Doppler Image

Doppler images were generated by first applying a short-time Fourier transform (STFT) to the full duration of each original radar recording, for example, the 12 min posture data from each participant. The STFT was computed using a 996 ms window, corresponding to 83 frames sampled at a 12 ms frame period. Within the STFT window, each frame was processed with a Hilbert transform along the fast time axis, and a Kaiser window (β = 6) was applied along the slow time axis. The STFT was then performed along the slow time axis, and the mean across the fast time axis was used to compute each row of the Doppler image. To improve temporal resolution, an overlap with a 9-frame increment (approximately 90% overlap) was applied between consecutive windows, effectively sliding the STFT window across the entire recording. The resulting Doppler representation shows the relative velocities of objects moving toward or away from the radar over the full recording duration. Finally, Doppler images were extracted as 4.8 s segments from the full Doppler representation using time windows matching those used for distance image construction. The resulting Doppler images have a resolution of 50 × 80, representing the number of time frames and Doppler frequency bins extracted from the STFT. The Doppler image generation pipeline is illustrated Figure 6.

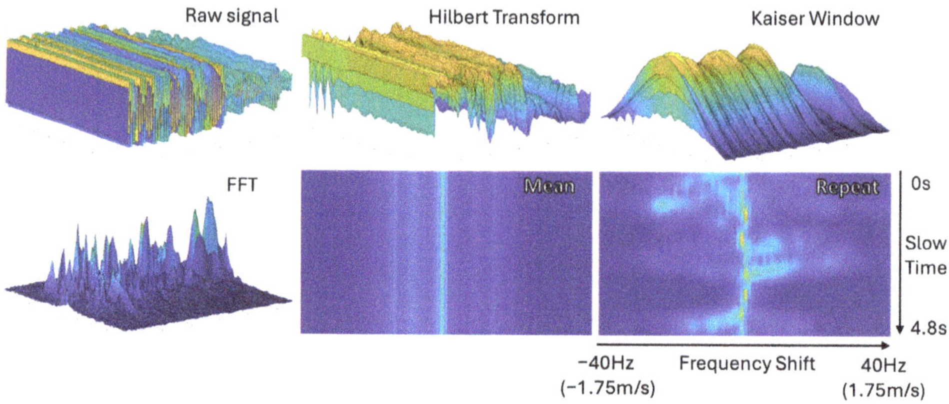

Figure 6. Step-by-step illustration of the Doppler image generation.

2.3.3. Normalization

Both the distance and Doppler images were normalized to the range 0–255 and saved as 8-bit single-channel images. These normalized images were then used as input to the classification models to distinguish between different postures and the empty environment.

2.4. Classification Models

The classification task aims to predict the class label based on dual-modality radar inputs: a distance image and a Doppler image. Each sample is represented as $\mathcal{X} = (\mathbf{X}_d, \mathbf{X}_v)$, where $\mathbf{X}_d \in \mathbb{R}^{1\times 96\times 288}$ is the single-channel distance image and $\mathbf{X}_v \in \mathbb{R}^{1\times 50\times 80}$ is the corresponding Doppler image. The associated label $y \in \mathcal{Y}$ denotes one of five classes: seated working, seated stretching, standing working, standing stretching, or empty environment. The training objective is to learn a function $f : \mathcal{X} = (\mathbf{X}_d, \mathbf{X}_v) \rightarrow y$ that maps each sample $\mathcal{X}$ to its corresponding class label y. Two deep learning models were developed for this classification task. Both models adopt a dual-stream convolutional neural network (CNN) architecture, in which modality-specific features are extracted from Doppler and distance representations using separate CNN blocks. The first model, *ConcatFusion*, implements a feature-level fusion approach in which modality-specific representations are concatenated prior to classification. The second model, *AttnFusion*, enhances this design by introducing spatial attention modules to emphasize informative regions in each modality and a deeper fusion block that integrates the refined features before classification. These models were implemented using Python 3.10.7 and PyTorch Lightning 2.5.1. Model performance was evaluated using leave-one-subject-out cross-validation (LOSO-CV), with accuracy, F1-score, precision, and recall as performance metrics.

2.4.1. *ConcatFusion*

The ConcatFusion model adopts a dual-stream CNN architecture that processes Doppler and distance images independently before fusing the learned features for classification. The architecture of the model is shown in Figure 7. The input images $\mathbf{X}_d, \mathbf{X}_v$ are passed through modality-specific CNN blocks:

$$\mathbf{F}_d = f_d(\mathbf{X}_d), \quad \mathbf{F}_v = f_v(\mathbf{X}_v) \tag{3}$$

where $f_d(\cdot)$ and $f_v(\cdot)$ are modality-specific CNN blocks, producing intermediate feature maps, $\mathbf{F}_d \in \mathbb{R}^{128\times 12\times 36}$ and $\mathbf{F}_v \in \mathbb{R}^{128\times 12\times 20}$. The Doppler CNN block uses a shallower architecture than the distance CNN block to account for the smaller input size of Doppler images. Each intermediate feature map is then passed through a global average pooling layer to generate global representations $\mathbf{G}_d, \mathbf{G}_v \in \mathbb{R}^{128\times1\times1}$. These are flattened to form the modality-specific embeddings $\mathbf{z}_d, \mathbf{z}_v \in \mathbb{R}^{128}$, which are then concatenated to produce a joint feature vector:

$$\mathbf{z} = [\mathbf{z}_d; \mathbf{z}_v] \in \mathbb{R}^{256} \tag{4}$$

The fused vector $\mathbf{z}$ is passed through a multilayer perceptron (MLP) classifier to produce the final classification result over the five predefined classes.

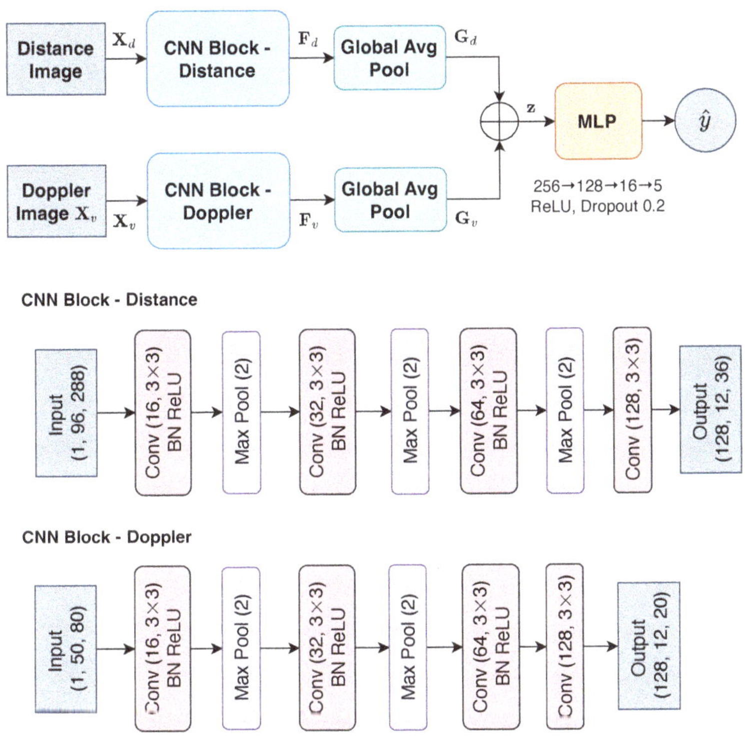

Figure 7. Architecture of the *ConcatFusion* model.

2.4.2. *AttnFusion*

The *AttnFusion* model extends the *ConcatFusion* architecture by incorporating spatial attention modules and a convolutional fusion block to enhance multimodal feature integration. The architecture of the model is shown in Figure 8. The distance and Doppler images are first passed through the same modality-specific CNN blocks as those used in the *ConcatFusion* model (Equation (3)). The outputs of the CNN blocks, $\mathbf{F}_d, \mathbf{F}_v$, are passed through an adaptive average pooling layer to produce fixed-size feature maps $\mathbf{F}_d^{\text{pool}}, \mathbf{F}_v^{\text{pool}} \in \mathbb{R}^{128\times4\times10}$. These pooled maps are then refined by a spatial attention module that creates a spatial attention mask that highlights informative regions by weighting spatial locations based on channel-wise statistics [18]. Specifically, the module first applies average and max pooling across the channel dimension, concatenates the results, and passes them through a shared convolutional layer with a 3×3 kernel and sigmoid activation. This convolutional layer has 2 input channels, corresponding to the pooled average and max features, and produces a single-channel attention mask $\mathcal{M}_s(\mathbf{F}) \in \mathbb{R}^{1\times4\times10}$:

$$\begin{aligned}\mathcal{M}_s(\mathbf{F}) &= \sigma\left(f^{3\times3}([\text{AvgPool}(\mathbf{F}); \text{MaxPool}(\mathbf{F})])\right) \\ &= \sigma\left(f^{3\times3}\left([\mathbf{F}_s^{\text{avg}}; \mathbf{F}_s^{\text{max}}]\right)\right), \quad \mathbf{F} \in \{\mathbf{F}_d^{\text{pool}}, \mathbf{F}_v^{\text{pool}}\}\end{aligned} \tag{5}$$

Then, $\mathbf{F}_d^{\text{pool}}$ and $\mathbf{F}_v^{\text{pool}}$ are multiplied element-wise with their corresponding attention mask across all channels to produce the attention-refined output, $\mathbf{F}_d^{\text{attn}}, \mathbf{F}_v^{\text{attn}} \in \mathbb{R}^{128\times4\times10}$, respectively. The attention-refined distance and Doppler features are concatenated along the channel dimension to form a fused representation:

$$\mathbf{F}_{\text{fused}} = [\mathbf{F}_d^{\text{attn}}; \mathbf{F}_v^{\text{attn}}] \in \mathbb{R}^{256\times4\times10} \tag{6}$$

This fused representation is processed by a convolutional fusion block, followed by global average pooling to generate a global presentation $\mathbf{G}_{\text{fused}} \in \mathbb{R}^{512\times1\times1}$. The output is then flattened to form a feature vector $\mathbf{z} \in \mathbb{R}^{512}$, which is passed through an MLP to produce the final classification result over the five predefined classes.

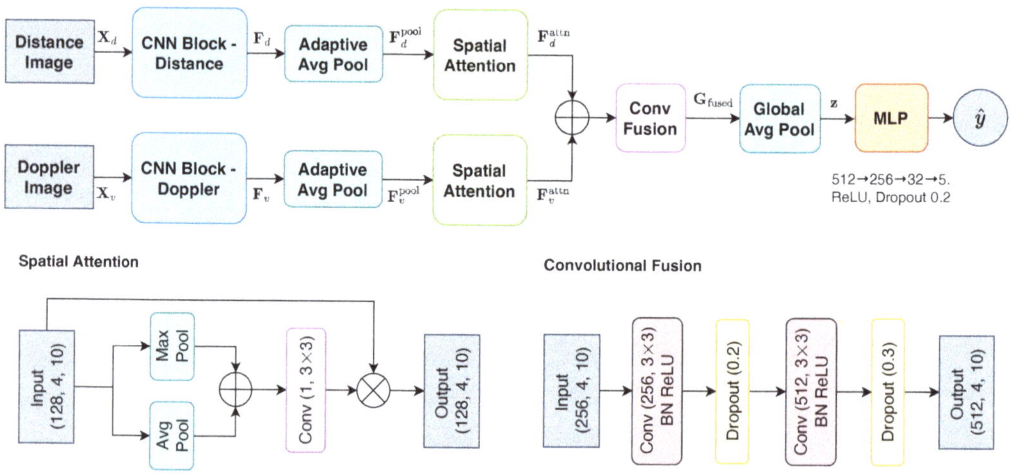

Figure 8. Architecture of the *AttnFusion*.

2.4.3. Training and Evaluation

Model performance was evaluated using LOSO-CV across 10 folds. In each fold, data from 10 participants were split into three groups: 8 for training, 1 for validation, and 1 for testing. This setup ensured that each participant was included once as the validation subject and once as the test subject, allowing for balanced evaluation across individuals. During each fold, the model was trained on the training subset, while the validation set was used to monitor convergence and apply early stopping to prevent overfitting. The model that achieved the highest validation accuracy was then evaluated on the held-out test subset. This process was repeated 10 times, producing 10 sets of performance metrics for each fold. The training hyperparameters are listed in the Appendix A (Table A1).

Performance metrics included accuracy, macro precision, macro recall, and macro F1-score, computed on the test subset of each fold. Let TP_k, FP_k, and FN_k denote the number of true positives, false positives, and false negatives for class k, respectively. Let K be the number of classes and N the total number of test samples. The accuracy is defined as:

$$\text{Accuracy} = \frac{1}{N}\sum_{k=1}^{K} TP_k \tag{7}$$

Macro precision, recall, and F1-score were computed by first evaluating each class independently and then averaging over the $K = 5$ classes. For class k, precision and recall are defined as:

$$\text{Precision}_k = \frac{TP_k}{TP_k + FP_k}, \quad \text{Recall}_k = \frac{TP_k}{TP_k + FN_k} \tag{8}$$

Macro precision, recall, and F1-score are then computed as:

$$\text{Macro Precision} = \frac{1}{K}\sum_{k=1}^{K} \text{Precision}_k, \quad \text{Macro Recall} = \frac{1}{K}\sum_{k=1}^{K} \text{Recall}_k \tag{9}$$

$$\text{Macro F1} = \frac{1}{K}\sum_{k=1}^{K} \frac{2 \cdot \text{Precision}_k \cdot \text{Recall}_k}{\text{Precision}_k + \text{Recall}_k} \tag{10}$$

To further assess the discriminative performance of the models for each class, aggregate receiver operating characteristic (ROC) curves were generated by combining all test samples from the 10 LOSO-CV folds. For each class, the ROC curve and corresponding area under the curve (AUC) were computed based on the aggregated test results, providing a summary of class-wise discriminative ability across all participants.

3. Results

This section presents the dataset details and overall model performance, including accuracy, F1-score, precision, and recall. Further analyses include per-class metrics, confusion matrices, ROC curves, and per-participant performance.

3.1. Dataset

A total of 26,000 samples were obtained from preprocessing the trial data, where each sample is represented as a pair of distance and Doppler images $\mathcal{X} = (\mathbf{X}_d, \mathbf{X}_v)$, along with a corresponding class label y. The dataset includes five categories: four postures (seated working, seated stretching, standing working, and standing stretching) and one empty condition, with 5200 samples per class. Each of the 10 participants contributed 520 samples per class, resulting in 2600 samples per participant. In the LOSO-CV setup, each fold uses 20,800 samples from 8 participants for training, 2600 samples from 1 participant for validation, and 2600 samples from 1 participant for testing.

3.2. Overall Performance

Overall performance was evaluated by averaging the test results across 10 test folds, with each fold corresponding to one participant held out for testing (Table 4). The *AttnFusion* model outperformed *ConcatFusion* across all metrics, achieving a higher accuracy ($90.6 \pm 4.2\%$) and F1-score ($90.5 \pm 4.3\%$). In comparison, *ConcatFusion* achieved an accuracy of $85.5 \pm 5.8\%$ and an F1-score of $85.4 \pm 6.0\%$, with a higher standard deviation across participants.

Table 4. Overall test performance of the proposed models. Values represent the mean ± standard deviation across 10 test folds.

Model	Accuracy (%)	Precision (%)	Recall (%)	F1-Score (%)
ConcatFusion	85.5 ± 5.8	87.0 ± 4.8	85.5 ± 5.8	85.4 ± 6.0
AttnFusion	90.6 ± 4.2	91.4 ± 3.7	90.6 ± 4.2	90.5 ± 4.3

3.3. Per-Class Performance

Confusion matrices were computed by aggregating the classification results across all test folds in LOSO-CV, showing the true labels versus predicted labels for each class (Figure 9). For the four posture classes, the *AttnFusion* model achieved higher diagonal values, indicating improved sensitivity for each class compared to the *ConcatFusion* model. Both models showed high sensitivity for the empty classes, with over 99% of empty samples classified correctly. When classifying seated stretching, *AttnFusion* achieved an accuracy of 86.8%, compared to 81.1% with *ConcatFusion*, reducing misclassification as standing stretching and working classes. A similar trend was observed for standing stretching, with *AttnFusion* achieving 86.3% correct classification versus 84.8% for *ConcatFusion*. Both models showed some confusion between stretching and working postures within the same desk configuration (seated or standing); however, this was less evident in the *AttnFusion* model. For seated working, *AttnFusion* classified 93.3% of instances correctly, compared to 87.6% for *ConcatFusion*, and for standing working, *AttnFusion* reached 87.1%, a significant improvement over *ConcatFusion*'s 74.5%. Off-diagonal values indicate that errors most often involved confusion between stretching and working postures in the same physical position, rather than between seated and standing. Overall, *AttnFusion* consistently improved per-class classification performance, particularly for working classes.

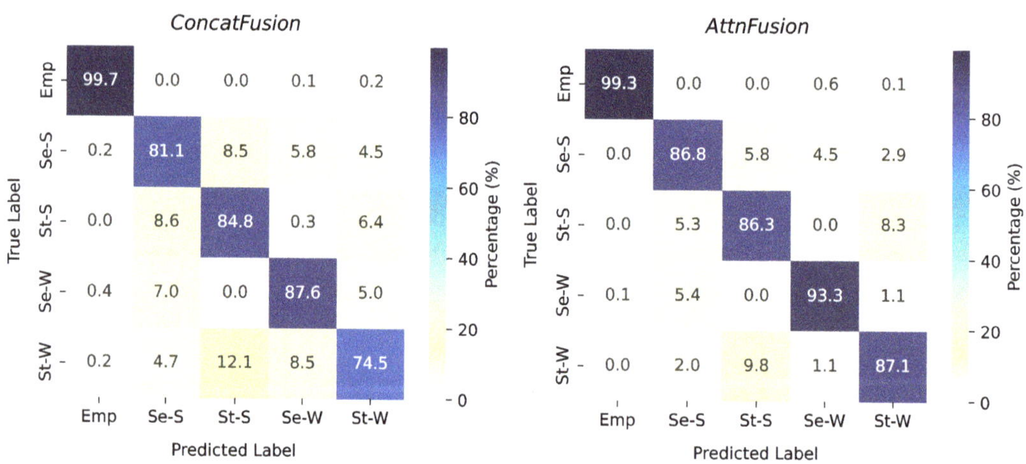

Figure 9. Cumulative confusion matrices for the *ConcatFusion* (**left**) and *AttnFusion* (**right**) models. The class labels are shown as: Emp (empty), Se-S (seated stretching), St-S (standing stretching), Se-W (seated working), and St-W (standing working).

ROC curves were computed for each class by combining all test samples across the 10 LOSO-CV folds (Figure 10). Both models achieved high AUC values for the empty class (AUC = 1.00). The *AttnFusion* model consistently outperformed *ConcatFusion* across the four posture classes, most notably for standing working (AUC = 0.98 vs. 0.94). Collectively, these results demonstrate robust class-wise discriminative ability and the benefits of modality-specific spatial attention and convolutional modality fusion in the *AttnFusion* model.

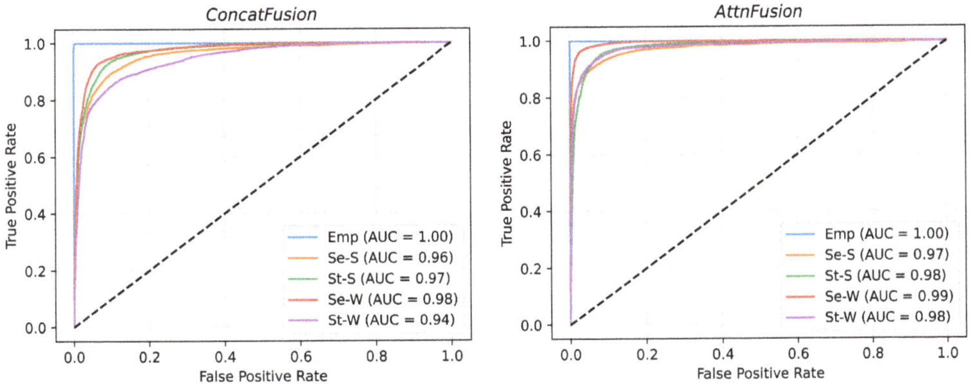

Figure 10. Aggregate ROC curves by class for the *ConcatFusion* (**left**) and *AttnFusion* (**right**) models. The class labels are shown as: Emp (empty), Se-S (seated stretching), St-S (standing stretching), Se-W (seated working), and St-W (standing working).

3.4. Per-Participant Performance

For each participant, accuracy and F1-score for both the *ConcatFusion* and *AttnFusion* models are reported in Figure 11. The *AttnFusion* model outperformed *ConcatFusion* for most participants. Notably, several participants (e.g., P2 and P3) showed larger gains with the *AttnFusion* model. While some inter-participant variability was observed, the overall trend indicates stable performance across individuals and consistent benefits from the *AttnFusion* model.

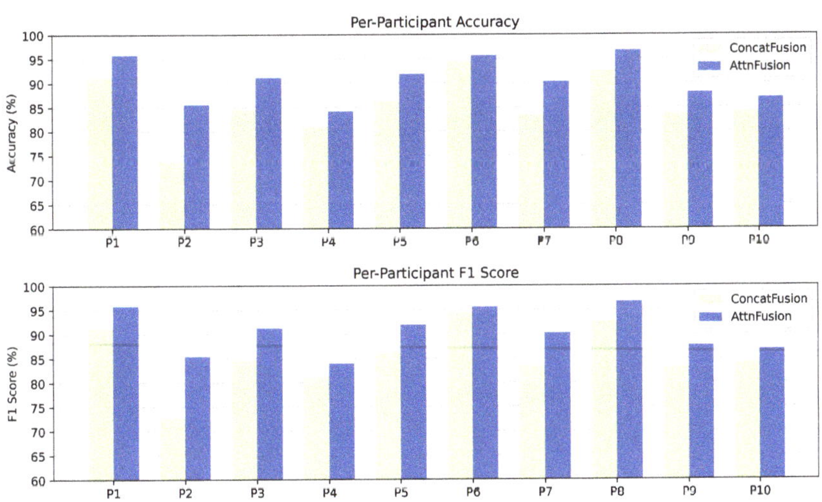

Figure 11. Per-participant accuracy (**top**) and F1-score (**bottom**) for the *ConcatFusion* and *AttnFusion* models. Each cluster of bars corresponds to one participant (P1–P10).

4. Discussion

This study demonstrates that a ceiling-mounted UWB radar system can differentiate both working and stretching postures in an office environment by combining distance and

Doppler information. The *AttnFusion* model demonstrated better overall performance, achieving a testing accuracy of 90.6% ± 4.2% and macro F1-score of 90.5% ± 4.3%, compared to 85.5% ± 5.8% and 85.4% ± 6.0% for *ConcatFusion*. The relatively lower standard deviation observed with *AttnFusion* also indicates greater consistency across different participants. At the class level, *AttnFusion* improved the classification of challenging postures, with seated stretching increasing from 81.1% to 86.8% and standing working from 74.8% to 87.1%, while maintaining high accuracy for other classes. When examined per participant, *AttnFusion* delivered more stable performance, with reduced variability in all performance metrics across all participants, highlighting its robustness to inter-individual differences. These results suggest that combining spatial attention with convolutional feature integration in a dual-modality framework can substantially improve the reliability of UWB radar-based posture recognition in office environments.

Our findings align with and extend recent radar-based human posture recognition research. Liu et al. achieved high accuracy in classifying five seated postures using FMCW radar, reporting an average accuracy above 98% [19]. Similarly, Zhao et al. proposed a deep learning pipeline for human motion and posture recognition using mmWave imaging radar, achieving robust angle-insensitive recognition by fusing point cloud and spectrogram representations [20]. Their system achieved an overall accuracy of 87.1% for six activities, including sitting down, standing up from sitting, bending over, standing up from bending, sitting still, and standing still. Zhang et al. evaluated several machine learning classifiers for posture identification using point clouds from FMCW radar [21]. Their best-performing MLP classifier achieved 94% accuracy in differentiating six postures, including sitting, lying, and four different standing postures. Additionally, some previous studies considered standing and sitting as two broad classes, without further dividing them into specific postural subclasses [22–24]. In comparison to the prior work, this study differs in several key aspects. First, in terms of activity recognition, our system aims to distinguish working and stretching postures in seated and standing conditions, but previous studies have often focused on a subset of postures, such as sitting postures or daily activities. Second, we employed a LOSO-CV protocol to assess performance and generalizability across different participants, while most previous studies on radar-based posture recognition relied on random splits of data from all participants or used data from a single individual, which may overestimate model generalization [19,21–24]. Finally, our use of a ceiling-mounted UWB radar offers unobtrusive monitoring with minimal occlusion, in contrast to previous studies employing side-mounted radars on desks or tripods, thereby enhancing practicality for office deployment [19–23]. Table 5 summarizes previous radar-based human posture recognition studies, comparing sensor location, number of participants, covered postures, validation methods, and reported accuracies.

Table 5. Comparison of previous studies on radar-based human posture recognition.

Study	Sensor Location	Number of Participants	Sitting and Standing [1]	Working and Stretching [1]	Subject-Wise Validation	Accuracy [2]
[19]	Side	5	✗	✗	✗	98.7%
[20]	Side	8	✓	✗	✓	97.9%
[21]	Side	1	✓	✗	✗	94.0%
[22]	Side	5	✓	✗	✗	84.9%
[23]	Side	9	✓	✗	✗	97.1%
[24]	Overhead	3	✓	✗	✗	98.9%
This study	Overhead	10	✓	✓	✓	90.6%

[1] Types of postures included in the study. [2] Accuracy of the best-performing model reported in each study; the calculation of accuracy varies according to the validation method employed.

The proposed radar-based approach offers several advantages over conventional camera-based and wearable office posture detection systems. Compared to camera-based systems, it enhances privacy by avoiding the capture of identifiable visual information and maintains consistent performance under varying lighting conditions, including low-light or dark environments [25]. Compared to wearable devices, the radar-based system requires no user compliance or physical attachment, allowing continuous monitoring without interfering with daily activities. In addition, UWB radar offers low power consumption, supporting energy-efficient operation suitable for long-term deployments. It is inherently resistant to narrowband interference, enabling reliable performance in environments with other wireless systems, and can sustain long-term continuous monitoring with minimal maintenance requirements [26].

Future research will build on the findings of this study while addressing its limitations. First, variations in body size and shape can affect the magnitude and distribution of reflected signals, while differences in movement patterns across age groups and genders may influence Doppler patterns. As the current dataset comprised ten participants with a relatively narrow age range, the results may not fully capture the variability present in broader populations. Future research should extend validation to more diverse participant groups, additional office environments, and a wider range of postures and stretching activities to improve the generalizability of the proposed system. Second, while the results demonstrated the feasibility of the proposed system, the signal processing pipeline and classification models were designed empirically. Both can be further optimized through tuning of signal processing parameters (e.g., data segmentation and filter settings), architecture refinement, and model hyperparameter optimization. A more comprehensive optimization process leveraging a larger dataset, incorporating explainable AI methods, and enabling lightweight deployment on edge devices could improve system transparency, performance, and overall utility. Third, the proposed system is designed to cover a single-person workspace, which does not address the presence of multiple individuals. Future work will explore the integration of additional sensing modules or dedicated radar signal processing pipelines capable of distinguishing between single- and multi-person occupancy in shared workspaces. Finally, real-world deployments are needed to assess the impact of environmental factors such as workspace clutter, reflective surfaces, and variations in ceiling height on system performance.

5. Conclusions

In this work, we propose a privacy-preserving and unobtrusive system for monitoring ergonomic behaviors in office environments using ceiling-mounted UWB radar. By integrating both distance and Doppler information extracted from UWB radar signals, our approach enables accurate detection of static and dynamic postures while minimizing the privacy concerns and workplace disruptions. This work provides a radar-based solution for scalable workplace interventions aimed at reducing musculoskeletal risks, prompting micro-breaks, and supporting healthier work routines. Further research should explore multi-person scenarios, extended environments, and real-world deployment to improve generalizability and impact.

Author Contributions: Conceptualization, W.L.; methodology, W.L. and C.B.; software, W.L. and C.B.; validation, W.L., C.B., M.S. and D.S.-T.; formal analysis, W.L. and C.B.; investigation, C.B.; resources, W.L., C.B., M.S. and D.S.-T.; data curation, W.L. and C.B.; writing—original draft preparation, W.L.; writing—review and editing, W.L., M.S., C.B. and D.S.-T.; visualization, W.L. and C.B.; supervision, W.L. and D.S.-T.; project administration, W.L., M.S. and D.S.-T.; funding acquisition, W.L. and D.S.-T. All authors have read and agreed to the published version of the manuscript.

Funding: This research was funded by Future Science Platforms, CSIRO.

Institutional Review Board Statement: This study was conducted under approval (2023_007_R) by the Health and Medical Human Research Ethics Committee of CSIRO.

Informed Consent Statement: Informed consent was obtained from all participants involved in the study.

Data Availability Statement: Data are unavailable due to privacy or ethical restrictions.

Acknowledgments: The authors would like to acknowledge the strategic investment of the Future Science Platform program at CSIRO.

Conflicts of Interest: The authors declare no conflicts of interest.

Abbreviations

The following abbreviations are used in this manuscript:

UWB	Ultra-wideband
CSIRO	Commonwealth Scientific and Industrial Research Organisation
GUI	Graphical user interface
STFT	Short-time Fourier transform
CNN	Convolutional neural network
LOSO-CV	Leave-one-subject-out cross-validation
MLP	Multilayer perceptron
ROC	Receiver operating characteristic
AUC	Area under the curve
Emp	Empty
Se-S	Seated stretching
St-S	Standing stretching
Se-W	Seated working
St-W	Standing working

Appendix A

Table A1. Model training hyperparameters.

Hyperparameter	Value
Optimizer	AdamW
Weight decay	1×10^{-4}
Batch size	64
Max epochs	200
Loss function	Cross Entropy
Learning rate scheduler	ReduceOnPlateau
Scheduler monitor	Validation loss
Scheduler factor	0.5
Scheduler patience	20
Early stopping monitor	Validation accuracy
Early stopping patience	20

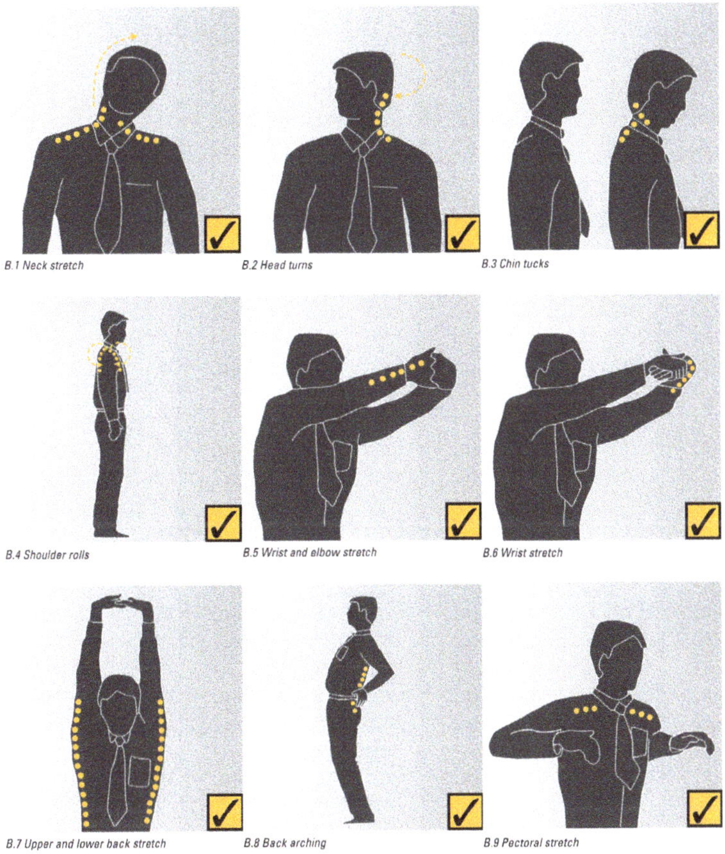

Figure A1. Stretching postures included in the study [17]. Shoulder rolls and back arching, shown as standing postures in the figure, were also performed by participants while seated.

References

1. Buckley, J.P.; Hedge, A.; Yates, T.; Copeland, R.J.; Loosemore, M.; Hamer, M.; Bradley, G.; Dunstan, D.W. The sedentary office: An expert statement on the growing case for change towards better health and productivity. *Br. J. Sport. Med.* **2015**, *49*, 1357–1362. [CrossRef] [PubMed]
2. Monsey, M.; Ioffe, I.; Beatini, A.; Lukey, B.; Santiago, A.; James, A.B. Increasing compliance with stretch breaks in computer users through reminder software. *Work* **2003**, *21*, 107–111.
3. Irmak, A.; Bumin, G.; Irmak, R. The effects of exercise reminder software program on office workers' perceived pain level, work performance and quality of life. *Work* **2012**, *41*, 5692–5695.
4. Martins, P.F.d.O.; Zicolau, E.A.A.; Cury-Boaventura, M.F. Stretch breaks in the work setting improve flexibility and grip strength and reduce musculoskeletal complaints. *Motriz Revista Educação Física* **2015**, *21*, 263–273.
5. Holzgreve, F.; Fraeulin, L.; Haenel, J.; Schmidt, H.; Bader, A.; Frei, M.; Groneberg, D.A.; Ohlendorf, D.; van Mark, A. Office work and stretch training (OST) study: Effects on the prevalence of musculoskeletal diseases and gender differences: A non-randomised control study. *BMJ Open* **2021**, *11*, e044453. [PubMed]
6. Adolf, J.; Kán, P.; Feuchtner, T.; Adolfová, B.; Doležal, J.; Lhotská, L. Offistretch: Camera-based real-time feedback for daily stretching exercises. *Vis. Comput.* **2025**, *41*, 1555–1571. [CrossRef]
7. Paliyawan, P.; Nukoolkit, C.; Mongkolnam, P. Prolonged sitting detection for office workers syndrome prevention using kinect. In Proceedings of the 2014 11th International Conference on Electrical Engineering/Electronics, Computer, Telecommunications and Information Technology (ECTI-CON), Nakhon Ratchasima, Thailand, 14–17 May 2014; pp. 1–6.

8. Tavares, C.; Silva, J.O.E.; Mendes, A.; Rebolo, L.; Domingues, M.D.F.; Alberto, N.; Lima, M.; Silva, H.P.; Antunes, P.F.D.C. Instrumented office chair with low-cost plastic optical fiber sensors for posture control and work conditions optimization. *IEEE Access* **2022**, *10*, 69063–69071. [CrossRef]
9. Odesola, D.F.; Kulon, J.; Verghese, S.; Partlow, A.; Gibson, C. Smart sensing chairs for sitting posture detection, classification, and monitoring: A comprehensive review. *Sensors* **2024**, *24*, 2940. [CrossRef]
10. Zhang, X.; Fan, J.; Peng, T.; Zheng, P.; Lee, C.K.; Tang, R. A privacy-preserving and unobtrusive sitting posture recognition system via pressure array sensor and infrared array sensor for office workers. *Adv. Eng. Inform.* **2022**, *53*, 101690. [CrossRef]
11. Zhang, X.; Fan, J.; Peng, T.; Zheng, P.; Zhang, X.; Tang, R. Multimodal data-based deep learning model for sitting posture recognition toward office workers' health promotion. *Sens. Actuators A Phys.* **2023**, *350*, 114150.
12. Zhang, X.; Zheng, P.; Peng, T.; Li, D.; Zhang, X.; Tang, R. Privacy-preserving activity recognition using multimodal sensors in smart office. *Future Gener. Comput. Syst.* **2023**, *148*, 27–38. [CrossRef]
13. Lai, D.K.H.; Zha, L.W.; Leung, T.Y.N.; Tam, A.Y.C.; So, B.P.H.; Lim, H.J.; Cheung, D.S.K.; Wong, D.W.C.; Cheung, J.C.W. Dual ultra-wideband (UWB) radar-based sleep posture recognition system: Towards ubiquitous sleep monitoring. *Eng. Regen.* **2023**, *4*, 36–43.
14. Lu, W.; Kumar, S.; Sandhu, M.; Zhang, Q. An unobtrusive fall detection system using ceiling-mounted ultra-wideband radar. In Proceedings of the 2023 45th Annual International Conference of the IEEE Engineering in Medicine & Biology Society (EMBC), Sydney, Australia, 24–27 July 2023; pp. 1–5.
15. Zhou, X.; Jin, T.; Dai, Y.; Song, Y.; Qiu, Z. Md-pose: Human pose estimation for single-channel uwb radar. *IEEE Trans. Biom. Behav. Identity Sci.* **2023**, *5*, 449–463.
16. Callaghan, J.P.; De Carvalho, D.; Gallagher, K.; Karakolis, T.; Nelson-Wong, E. Is standing the solution to sedentary office work? *Ergon. Des.* **2015**, *23*, 20–24. [CrossRef]
17. Ruseckaite, R.; Collie, A. The incidence and impact of recurrent workplace injury and disease: A cohort study of WorkSafe Victoria, Australia compensation claims. *BMJ Open* **2013**, *3*, e002396. [CrossRef] [PubMed]
18. Woo, S.; Park, J.; Lee, J.Y.; Kweon, I.S. Cbam: Convolutional block attention module. In Proceedings of the European Conference on Computer Vision (ECCV), Munich, Germany, 8–14 September 2018; pp. 3–19.
19. Liu, G.; Li, X.; Xu, C.; Ma, L.; Li, H. FMCW radar-based human sitting posture detection. *IEEE Access* **2023**, *11*, 102746–102756. [CrossRef]
20. Zhao, Y.; Yarovoy, A.; Fioranelli, F. Angle-insensitive human motion and posture recognition based on 4D imaging radar and deep learning classifiers. *IEEE Sens. J.* **2022**, *22*, 12173–12182.
21. Zhang, G.; Li, S.; Zhang, K.; Lin, Y.J. Machine learning-based human posture identification from point cloud data acquisitioned by FMCW millimetre-wave radar. *Sensors* **2023**, *23*, 7208. [CrossRef] [PubMed]
22. Baird, Z.; Rajan, S.; Bolic, M. Classification of human posture from radar returns using ultra-wideband radar. In Proceedings of the 2018 40th Annual International Conference of the IEEE Engineering in Medicine and Biology Society (EMBC), Honolulu, HI, USA, 18–21 July 2018; pp. 3268–3271.
23. Mahajan, P.; Chaudhary, D.; Khan, M.; Khan, M.H.; Wajid, M.; Srivastava, A. A point cloud-based non-intrusive approach for human posture classification by utilizing 77 ghz fmcw radar and deep learning models. In Proceedings of the 2024 IEEE International Symposium on Circuits and Systems (ISCAS), Singapore, 19–22 May 2024; pp. 1–5.
24. Wu, J.; Dahnoun, N. A health monitoring system with posture estimation and heart rate detection based on millimeter-wave radar. *Microprocess. Microsyst.* **2022**, *94*, 104670. [CrossRef]
25. Wang, D.; Yoo, S.; Cho, S.H. Experimental comparison of IR-UWB radar and FMCW radar for vital signs. *Sensors* **2020**, *20*, 6695. [CrossRef]
26. Cheraghinia, M.; Shahid, A.; Luchie, S.; Gordebeke, G.J.; Caytan, O.; Fontaine, J.; Van Herbruggen, B.; Lemey, S.; De Poorter, E. A comprehensive overview on UWB radar: Applications, standards, signal processing techniques, datasets, radio chips, trends and future research directions. *IEEE Commun. Surv. Tutor.* **2024**, *27*, 2283–2324. [CrossRef]

sensors

MDPI

Article

Replication of Sensor-Based Categorization of Upper-Limb Performance in Daily Life in People Post Stroke and Generalizability to Other Populations

Chelsea E. Macpherson [1], Marghuretta D. Bland [1,2,3], Christine Gordon [1], Allison E. Miller [1], Caitlin Newman [4], Carey L. Holleran [1,2], Christopher J. Dy [5], Lindsay Peterson [6], Keith R. Lohse [1,2] and Catherine E. Lang [1,2,3,*]

1 Program in Physical Therapy, Washington University School of Medicine, St. Louis, MO 63110, USA; mchelsea@wustl.edu (C.E.M.); blandm@wustl.edu (M.D.B.); gordon.christine@wustl.edu (C.G.); miller.allison@wustl.edu (A.E.M.); cholleran@wustl.edu (C.L.H.); lohse@wustl.edu (K.R.L.)
2 Department of Neurology, Washington University School of Medicine, St. Louis, MO 63110, USA
3 Program in Occupational Therapy, Washington University School of Medicine, St. Louis, MO 63110, USA
4 Shirley Ryan AbilityLab, Chicago, IL 60611, USA; cnewman@sralab.org
5 Department of Orthopedic Surgery, Washington University School of Medicine, St. Louis, MO 63110, USA; dyc@wustl.edu
6 Department of Medicine, Washington University School of Medicine, St. Louis, MO 63110, USA; llpeterson@wustl.edu
* Correspondence: langc@wustl.edu

Highlights

What are the main findings?

- A five-variable, five-cluster model was replicated in people with stroke and controls, and it generalized to musculoskeletal and other neurological conditions affecting the upper limb.
- Compared to clusters, two principal components and individual accelerometry variables showed higher convergent validity with self-report outcomes of upper limb performance and disability.

What is the implication of the main finding?

- Upper limb performance in daily life, quantified by wearable movement sensors, may be better represented on a continuum of functional recovery, rather than with discrete categories.
- This application of wearable movement sensors supports a unified, data-driven approach to monitor upper limb recovery across conditions and severity of functional deficits in rehabilitation.

Abstract

Background: Wearable movement sensors can measure upper limb (UL) activity, but single variables may not capture the full picture. This study aimed to replicate prior work identifying five multivariate categories of UL activity performance in people with stroke and controls and expand those findings to other UL conditions. Methods: Demographic, self-report, and wearable sensor based UL activity performance variables were collected from 324 participants (stroke $n = 49$, multiple sclerosis $n = 19$, distal UL fracture $n = 40$, proximal UL pain $n = 55$, post-breast cancer $n = 23$, control $n = 138$). Principal component (PC) analyses (12, 9, 7, or 5 accelerometry input variables) were followed by cluster analyses and numerous assessments of model fit across multiple subsets of the total sample. Results: Two PCs explained 70–90% variance: PC1 (overall UL activity performance) and PC2 (preferred-limb use). A five-variable, five-cluster model was optimal across samples. In

https://doi.org/10.3390/s25154618

comparison to clusters, two PCs and individual accelerometry variables showed higher convergent validity with self-report outcomes of UL activity performance and disability. Conclusions: A five-variable, five-cluster model was replicable and generalizable. Convergent validity data suggest that UL activity performance in daily life may be better conceptualized on a continuum, rather than categorically. These findings highlight a unified, data-driven approach to tracking functional changes across UL conditions and severity of functional deficits.

Keywords: activities of daily living; measurement; musculoskeletal; neurology; rehabilitation; upper limb; wearable sensors

1. Introduction

Upper limb (UL) use is integral for engagement in activities of daily life. When one or both ULs are affected due to conditions such as stroke or shoulder pain, the ability to perform daily activities may become challenging. This can substantially disrupt one's functional independence and participation, leading to disability [1]. People often seek out rehabilitation services to improve their ability to perform activities in daily life [2]. In-clinic measurement tools accurately quantify a person's capacity for UL activities within a clinical setting (i.e., activity capacity), but these measures do not quantify what a person actually does in an unstructured, free-living environment (i.e., activity performance in daily life) [3,4]. In recent years, wearable movement sensors such as accelerometers have emerged as a research tool to quantify UL activity performance in daily life and their potential for integration in clinical rehabilitation continues to grow [5,6].

Rehabilitation clinicians manage diverse patient populations and require measurement tools that are efficient, easily understood by themselves and their patients, and adaptable to the time constraints of high-demand care environments. As wearable movement sensors transition into the clinical space, there are multiple challenges that need to be addressed: (1) the number of single variables used across studies, often with different definitions or algorithms, creates inconsistency in the description of UL activity performance in daily life; (2) the mathematical complexity and interpretability of some variables complicates their clinical use; (3) the lack of validation data hinders understanding of how UL accelerometry variables may relate to self-reported UL use in daily life; and (4) the generalizability across various clinical populations and severity of functional deficits remains unclear [7,8]. A potential solution to overcome some of these challenges would be to transition from using multiple single variables that describe unique populations to multivariate categories of UL activity performance in daily life that could span clinical populations.

Several single sensor variables have been validated to capture UL activity performance in daily life in people post stroke [8]. While single variables may be highly useful, UL activity performance in daily life is likely multi-dimensional [9]. Thus, quantifying UL activity performance with single variables may not fully represent UL activity performance in daily life [9,10]. In prior work, we identified five distinct multivariate categories that characterized UL activity performance in daily life in a sample of people with stroke and people without UL disability. Using different numbers of accelerometry input variables, two principal components consistently accounted for the majority of the variance, and a five-cluster solution provided the best model fit by maximizing the overall variance explained [11]. Although these results were promising, additional studies are needed to replicate and validate the findings. Further, if a solution for the clinical environment involves multivariate categories, then they should generalize beyond stroke to other conditions affecting one or both ULs, thus improving clinical utility through broader applicability [7,8].

This manuscript is organized according to the primary purposes of this study, which were to (1) replicate the multivariate categories of UL activity performance in a separate sample of people with stroke and people without UL disability; (2) determine the generalizability of the categories beyond stroke to other conditions for which people seek out UL rehabilitation; and (3) evaluate the convergent validity between sensor-based categories and self-reported measures of daily UL activity and quality of life. To enhance generalization, we aimed to include a heterogeneous sample of clinical populations known to cause UL disability who seek rehabilitation services. Since it would be impossible to study every condition, we intentionally selected candidate conditions that varied in their biological underpinnings (i.e., neurological: stroke, multiple sclerosis; musculoskeletal: shoulder pain, fractures; and medical: post curative breast cancer treatment), region of impact (e.g., proximal, distal, or entire limb), and range of functional severity and chronicity (e.g., distal radius fracture, multiple sclerosis). We hypothesized that five multivariate categories would be replicable in a new sample of people with stroke and people without UL disability and that these categories would be generalizable across conditions and severity of functional deficits despite variable biological causes and patterns of UL impairment and capacity. We further hypothesized that convergent validity of the categories would be evident between condition-specific and generic self-report measures of UL activity performance and disability. If confirmed, defined categories from wearable movement sensor data that can be used across clinical populations and functional levels of severity could dually promote personalized care and clinical efficiency within rehabilitation settings.

2. Materials and Methods

This study enrolled two groups of people into a prospective, longitudinal, observational cohort: (1) adults referred to physical or occupational therapy services for UL problems and (2) adults who had no history of neurological or musculoskeletal conditions that affected their ULs to serve as controls. The data used in this report were from the first assessment, which occurred within 2 weeks of starting rehabilitation care for those receiving services. By nature of its design, this study could either be administered in-person during a clinic visit or fully remotely depending on participant preference. This study used a single Institutional Review Board (IRB) at Washington University (WashU IRB# 202207003-1001, approval date 21 July 2022). All participants provided informed consent, with most consenting electronically via REDCap version 15 [12–15].

2.1. Participants

Participants included people seeking rehabilitation services for conditions affecting the UL (e.g., stroke, multiple sclerosis, UL fracture, shoulder pain, breast cancer) and people without UL disability as comparators. Participants with conditions affecting the UL were recruited from rehabilitation and medical clinics at WashU Medicine in St. Louis, Missouri, and Shirley Ryan Ability Lab in Chicago, Illinois, or from outside either medical network across the United States via electronic flyers, condition-specific websites, and social media advertisements. An additional source to recruit control participants was the Recruitment Enhancement Core through the Institute of Clinical and Translational Sciences services at Washington University.

2.1.1. Participants with Conditions Affecting the Upper Limb

General inclusion criteria:

1. Age > 18 years.

2. UL disability determined by the referring physician or surgeon.
3. Referred to rehabilitation to address UL disability.
4. Documented goals of service (rehabilitation and/or surgery) to increase or restore UL function.

Condition specific inclusion criteria:

1. Stroke: Confirmed ischemic or hemorrhagic stroke diagnosis by neurologist, consistent with imaging; unilateral UL sensorimotor impairments due to stroke.
2. Multiple sclerosis (MS): Confirmed diagnosis of MS by neurologist; sensorimotor impairments in at least one UL.
3. Distal UL fracture: Unilateral, radiographically confirmed, distal radius fracture, either treated with surgery or non-operatively.
4. Proximal UL Pain: Unilateral, radiographically confirmed, proximal humerus or clavicle fracture, either treated with surgery or non-operatively or physician diagnosis of shoulder pain of musculoskeletal origin; limitations in shoulder range of motion; and reported problems using the limb for functional activities.
5. Breast Cancer: Confirmed diagnosis of breast cancer, stage 0–III, by oncology provider; >4 weeks post curative-intent breast cancer treatment (treatment could include one or more of surgery, chemotherapy, and radiation). This could be a new or older diagnosis of breast cancer. Participants could have unilateral or bilateral UL involvement and were not excluded if lymphedema was present.

General exclusion criteria for participants with UL conditions:

1. Other concurrent neurologic, musculoskeletal, or medical conditions that affected the UL (e.g., exclude if both stroke plus distal radius fracture) or general physical activity.
2. Other co-morbid conditions that indicate a minimal chance for functional improvement (e.g., end-stage cancer, end-stage renal disease).
3. Pregnant or planning to become pregnant.
4. Cognitive impairment or disorders of communication that would prevent informed consent and study completion as indicated in their medical record.

2.1.2. Participants Without UL Disability Serving as Controls

Eligibility criteria:

1. Age > 18 years.
2. No neurological, musculoskeletal, or medical conditions that affect the UL, or that significantly affect the ability to engage in physical activity as reported by the participant.

Once enrolled, participants chose the most feasible method of study participation. Depending on participant choice, the described data collection and assessment procedures could occur (1) remotely via mailing of sensors, electronic questionnaires (via REDCap version 15), and secure telephone or zoom calls; (2) during an in-person home visit; or (3) during an in-person clinic visit. Study participants could also opt to have some aspects administered remotely with others administered in person.

2.2. Study Assessments

UL activity performance in daily life was quantified directly from bilateral wrist worn accelerometers and indirectly from self-report. Descriptive demographic and quality of life data were collected via self-report or via the electronic health record.

2.2.1. Accelerometry Measurement of Upper Limb Performance in Daily Life

The devices used were the tri-axial ActiGraph GT9x-BT Links. Ametris (formerly ActiGraph LLC, Pensacola, FL, USA) is a Class II FDA-Approved Medical Device which has established reliability and validity standards and conforms with requirements of the International Standardization Organization [16] to meet regulatory requirements and ensure high quality medical devices. Participants were instructed to continuously wear the accelerometers on both wrists, with wrist straps comfortably taught, and positioned just proximal to the ulnar styloid for two consecutive days [17]. Past literature has indicated that a minimum of 24 h is sufficient to show stability of UL activity performance variables in adults [17,18] and that shorter durations of prescribed wear time often indicate greater adherence [19]. Participants were also asked to keep a log of wear time, rate their activity level over the course of the two days, document any times the sensors were removed, and report any difficulty wearing the devices. After two days, participants returned the accelerometers to their research facility (in person, by mail).

Once accelerometers were returned, recorded data were downloaded using ActiLife 6 (ActiGraph LLC, Pensacola, FL, USA), visually inspected, and processed using custom code programmed in R software version 4.4.2 (R Core Team, Vienna, Austria) [11,17,20]. The processing code can be found on the following Zenodo repository: https://doi.org/10.5281/zenodo.10999195 [21,22]. For inclusion in analyses, participants had to have at least one valid day (≥24 h) on bilateral devices [18]. There were two data files extracted from ActiLife 6 software: a 1 Hz data file (activity counts) and a 30 Hz data file (gravitational units). Data processing methods were replicated from Barth et al., 2021, [11] where most variables were computed from the vector magnitude of the x, y, and z axes accelerations after bandpass filtering (between 0.25 and 2.5 Hz), converting to activity counts, and down sampling into 1-s epochs using proprietary ActiLife software [17,23]. A few variables (e.g., Preferred/Non-Preferred Spectral Arc Length, and Jerk Asymmetry Index) that required higher sampling frequencies were computed from 30 Hz data using the vector magnitude of the x, y, and z accelerations in gravitational units after bandpass filtering (0.2–12 Hz).

Twelve UL activity performance variables, identical to those described by Barth et al., 2021, were included in this analysis (Table 1) [11]. In contrast to Barth et al., the current report uses the terms preferred and non-preferred limbs for simplicity [11]. The preferred limb is the dominant limb of the control participants and the non-affected/non-injured limb of the patient participants. Likewise, the non-preferred limb is the non-dominant limb or the affected/injured limb, respectively.

Table 1. Description of UL wearable movement sensor variables, adapted from Barth et al. (2021) [11].

	Data Source	UL Accelerometry Performance Variable Name	Description and Interpretation	Accelerometry Input Variable Set
Duration (h)	1 Hz	Preferred time	Total time that the preferred limb is moving, as determined by activity counts > 2 for each second [24].	12, 9, 7, 5
	1 Hz	Non-preferred time	Total time that the non-preferred limb is moving, as above.	12, 9, 7, 5
	1 Hz	Preferred-only time	Total time that only the preferred limb is moving, as above.	12, 9
	1 Hz	Non-preferred-only time	Total time that only the non-preferred limb is moving, as above.	12, 9

Table 1. *Cont.*

	Data Source	UL Accelerometry Performance Variable Name	Description and Interpretation	Accelerometry Input Variable Set
Intensity (acs)	1 Hz	Non-preferred magnitude	Median of the accelerations for the non-preferred limb when it was moving (excluding non-movement time). Higher movement counts indicate greater movement intensity of the non-preferred limb.	12, 9, 7
	1 Hz	Bilateral magnitude	Sum of the non-preferred and preferred magnitudes, as above. Higher activity counts indicate greater intensity of movement across both limbs.	12, 9, 7
Variability	1 Hz	Non-preferred variance	Standard deviation of the magnitude of accelerations for the non-preferred limb when it was moving. Higher activity counts indicate greater movement variability of movement for the non-preferred limb.	12, 9, 7, 5
	1 Hz	Use ratio	Ratio of hours of non-preferred time to preferred time. Values are generally between 0 and 1, with values close to 1 indicating equal integration of both limbs into daily activities.	12, 9, 7, 5
	1 Hz	Magnitude ratio	Ratio of the magnitude of non-preferred versus preferred limb accelerations (intensity). Interpretation as above, except with magnitudes instead of durations.	12, 9, 7
Symmetry	30 Hz	Jerk asymmetry index [25]	Ratio of the jerk of the non-preferred and preferred limbs but calculated as $((jerk_{non\text{-}preferred} - jerk_{preferred})/jerk_{non\text{-}preferred} + jerk_{preferred}))$. Values range from −1 and +1, with values around 0 indicating similar smoothness of movement in the limbs. Values closer to +1 or −1 reflect greater jerk for the non-preferred limb and the preferred limb, respectively.	12
Movement Quality	30 Hz	Preferred spectral arc length [26,27]	Measurement of the "arc length" of the Fourier magnitude spectrum within a certain frequency range. This measure is independent of the movement's amplitude and duration and indicates smoothness of movement by quantifying movement interruptions. More negative spectral arc lengths are reflective of less smooth or less coordinated movement in the preferred/non-preferred limbs.	12
	30 Hz	Non-preferred spectral arc length		12

Abbreviations: acs, activity counts; h, hours. Legend: The *Accelerometry Input Variable Set* column describes groups of single accelerometry input variables that were systematically reduced based on perceived clinical utility. These variable sets are based on prior work by Barth et al., 2021 [11].

2.2.2. Self-Report Measurements of Upper Limb Performance in Daily Life

Most participants completed online questionnaires remotely via REDCap (Vanderbilt University, Nashville, TN, USA), with a few participants who completed them either on paper or on a computer with assistance from study personnel. All surveys were completed by participants with the exception of the Disability of the Shoulder Arm and Hand (DASH) survey, which was only completed by people with musculoskeletal conditions affecting the UL (e.g., breast cancer, proximal shoulder pain or fracture, and distal fracture groups), and the Motor Activity Log–Amount of Use Scale (MAL-AoU), which was only completed by people with neurological conditions affecting the UL (e.g., stroke and multiple sclerosis groups).

2.2.3. Patient-Reported Outcome Measurement Information System Upper Extremity Bank 2.0 via Computer Adaptive Test (PROMIS)

The PROMIS is a system of self-reported measurement tools that evaluate health status for physical, mental, and social well-being. This study used the computer adaptive test for the UL as the primary measure to quantify participant perception of UL activity performance in daily life. The Upper Extremity Bank 2.0 consists of 126 items, with participants typically answering only 5–6 questions for the computerized adapted testing version. Scores are reported as T-scores, where the normative sample without any conditions has a mean ± SD of 50 ± 10 points [28]. PROMIS tools have excellent test–retest reliability and internal consistency [28–30], and they have been used across a wide variety of chronic diseases and conditions and in the general population [29].

2.2.4. Motor Activity Log–Amount of Use Scale (MAL-AoU)

The MAL-AoU is a questionnaire that measures perceived UL activity performance in daily life for persons with neurologic conditions. The MAL-AoU was used here as a condition-specific tool for quantifying UL activity performance in daily life by participants with stroke and multiple sclerosis. The MAL-AoU asks participants to report the amount of UL use in 30 functional activities. Each item is scored on a 6-point ordinal scale that ranges from 0 ("I did not use my affected arm") to 5 ("I used my affected arm as much as before my condition [stroke, multiple sclerosis])." Item scores are averaged, with overall scores ranging from 0 to 5, with higher scores indicating greater reported use of the affected UL in daily life. The MAL has excellent psychometric properties for test–retest reliability and internal consistency as well as criterion validity [31,32].

2.2.5. Disability of the Arm, Shoulder, and Hand Scale (DASH)

The DASH scale is a 30-item questionnaire that measures perceived UL activity performance in daily life for persons with musculoskeletal conditions. The DASH scale was used here as a condition-specific tool for quantifying UL activity performance in daily life from the participants with UL fractures, shoulder pain, and breast cancer. The DASH survey has 30 items, and each item is rated on a 5-point Likert scale where 1 means no difficulty with the task and 5 means being unable to perform that task. Items scores are summed with total scores range from 0 to 100, with lower scores indicating less disability. The DASH has excellent test–retest reliability, internal consistency, and construct validity [33–35].

2.2.6. Activity Card Sort Test (ACS)

The ACS measures participation in four domains of activities across daily life: instrumental, social, low-demand physical leisure and high-demand physical leisure [36,37]. The ACS was used here to quantify participant perception of return to activities involving the UL. Participants are shown pictures of various activities and asked to rate each activity as either: 0 meaning they never engaged in the activity, or they gave up on the activity after their diagnosis; 0.5 meaning that they partially engage in that activity now since their diagnosis; or 1 meaning that they continue to engage in that activity or have now started to engage in that activity since their diagnosis. For this study, we used 65 of 89 activities that involve the UL, as done previously in a clinical trial [38,39]. We were most interested in the ACS Global Score encompassing all four domains, as well as the ACS Instrumental Activities of Daily Living (ACS IADL) score, which here was a subset of 17 items. The ACS has been used across a wide variety of chronic diseases and conditions and in the general population, and shows acceptable to excellent test–retest reliability and internal consistency [40–43].

2.2.7. European Quality of Life Scale—5 Dimensions 3 Levels (EuroQoL)

The EuroQoL is a descriptive, standardized self-report measure of overall quality of life in 5 dimensions: mobility, self-care, usual activities, pain/discomfort, and anxiety/depression. The EuroQoL self-care scale was used here to capture aspects of UL activity performance in daily life, with the rationale that most self-care activities require the use of the ULs. There are 5 items on this scale; participants rate each item as presenting no problems, some problems, or more extreme problems. Lower scores indicate better function. The EuroQoL has been used across a wide variety of chronic diseases and conditions and in the general population [44]. The EuroQoL has excellent psychometric properties for test–retest reliability and convergent validity [44].

2.2.8. Demographic and Other Data

Demographic and descriptive data were obtained by self-report or, for participants in clinical subgroups, by review of electronic medical records or from the referring medical providers when available. Additional self-report measures were collected to describe comorbid status (Charlson Comorbidity Index [45,46], score range = 0–29, higher scores = more disease burden) and depressive symptomatology (Center for Epidemiological Studies Depression Scale (CES-D), score range = 0–60, higher scores = greater depressive symptoms [47–50]). For this study, the CES-D was also used as a tool to confirm divergent/discriminant validity of the accelerometry measures.

2.3. *Statistical Analysis*

2.3.1. Software Used and Data Availability Statement

All data were managed and analyzed in R (version 4.4.2), an open-source statistical computing software [20]. Data were managed with the *tidyverse* [51] package, analyzed using the *factoextra* [52] and *stats* [20] packages, and then visualized using both the *tidyverse* [51] and *patchwork* [53] packages in R. De-identified data are available from the lead authors upon request. Once the overall study is completed, all data will be publicly shared through the NIH-NICHD Data and Specimen Hub (DASH) repository. R code for all statistical analyses is available from the lead author's GitHub repository: https://github.com/cem2183/sensor_categories (accessed on 11 June 2025).

2.3.2. Sample Size

Determination of sample size for this study was based on a sensitivity analysis informed by preliminary data in a sample of people with stroke and people without UL disability that yielded a 5-variable, 5-cluster solution [11]. Simulations showed that $N \geq 200$ would yield >80% classification accuracy to detect a range of differences between 5 cluster centroids across 5 standardized variables [54].

2.3.3. Replication and Generalizability Analyses

The first two purposes of this study were to (1) replicate prior findings in a new sample of people with stroke and people without UL disability and (2) generalize those findings beyond stroke to other conditions for which people seek out UL rehabilitation. Multiple principal component analyses (PCAs) and cluster analyses were used to achieve these purposes. As such, the replication analysis was performed first with a sample of people with stroke (n = 49) and people without UL disability who served as controls (n = 138). A second replication analysis was performed on a sample that had matching stroke (64%) and proportionate control (36%) to the sample from Barth et al. (2021) [11]. The second sample retained all the participants with stroke (n = 49), while people without UL disability were sampled to produce an age-matched distribution (n = 20). After replication was confirmed, analytic methods were repeated using a third sample of people with distal UL fracture, proximal UL pain, breast cancer, multiple sclerosis, and people without UL disability to determine initial generalizability of findings without people with stroke. Finally, the analysis was repeated on a fourth sample using all participants (N = 324).

2.3.4. Principal Component Analyses

Principal components were derived from sets of accelerometry input variables (12, 9, 7, and 5). Prior to conducting PCAs, all accelerometry variables were standardized using z-scores due to different measurement scales (e.g., counts, hours, ratios). All 12 accelerometry input variables were then visualized in density plots stratified by diagnosis (Figure 1). To replicate work by Barth et al., 2021 [11], the PCA was conducted using the *prcomp* function as part of the *stats* [20] package on sets of 12, 9, 7, and then 5 accelerometry input variables, as indicated in the last column in Table 1. Accelerometry input variables were sequentially excluded from analyses according to computational complexity, validation in clinical populations, and clinical interpretation [11]. Additionally, each model had at least one accelerometry input variable from constructs of duration, intensity, variability, and symmetry to best capture the dimensionality of UL activity performance in daily life [11]. For each variable model (12, 9, 7, and 5), scree plots were evaluated to determine the appropriate number of PCs to explain variance among the accelerometry input variables. Importantly, because the sign of a PC is arbitrary, we manually set the direction of the PC to load positively on preferred time across all analyses (e.g., if the loading of PC1 on preferred time was negative, all loadings for PC1 were multiplied by −1). This alignment does not alter the internal structure of the loadings but ensures directional consistency across variable sets.

2.3.5. Cluster Analyses

Following the PCAs, we used the *factoextra* [52] package to perform a k-means cluster analysis as an efficient means to identify potential subgroups of participants within the data (k tested from 1 to 10). Previously, a 5-variable, 5-cluster solution was sufficient for people with stroke and people without UL disability [11]. However, with replication and generalization to other conditions, we estimated that upwards of 8 clusters may be necessary to explain the data. We used several statistical methods to determine the most appropriate number of clusters for a given set of input variables: (1) the elbow method on a scree plot of the within cluster sum of squares (WSS) [55], (2) the silhouette statistic [56], and the (3) gap statistic [57]. Collectively, from the scree plot, silhouette statistic, and the gap statistic, 2–5 cluster solutions progressively explained the data, and so we focused on these cluster sizes for further analyses.

To adjudicate between 2- to 5-cluster solutions, we extracted cluster membership from each solution for each variable set (12, 9, 7, and 5 input variables). Treating cluster membership as a categorical factor, we assessed model fit via multivariate analysis of variance (MANOVA) via the *stats* [20] package. MANOVA produced the percentage of total variance explained by the number of clusters, allowing for the assessment of model fit [58]. To penalize for overfitting, MANOVA also allowed us to calculate the Akaike Information Criterion (AIC) via the *stats* package for each number of clusters and input variables [58]. The AIC imposes a penalty for additional model parameters, so the model with the lowest AIC value was chosen to avoid overfitting and enhance generalizability [58].

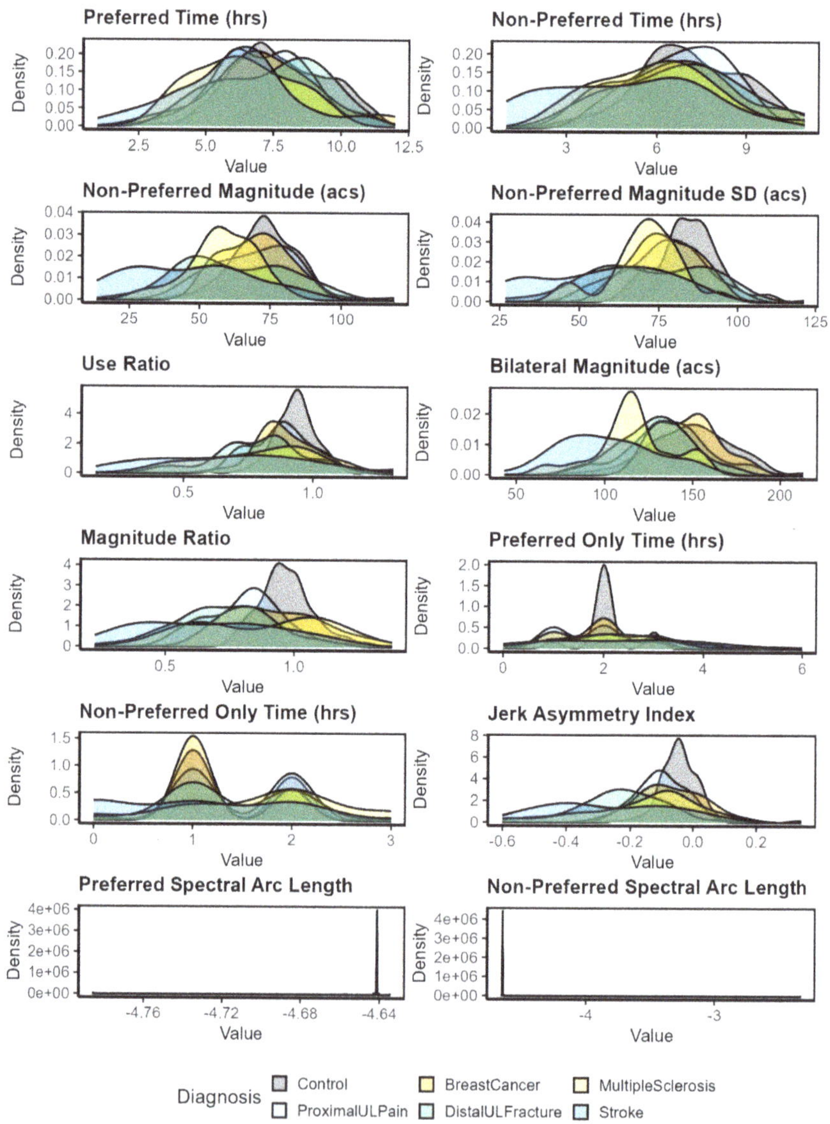

Figure 1. Density plots for each accelerometry input variable by diagnosis. Abbreviations: acs, activity counts; hrs, hours; ProximalULPain, proximal upper limb pain; DistalULFracture, distal upper limb fracture.

2.3.6. Determining Convergent and Divergent Validity

The third purpose of this study was to evaluate the convergent validity between sensor-based categories, self-reported daily UL activity, and other related measures. The convergent validity of generic (i.e., PROMIS UE score) and condition-specific (i.e., MAL-AoU, DASH) self-report of UL activity performance and disability were compared against (1) 2 PCs, (2) the 5-cluster model, and then (3) individual accelerometry variables using the *lm* function of the *stats* [20] package to obtain R^2. As some models rely on multiple predictors (e.g., multiple clusters or principal components) and other models use a single predictor (e.g., paretic arm time or the use ratio), we focused on the R^2 of all models to understand how these self-report outcomes related to accelerometry-derived values. For convergent validity of single predictors, we regressed condition-specific outcomes (i.e., MAL-AoU, DASH) onto individual accelerometry measures. As a test of divergent validity, we regressed a measure of depressive symptoms (CES-D) onto individual accelerometry measures. Measures of depressive symptoms should have little to no relation to accelerometry measures [59].

3. Results

A total sample of $N = 324$ participants were included in the various analyses. Demographic and participant characteristics for the five clinical sub-groups and people without UL disability are provided in Table 2. Baseline scores across self-report measures are provided in Table 3. People with proximal UL pain generally had the highest incidence of concordance (where the dominant limb is the affected upper limb) followed by people with multiple sclerosis, distal UL fracture, stroke, and then breast cancer. Figure 1 displays density plots for each accelerometry input variable, by diagnosis.

Table 2. Demographics of the sample. Values are presented as percentage [*n*] or median [IQR].

		Total Sample (n = 324)	**People Without UL Disability (n = 138)**	**People with Stroke (n = 49)**	**People with Proximal UL Pain (n= 55)**	**People with Distal UL Fracture (n= 40)**	**People with Breast Cancer (n= 23)**	**People with Multiple Sclerosis (n= 19)**
Age		53 [40, 67]	41 [29, 60]	59 [52, 70]	59 [49, 68]	63 [51, 68]	56 [43, 64]	49 [43, 53]
Sex	Male	28% [91]	25% [34]	59% [29]	35% [19]	12% [5]	NA	21% [4]
	Female	72% [233]	75% [104]	41% [20]	65% [36]	88% [35]	100% [23]	79% [15]
Race	American Indian or Alaska Native	<1% [1]	<1% [1]	NA	NA	NA	NA	NA
	Asian	6% [21]	12% [17]	NA	5% [3]	NA	NA	5% [1]
	Black or African American	23% [76]	20% [28]	43% [21]	20% [11]	3% [1]	17% [4]	58% [11]
	Native Hawaiian or Other Pacific Islander	<1% [3]	NA	NA	NA	3% [1]	NA	5% [1]
	White	69% [224]	67% [92]	57% [28]	75% [41]	94% [38]	83% [19]	32% [6]
Ethnicity	Hispanic, Latinx	5% [15]	4% [6]	8% [4]	8% [4]	6% [2]	9% [2]	6% [1]
	Non-Hispanic, Non-Latinx	99% [309]	96% [132]	92% [45]	82% [45]	94% [38]	91% [21]	94% [16]

Table 2. *Cont.*

		Total Sample (n = 324)	People Without UL Disability (n = 138)	People with Stroke (n = 49)	People with Proximal UL Pain (n= 55)	People with Distal UL Fracture (n= 40)	People with Breast Cancer (n= 23)	People with Multiple Sclerosis (n= 19)
Employment Status	Not working for paid employment	46% [148]	31% [43]	86% [42]	36% [20]	42% [17]	48% [11]	79% [15]
	Working < 20 h/week	8% [25]	11% [15]	2% [1]	7% [4]	10% [4]	4% [1]	NA
	Working part-time ≥ 20 h/week	6% [18]	6% [8]	4% [2]	4% [2]	10% [4]	4% [1]	5% [1]
	Woking full-time ≥ 37.5 h/week	40% [133]	52% [72]	8% [4]	53% [29]	38% [15]	44% [10]	16% [3]
Hand Dominance	Right	90% [292]	93% [129]	88% [43]	93% [51]	85% [34]	78% [18]	89% [17]
	Left	9% [29]	7% [9]	10% [5]	7% [4]	10% [4]	22% [5]	11% [2]
	Ambidextrous	1% [3]	NA	2% [1]	NA	5% [2]	NA	NA
Affected Side	Right	NA	NA	45% [22]	56% [31]	42% [17]	52% [12]	53% [10]
	Left	NA	NA	55% [27]	44% [24]	58% [23]	47% [11]	47% [9]
Time Since UL Dysfunction/Pain		NA	NA	3 mo [1.5, 12]	2 yrs [1, 4]	1.6 mo [1.1, 1.8]	12 mo [5.75, 30]	13 yrs [8, 22]
Concordance *	Yes	NA	NA	41% [20]	53% [29]	42% [17]	39% [9]	42% [8]
	No	NA	NA	59% [29]	47% [26]	58% [23]	61% [14]	58% [11]
Total Charleson Comorbidity Index Score		1 [0, 3]	1 [0, 3]	3 [2, 4]	3 [1, 4]	3 [1, 3]	3 [2, 4]	2 [1, 2]
Average Accelerometry Weartime †		100% [324]	100% [138]	100% [49]	100% [55]	100% [40]	100% [23]	100% [19]

* Concordance: dominant limb = paretic limb. † Adherence to wearing for this cohort was 96% for at least a single day. Data from participants with <1 day of recording were excluded from this report. Abbreviations: ADL, Activities of Daily Living; IQR, inter-quartile range; mo, months; *n*, number of participants; NA, Not Applicable; SD, standard deviation; yrs, years.

Table 3. Baseline data for self-report measures. Values are median [IQR].

Self-Report Measure (Points)	Total Sample	People Without UL Disability	People with Stroke	People with Proximal UL Pain	People with Distal UL Fracture	People with Breast Cancer	People with Multiple Sclerosis
PROMIS Upper Extremity Score	42 [32, 52]	55 [47, 61]	34 [29, 39]	36 [30, 38]	32 [28, 38]	37 [34, 44]	32 [27, 39]
MAL—Amount of Use Scale Score	NA	NA	3 [2, 4]	NA	NA	NA	2 [2, 4]
DASH Score	NA	NA	NA	40 [23, 53]	41 [30, 60]	35 [9, 49]	NA
ACS Global Score	31 [24, 38]	36 [31, 43]	21 [15, 26]	30 [25, 34]	27 [22, 34]	31 [23, 40]	21 [15, 28]
ACS IADL Score	12 [9, 14]	14 [12, 15]	6 [3, 9]	13 [9, 15]	11 [8, 13]	12 [10, 14]	7 [3, 9]

Table 3. *Cont.*

Self-Report Measure (Points)	Total Sample	People Without UL Disability	People with Stroke	People with Proximal UL Pain	People with Distal UL Fracture	People with Breast Cancer	People with Multiple Sclerosis
Euro-QofL—Self Care Score	1 [1, 1]	1 [1, 1]	2 [1, 2]	1 [1, 2]	1 [1, 2]	1 [1, 1]	1 [1, 2]
Euro-QofL—Usual Activities Score	1 [1, 2]	1 [1, 1]	2 [2, 2]	2 [1, 2]	2 [2, 2]	2 [1, 2]	2 [2, 2]
CES-D Score	9 [4, 17]	8 [4, 15]	13 [8, 23]	8 [3, 15]	7 [3, 13]	11 [5, 16]	12 [8, 26]

Abbreviations: ACS, Activity Card Sort; CES-D, Center for Epidemiological Studies–Depression Scale; DASH, Disabilities of the Arm, Shoulder, and Hand Scale; Euro-QofL, European Quality of Life Scale; IADL, Instrumental Activities of Daily Living; MAL, Motor Activity Log; NA, Not Applicable; PROMIS, Patient-Reported Outcome Measure Information System; IQR, inter-quartile range; *n*, number.

Despite differing numbers of accelerometry input variables, two principal components (PC1, PC2) consistently explained the majority of variance for each sample in our analysis. Statistics from the PCs and two-, three-, four-, or five-cluster evaluations across 12, 9, 7, or 5 accelerometry input variables are displayed along with the variance explained and model fit criteria in Table 4. The most parsimonious model used five accelerometry input variables. Using this five-variable model, PC1 explained most of the variance for all samples (range 53.0–76.4) and consistently showed moderate loadings across all five accelerometry input variables. PC loadings represent the contribution of each original accelerometry input variable to the principal component. PC1 appears to capture overall UL activity level. PC2 explained considerably less variance across all samples (range 17.6–25.7). PC2 appears to reflect the duration of unilateral activity of the preferred limb (dominant limb in control participants, non-affected limb in patient participants), based on the strong (positive) loading response from preferred time (Figure 2).

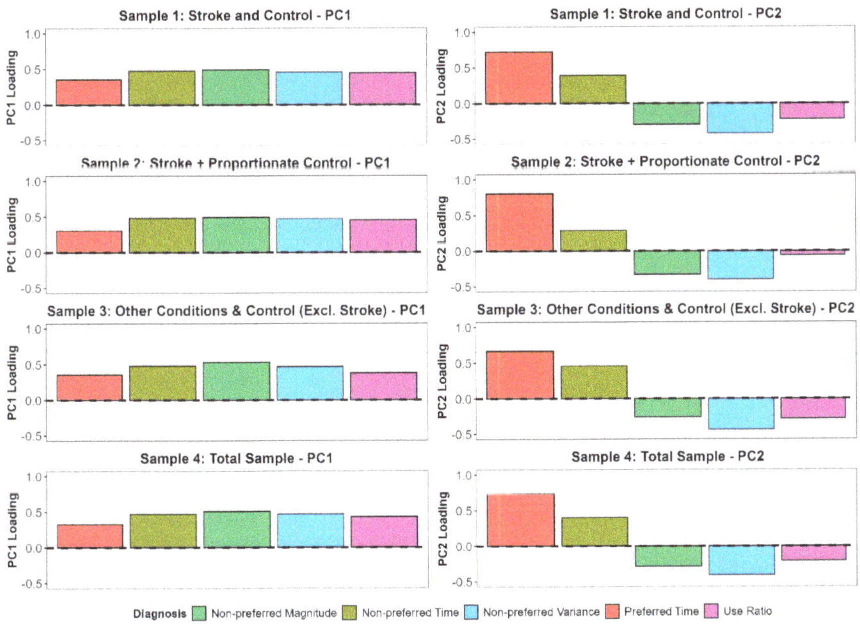

Figure 2. Principal component variance explained. Abbreviations: Excl, excluding; PC, principal component.

A five-cluster solution consistently explained the most overall variance in comparison to two-, three-, or four-cluster solutions for each sample in our analysis, regardless of the number of accelerometry input variables. Cluster statistics are shown in the last two columns of Table 4 and represented graphically in Figure 3. For samples that included participants with stroke and people without UL disability, the analyses replicated prior work [11]. AIC values (last column, Table 4) determined that a five-variable five-cluster solution provided the best model fit in comparison to the two-, three-, or four- cluster solutions across different accelerometry input variables (12, 9, 7 and 5). This held consistent across all samples. While each cluster solution (2-, 3-, 4-, 5-) was statistically feasible, the final, most parsimonious solution included five clusters, with five accelerometry input variables of non-preferred magnitude, non-preferred time, non-preferred variance, preferred time, and the use ratio, consistent with prior work. Figure 3 displays a five-variable, five-cluster solution within a two-dimensional PC space for each of the four samples in this analysis. The x-axis represents PC1, which captures overall UL activity, while the y-axis represents PC2, which represents the duration of preferred limb use. Each axis reflects a continuous gradient, with participants distributed according to their clustered UL performance profiles. To aid interpretation, consider the following examples in Figure 3: Cluster 1 (shown in blue) comprises individuals with high preferred UL use but low overall UL activity, suggesting limited engagement of the non-preferred limb in daily tasks, and likely greater severity of UL functional deficits. Cluster 5 (shown in purple includes individuals with both high preferred UL use and high overall UL activity, consistent with more symmetrical and frequent UL use throughout the day, and likely less severe or no impairments. Cluster 2 (shown in orange) consists of individuals with low preferred UL use and low-to-moderate overall UL activity, indicating either impairment with the preferred UL, or reduced overall upper limb engagement. Overall, clusters show remarkable similarities across each sample, despite differing compositions of clinical populations and severity of functional deficits.

Table 4. Cluster statistics are shown per sample sub-set and listed in ascending order by accelerometry input variable. Values are to be compared within each row of data.

Sample	Number of Accelerometry Input Variables	Variance Explained by Each PC (%)		Total Variance Explained by Number of Clusters (%)				AIC by # of Clusters			
		PC1	PC2	2	3	4	5	2	3	4	5
Sample 1: Stroke + Control (n = 192, replication)	12	57.4	13.1	35.9	45.2	53.8	59.4	1462.7	1281.9	1116.6	1017.2
	9	68.5	16.5	40.6	53.2	59.8	64.6	1019.7	829.9	738.1	677.0
	7	75.6	14.1	46.8	61.4	67.7	70.8	713.3	539.4	471.6	445.7
	5	76.4	17.6	45.7	62.7	69.4	73.9	519.6	373.1	321.6	289.7
Sample 2: Stroke + Proportionate Control (n = 69, replication)	12	49.6	13.2	39.5	48.5	55.3	60.1	527.0	479.9	450.4	436.1
	9	58.9	17.5	46.6	58.1	65.2	69.7	353.4	302.7	278.6	270.3
	7	66.9	15.0	51.1	63.0	68.9	73.6	254.0	213.0	199.8	192.1
	5	67.1	19.5	49.9	64.8	70.9	75.8	185.3	146.1	136.0	129.9
Sample 3: Other conditions +Control excluding stroke (n = 275, generalization)	12	34.2	15.5	20.9	30.6	39.4	46.4	2638.5	2343.9	2080.2	1876.1
	9	40.4	19.8	25.5	37.4	45.1	50.5	1865.4	1593.4	1420.4	1306.5
	7	49.5	21.2	31.2	44.3	51.1	56.0	1343.4	1107.4	990.7	911.7
	5	53.0	25.7	58.0	72.1	78.2	81.6	935.4	720.6	645.5	588.0
Sample 4: Total Sample (n = 324, generalization)	12	42.9	13.7	28.0	37.9	46.5	52.2	2823.4	2465.7	2158.4	1868.0
	9	50.6	18.0	32.1	45.0	51.9	62.1	1997.2	1643.2	1460.7	1305.2
	7	59.5	17.5	37.2	51.4	58.7	63.7	1440.0	1134.8	984.2	885.9
	5	67.6	19.5	38.4	53.8	62.7	68.0	1008.1	772.1	637.7	563.5

Abbreviations: Akaike Information Criterion (AIC), principal component (PC).

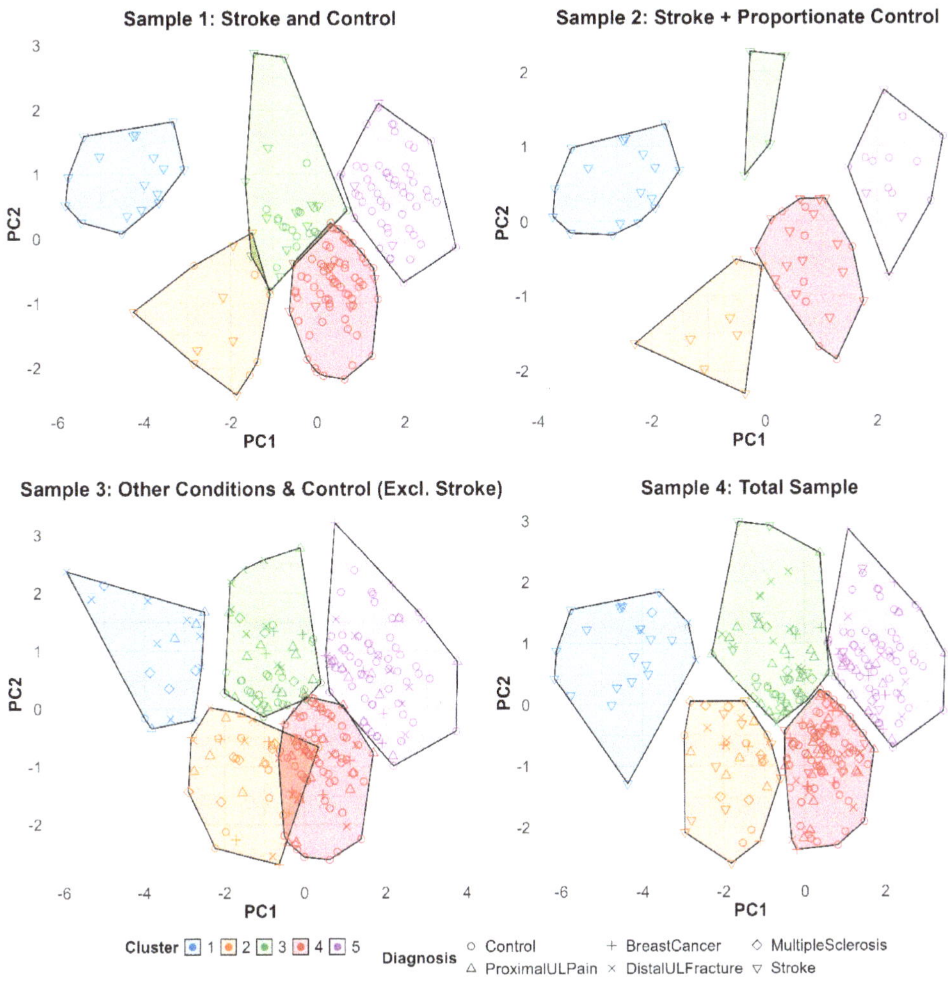

Figure 3. Five-variable, five-cluster plot across samples. Abbreviations: Excl., excluding; PC, principal component; ProximalULPain, proximal upper limb pain; DistalULFracture, distal upper limb fracture.

Surprisingly, there was better convergent validity of the two continuous PCs and individual continuous UL accelerometry variables compared to the five categorical subgroups from our clustering algorithm. Continuous variables generally explained more variance in generic and condition-specific self-report outcomes of UL activity performance and disability, compared to the categorical clusters. Figure 4 visually illustrates this by showing the lack of relationship between the cluster solutions and the PROMIS Upper Extremity measure and the ACS IADL measure in the top row (Figure 4A,B) compared to scatter plots of PC 1 (Figure 4C,D) and example single variables (Figure 4E,H). Table 5 shows the R^2 values that quantify these relationships. Of note, there are no universally defined thresholds for interpreting R^2 values; rather, they should be evaluated in relation to the construct being measured and the methods used. In the context of this work, each accelerometry input variable captures a single aspect of a broader construct being that of performance of UL activity in daily life. Accordingly, modest R^2 values across multiple variables may still provide meaningful evidence of convergent validity when considered collectively. For example, many single UL accelerometry variables (e.g., non-preferred magnitude, bilateral magnitude, non-preferred variance, use ratio, and magnitude ratio) showed convergent validity with self-report outcomes of UL activity performance (column 2, Table 5) and UL disability (columns 5–6, Table 5). Three UL accelerometry variables (e.g., spectral arc length and preferred/non-preferred-only times) consistently showed the weakest convergent validity across self-report outcomes of UL activity performance and disability. Evaluation of condition-specific measures revealed no convergent validity across UL accelerometry variables for the DASH scale. However, we observed significant relations for convergent validity on the MAL (e.g., non-preferred magnitude, bilateral magnitude, non-preferred variance, use ratio, magnitude ratio, and jerk asymmetry index). Additionally, the relationship between the PROMIS Upper Extremity measure and the two PCs is represented as an R^2 of 0.190 indicating significance, while clusters showed essentially no relationship with this measure as an R^2 0.030. Divergent validity was established using the CES-D, wherein low values of R^2 were observed across five clusters, two PCs, and individual UL accelerometry variables.

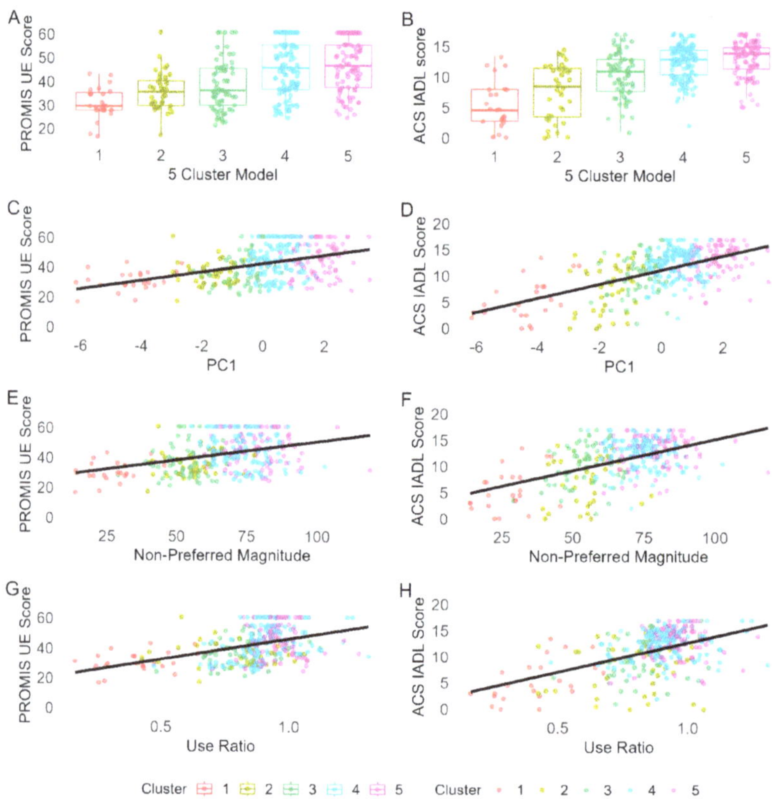

Figure 4. Scatterplots of convergent validity analysis. (**A**) Scatterplot of PROMIS UE score and 5 Cluster Model. (**B**) Scatterplot of ACS IADL score and 5 Cluster Model. (**C**) Scatterplot of PROMIS UE and PC1 (which represents overall UL activity performance). (**D**) Scatterplot of ACS IADL score and PC1 (which represents overall UL activity performance). (**E**) Scatterplot of PROMIS UE score and Non-Preferred Magnitude. (**F**) Scatterplot of ACS IADL score and Non-Preferred Magnitude. (**G**) Scatterplot of PROMIS UE score and Use Ratio. (**H**) Scatterplot of ACS IADL score and Use Ratio. Abbreviations: ACS IADL score, Activity Card Sort–Instrumental Activities of Daily Living score; PC, principal component; PROMIS UE Score, Patient-Reported Outcome Measurement Information System Score for the Upper Extremity.

Table 5. Convergent and divergent validity statistics.

Accelerometry Input Variable (R^2)	Universal Self-Report of UL Activity	Condition Specific Self-Report of UL Activity		Common Self-Report of Activity and Quality of Life				Self-Report of Depressive Symptoms
	PROMIS UE	**MAL (Stroke, MS)**	**DASH (Breast Cancer, Distal UL Fracture, Proximal UL Pain)**	**ACS Global**	**ACS IADL**	**Euro QofL Self-Care**	**Euro QofL Usual Activities**	**CES-D**
5 Clusters	0.030	**0.210**	**0.150**	0.015	0.027	0.065	0.025	0.007
2 PCs	**0.190**	**0.260**	0.010	**0.260**	**0.340**	**0.150**	**0.140**	0.063
Preferred time	0.036	0.057	0.002	**0.144**	**0.152**	0.053	0.048	0.040
Non-preferred time	0.057	0.012	0.023	**0.152**	**0.116**	0.068	0.063	0.063
Preferred only time	4.0×10^{-4}	0.053	0.048	0.012	0.026	0.003	2.5×10^{-5}	4.0×10^{-6}
Non-preferred only time	0.004	0.053	0.004	0.004	0.023	4.9×10^{-5}	0.004	0.005
Non-preferred magnitude	**0.130**	**0.212**	4.0×10^{-4}	**0.168**	**0.260**	0.090	0.090	0.005
Bilateral magnitude	**0.203**	**0.194**	0.068	**0.240**	**0.325**	**0.152**	**0.152**	0.014
Non-preferred variance	**0.194**	**0.203**	0.006	**0.176**	**0.270**	**0.109**	**0.110**	0.004
Use ratio	**0.176**	**0.260**	0.058	**0.176**	**0.260**	**0.160**	**0.144**	1.0×10^{-4}
Magnitude ratio	**0.212**	**0.230**	0.090	**0.102**	**0.144**	**0.102**	**0.116**	2.0×10^{-4}
Jerk asymmetry index	**0.212**	**0.270**	0.090	**0.144**	**0.203**	**0.144**	**0.168**	1.0×10^{-4}
Preferred spectral arc length	1.0×10^{-4}	4.0×10^{-4}	0.008	0.030	0.003	1.6×10^{-4}	1.6×10^{-4}	1.6×10^{-4}
Non-preferred spectral arc length	2.0×10^{-4}	0.040	0.017	9.0×10^{-4}	4.0×10^{-4}	1.6×10^{-4}	1.6×10^{-5}	4.9×10^{-4}

Values in bold are statistically significant from zero. Preferred limb refers to the dominant limb in participants without UL disability, and the non-affected limb in participants with clinical conditions. Non-preferred limb refers to the non-dominant limb in participants without UL disability and the affected limb in participants with clinical conditions. Abbreviations: ACS, Activity Card Sort; CES-D, Center for Epidemiologic Studies Depression Scale; DASH, Disability of the Arm, Shoulder, and Hand Scale; EuroQoL, European Quality of Life Scale; IADL, Instrumental Activities of Daily Living; MAL, Motor Activity Log; Multiple Sclerosis; PROMIS, Patient-Reported Outcomes Measurement Information System; UL, upper limb.

4. Discussion

A five-variable, five-cluster solution for UL activity performance in daily life was replicated in a new independent sample of people with stroke and people without UL disability. Furthermore, the relationships between variables (PCA) and clustering of people into roughly five multivariate groups (k-means), generalized across neurological, musculoskeletal, and other medical conditions and across severity of functional deficits, were studied. Expanding the analyses from stroke to other conditions resulted in remarkable similarities across samples. This suggests that UL activity performance in daily life can be quantified in a similar manner regardless of the biological cause or severity of functional deficits. However, across generic and condition-specific self-report outcomes of UL activity performance and disability, convergent validity was much higher for PCs and individual UL accelerometry variables treated continuously than for the five clusters treated categorically. Thus, although there is empirical support to divide people into clusters, when it comes to explaining individual differences in UL activity performance and disability, treating these measures continuously may be the more powerful approach. Overall, these findings underscore the potential for more efficient and personalized rehabilitative care by streamlining wearable sensor-based assessment of UL activity performance into a focused, generalizable tool that is applicable across diverse conditions of the UL as well as severity of functional deficits and salient to clinicians and patients alike.

Replication of a five-variable, five-cluster solution in a sample of people with stroke and people without UL disability was confirmed. This analysis demonstrated the stability of original findings from Barth et al. (2021) [11] across two new samples of people with stroke and people without UL disability. Although both replication samples included the same conditions, their compositions differed substantially, which provided an opportunity to assess the robustness of the model across contrasting clinical profiles. Irrespective of sample composition (one sample had a higher frequency of people without UL disability than the other), two PCs consistently emerged from the data with comparable variance explained, and the five-variable, five-cluster model was preserved (samples 1 and 2, Table 4).

Replication of the same solution suggests the findings are real, as many findings in the biomedical literature cannot be replicated [60,61], especially with statistical models such as the ones used here.

A five-variable, five-cluster solution was generalizable beyond people with stroke and people without UL disability, to people with other neurologic, musculoskeletal, and medical conditions that affect the ULs to varying degrees of functional severity. This generalizability is visually supported by the consistent spatial patterns observed across samples in both the PC space (Figure 2) and cluster distributions (Figure 3). There are two intertwined reasons that may account for this generalizability. First, all people need to perform similarly complex UL activities in daily life. And second, accelerometry-derived sensor variables quantify general characteristics of movement (e.g., duration, magnitude, quality) [62], but they do not yet quantify how and when specific tasks are performed by a person [18]. While efforts are underway in other research groups to quantify specific, individual tasks performed in daily life, it may be decades before the library of algorithms is large and accurate enough to be used in an unsupervised clinical setting across patient populations and severity of functional deficits [63–66]. Taken together, the generalizability observed for both PCA and cluster analyses suggests a practical and scalable solution for characterizing UL activity performance in daily life across diverse clinical conditions and severity of functional deficits.

Assessment of convergent validity revealed PC and individual UL accelerometry variables had significant relationships with both generic and condition-specific self-report measures of UL activity performance and disability, while cluster membership did not. Five categorical clusters showed trivial relationships with PROMIS UE and ACS IADL scores (Figure 4A,B; $R^2 \leq 0.03$), suggesting that although these people may consistently move similarly based on their accelerometry recorded in daily life, cluster membership was unrelated to perceptions of UL activity in daily life. In contrast, PCs showed significant relations with self-report measures (Figure 4C,D), particularly condition-specific instruments like the MAL ($R^2 = 0.26$–0.27), and broader indices of activity and participation ($R^2 = 0.26$–0.34). While the data support consistent groups of people with similar movement profiles, there remains important variability within each group. This variability is meaningfully associated with clinically validated outcomes but is lost when continuous data are reduced to categorical classifications. Similarly, among individual accelerometry variables, those reflecting movement magnitude (e.g., bilateral magnitude) and symmetry (e.g., magnitude ratio, jerk asymmetry index) showed significant relations with self-reported activity (R^2 up to 0.27), while duration (e.g., preferred/non-preferred only time) and quality of movement (e.g., spectral arc length) did not. The magnitude of the significant relationships aligns with prior findings in people with stroke, though it is presented here as R^2 rather than correlation coefficients [66], to allow comparison with multivariable constructs such as the categorical clusters and two PCs. Overall, these findings suggest that upper limb performance may be better represented along a continuum of functional recovery using 2PCs, rather than with discrete categories using clusters. In the future, a five-variable model could be implemented clinically using onboard processing in either wearable movement sensors or mobile devices to map an individual's performance within a two-dimensional PC space. This approach may offer several benefits: it can be generalized across conditions and severity of functional deficits, avoids reliance on condition-specific clinical assessments, and reduces the need for recall of diagnostic-specific details. However, certain clinical populations may still benefit from targeted examination of specific variables, for example, the use ratio in stroke or jerk asymmetry in ataxia, highlighting the potential need for hybrid approaches in some contexts or environments.

This study had two primary limitations, which influence interpretation of the data. First, the proportion of participants people without UL disability relative to individual clinical groups was high. While the total sample was predominantly composed of clinical populations (57%), the relatively high proportion of people without UL disability (43%) may have biased results towards lower levels of disability. The inclusion of people without UL disability, however, served a critical role by providing a reference point for normative functional status, given that the aims of this work were to replicate and generalize prior findings to additional clinical populations. Second, the aim of replication required use of the same composition of (12, 9, 7, and 5) accelerometry input variables for each stage of analysis. This approach may have limited discovery of other relevant variables or combinations that could reveal additional patterns across clinical populations and severity of functional deficits. This limitation was further amplified in the assessment of convergent validity, where some individual accelerometry variables demonstrated comparable associations with self-reported outcomes as the multivariate PCs. It is possible that other, multivariate combinations could be identified in the future and might be more strongly related to perception of UL activity performance in daily life.

5. Conclusions

This work demonstrates that while a five-variable, five-cluster solution can be reliably reproduced and generalized across a diverse group of clinical populations and severity of functional deficits, it does not fully capture the clinically meaningful variation of UL activity performance in daily life. Stronger associations between self-reported outcomes and both PC and individual accelerometry variables indicated that key aspects of functional recovery are lost when continuous data are reduced to categories. These findings support a shift toward models that quantify UL recovery along a continuum, which may offer greater sensitivity to individual differences and broader applicability across diagnostic groups and functional levels of severity. This approach lays the foundation for the development of efficient and scalable tools to monitor UL function in real-world rehabilitation settings.

Author Contributions: Conceptualization, C.E.L., M.D.B. and C.L.H.; Methodology, C.E.L., M.D.B., A.E.M., C.L.H. and K.R.L.; Software, K.R.L.; Validation, K.R.L. and C.E.M.; Formal analysis, C.E.M., K.R.L. and C.E.L.; Investigation, C.G., C.N., A.E.M. and M.D.B.; Resources, C.E.L.; Data curation, M.D.B.; Writing—original draft preparation, C.E.M., C.E.L. and K.R.L.; Writing—review and editing, C.E.M., C.E.L., K.R.L., A.E.M., C.L.H., C.N., C.G., C.J.D. and L.P.; Visualization, C.E.M., A.E.M. and K.R.L.; Supervision, C.E.L. and K.R.L.; Project administration, M.D.B.; Funding acquisition, C.E.L. All authors have read and agreed to the published version of the manuscript.

Funding: This manuscript is the result of funding in whole or in part by the National Institutes of Health (NIH, R37HD068290). It is subject to the NIH Public Access Policy. Through acceptance of this federal funding, the NIH has been given a right to make this manuscript publicly available in PubMed Central upon the official date of publication, as defined by NIH. The views expressed are those of the authors and do not necessarily represent the official views of the National Institutes of Health.

Institutional Review Board Statement: The study was conducted in accordance with the Declaration of Helsinki and approved by the Institutional Review Board at WashU Medicine (WUSTL IRB# 202207003-1001, 21 July 2022).

Informed Consent Statement: Informed consent was obtained from all subjects involved in the study.

Data Availability Statement: Informed consent was obtained from all subjects involved in the study.

Acknowledgments: We would like to thank Kayla Bell, Makenna Dixon, and Brandon Jensen for their assistance with processing data for this study.

Conflicts of Interest: The authors declare no conflicts of interest. The funders had no role in the design of the study; in the collection, analyses, or interpretation of data; in the writing of the manuscript; or in the decision to publish the results.

Abbreviations

The following abbreviations are used in this manuscript:

N/n	Number
UL	Upper Limb
PC	Principal Component
PCA	Principal Component Analysis
IRB	Institutional Review Board
MS	Multiple Sclerosis
h	Hours
acs	Activity Count
DASH	Disability of the Shoulder Arm and Hand Scale
MAL-AoU	Motor Activity Log–Amount of Use Scale
PROMIS	Patient-Reported Outcome Measurement Information System Upper Extremity Bank 2.0 via Computer Adaptive Test
ACS	Activity Card Sort
EuroQoL	European Quality of Life Scale—5 dimensions 3 Levels
CES-D	Center for Epidemiological Studies Depression Scale
NIH-NICHD	National Institutes of Health: Eunice Kennedy Shriver National Institute of Child Health and Human Development
WSS	Within-Cluster Sum of Squares
MANOVA	Multivariate Analysis of Variance
AIC	Akaike Information Criterion
IQR	Inter-Quartile Range
ADL	Activities of Daily Living
Mo	Months
SD	Standard Deviation
Yrs	Years
IADL	Instrumental Activities of Daily Living
ProximalULPain	Proximal Upper Limb Pain
DistalULFracture	Distal Upper Limb Fracture
Excl.	Excluding
UE	Upper Extremity

References

1. Huang, G.D.; Feuerstein, M.; Berkowitz, S.M.; Peck, C.A. Occupational upper-extremity-related disability: Demographic, physical, and psychosocial factors. *Mil. Med.* **1998**, *163*, 552–558. [CrossRef] [PubMed]
2. Waddell, K.J.; Birkenmeier, R.L.; Bland, M.D.; Lang, C.E. An exploratory analysis of the self-reported goals of individuals with chronic upper-extremity paresis following stroke. *Disabil. Rehabil.* **2016**, *38*, 853–857. [CrossRef] [PubMed]
3. International Classification of Functioning, Disability and Health (ICF). Available online: https://www.who.int/standards/classifications/international-classification-of-functioning-disability-and-health (accessed on 6 May 2025).
4. Towards a Common Language for Functioning, Disability and Health: IC. Available online: https://www.medbox.org/document/towards-a-common-language-for-functioning-disability-and-health-icf-the-international-classification-of-functioning-disability-and-health (accessed on 6 May 2025).
5. Patel, S.; Park, H.; Bonato, P.; Chan, L.; Rodgers, M. A review of wearable sensors and systems with application in rehabilitation. *J. Neuroeng. Rehabil.* **2012**, *9*, 21. [CrossRef]
6. Porciuncula, F.; Roto, A.V.; Kumar, D.; Davis, I.; Roy, S.; Walsh, C.J.; Awad, L.N. Wearable Movement Sensors for Rehabilitation: A Focused Review of Technological and Clinical Advances. *PM&R* **2018**, *10* (Suppl. S2), S220–S232. [CrossRef] [PubMed]
7. Cain, A.; Gunby, T.; Winstein, C.; Demers, M. Advancing stroke rehabilitation: The role of wearable technology according to research experts. *Disabil. Rehabil. Assist. Technol.* **2025**, *20*, 1460–1469. [CrossRef]

8. Lang, C.E.; Barth, J.; Holleran, C.L.; Konrad, J.D.; Bland, M.D. Implementation of Wearable Sensing Technology for Movement: Pushing Forward into the Routine Physical Rehabilitation Care Field. *Sensors* **2020**, *20*, 5744. [CrossRef]
9. Wang, S.; Liu, J.; Chen, S.; Wang, S.; Peng, Y.; Liao, C.; Liu, L. Recognizing wearable upper-limb rehabilitation gestures by a hybrid multi-feature neural network. *Eng. Appl. Artif. Intell.* **2024**, *127*, 107424. [CrossRef]
10. Lang, C.E.; Cade, W.T. A step toward the future of seamless measurement with wearable sensors in pediatric populations with neuromuscular diseases. *Muscle Nerve* **2020**, *61*, 265–267. [CrossRef]
11. Barth, J.; Lohse, K.R.; Konrad, J.D.; Bland, M.D.; Lang, C.E. Sensor-Based Categorization of Upper Limb Performance in Daily Life of Persons With and Without Neurological Upper Limb Deficits. *Front. Rehabil. Sci.* **2021**, *2*, 741393. [CrossRef]
12. Harris, P.A.; Taylor, R.; Minor, B.L.; Elliott, V.; Fernandez, M.; O'Neal, L.; McLeod, L.; Delacqua, G.; Delacqua, F.; Kirby, J.; et al. The REDCap consortium: Building an international community of software platform partners. *J. Biomed. Inform.* **2019**, *95*, 103208. [CrossRef]
13. Harris, P.A.; Taylor, R.; Thielke, R.; Payne, J.; Gonzalez, N.; Conde, J.G. Research electronic data capture (REDCap)—A metadata-driven methodology and workflow process for providing translational research informatics support. *J. Biomed. Inform.* **2009**, *42*, 377–381. [CrossRef]
14. Obeid, J.S.; McGraw, C.A.; Minor, B.L.; Conde, J.G.; Pawluk, R.; Lin, M.; Wang, J.; Banks, S.R.; Hemphill, S.A.; Taylor, R.; et al. Procurement of shared data instruments for Research Electronic Data Capture (REDCap). *J. Biomed. Inform.* **2013**, *46*, 259–265. [CrossRef]
15. Lawrence, C.E.; Dunkel, L.; McEver, M.; Israel, T.; Taylor, R.; Chiriboga, G.; Goins, K.V.; Rahn, E.J.; Mudano, A.S.; Roberson, E.D.; et al. A REDCap-based model for electronic consent (eConsent): Moving toward a more personalized consent. *J. Clin. Transl. Sci.* **2020**, *4*, 345–353. [CrossRef]
16. *ISO 13485:2016*; International Standardization Organization Medical Device Single Audit Program. ISO: Geneva, Switzerland, 2016.
17. Lang, C.E.; Waddell, K.J.; Klaesner, J.W.; Bland, M.D. A Method for Quantifying Upper Limb Performance in Daily Life Using Accelerometers. *J. Vis. Exp. JoVE* **2017**, 55673. [CrossRef]
18. Bailey, R.R.; Lang, C.E. Upper extremity activity in adults: Referent values using accelerometry. *J. Rehabil. Res. Dev.* **2014**, *50*, 1213–1222. [CrossRef] [PubMed]
19. Barak, S.; Wu, S.S.; Dai, Y.; Duncan, P.W.; Behrman, A.L. Adherence to Accelerometry Measurement of Community Ambulation Poststroke. *Phys. Ther.* **2014**, *94*, 101–110. [CrossRef] [PubMed]
20. R Core Team. *R: A Language and Environment for Statistical Computing*; R Core Team: Vienna, Austria, 2023.
21. Miller, A.E.; Lohse, K.R.; Bland, M.D.; Konrad, J.D.; Hoyt, C.R.; Lenze, E.J.; Lang, C.E. A Large Harmonized Upper and Lower Limb Accelerometry Dataset: A Resource for Rehabilitation Scientists. *medRxiv* **2024**. [CrossRef]
22. Lohse, K. keithlohse/HarmonizedAccelData: Harmonized Upper and Lower Limb Accelerometry Data. 2024. Available online: https://zenodo.org/records/10999195 (accessed on 1 June 2025).
23. Neishabouri, A.; Nguyen, J.; Samuelsson, J.; Guthrie, T.; Biggs, M.; Wyatt, J.; Cross, D.; Karas, M.; Migueles, J.H.; Khan, S.; et al. Quantification of acceleration as activity counts in ActiGraph wearable. *Sci. Rep.* **2022**, *12*, 11958. [CrossRef]
24. Uswatte, G.; Miltner, W.H.; Foo, B.; Varma, M.; Moran, S.; Taub, E. Objective measurement of functional upper-extremity movement using accelerometer recordings transformed with a threshold filter. *Stroke* **2000**, *31*, 662–667. [CrossRef]
25. Lang, C.E.; Hoyt, C.R.; Konrad, J.D.; Bell, K.R.; Marrus, N.; Bland, M.D.; Lohse, K.R.; Miller, A.E. Referent data for investigations of upper limb accelerometry: Harmonized data from three cohorts of typically-developing children. *Front. Pediatr.* **2024**, *12*, 1361757. [CrossRef]
26. Balasubramanian, S.; Melendez-Calderon, A.; Roby-Brami, A.; Burdet, E. On the analysis of movement smoothness. *J. Neuroeng. Rehabil* **2015**, *12*, 112. [CrossRef]
27. Balasubramanian, S.; Melendez-Calderon, A.; Burdet, E. A Robust and Sensitive Metric for Quantifying Movement Smoothness. *IEEE Trans. Biomed. Eng.* **2011**, *59*, 2126–2136. Available online: https://ieeexplore.ieee.org/document/6104119 (accessed on 6 May 2025). [CrossRef]
28. Horn, M.E.; Reinke, E.K.; Couce, L.J.; Reeve, B.B.; Ledbetter, L.; George, S.Z. Reporting and utilization of Patient-Reported Outcomes Measurement Information System® (PROMIS®) measures in orthopedic research and practice: A systematic review. *J. Orthop. Surg.* **2020**, *15*, 553. [CrossRef]
29. Kaat, A.J.; Buckenmaier, C.T., III; Cook, K.F.; Rothrock, N.E.; Schalet, B.D.; Gershon, R.C.; Vrahas, M.S. The expansion and validation of a new upper extremity item bank for the Patient-Reported Outcomes Measurement Information System® (PROMIS). *J. Patient-Rep. Outcomes* **2019**, *3*, 69. [CrossRef]
30. Crins, M.H.P.; van der Wees, P.J.; Klausch, T.; van Dulmen, S.A.; Roorda, L.D.; Terwee, C.B. Psychometric properties of the PROMIS Physical Function item bank in patients receiving physical therapy. *PLoS ONE* **2018**, *13*, e0192187. [CrossRef]
31. van der Lee, J.H.; Beckerman, H.; Knol, D.L.; de Vet, H.C.W.; Bouter, L.M. Clinimetric properties of the motor activity log for the assessment of arm use in hemiparetic patients. *Stroke* **2004**, *35*, 1410–1414. [CrossRef] [PubMed]

32. Uswatte, G.; Taub, E.; Morris, D.; Vignolo, M.; McCulloch, K. Reliability and validity of the upper-extremity Motor Activity Log-14 for measuring real-world arm use. *Stroke* **2005**, *36*, 2493–2496. [CrossRef] [PubMed]
33. Beaton, D.E.; Katz, J.N.; Fossel, A.H.; Wright, J.G.; Tarasuk, V.; Bombardier, C. Measuring the whole or the parts? Validity, reliability, and responsiveness of the Disabilities of the Arm, Shoulder and Hand outcome measure in different regions of the upper extremity. *J. Hand Ther. Off. J. Am. Soc. Hand Ther.* **2001**, *14*, 128–146. [CrossRef]
34. Schmitt, J.S.; Di Fabio, R.P. Reliable change and minimum important difference (MID) proportions facilitated group responsiveness comparisons using individual threshold criteria. *J. Clin. Epidemiol.* **2004**, *57*, 1008–1018. [CrossRef]
35. Gummesson, C.; Atroshi, I.; Ekdahl, C. The disabilities of the arm, shoulder and hand (DASH) outcome questionnaire: Longitudinal construct validity and measuring self-rated health change after surgery. *BMC Musculoskelet. Disord.* **2003**, *4*, 11. [CrossRef]
36. Boone, A.E.; Wolf, T.J.; Baum, C.M. Development and Initial Testing of the Electronic Activity Card Sort (ACS3) Among Community-Dwelling Adults. *Am. J. Occup. Ther.* **2022**, *76*, 7603345030. [CrossRef] [PubMed]
37. Baum, C.M.; Edwards, D. *Activity Card Sort*, 2nd ed.; American Occupational Therapy Association: Bethesda, MD, USA, 2008.
38. Barth, J.; Geed, S.; Mitchell, A.; Brady, K.P.; Giannetti, M.L.; Dromerick, A.W.; Edwards, D.F. The Critical Period After Stroke Study (CPASS) Upper Extremity Treatment Protocol. *Arch. Rehabil. Res. Clin. Transl.* **2023**, *5*, 100282. [CrossRef] [PubMed]
39. Dromerick, A.W.; Edwardson, M.A.; Edwards, D.F.; Giannetti, M.L.; Barth, J.; Brady, K.P.; Chan, E.; Tan, M.T.; Tamboli, I.; Chia, R.; et al. Critical periods after stroke study: Translating animal stroke recovery experiments into a clinical trial. *Front. Hum. Neurosci.* **2015**, *9*, 231. [CrossRef] [PubMed]
40. Hartman-Maeir, A.; Eliad, Y.; Kizoni, R.; Nahaloni, I.; Kelberman, H.; Katz, N. Evaluation of a long-term community based rehabilitation program for adult stroke survivors. *NeuroRehabilitation* **2007**, *22*, 295–301. [CrossRef]
41. Doney, R.M.; Packer, T.L. Measuring changes in activity participation of older Australians: Validation of the Activity Card Sort-Australia. *Australas. J. Ageing* **2008**, *27*, 33–37. [CrossRef]
42. Hamed, R.; Holm, M.B. Psychometric Properties of the Arab Heritage Activity Card Sort. *Occup. Ther. Int.* **2013**, *20*, 23–34. [CrossRef]
43. Gustafsson, L.; Hung, I.H.M.; Liddle, J. Test–Retest Reliability and Internal Consistency of the Activity Card Sort–Australia (18-64). *OTJR Occup. Particip. Health* **2017**, *37*, 50–56. [CrossRef]
44. Feng, Y.-S.; Kohlmann, T.; Janssen, M.F.; Buchholz, I. Psychometric properties of the EQ-5D-5L: A systematic review of the literature. *Qual. Life Res.* **2021**, *30*, 647–673. [CrossRef]
45. Charlson, M.E.; Carrozzino, D.; Guidi, J.; Patierno, C. Charlson Comorbidity Index: A Critical Review of Clinimetric Properties. *Psychother. Psychosom.* **2022**, *91*, 8–35. [CrossRef]
46. Charlson, M.E.; Pompei, P.; Ales, K.L.; MacKenzie, C.R. A new method of classifying prognostic comorbidity in longitudinal studies: Development and validation. *J. Chronic Dis.* **1987**, *40*, 373–383. [CrossRef]
47. Cosco, T.D.; Prina, M.; Stubbs, B.; Wu, Y.-T. Reliability and Validity of the Center for Epidemiologic Studies Depression Scale in a Population-Based Cohort of Middle-Aged, U.S. Adults. *J. Nurs. Meas.* **2017**, *25*, 476–485. [CrossRef]
48. Radloff, L.S. The CES-D Scale: A Self-Report Depression Scale for Research in the General Population. *Appl. Psychol. Meas.* **1977**, *1*, 385–401. [CrossRef]
49. Shinar, D.; Gross, C.R.; Price, T.R.; Banko, M.; Bolduc, P.L.; Robinson, R.G. Screening for depression in stroke patients: The reliability and validity of the Center for Epidemiologic Studies Depression Scale. *Stroke* **1986**, *17*, 241–245. [CrossRef]
50. Gillen, R.; Eberhardt, T.L.; Tennen, H.; Affleck, G.; Groszmann, Y. Screening for depression in stroke: Relationship to rehabilitation efficiency. *J. Stroke Cerebrovasc. Dis.* **1999**, *8*, 300–306. [CrossRef]
51. Wickham, H.; Averick, M.; Bryan, J.; Chang, W.; McGowan, L.; François, R.; Grolemund, G.; Hayes, A.; Henry, L.; Hester, J.; et al. Welcome to Tidyverse. *J. Open Source Softw.* **2019**, *4*, 1686. [CrossRef]
52. Kassambara, A.; Mundt, F. factoextra: Extract and Visualize the Results of Multivariate Data Analyses 2020. Available online: https://CRAN.R-project.org/package=factoextra (accessed on 14 October 2024).
53. Pedersen, T. patchwork: The Composer of Plots 2024. Available online: https://CRAN.R-project.org/package=patchwork (accessed on 5 December 2024).
54. Dalmaijer, E.S.; Nord, C.L.; Astle, D.E. Statistical power for cluster analysis. *BMC Bioinform.* **2021**, *23*, 205. [CrossRef] [PubMed]
55. Bholowalia, P. EBK-Means: A Clustering Technique based on Elbow Method and K-Means in WSN. *Int. J. Comput. Appl.* **2014**, *105*, 9.
56. Rousseeuw, P.J. Silhouettes: A graphical aid to the interpretation and validation of cluster analysis. *J. Comput. Appl. Math.* **1987**, *20*, 53–65. [CrossRef]
57. Tibshirani, R.; Walther, G.; Hastie, T. Estimating the Number of Clusters in a Data Set Via the Gap Statistic. *J. R. Stat. Soc. Ser. B Stat. Methodol.* **2001**, *63*, 411–423. [CrossRef]
58. James, G.; Witten, D.; Hastie, T.; Tibshirani, R. *An Introduction to Statistical Learning: With Applications in R*, 2nd ed.; Springer: New York, NY, USA, 2021.

59. Bailey, R.R.; Birkenmeier, R.L.; Lang, C.E. Real-World Affected Upper Limb Activity in Chronic Stroke: An Examination of Potential Modifying Factors. *Top. Stroke Rehabil.* **2015**, *22*, 26–33. [CrossRef]
60. Autzen, B. Is the replication crisis a base-rate fallacy? *Theor. Med. Bioeth.* **2021**, *42*, 233–243. [CrossRef]
61. Gannot, G.; Cutting, M.A.; Fischer, D.J.; Hsu, L.J. Reproducibility and transparency in biomedical sciences. *Oral Dis.* **2017**, *23*, 813–816. [CrossRef]
62. Barth, J.; Klaesner, J.W.; Lang, C.E. Relationships between accelerometry and general compensatory movements of the upper limb after stroke. *J. Neuroeng. Rehabil.* **2020**, *17*, 138. [CrossRef] [PubMed]
63. Kim, G.J.; Parnandi, A.; Eva, S.; Schambra, H. The use of wearable sensors to assess and treat the upper extremity after stroke: A scoping review. *Disabil. Rehabil.* **2022**, *44*, 6119–6138. [CrossRef] [PubMed]
64. Schambra, H.M.; Parnandi, A.; Pandit, N.G.; Uddin, J.; Wirtanen, A.; Nilsen, D.M. A Taxonomy of Functional Upper Extremity Motion. *Front. Neurol.* **2019**, *10*, 857. [CrossRef] [PubMed]
65. Parnandi, A.; Uddin, J.; Nilsen, D.M.; Schambra, H.M. The Pragmatic Classification of Upper Extremity Motion in Neurological Patients: A Primer. *Front. Neurol.* **2019**, *10*, 996. [CrossRef]
66. Hayward, K.S.; Eng, J.J.; Boyd, L.A.; Lakhani, B.; Bernhardt, J.; Lang, C.E. Exploring the Role of Accelerometers in the Measurement of Real World Upper-Limb Use After Stroke. *Brain Impair.* **2016**, *17*, 16–33. [CrossRef]

sensors

MDPI

Article

An EMG-Based GRU Model for Estimating Foot Pressure to Support Active Ankle Orthosis Development

Praveen Nuwantha Gunaratne [1] and Hiroki Tamura [2,*]

[1] Interdisciplinary Graduate School of Agriculture and Engineering, University of Miyazaki, 1-1 Gakuen Kibanadai-nishi, Miyazaki 889-2192, Japan

[2] Faculty of Engineering, University of Miyazaki, 1-1 Gakuen Kibanadai-nishi, Miyazaki 889-2192, Japan

* Correspondence: htamura@cc.miyazaki-u.ac.jp

Abstract

As populations age, particularly in countries like Japan, mobility impairments related to ankle joint dysfunction, such as foot drop, instability, and reduced gait adaptability, have become a significant concern. Active ankle–foot orthoses (AAFO) offer targeted support during walking; however, most existing systems rely on rule-based or threshold-based control, which are often limited to sagittal plane movements and lacking adaptability to subject-specific gait variations. This study proposes an approach driven by neuromuscular activation using surface electromyography (EMG) and a Gated Recurrent Unit (GRU)-based deep learning model to predict plantar pressure distributions at the heel, midfoot, and toe regions during gait. EMG signals were collected from four key ankle muscles, and plantar pressures were recorded using a customized sandal-integrated force-sensitive resistor (FSR) system. The data underwent comprehensive preprocessing and segmentation using a sliding window method. Root mean square (RMS) values were extracted as the primary input feature due to their consistent performance in capturing muscle activation intensity. The GRU model successfully generalized across subjects, enabling the accurate real-time inference of critical gait events such as heel strike, mid-stance, and toe off. This biomechanical evaluation demonstrated strong signal compatibility, while also identifying individual variations in electromechanical delay (EMD). The proposed predictive framework offers a scalable and interpretable approach to improving real-time AAFO control by synchronizing assistance with user-specific gait dynamics.

Keywords: surface EMG; GRU neural network; foot pressure estimation; gait analysis; AAFO

1. Introduction

Japan, like many developed nations, is facing an unprecedented demographic transformation. With over 29% of its population aged 65 years and above, age-related mobility impairments are becoming increasingly prevalent [1]. Among the elderly, lower limb dysfunction, including weakness in ankle dorsiflexion, imbalance, and reduced gait speed, has emerged as a primary contributor to falls, limited mobility, and reduced independence [2,3]. These challenges have created an urgent demand for advanced assistive technologies and targeted rehabilitation solutions capable of addressing an aging society's complex biomechanical and neuromuscular needs [4]. Among the critical areas of focus, the ankle joint complex plays a key role in enabling a safe, stable, and efficient gait. It acts as a dynamic interface between the body and ground, bearing weight and modulating movement across three anatomical planes: sagittal (dorsiflexion and plantarflexion), frontal (inversion and eversion), and transverse (abduction and adduction) [5]. While sagittal plane dynamics, especially dorsiflexion and plantarflexion, have been the primary focus in both clinical assessments and device control strategies [6], recent studies highlight the essential contribution of frontal and transverse movements in ensuring balance, adaptability to uneven surfaces, and overall gait symmetry [7]. The inability to coordinate these multi-planar movements can result in abnormal gait patterns, poor load distribution, and an increased risk of injury [8].

In response to these challenges, ankle–foot orthoses (AFO), especially AAFO, have been developed to assist or restore ankle joint function [9–11]. These devices use sensors and actuators to detect gait events and provide timely mechanical support (see Figure 1), particularly during dorsiflexion failure as observed in foot drop [12]. Traditional rigid AFO offer joint immobilization and passive correction, while articulated AFO provide limited dynamic control by allowing a partial range of motion [13].

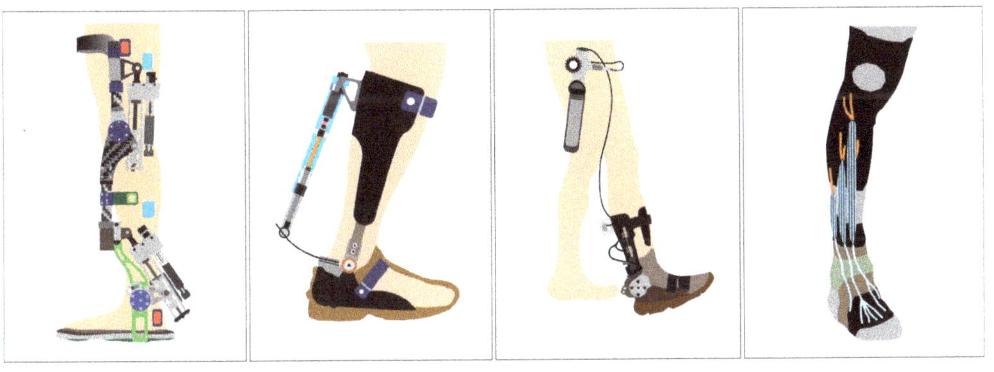

Figure 1. Example AAFO designs proposed by previous researchers featuring integrated sensor–actuator systems for gait event detection and providing ankle joint assistance [9].

However, both types often restrict natural joint kinematics and fail to deliver phase-specific assistance [14]. To overcome these limitations, modern robotic AAFO integrate active control mechanisms and aim to replicate physiological ankle movement [15]. However, some significant challenges persist in both hardware (e.g., actuator miniaturization, power efficiency, and sensor integration) and control architecture (e.g., real-time adaptability, multi-planar movement estimation, and subject-specific variability) [16,17]. A primary limitation of existing AAFO is the use of simplified control strategies, typically based on fixed thresholds, rule-based algorithms, or pre-programmed assistance limited to sagittal plane movements [18]. These methods are inadequate for addressing complex gait deviations, particularly when multi-directional ankle actions like inversion, eversion, or plantarflexion during push off are involved [19]. Additionally, there is often a lack of robust real-time estimation of foot–ground interaction forces, which is essential for adaptive and intuitive control [20]. Addressing this gap requires a predictive approach that can infer spatial plantar pressure distributions from neuromuscular activity in a dynamic, subject-independent manner.

Several studies have explored advanced control strategies to overcome these limitations. For instance, non-parametric neural network models such as multilayer perceptrons (MLPs) have been applied to model AFO dynamics and estimate ground reaction forces with high accuracy [21,22]. While these systems showed low prediction errors, they primarily focused on mechanical system identification and did not utilize EMG-based neuromuscular inputs. Other research integrated EMG and inertial measurement unit

(IMU) data with classifiers and sequential models such as long short-term memory (LSTM) and transformer networks for gait event detection or abnormality classification [23,24]. Despite achieving high accuracy in phase classification, these approaches did not predict continuous, region-specific plantar pressure in real time. Furthermore, data-driven predictive controllers, including model predictive control (MPC) and disturbance rejection strategies, have been proposed for AAFO [25,26], but these designs remain largely reactive and do not incorporate proactive neuromuscular prediction. Collectively, these efforts underscore a significant research gap, namely, the absence of interpretable, temporally aligned models that leverage EMG signals to estimate continuous foot–ground pressure distributions for adaptive AAFO control.

This study proposes a GRU-based deep learning model for predicting plantar pressure values at key foot regions (heel, midfoot, and toe) using surface EMG signals. The model is designed to estimate the temporal relationship between muscle activation patterns and foot pressure dynamics, thereby enabling the real-time inference of gait events and associated ankle joint functions [27]. EMG signals are inherently noisy and exhibit inter-subject variability; therefore, we applied comprehensive signal preprocessing, including band pass filtering, notch filtering, rectification, and normalization [28]. A sliding window approach was used to segment the EMG time series, and the RMS feature was extracted from each window as it consistently demonstrated the strongest correlation with FSR pressure outputs among other time-domain and frequency-domain features [29]. The model architecture is centered on a GRU network, selected for its ability to model temporal dependencies in EMG signals with a lightweight structure suitable for embedded systems. The model was trained using data from multiple subjects and evaluated based on mean squared error (MSE) and mean absolute error (MAE). The time lag between EMG activity and corresponding foot pressure, a common challenge in neuromuscular modeling, was manually addressed during feature alignment. While this method assumes temporal consistency across subjects, the analysis revealed individual variations, underscoring the need for the future development of adaptive alignment strategies [30,31]. This modeling approach is directly applicable to AAFO control systems, enabling real-time pressure prediction to identify gait phases such as initial contact (heel strike), mid-stance, and push off (toe off), each corresponding to specific ankle joint actions [32]. This information can be used to trigger actuator responses for specific gait assistance scenarios, such as compensating for foot drop during the swing phase, enhancing plantarflexion during propulsion, or stabilizing inversion/eversion movements on uneven terrain. Unlike conventional AAFO systems, which rely on mechanical sensing or phase detection algorithms, this EMG-based predictive framework offers a personalized control approach driven by neuromuscular signals [33].

In conclusion, this study presents an interpretable GRU-based model for predicting plantar pressure from EMG signals, addressing key limitations in current AAFO control strategies. While previous studies have utilized combinations of EMG and IMU signals for gait phase classification or joint trajectory estimation [23,24], the present work emphasizes the continuous prediction of spatially distributed plantar pressure patterns using surface EMG signals as the primary input modality. Rather than classifying discrete gait phases, the model captures temporally aligned pressure dynamics at anatomically segmented foot regions, namely the heel, midfoot, and toe, enabling the fine-grained inference of gait events. This temporal modeling approach, driven by neuromuscular activation patterns, offers a physiologically relevant and computationally efficient solution that supports adaptive, multi-phase, and directionally responsive assistance. Accordingly, the proposed framework contributes to the development of personalized AAFO systems that synchronize actuator output with real-time muscle intent, facilitating more natural and effective gait rehabilitation.

2. Considerations for Evaluation

2.1. Gait Cycle

Human walking is characterized by a repetitive, coordinated sequence of lower limb movements collectively known as the gait cycle. A single gait cycle is defined as the time interval between two successive occurrences of an initial heel strike (HS) of the same foot [34]. This cyclical pattern allows the body to move forward in a stable and energy-efficient manner, involving alternating periods of support and limb advancement. Figure 2 presents a schematic representation of the human gait cycle, illustrating key temporal events and associated joint movements across different anatomical planes. The gait cycle is broadly divided into two main phases: the stance phase and the swing phase. The stance phase, which accounts for approximately 60% of the total cycle, begins at HS and ends at toe off (TO), during which the foot remains in contact with the ground. The swing phase follows, occupying the remaining 40%, and represents the period during which the foot is lifted from the ground and progresses forward in preparation for the next HS [3]. Within these two broad phases, the gait cycle can be further segmented into several key gait events, including foot flat (FF), mid-stance (MST), heel off (HO), TO, and terminal swing, each representing important transitional points in lower limb mechanics (see Figure 2a) [35].

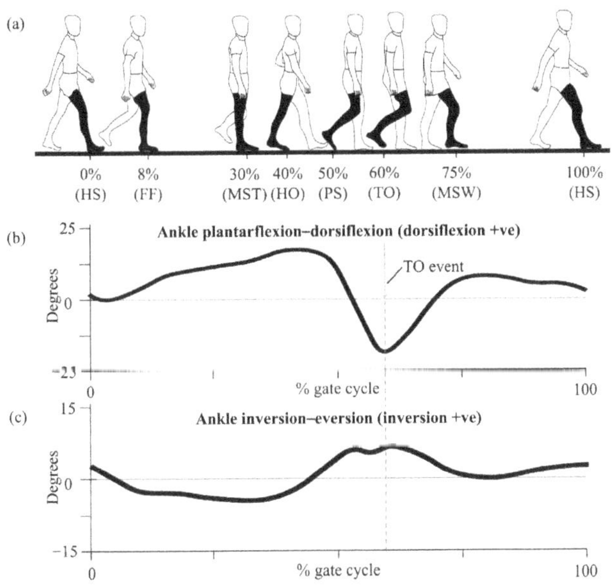

Figure 2. Schematic of the human gait cycle: (**a**) key temporal events including heel strike (HS), foot flat (FF), mid-stance (MST), heel off (HO), pre-swing (PS), toe off (TO), and mid-swing (MSW); (**b**) representative ankle joint movements in the sagittal plane; (**c**) corresponding movements in the frontal plane.

In the sagittal plane, the cycle begins at HS, where the ankle is positioned in slight plantarflexion to absorb ground reaction forces. As the foot transitions to an FF position, the ankle moves into dorsiflexion, enabling shock absorption and body weight acceptance. During MST, dorsiflexion continues as the body's center of mass shifts forward over the supporting foot. Toward the end of the stance phase, the ankle initiates plantarflexion, reaching its peak at the TO event, which generates the propulsive force required for forward progression. During the swing phase, the ankle returns to dorsiflexion to achieve ground clearance and then transitions into slight plantarflexion in preparation for the next HS (see Figure 2b) [36].

Although sagittal plane movements, especially dorsiflexion and plantarflexion, are the most visually evident and frequently analyzed, frontal plane movements such as inversion and eversion are equally critical for maintaining lateral stability [37]. As the foot approaches HS, it typically lands in a slightly inverted position, improving lateral stability upon contact. As the body progresses into MST, the foot transitions into eversion, helping to distribute plantar pressures more evenly and adapt to irregular surfaces, which is vital for balance and preventing falls [38]. Before TO, the foot once again moves into inversion, forming a rigid lever necessary for effective propulsion and efficient energy transfer into the swing phase (see Figure 2c). These controlled mediolateral movements, typically occurring within ±15 degrees, are particularly important in individuals with impaired gait stability [39,40].

Movements in the transverse plane involve subtle internal and external rotations of the foot and ankle, often overshadowed by the more dominant sagittal and frontal plane actions. Though less prominent, transverse plane adjustments are especially relevant in complex tasks such as turning, obstacle negotiation, and adapting to sloped surfaces [41]. From our standpoint, the ability to precisely identify and respond to these key gait events is essential, particularly in the development of intelligent AAFO. The real-time recognition of gait transitions enables orthotic systems to synchronize assistance with user intent and gait phase demands [42]. Detecting TO allows timely plantarflexion support to aid propulsion while identifying HS, which can trigger dorsiflexion assistance to stabilize the ankle during loading. Similarly, understanding MST dynamics can inform balance-oriented corrections through inversion/eversion support, which is especially critical in populations at risk of lateral instability or falls [43]. In the context of this study, this EMG-based GRU model is capable of predicting FSR pressure values at the heel, midfoot, and toe regions—corresponding to critical gait events throughout the walking cycle. These predicted pressure profiles function as real-time indicators of events such as HS, MST, and TO, enabling targeted and phase-specific actuation in AAFO systems [44]. These specific gait events were prioritized in our model design due to their biomechanical significance; each event represents a transition point involving rapid changes in ankle loading or unloading, where timely neuromuscular assistance can meaningfully enhance gait safety, propulsion, and postural stability [45].

2.2. Anatomy of the Ankle Joint Complex

The ankle joint complex is fundamental in human locomotion, serving as the dynamic interface between the lower limb and the ground. Structurally, it comprises three primary articulations: the talocrural joint, the subtalar joint, and the transverse-tarsal joint. Each contributes to the intricate multidirectional mobility required for efficient gait and balance. These articulations work in a coordinated fashion to accommodate changes in terrain, absorb impact forces, and maintain postural control functions that are especially critical in developing responsive AAFO [46]. The talocrural joint is traditionally characterized as a hinge type synovial joint formed by the articulation between the distal tibia and fibula with the talus. This joint primarily enables plantarflexion and dorsiflexion key movements in forward propulsion and foot clearance during gait. However, its axis of rotation is not purely aligned with the sagittal plane; instead, it follows an oblique trajectory, slanting slightly downward and laterally (see Figure 3a) [47]. This obliquity introduces subtle components of transverse and frontal plane motion, increasing the joint's biomechanical complexity and making it more functionally adaptable than a simple hinge would suggest [48].

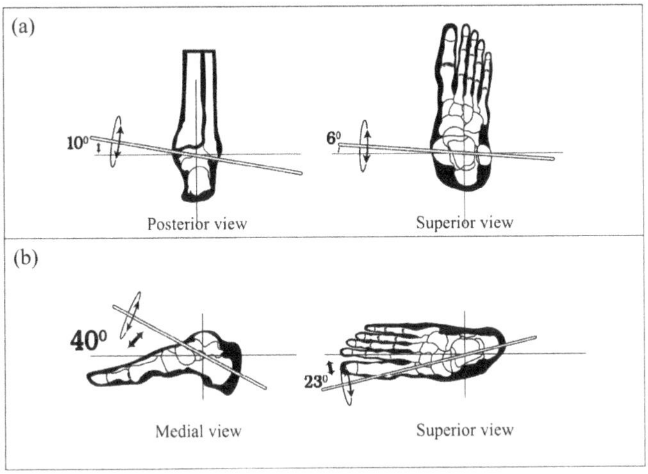

Figure 3. Oblique orientation of the rotational axes in ankle joint complex illustrating their multiplanar contributions to ankle joint motion: (**a**) the talocrural joint; (**b**) the subtalar joint.

Inferior to the talocrural joint lies the subtalar joint, which facilitates the inversion and eversion of the foot. This articulation, formed between the talus and calcaneus, also operates around an oblique axis (see Figure 3b) angled medially and anteriorly, which enables it to contribute to compound motions such as pronation and supination [49]. These combined actions are essential for mediolateral stability, particularly during stance phase transitions [50]. The subtalar joint also interacts functionally with the transverse-tarsal joint, comprising the talonavicular and calcaneocuboid joints. The combined mobility of these two joints enhances the foot's ability to adjust to varying ground surfaces and maintain dynamic equilibrium. This coupling is critical during tasks that require rapid adaptation, such as turning or walking on uneven terrain [51,52].

The complexity of the ankle joint's mechanical behavior is mirrored in its neuromuscular control architecture. Twelve extrinsic muscles control foot and ankle motions and are categorized into four functional compartments [53]. The anterior compartment includes the tibialis anterior (TA), a key muscle in dorsiflexion and a frequent focus in EMG-based foot drop analysis [54]. The lateral compartment, containing the fibularis longus (FL) and brevis, facilitates plantarflexion and eversion [55]. The posterior compartments are further divided into superficial and deep layers. The superficial posterior compartment, including the gastrocnemius (GA) and soleus (SOL), is primarily responsible for plantarflexion, especially during the push off event that occurs in the pre-swing phase of the gait cycle [56]. The deep posterior compartment, including the tibialis posterior, contributes to inversion and stabilization of the medial arch [57].

This anatomical arrangement reflects not only the mechanical interdependence but also the electromyographic complexity involved in generating and controlling ankle motion. From a modeling perspective, this has direct implications. Since our study utilizes surface EMG signals to estimate plantar pressure distributions, understanding which muscles contribute to which movement directions and how these movements manifest during different gait phases is essential [28]. Moreover, the overlapping functions of certain muscles across multiple planes (e.g., TA in dorsiflexion and inversion) present challenges for signal interpretation and movement differentiation, especially in real-time control systems of AAFO [58,59].

3. Methodology

3.1. Participants

This study involved primarily a cohort of four healthy male participants (subjects I–IV), all of whom voluntarily participated after providing written informed consent. One additional participant (subject V) with similar demographic characteristics and inclusion criteria was reserved exclusively for test data acquisition to evaluate model generalization performance. The subjects I–V had a mean age of 23.6 $\pm$ 1.52 years, mean weight of 60.4 $\pm$ 7.09 kg, mean height of 166.6 $\pm$ 3.51 cm, and mean BMI of 21.77 $\pm$ 2.58 kg/m^2. Subjects were screened before inclusion to ensure the absence of any musculoskeletal, neurological, or systemic conditions that could affect gait performance. All data were collected from the right leg to maintain consistency, as all participants self-reported right leg dominance. The experimental procedures were conducted in accordance with the ethical standards and protocols approved by Prof. Tamura's laboratory at the University of Miyazaki.

3.2. Experimental Setup

The experimental system was designed to simultaneously collect surface EMG and plantar pressure data during normal walking trials. Two primary sensor platforms were utilized:

- four wireless surface EMG sensors (Trigno, Delsys Inc., Natick, MA, USA);
- a four-channel FSR sensor system using the Delsys Trigno 4-Ch FSR Adapter (Delsys Inc., Natick, MA, USA).

The surface EMG sensors were positioned over the muscle bellies of four key muscles of the right lower leg: the TA, FL, SOL, and GA. These muscles were selected based on their primary roles in ankle biomechanics, particularly dorsiflexion (TA), eversion and lateral stabilization (FL), and plantarflexion (SOL and GA), all of which are critical during different gait events. Sensor placement was performed by established anatomical landmarks to ensure signal reliability and repeatability across subjects. The sensor configuration used for data collection is shown in Figure 4, including the wireless sEMG and FSR systems.

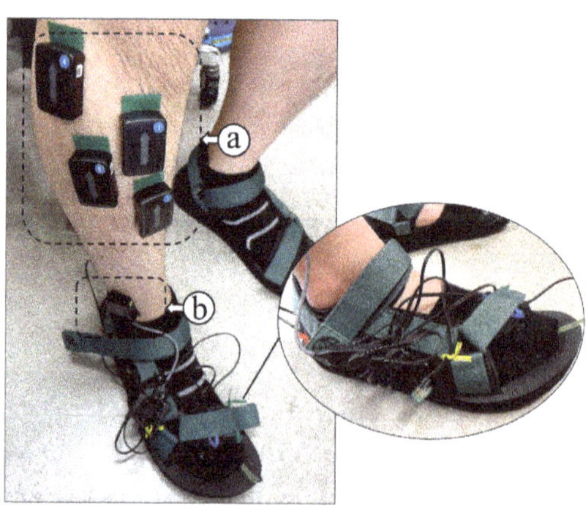

Figure 4. Sensor configuration used for data acquisition: (a) wireless surface EMG sensor placement over target lower limb muscles; (b) wireless FSR sensor unit with attached FSR membrane for plantar pressure measurement.

Each Delsys surface EMG sensor featured a compact body size of 27 × 37 × 13 mm and a mass of 14 g, offering a lightweight and unobtrusive profile suitable for gait trials. The surface EMG signals were acquired at a sampling rate of 1926 samples/s, with a bandwidth ranging from 20 to 450 Hz, enabling high-fidelity recording of muscle activation patterns during dynamic activities. The four-channel FSR system, integrated into a customized wearable sandal, was used to capture localized plantar pressure values beneath the heel, midfoot, and toe regions. Individual adjustments were made to the sandal structure for each participant to ensure the proper alignment of the FSR membranes with anatomical landmarks of the foot (see Figure 5).

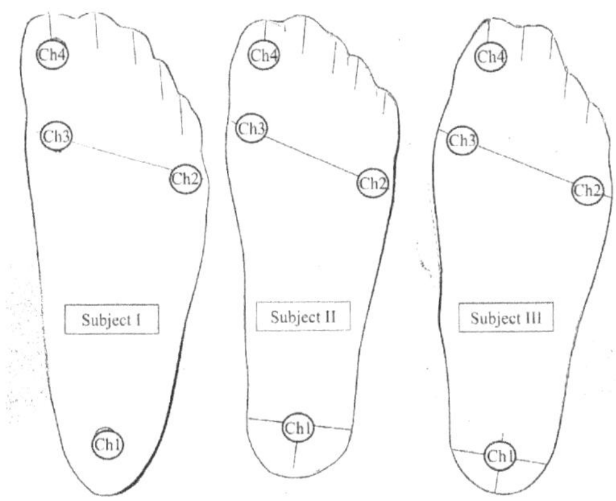

Figure 5. Placement of FSR membranes customized to subject-specific foot geometry, aligned with anatomical pressure zones corresponding to channels 1–4 (heel, midfoot, and toe regions).

The FSR sensor unit had a body size of 27 × 46 × 13 mm and a mass of 19 g. The pressure values from FSR channel 1 (heel) were sampled at 1926 samples/s, while FSR channels 2–4 (midfoot and forefoot regions) were sampled at 148 samples/s, all within a consistent 50 Hz bandwidth. Though hardware dependent, this mixed sampling configuration allowed sufficient temporal resolution for initial contact and push off phase analysis.

EMG and FSR data streams were wirelessly transmitted to a workstation via EMGworks Acquisition v4.8.0 software (Delsys Inc., USA), enabling real-time synchronization and continuous monitoring throughout the experiments. The synchronized acquisition of neuromuscular and plantar pressure signals enabled the precise identification of gait events. It provided the foundational dataset for developing the EMG-driven CRU model discussed in this study.

3.3. Experimental Procedure

To collect reliable, multi-modal gait data for plantar pressure prediction, each participant was asked to walk at a natural, self-selected pace along a fixed 12 m straight walkway within a controlled indoor environment. The walkway surface was clean, level, and free of obstacles to minimize environmental influence on gait dynamics. Participants completed five walking trials, with brief 30 s rest intervals between trials to prevent muscle fatigue while preserving consistent physical conditions across sessions.

To ensure symmetry and natural gait, all participants wore a pair of customized sandals during the trials. Only the right sandal, however, was instrumented with a 4-channel FSR system integrated into the insole to capture localized plantar pressure values at the heel, midfoot, and toe regions. The left sandal was identical in shape and material but non-instrumented, ensuring that footwear conditions were consistent without introducing functional asymmetry. Each right sandal was individually fitted to align the FSR membranes precisely with anatomical pressure zones, enhancing the reliability of pressure readings during gait.

Each trial began with the right foot and ended at the 12 m mark, also stepping with the right foot to ensure uniformity in stride segmentation. While walking, the synchronized EMG and FSR systems recorded neuromuscular activation and plantar pressure distributions across complete gait cycles. This dual-sensor setup enabled the precise identification of key gait events, specifically HS, MST, and TO. These events were selected as focal points for pressure prediction due to their biomechanical relevance and functional applicability in AAFO control.

After each walking session, raw signals were reviewed to verify signal integrity. Any trials affected by sensor detachment, excessive noise, or motion artifacts were excluded from further analysis. The resulting dataset provided high-resolution EMG and pressure profiles suitable for training and validating the proposed GRU-based model to predict plantar pressure values from EMG features. This model is intended to inform future real-time gait phase recognition and event-triggered actuation in active ankle–foot orthoses.

3.4. Data Filtering and Preparation

The raw EMG and FSR signals underwent preprocessing to enhance signal clarity and enable accurate temporal alignment for model development. All processing steps were implemented using a custom Python-based script (Python 3.12). The EMG signals, recorded at 1926 Hz with a 20–450 Hz bandwidth, were filtered using a band pass filter to remove motion artifacts and high-frequency noise. A 50 Hz notch filter was applied to eliminate power line interference. The signals were then rectified and smoothed to generate clear EMG envelopes, which were normalized to reduce variability between subjects and prepare the data for biomechanical interpretation and machine learning input.

The FSR signals were processed based on their respective sampling rates. A low-pass filter (cutoff at 20 Hz) and baseline correction were applied to reduce noise and highlight foot–ground interactions. The pressure signals were then normalized between 0 and 1 to align with the EMG feature scale and ensure compatibility for training the GRU model. The resulting preprocessed datasets were time-aligned and segmented according to gait cycles, forming a reliable foundation for the subsequent biomechanical signal comparisons and the EMG-based pressure prediction model introduced in the following sections.

3.5. Biomechanical Signal Compatibility Evaluation

The suitability of surface EMG and FSR signals for capturing physiologically relevant ankle joint behavior was evaluated across three key movement types: plantarflexion, dorsiflexion, and inversion. This simple analysis confirmed that the acquired neuromuscular and mechanical signals reflect well-aligned, phase-specific activity consistent with expected gait biomechanics, establishing a reliable foundation for pressure estimation modeling. During plantarflexion, EMG activity from the FL, SOL, and GA muscles (sensors 2–4) was compared with data from FSR channel 4, located at the toe region. Due to the inherent delays between muscle activation and force output, a cross-correlation-based approach was used to determine the EMD between each EMG signal and the corresponding FSR segment. This alignment process enabled the precise synchronization of neuromuscular and mechanical data. After temporal alignment, the GA muscle (sensor 4) exhibited the most prominent and sharply timed activation peaks relative to toe pressure maxima (see Figure 6), reinforcing its critical role in generating plantarflexion force during the TO event. The FL and SOL muscles also displayed well-aligned activation patterns, consistent with their lateral stabilization and postural support functions.

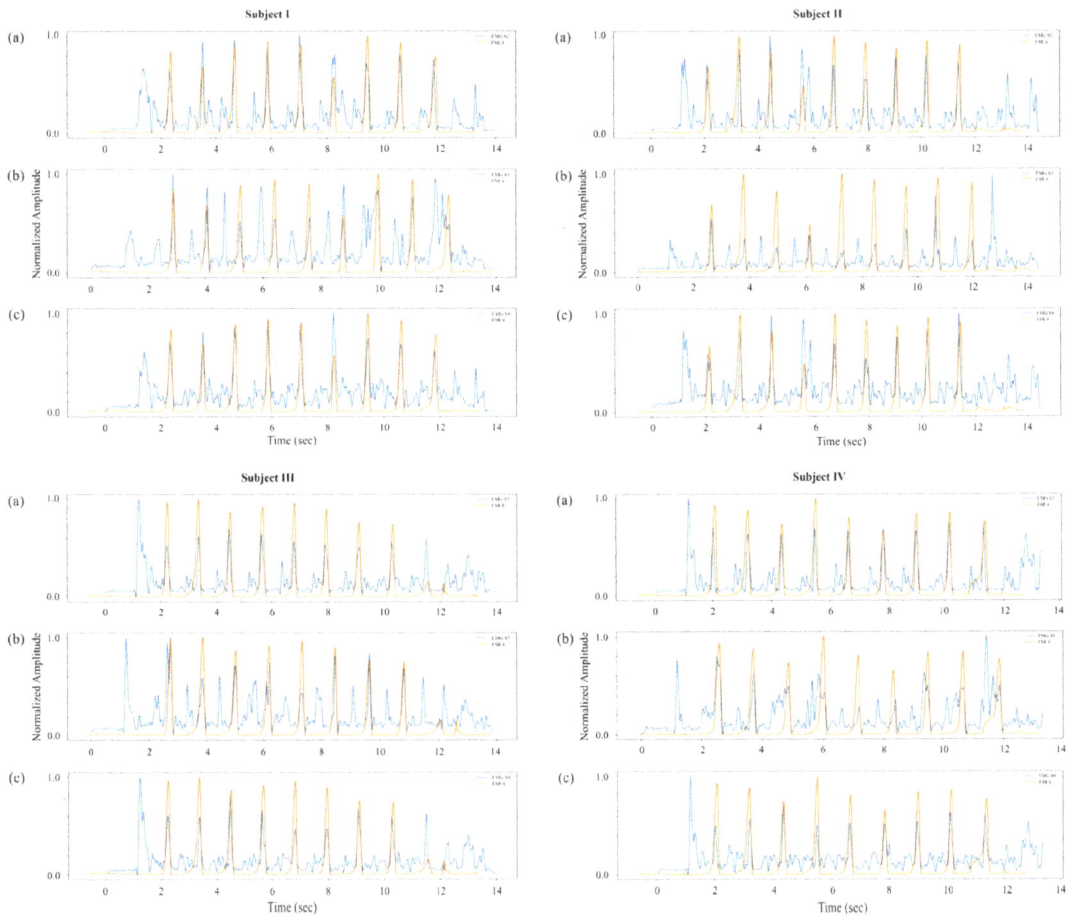

Figure 6. Comparison of representative normalized EMG envelopes (blue) with interpolated FSR channel 4 (toe region) outputs (orange) for subjects I–IV: (a) EMG sensor 2 positioned over the FL; (b) EMG sensor 3 over the SOL; (c) EMG sensor 4 over the GA muscle.

In the case of dorsiflexion, EMG signals from the TA muscle (sensor 1) were compared with FSR channel 1, positioned beneath the heel. The analysis revealed distinct EMG amplitude increases immediately preceding the heel pressure decline during the HO transition (see Figure 7). This activation reflects the initiation of dorsiflexion to lift the foot into the swing.

The EMD estimated in the previous phase was subsequently applied to time align the TA activity with midfoot pressure data for inversion analysis based on the shared functional involvement of the TA muscle in both motions. EMG sensor 1 was analyzed with FSR channel 2, which monitors midfoot pressure for inversion. Using the EMD from the dorsiflexion comparison, the signals were synchronized to isolate inversion-related activity. Following the primary dorsiflexion-associated activation, a secondary EMG activation pattern emerged during mid-to-late stance, aligned with rising pressure in the midfoot region (see Figure 8). This secondary activity reflects the TA muscle's role in medial foot stabilization, contributing to inversion control as the body transitions through the stance phase. Despite inter-subject variability in signal morphology, the observed activation–pressure relationship remained consistent across all four participants.

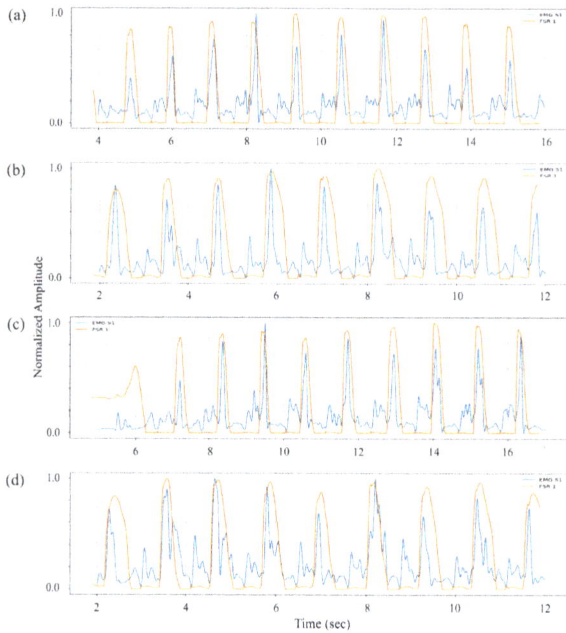

Figure 7. Comparison of normalized EMG signals (blue) from sensor 1 placed over the TA muscle with interpolated FSR channel 1 outputs (orange) from the heel region for dorsiflexion analysis. Subplots (**a–d**) correspond to subjects I–IV, respectively.

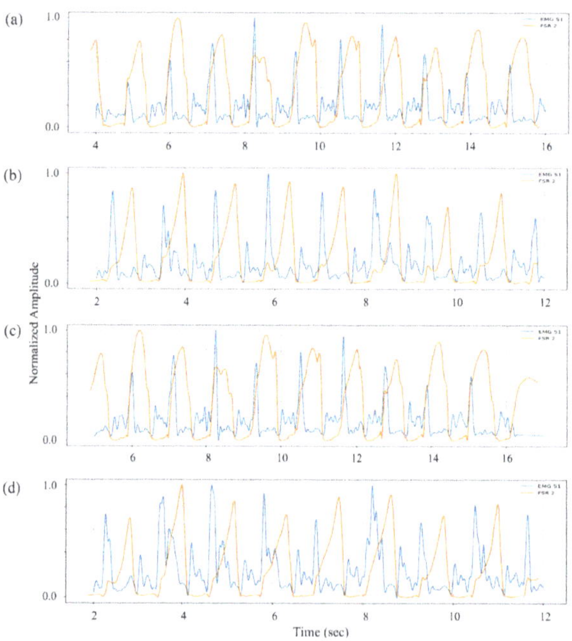

Figure 8. Comparison of normalized EMG signals (blue) from sensor 1 placed over the TA muscle with interpolated FSR channel 2 outputs (orange) from the midfoot region for inversion analysis. Subplots (**a–d**) correspond to subjects I–IV, respectively.

Overall, these evaluations demonstrate precise and repeatable neuromechanical relationships between EMG signals and plantar pressure across the three movement types. The use of EMD-based alignment, particularly the pairing of sensor 4 and FSR channel 4 for plantarflexion calibration, proved essential in establishing temporal compatibility between muscle activation and ground contact forces (e.g., given that the TO event, as represented in Figure 2, is commonly associated with the point of maximum plantarflexion during the gait cycle). These results affirm the validity of the recorded signals and justify their integration into the EMG-based GRU model for real-time plantar pressure estimation introduced in the subsequent section.

4. Predictive Model Development

4.1. Model Architecture

The primary objective of this study is to design and implement a machine learning model capable of predicting plantar pressure values captured via FSR sensors based on time series EMG signals. These signals reflect the electrical activity of the muscles surrounding the ankle joint and are inherently temporal. Given the dynamic structure of EMG signals and the need to learn sequential dependencies across time, a Recurrent Neural Network (RNN) approach was adopted. Specifically, a GRU-based architecture was employed due to its ability to effectively capture long-term dependencies with reduced computational complexity compared with LSTM networks. The predictive pipeline integrated several key components: rigorous signal preprocessing, a sliding window segmentation strategy, focused feature extraction using RMS values, and an optimized GRU model trained to output synchronized FSR pressures corresponding to the heel, midfoot, and toe regions. This model contributes to the broader objective of neuromechanical modeling for real-time applications in assistive technologies such as AAFO, as discussed previously.

The final GRU-based model architecture was designed to efficiently process temporally segmented EMG data and produce multi-channel FSR output predictions. The model comprised the following layers:

- Input Layer: Accepts sequences of RMS values extracted from sliding windows of EMG data.
- GRU Layer: Includes 64 units with 'return_sequences = True' to preserve the temporal resolution across all time steps, ReLU activation was subsequently applied to the GRU outputs to introduce non-linearity.
- Dropout Layer: Applied with a rate of 0.4 to prevent overfitting by randomly disabling 40% of neurons during training.
- Dense Layer: A fully connected output layer with four units corresponding to the four FSR channels.
- Optimizer: The Adam optimizer with a learning rate of 0.0005 was selected for its adaptive learning rate capabilities and robust convergence behavior.

The overall architecture of the proposed GRU-based predictive model, designed to map EMG signal features to FSR pressure outputs, is depicted in Figure 9. A detailed summary of the layer configuration and parameter distribution is provided in Table 1. The model comprises a total of 13,700 trainable parameters with no non-trainable parameters. This compact and efficient structure balances learning capacity with computational demands, facilitating real-time application potential for gait event prediction and control.

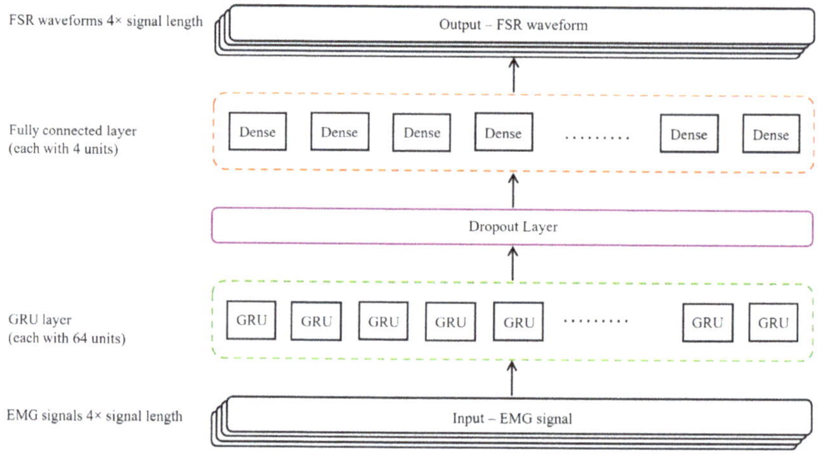

Figure 9. Architecture of the GRU-based predictive model.

Table 1. Summary of model architecture and parameter distribution.

Layer (Type)	Output Shape	No. of Parameters	Description
GRU (64 units)	(None, 2513, 64)	13,440	Sequential feature extraction and temporal dependency modeling
Dropout (rate = 0.4)	(None, 2513, 64)	0	Regularization to prevent overfitting
Dense (4 units)	(None, 2513, 4)	260	Output layer for predicting four FSR pressure values

4.2. Model Training

The model was trained on a dataset comprising synchronized EMG and FSR signals recorded across multiple walking trials from different subjects. A total of 200 training epochs were used, with a batch size of 1 to preserve sequence integrity. The MSE was employed as the primary loss function, and the MAE served as the evaluation metric. Noisy or corrupted trials were excluded to maintain training quality. Additionally, subject V, who met the same inclusion criteria and demographic profile as the primary cohort, was included for further validation through multiple test cases, demonstrating the model's robustness in handling inter-subject variability.

The outcomes of the training and validation processes are presented in the following section, highlighting the model's predictive performance and generalization capabilities across subjects.

5. Results

During training, the model achieved a low MSE of 0.0162 and an MAE of 0.0848, indicating a strong ability to map EMG-derived RMS features to FSR pressure values with minimal deviation. These results demonstrate that the model effectively captured the underlying neuromechanical relationships between muscle activation patterns and plantar pressure distributions throughout the gait cycle. Figure 10 depicts the evolution of the training loss MSE and MAE across 200 epochs. Both metrics show a clear downward trend, reflecting stable model convergence without signs of overfitting. Notably, the MAE curve exhibits a smooth decline and plateau behavior after approximately 150 epochs, suggesting that the model successfully optimized its internal parameters to achieve consistent predictive performance.

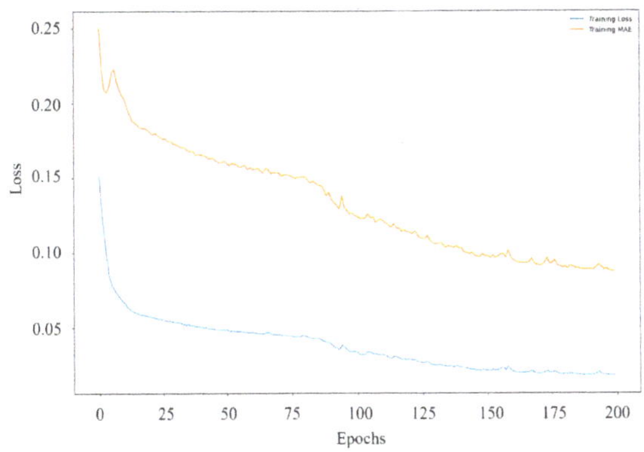

Figure 10. Training loss MSE (blue) and MAE (orange) trends over 200 epochs, indicating stable model convergence.

Figure 11 presents the comparison between predicted and ground-truth FSR pressure waveforms across the four sensing regions (heel, midfoot medial, midfoot lateral, and toe). The normalized pressure profiles reveal a high degree of temporal and amplitude alignment across multiple gait cycles. The predicted waveforms successfully reproduce major mechanical events such as HS, MST, and TO, demonstrating strong temporal fidelity. Minor discrepancies, primarily during rapid transition phases, are expected due to physiological variability, ambient noise, and the inherent electromechanical delay between neural activation and mechanical force output.

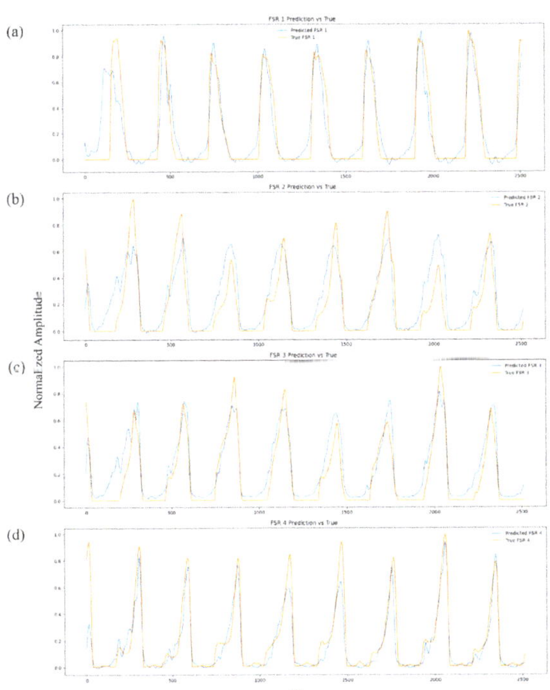

Figure 11. Comparison of predicted (blue) and ground-truth (orange) FSR waveforms across channels 1–4 (**a**–**d**), demonstrating accurate plantar pressure prediction over multiple gait cycles.

The evaluation of the test dataset, which consisted of unseen walking trials from subject V, who met the same inclusion criteria and demographic profile as the primary cohort, resulted in a comparable MSE of 0.0171 and MAE of 0.0832. The close alignment between training and test errors confirms that the model generalized effectively beyond the training data, maintaining predictive accuracy across the different individuals. This is particularly notable given the well-known variability in EMG signals associated with factors such as muscle morphology, activation strategies, and gait kinematics across subjects. Figure 12 further illustrates the model's predictive performance on three independent walking trials from subject V (test cases 1–3).

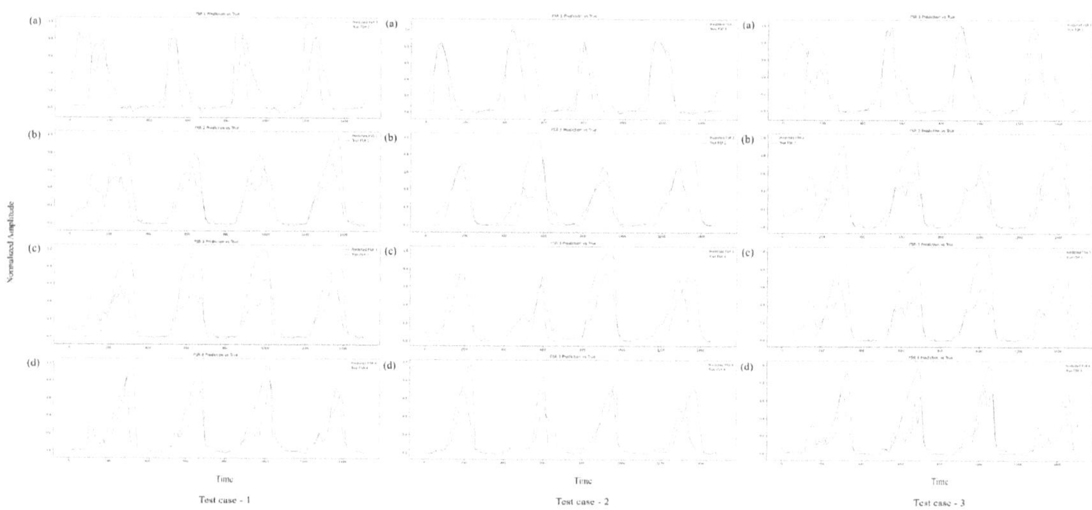

Figure 12. Comparison of predicted (blue) and actual (orange) FSR signals for subject V across three independent test cases. FSR channels 1–4 (a–d).

Across all four FSR channels, the model consistently tracks the pressure dynamics over several gait cycles, capturing both the timing and amplitude of critical events. In particular, the model accurately reproduces pressure peaks associated with toe off (maximum plantarflexion) and midfoot loading during MST. Although minor amplitude mismatches are observed during certain transitions, these deviations predominantly occur during rapid loading and unloading phases, where dynamic changes in ground reaction forces are most pronounced. In the context of gait analysis, the loading phase corresponds to the period immediately following HS, when body weight is transferred onto the foot, while the unloading phase represents the progressive reduction in ground contact forces as the foot prepares for TO and transitions into the swing phase.

Despite these slight deviations, the overall temporal patterns and pressure dynamics remain accurately preserved, demonstrating the model's ability to maintain biomechanical relevance even under inter-subject testing conditions.

6. Discussion

This study is positioned within the broader domain of developing an intelligent and adaptive AAFO system capable of delivering phase-specific, real-time assistance across multiple planes of ankle motion. To facilitate such functionality, we investigated the viability of leveraging neuromuscular signals, specifically surface EMG as input features for the prediction of spatially distributed plantar pressure patterns via a temporally responsive deep learning framework. The primary research objective was to determine whether temporal dependencies encoded within multi-sensory EMG signals could be effectively exploited to estimate continuous plantar loading profiles across anatomically defined foot regions during locomotion. We hypothesized that a GRU-based architecture, trained on systematically preprocessed EMG signals, could record physiologically meaningful neuromechanical associations under controlled experimental conditions. Although inter-subject variability in EMD was observed, the proposed model exhibited stable predictive performance across multiple healthy participants, indicating its generalization potential within normative populations. Ultimately, the proposed framework is intended to inform the control logic of next-generation AAFO by overcoming the limitations inherent to threshold-based or rule-based approaches, thereby enabling the fine-grained, data-driven modulation of orthotic support in response to the dynamic demands of human gait.

6.1. Predictive Model Performance and Generalization

The results obtained in this study highlight the feasibility and effectiveness of employing a GRU-based deep learning approach to predict plantar pressure distributions from EMG signals. This work followed a structured methodology, starting from biomechanical signal validation to predictive model development and evaluation, ensuring that the approach remained both technically sound and meaningful. Prior to model development, a Biomechanical Signal Compatibility Evaluation was performed to assess whether surface EMG signals from key ankle-related muscles appropriately reflected corresponding plantar pressure changes during major ankle joint movements. Through cross-correlation-based alignment techniques, it was confirmed that muscle activation patterns could reliably predict pressure variations related to plantarflexion, dorsiflexion, and inversion across different gait phases. This preliminary analysis provided strong justification for utilizing EMG signals as predictors of foot–ground interaction forces.

Building upon this foundation, a compact GRU-based predictive model was developed. The model utilized RMS values extracted from sliding windows of EMG signals, preserving temporal dependencies while simplifying feature space complexity. During training, the model achieved a low MSE of 0.0162 and an MAE of 0.0848, demonstrating the ability to learn robust mappings between neuromuscular activity and plantar pressure outputs. Evaluation on unseen walking trials from subject V, who met the same inclusion criteria as the primary cohort, resulted in comparably low errors (MSE = 0.0171, MAE = 0.0832), confirming the model's generalization capability across individuals. The temporal patterns of predicted FSR signals closely tracked ground truth measurements, effectively capturing key gait events such as HS, MST, and TO. Minor deviations were observed during rapid loading and unloading transitions, which are common sources of variability due to the dynamic nature of gait and inherent EMD.

6.2. Electromechanical Delay and Timing Alignment

A notable technical consideration in this study involves the EMD observed between muscle activation (EMG) and the resulting mechanical response (FSR). Cross-correlation analysis revealed subject-specific time lags for each EMG sensor, summarized in Table 2:

Table 2. Subject-specific EMD values (seconds) between EMG signals and FSR outputs.

Subject	EMG Sensor 1	EMG Sensor 2	EMG Sensor 3	EMG Sensor 4
I	−0.108	−0.626	−0.112	−0.623
II	−0.146	−0.590	—	−0.636
III	−0.124	−0.607	−0.096	−0.631
IV	−0.156	−0.686	−0.673	−0.687

The observed EMD values, ranging approximately from −0.096 to −0.687 s (−96 to −687 ms), indicate that muscle activation (EMG) consistently preceded the mechanical response (FSR) across the subjects, aligning with expected neuromechanical timing. These values are physiologically reasonable for dynamic lower limb movements. Previous studies have reported that EMD typically ranges from approximately 30 to 200 ms during simple tasks such as isometric contractions, whereas longer delays up to 500–600 ms have been observed during complex dynamic activities like human gait [60,61]. Therefore, the delays found in this study align well with known physiological norms, particularly considering the multi-muscle, multi-phase characteristics of standard walking. While these variations are within expected ranges, they also suggest that a fixed time alignment approach may not fully account for individual neuromuscular differences. Future refinements could involve subject-specific dynamic alignment strategies to enhance prediction accuracy, especially in personalized orthotic device applications. Despite these distinctions, the model demonstrated consistently strong predictive performance across multiple subjects and trials. The relatively low MAE values indicate that predicted plantar pressures remained within acceptable error margins, ensuring that key gait transitions such as loading and unloading phases were accurately detected.

6.3. Predictive Robustness and Future Applicability

While the model's predictive accuracy was validated within the current subject cohort, several methodological factors also suggest a strong potential for generalization to future data. The preprocessing steps, including band pass filtering (20–450 Hz), notch filtering, rectification, and RMS envelope extraction with a 10 Hz low-pass filter, standardized EMG signals and minimized subject-specific artifacts. The use of 200 sample sliding windows with 75% overlap produced over 50,000 sequences per subject, increasing temporal variability in the training data. The GRU architecture, with approximately 13,000 trainable parameters and 40% dropout, further reduced the overfitting risk. Notably, the model's receptive field (251 samples) accommodated the observed electromechanical delay variability (−96 to −687 ms), enabling robust timing alignment across the subjects. These design choices are expected to sustain prediction accuracy (MAE 0.08–0.10) even when applied to future datasets processed under similar conditions.

6.4. EMG Input Variability on Predictive Performance

The number of EMG sensors also influenced the model's predictive accuracy. Using a single sensor limited the model's ability to capture co-activation patterns, increasing error rates by approximately 35–40% due to difficulties in distinguishing synergistic and antagonistic muscle activity. In contrast, employing 3–4 sensors targeting key agonist–antagonist groups such as TA, FL, SOL, and GA provided sufficient information on muscle coordination while maintaining minimal redundancy, resulting in MAE values around 0.08. Adding more sensors (up to 6–8) offered modest further reductions in error (3–5%) when large and diverse training datasets were available. However, increasing the number of sensor inputs also raised the risk of overfitting and roughly doubled the training time and computational load. When more than 6 sensors were used, the small accuracy gains were often outweighed by increased susceptibility to crosstalk between muscle signals and variability in sensor placement. Based on these considerations, the 4-sensor configuration adopted in this study provided a practical balance between predictive accuracy and model complexity.

6.5. Limitations and Future Directions

While the GRU-based model demonstrated consistent accuracy across the trials and the subjects, several important limitations should be acknowledged. First, the model was developed using data collected exclusively from four healthy male participants, with a fifth subject used for external validation. While this cohort allowed for controlled experimentation and cross-subject testing, the small sample size limits the statistical and clinical generalizability of the findings. Future work should extend the dataset to include a more diverse population, particularly individuals with neuromuscular disorders or pathological gait patterns. Such populations often exhibit irregular muscle activation profiles and altered gait timing, providing essential test cases for evaluating the robustness and clinical applicability of the proposed predictive model.

A second notable constraint involves the reliance on manual signal alignment via cross-correlation to synchronize EMG and FSR data. Although this method enabled the clear identification of subject-specific EMDs and ensured repeatable alignment during initial feasibility testing, it assumes fixed timing across all gait cycles. This limits its adaptability to intra-subject gait variability. In real-world conditions, especially in patients with impaired gait, these factors can introduce temporal misalignments that degrade prediction accuracy. Addressing this issue is critical for deploying EMG-driven models in dynamic, real-time control applications. To overcome this limitation, future studies will incorporate automated, subject-adaptive alignment strategies. Techniques such as dynamic time warping (DTW) can be used to non-linearly align EMG and pressure sequences on a cycle-by-cycle basis, keeping biomechanical phase relationships even under varying timing conditions. Additionally, delay-aware neural network architectures, such as GRUs or LSTMs enhanced with time shift embeddings, may allow the model to learn and compensate for timing mismatches directly from the data. These approaches would enable more robust and generalizable alignments, facilitating reliable real-time prediction across varying gait styles and subject populations.

Another methodological limitation is the exclusive use of surface EMG signals which, while informative, only reflect muscle activation but not limb orientation or joint kinematics. Future extensions may integrate IMUs or joint angle data to enhance the spatial understanding of foot–ground interactions, particularly on uneven terrain or in turning maneuvers. A multimodal sensor fusion approach could provide more comprehensive inputs for gait phase classification and orthotic control logic.

The number of EMG inputs required for the accurate prediction of pressure also warrants consideration. While our results showed that using three to four EMG channels offered a balance between prediction accuracy and model complexity, reducing the inputs to only one or two muscles led to a substantial increase in prediction error. This indicates that individual muscles provide distinct and non-redundant information. At the same time, the marginal improvement in accuracy beyond four sensors suggests that some of the neuromuscular coordination can be captured with a minimal sensor set. Future research may explore dimensionality reduction techniques, such as principal component analysis or feature selection algorithms, to identify a compact yet effective combination of muscle inputs. This line of investigation could further support the development of simplified, low-power, and wearable orthotic control systems.

Finally, this study's design focused on offline prediction. While the current architecture is compact and optimized for real-time deployment, it has not yet been validated in live control scenarios. Future work will implement the trained model in embedded platforms and evaluate its real-time inference performance, latency, and responsiveness when integrated with active orthotic hardware.

In conclusion, this work presents a compact and computationally efficient GRU-based framework that enables the accurate estimation of plantar loading distributions from surface EMG signals. The model demonstrated strong predictive performance, capturing muscle-activation-to-pressure dynamics with low error margins across multiple gait cycles and test subjects. A four-sensor EMG configuration was shown to offer a pragmatic trade off between accuracy and system complexity, underscoring the potential for wearable implementation. Importantly, the framework lays the foundation for future AAFO control strategies aimed at restoring gait function, particularly in populations affected by neuromuscular impairments. Although the validation was limited to healthy young adults, the findings suggest translational potential in older individuals with mobility challenges, where adaptive orthotic control based on real-time muscle activation could improve gait stability and reduce fall risk. Further investigations involving clinical populations and real-time deployment will be essential to realize these applications.

Author Contributions: Conceptualization, P.N.G. and H.T.; methodology, P.N.G.; software, P.N.G.; validation, P.N.G. and H.T.; formal analysis, P.N.G.; investigation, P.N.G.; resources, P.N.G.; data curation, P.N.G.; writing—original draft preparation, P.N.G.; writing—review and editing, P.N.G. and H.T.; visualization, P.N.G.; supervision, H.T.; project administration, H.T.; funding acquisition, H.T. All authors have read and agreed to the published version of the manuscript.

Funding: This work was supported by JST SPRING, Grant Number JPMJSP2105.

Institutional Review Board Statement: Not applicable.

Informed Consent Statement: Informed consent was obtained from all subjects involved in the study.

Data Availability Statement: The data presented in this study are available on request.

Conflicts of Interest: The authors declare no conflicts of interest.

Abbreviations

The following abbreviations are used in this manuscript:

AAFO	active ankle–foot orthoses
AFO	ankle–foot orthoses
DTW	dynamic time warping
EMD	electromechanical delay
EMG	electromyography
FF	foot flat
FL	fibularis longus
FSR	force-sensitive resistor
GA	gastrocnemius
GRU	Gated Recurrent Unit
HO	heel off
HS	heel strike
IMU	inertial measurement unit
LSTM	long short-term memory
MAE	mean absolute error
MLP	multilayer perceptron
MPC	model predictive control
MSW	mid-swing
MSE	mean squared error
MST	mid stance
PS	pre-swing
RMS	root mean square
SOL	soleus
TA	tibialis anterior
TO	toe off

References

1. Cabinet Office, Japan. Annual Report on the Ageing Society [Summary] FY2024. Available online: https://www8.cao.go.jp/kourei/english/annualreport/2024/pdf/2024.pdf (accessed on 20 January 2025).
2. Tinetti, M.E.; Speechley, M.; Ginter, S.F. Risk Factors for Falls among Elderly Persons Living in the Community. *N. Engl. J. Med.* **1988**, *319*, 1701–1707. [CrossRef] [PubMed]
3. Perry, J.; Burnfield, J.M. *Gait Analysis: Normal and Pathological Function*; Slack: Thorofare, NJ, USA, 2010; ISBN 9781556427664.
4. Wren, T.A.L.; Gorton, G.E.; Õunpuu, S.; Tucker, C.A. Efficacy of Clinical Gait Analysis: A Systematic Review. *Gait Posture* **2011**, *34*, 149–153. [CrossRef] [PubMed]
5. Leardini, A.; O'Connor, J.J.; Giannini, S. Biomechanics of the Natural, Arthritic, and Replaced Human Ankle Joint. *J. Foot Ankle Res.* **2014**, *7*, 8. [CrossRef] [PubMed]
6. Bregman, D.J.J.; van der Krogt, M.M.; de Groot, V.; Harlaar, J.; Wisse, M.; Collins, S.H. The Effect of Ankle Foot Orthosis Stiffness on the Energy Cost of Walking: A Simulation Study. *Clin. Biomech.* **2011**, *26*, 955–961. [CrossRef]
7. Neptune, R.R.; Wright, I.C.; van den Bogert, A.J. Muscle Coordination and Function during Cutting Movements. *Med. Sci. Sports Exerc.* **1999**, *31*, 294–302. [CrossRef]
8. Ippersiel, P.; Robbins, S.M.; Dixon, P.C. Lower-Limb Coordination and Variability during Gait: The Effects of Age and Walking Surface. *Gait Posture* **2021**, *85*, 251–257. [CrossRef]
9. Gunaratne, P.N.; Tamura, H. A Review: Developments in Hardware Systems of Active Ankle Orthoses. *Sensors* **2024**, *24*, 8153. [CrossRef]
10. Esquenazi, A.; Talaty, M.; Packel, A.; Saulino, M. The ReWalk Powered Exoskeleton to Restore Ambulatory Function to Individuals with Thoracic-Level Motor-Complete Spinal Cord Injury. *Am. J. Phys. Med. Rehabil.* **2012**, *91*, 911–921. [CrossRef]
11. Veneman, J.F.; Kruidhof, R.; Hekman, E.E.G.; Ekkelenkamp, R.; Van Asseldonk, E.H.F.; van der Kooij, H. Design and Evaluation of the LOPES Exoskeleton Robot for Interactive Gait Rehabilitation. *IEEE Trans. Neural Syst. Rehabil. Eng.* **2007**, *15*, 379–386. [CrossRef]
12. Maqbool, H.F.; Husman, M.A.B.; Awad, M.I.; Abouhossein, A.; Mehryar, P.; Iqbal, N.; Dehghani-Sanij, A.A. Real-Time Gait Event Detection for Lower Limb Amputees Using a Single Wearable Sensor. In Proceedings of the 2016 38th Annual International Conference of the IEEE Engineering in Medicine and Biology Society (EMBC), Orlando, FL, USA, 16–20 August 2016. [CrossRef]
13. Fatone, S.; Owen, E.; Gao, F.; Shippen, G.; Orendurff, M.S.; Bjornson, K. Comparison of Sagittal Plane Stiffness of Nonarticulated Pediatric Ankle-Foot Orthoses Designed to Be Rigid. *JPO J. Prosthet. Orthot.* **2021**, *34*, e44–e49. [CrossRef]
14. Jiménez-Fabián, R.; Verlinden, O. Review of Control Algorithms for Robotic Ankle Systems in Lower-Limb Orthoses, Prostheses, and Exoskeletons. *Med. Eng. Phys.* **2012**, *34*, 397–408. [CrossRef] [PubMed]
15. Shamaei, K.; Napolitano, P.C.; Dollar, A.M. A Quasi-Passive Compliant Stance Control Knee-Ankle-Foot Orthosis. In Proceedings of the 2013 IEEE 13th International Conference on Rehabilitation Robotics (ICORR), Seattle, WA, USA, 24–26 June 2013. [CrossRef]
16. Sawicki, G.S.; Ferris, D.P. Powered Ankle Exoskeletons Reveal the Metabolic Cost of Plantar Flexor Mechanical Work during Walking with Longer Steps at Constant Step Frequency. *J. Exp. Biol.* **2008**, *212*, 21–31. [CrossRef] [PubMed]
17. Tao, W.; Liu, T.; Zheng, R.; Feng, H. Gait Analysis Using Wearable Sensors. *Sensors* **2012**, *12*, 2255–2283. [CrossRef] [PubMed]
18. Chen, B.; Ma, H.; Qin, L.-Y.; Gao, F.; Chan, K.-M.; Law, S.-W.; Qin, L.; Liao, W.-H. Recent Developments and Challenges of Lower Extremity Exoskeletons. *J. Orthop. Transl.* **2016**, *5*, 26–37. [CrossRef]
19. Gao, Y.; Zheng, J.; Yang, C.; Yan, R.; Wang, C.; Tang, J.; Jiang, Z. Real-Time Gait Phase Detection Based on LSTM-ResMLP-LightGBM Approach for Exoskeleton in Outdoor Activity. *IEEE Access* **2025**, *13*, 39993–40011. [CrossRef]
20. Panizzolo, F.A.; Galiana, I.; Asbeck, A.T.; Siviy, C.; Schmidt, K.; Holt, K.G.; Walsh, C.J. A Biologically-Inspired Multi-Joint Soft Exosuit That Can Reduce the Energy Cost of Loaded Walking. *J. Neuroeng. Rehabil.* **2016**, *13*, 43. [CrossRef]
21. Jamali, A.; Abdul Razak, A.S.; Mohamaddan, S. Imposing Neural Networks and PSO Optimization in the Quest for Optimal Ankle-Foot Orthosis Dynamic Modelling. *TELKOMNIKA Telecommun. Comput. Electron. Control* **2025**, *23*, 484. [CrossRef]
22. Jamali, A.; Abdul Razak, A.S.; Mohamaddan, S. An In-Depth Study of Ankle-Foot Orthosis Dynamics Modeling: Leveraging Non-Parametric Approach via Artificial Neural Networks. In Proceedings of the 2023 IEEE 9th International Conference on Smart Instrumentation, Measurement and Applications (ICSIMA), Kuala Lumpur, Malaysia, 17–18 October 2023; pp. 170–175. [CrossRef]
23. Shefa, F.R.; Sifat, F.H.; Uddin, J.; Ahmad, Z.; Kim, J.-M.; Kibria, M.G. Deep Learning and IoT-Based Ankle–Foot Orthosis for Enhanced Gait Optimization. *Healthcare* **2024**, *12*, 2273. [CrossRef]
24. Shefa, F.R.; Sifat, F.H.; Shah, S.C.; Kibria, M.G. IoT-Based Smart Ankle-Foot Orthosis for Patients with Gait Imbalance. In Proceedings of the 2023 23rd International Conference on Control, Automation and Systems (ICCAS), Yeosu, Republic of Korea, 17–20 October 2023; pp. 969–974. [CrossRef]
25. Ulkir, O.; Akgun, G.; Nasab, A.; Kaplanoglu, E. Data-Driven Predictive Control of a Pneumatic Ankle Foot Orthosis. *Adv. Electr. Comput. Eng.* **2021**, *21*, 65–74. [CrossRef]

26. DeBoer, B.; Hosseini, A.; Rossa, C. Model Predictive Control of an Active Ankle-Foot Orthosis with Non-Linear Actuation Constraints. *Control Eng. Pract.* **2023**, *136*, 105538. [CrossRef]
27. Jun, K.; Lee, S.; Lee, D.-W.; Kim, M.S. Deep Learning-Based Multimodal Abnormal Gait Classification Using a 3D Skeleton and Plantar Foot Pressure. *IEEE Access* **2021**, *9*, 161576–161589. [CrossRef]
28. Phinyomark, A.; Khushaba, R.N.; Scheme, E. Feature Extraction and Selection for Myoelectric Control Based on Wearable EMG Sensors. *Sensors* **2018**, *18*, 1615. [CrossRef] [PubMed]
29. Hudgins, B.; Parker, P.; Scott, R.N. A New Strategy for Multifunction Myoelectric Control. *IEEE Trans. Biomed. Eng.* **1993**, *40*, 82–94. [CrossRef] [PubMed]
30. Cho, K.; van Merriënboer, B.; Gulcehre, C.; Bahdanau, D.; Bougares, F.; Schwenk, H.; Bengio, Y. Learning Phrase Representations Using RNN Encoder-Decoder for Statistical Machine Translation. *arXiv* **2014**, arXiv:1406.1078. [CrossRef]
31. Saponas, T.S.; Tan, D.S.; Morris, D.; Balakrishnan, R.; Turner, J.; Landay, J.A. Enabling Always-Available Input with Muscle-Computer Interfaces. In Proceedings of the UIST '09: Proceedings of the 22nd Annual ACM Symposium on User Interface Software and Technology, Victoria, BC, Canada, 4–7 October 2009. [CrossRef]
32. Vrieling, A.H.; van Keeken, H.G.; Schoppen, T.; Otten, E.; Halbertsma, J.P.K.; Hof, A.L.; Postema, K. Gait Initiation in Lower Limb Amputees. *Gait Posture* **2008**, *27*, 423–430. [CrossRef]
33. Hoover, C.D.; Fulk, G.D.; Fite, K.B. Stair Ascent with a Powered Transfemoral Prosthesis under Direct Myoelectric Control. *IEEE/ASME Trans. Mechatron.* **2013**, *18*, 1191–1200. [CrossRef]
34. Whittle, M. *Gait Analysis: An Introduction*; Butterworth-Heinemann Ltd.: Oxford, UK, 2007; ISBN 9781483183732.
35. Winter, D.A. *Biomechanics and Motor Control of Human Movement*; Wiley: Hoboken, NJ, USA, 2009; ISBN 9780470398180.
36. Nigg, B.M. *Biomechanics of the Musculo-Skeletal System*; Wiley: Chichester, UK, 2006; ISBN 9780470017678.
37. MacKinnon, C.D.; Winter, D.A. Control of Whole Body Balance in the Frontal Plane during Human Walking. *J. Biomech.* **1993**, *26*, 633–644. [CrossRef]
38. Mueller, M.J.; Sinacore, D.R.; Hoogstrate, S.; Daly, L. Hip and Ankle Walking Strategies: Effect on Peak Plantar Pressures and Implications for Neuropathic Ulceration. *Arch. Phys. Med. Rehabil.* **1994**, *75*, 1196–1200. [CrossRef]
39. Dugan, S.A.; Bhat, K.P. Biomechanics and Analysis of Running Gait. *Phys. Med. Rehabil. Clin. N. Am.* **2005**, *16*, 603–621. [CrossRef]
40. Kulmala, J.-P.; Korhonen, M.T.; Kuitunen, S.; Suominen, H.; Heinonen, A.; Mikkola, A.; Avela, J. Whole Body Frontal Plane Mechanics across Walking, Running, and Sprinting in Young and Older Adults. *Scand. J. Med. Sci. Sports* **2016**, *27*, 956–963. [CrossRef]
41. Avers, D.; Wong, R.A. *Guccione's Geriatric Physical Therapy*; Elsevier: St. Louis, MO, USA, 2020; ISBN 9780323609128.
42. Liu, J.; Tan, X.; Jia, X.; Li, T.; Li, W. A Gait Phase Recognition Method for Obstacle Crossing Based on Multi-Sensor Fusion. *Sens. Actuators A Phys.* **2024**, *376*, 115645. [CrossRef]
43. Dollar, A.M.; Herr, H. Lower Extremity Exoskeletons and Active Orthoses: Challenges and State-of-The-Art. *IEEE Trans. Robot.* **2008**, *24*, 144–158. [CrossRef]
44. Morbidoni, C.; Cucchiarelli, A.; Agostini, V.; Knaflitz, M.; Fioretti, S.; Di Nardo, F. Machine-Learning-Based Prediction of Gait Events from EMG in Cerebral Palsy Children. *IEEE Trans. Neural Syst. Rehabil. Eng.* **2021**, *29*, 819–830. [CrossRef] [PubMed]
45. Dimitrov, H.; Bull, J.; Farina, D. Real-Time Interface Algorithm for Ankle Kinematics and Stiffness from Electromyographic Signals. *IEEE Trans. Neural Syst. Rehabil. Eng.* **2020**, *28*, 1416–1427. [CrossRef] [PubMed]
46. Brockett, C.L.; Chapman, G.J. Biomechanics of the Ankle. *Orthop. Trauma* **2016**, *30*, 232–238. [CrossRef]
47. Lundberg, A.; Svensson, O.; Nemeth, G.; Selvik, G. The Axis of Rotation of the Ankle Joint. *J. Bone Jt. Surg. Br. Vol.* **1989**, *71-B*, 94–99. [CrossRef]
48. Barnett, C.H.; Napier, J.R. The Axis of Rotation at the Ankle Joint in Man; Its Influence upon the Form of the Talus and the Mobility of the Fibula. *J. Anat.* **1952**, *86*, 1–9.
49. Manter, J.T. Movements of the Subtalar and Transverse Tarsal Joints. *Anat. Rec.* **1941**, *80*, 397–410. [CrossRef]
50. Procter, P.; Paul, J.P. Ankle Joint Biomechanics. *J. Biomech.* **1982**, *15*, 627–634. [CrossRef]
51. Hicks, J.H. The Mechanics of the Foot. II. The Plantar Aponeurosis and the Arch. *J. Anat.* **1954**, *88*, 25–30.
52. Kirby, K. Biomechanics of the Normal and Abnormal Foot. *J. Am. Podiatr. Med. Assoc.* **2000**, *90*, 30–34. [CrossRef] [PubMed]
53. Moore, K.L.; Dalley, A.F.; Agur, A.M.R. *Clinically Oriented Anatomy*; Lippincott Williams & Wilkins: Philadelphia, PA, USA, 2017; ISBN 9781496389404.
54. Hermens, H.J.; Freriks, B.; Disselhorst-Klug, C.; Rau, G. Development of Recommendations for SEMG Sensors and Sensor Placement Procedures. *J. Electromyogr. Kinesiol.* **2000**, *10*, 361–374. [CrossRef] [PubMed]
55. Perotto, A.; Delagi, E.F. *Anatomical Guide for the Electromyographer: The Limbs and Trunk*; Charles, C., Ed.; Thomas: Springfield, IL, USA, 2005; ISBN 9780398075774.
56. Winter, D.A. *The Biomechanics and Motor Control of Human Gait: Normal, Elderly and Pathological*; University of Waterloo Press: Waterloo, ON, Canada, 1991.

57. Rhim, H.C.; Dhawan, R.; Gureck, A.E.; Lieberman, D.E.; Nolan, D.C.; Elshafey, R.; Tenforde, A.S. Characteristics and Future Direction of Tibialis Posterior Tendinopathy Research: A Scoping Review. *Medicina* **2022**, *58*, 1858. [CrossRef] [PubMed]
58. Clancy, E.A.; Morin, E.L.; Merletti, R. Sampling, Noise-Reduction and Amplitude Estimation Issues in Surface Electromyography. *J. Electromyogr. Kinesiol.* **2002**, *12*, 1–16. [CrossRef]
59. Farina, D.; Merletti, R.; Enoka, R.M. The Extraction of Neural Strategies from the Surface EMG. *J. Appl. Physiol.* **2004**, *96*, 1486–1495. [CrossRef]
60. Cavanagh, P.R.; Komi, P.V. Electromechanical Delay in Human Skeletal Muscle under Concentric and Eccentric Contractions. *Eur. J. Appl. Physiol. Occup. Physiol.* **1979**, *42*, 159–163. [CrossRef]
61. Norman, R.W.; Komi, P.V. Electromechanical Delay in Skeletal Muscle under Normal Movement Conditions. *Acta Physiol. Scand.* **1979**, *106*, 241–248. [CrossRef]

sensors MDPI

Article

IMU Sensor-Based Worker Behavior Recognition and Construction of a Cyber–Physical System Environment

Sehwan Park, Minkyo Youm * and Junkyeong Kim *

Advanced Institute of Convergence Technology, 145 Gwanggyo-ro, Yeongtong-gu, Suwon-si 16229, Gyeonggi-do, Republic of Korea; sehwan0721@snu.ac.kr
* Correspondence: tomsmith850918@snu.ac.kr (M.Y.); junkyeong@snu.ac.kr (J.K.)

Abstract

According to South Korea's Ministry of Employment and Labor, approximately 25,000 construction workers suffered from various injuries between 2015 and 2019. Additionally, about 500 fatalities occur annually, and multiple studies are being conducted to prevent these accidents and quickly identify their occurrence to secure the golden time for the injured. Recently, AI-based video analysis systems for detecting safety accidents have been introduced. However, these systems are limited to areas where CCTV is installed, and in locations like construction sites, numerous blind spots exist due to the limitations of CCTV coverage. To address this issue, there is active research on the use of MEMS (micro-electromechanical systems) sensors to detect abnormal conditions in workers. In particular, methods such as using accelerometers and gyroscopes within MEMS sensors to acquire data based on workers' angles, utilizing three-axis accelerometers and barometric pressure sensors to improve the accuracy of fall detection systems, and measuring the wearer's gait using the x-, y-, and z-axis data from accelerometers and gyroscopes are being studied. However, most methods involve use of MEMS sensors embedded in smartphones, typically attaching the sensors to one or two specific body parts. Therefore, in this study, we developed a novel miniaturized IMU (inertial measurement unit) sensor that can be simultaneously attached to multiple body parts of construction workers (head, body, hands, and legs). The sensor integrates accelerometers, gyroscopes, and barometric pressure sensors to measure various worker movements in real time (e.g., walking, jumping, standing, and working at heights). Additionally, incorporating PPG (photoplethysmography), body temperature, and acoustic sensors, enables the comprehensive observation of both physiological signals and environmental changes. The collected sensor data are preprocessed using Kalman and extended Kalman filters, among others, and an algorithm was proposed to evaluate workers' safety status and update health-related data in real time. Experimental results demonstrated that the proposed IMU sensor can classify work activities with over 90% accuracy even at a low sampling rate of 15 Hz. Furthermore, by integrating internal filtering, communication modules, and server connectivity within an application, we established a cyber–physical system (CPS), enabling real-time monitoring and immediate alert transmission to safety managers. Through this approach, we verified improved performance in terms of miniaturization, measurement accuracy, and server integration compared to existing commercial sensors.

Keywords: IMU sensor; behavior recognition; real-time monitoring; CPS

1. Introduction

According to the Occupational Safety and Health Administration (OSHA), the construction industry accounted for 5486 fatal work injuries in 2022, equating to a rate of 3.7 fatalities per 100,000 full-time equivalent workers [1]. Similarly, the Health and Safety Executive (HSE) in Great Britain reports that the construction sector continues to account for the greatest number of workers killed in fatal accidents each year [2]. Common accident types include falls, slips, crush injuries, entanglements, and collisions. Particularly, workers at construction sites are exposed to various risks such as collisions with construction equipment, falls from heights, and slips. Most safety accidents occurring at construction sites are caused not by unsafe facilities and infrastructure but by unsafe work practices of the workers themselves.

Various studies are being conducted to prevent accidents resulting from such unsafe work practices. One of these technologies involves monitoring techniques using computer vision (CV), which is being developed by training and applying monitoring systems through advancements in deep learning technology. However, there are areas that CV technology cannot cover. Monitoring accuracy significantly decreases when workers are in complex environments, areas with obstructed views, low lighting conditions, or when the imaging equipment is far from the worker. To address these blind spots in worker monitoring methods using CV, this study aimed to assess the worker's status using sensors.

To evaluate a worker's status, accelerometers, gyroscopes, and barometric pressure sensors are primarily used, all of which belong to the category of MEMS sensors. An IMU sensor is a device that integrates these MEMS sensors into a single module to measure changes in the position and posture of an object (or the human body). The IMU sensor includes a three-axis accelerometer and a three-axis gyroscope and can incorporate additional sensors such as a magnetometer or barometric pressure sensor when necessary to obtain diverse motion information. Accordingly, various studies have been conducted using MEMS and IMU sensors to evaluate users' conditions. For instance, R. Zhong et al. explored gait patterns between young adults and the elderly by having subjects wear a smart bracelet embedded with an accelerometer and gyroscope to record acceleration and Euler angles in real time [3]. S. Chen et al. proposed a method for real-time gait detection and pose estimation when walking on flat terrain and slopes using a single wearable IMU sensor [4]. Additionally, N. Yodpijit et al. designed a system to analyze gait characteristics using smartphone accelerometers as wireless motion sensors. The study quantifies human motion through four main stages: data acquisition, feature extraction, classifier design, and decision-making. Using a peak detection algorithm, the system extracted features such as stride time, stance time, swing time, and cadence to evaluate gait patterns [5].

Studies have also been conducted to monitor poses and behaviors. M. Awais et al. extracted features for sitting, standing, walking, and lying down by having 20 elderly subjects wear accelerometers, gyroscopes, and magnetometers on the chest, wrist, waist, and thigh, and classified these behaviors [6]. H. Li et al. conducted a study to classify actions such as walking, sitting, and bending by having subjects wear IMU sensors composed of three MEMS sensors (accelerometer, gyroscope, magnetometer) on the wrist, waist, and ankle [7]. Y. Lee et al. conducted studies on data poses by measuring inertial data by attaching MEMS sensors to the hands, pelvis, head, and other body parts [8]. N.G. Nia et al. aimed to effectively classify a wide range of human activities using machine learning algorithms, artificial neural networks (ANN), decision tree classifiers (DTC), and k-nearest neighbors (KNN) with IMU sensors composed of three MEMS sensors [9].

In terms of detecting and preventing falls using MEMS sensors, A. Singh et al. reviewed various fall detection systems, classifying them into three main categories: wearable, ambiance-based, and hybrid-sensing detectors. The study analyzed competing sensor technologies, including accelerometers, pressure sensors, radar, and camera-based solutions, and highlighted their strengths and limitations in feature extraction, classification, and real-world applicability [10]. Additionally, N. Shibuya et al. developed a real-time fall detection system using a wearable gait analysis sensor (WGAS) equipped with a tri-axial accelerometer, gyroscopes, and an MSP430 microcontroller. The system utilized a support vector machine (SVM) classifier to extract six features for fall classification, achieving accuracies of 98.8% and 98.7% at different sensor positions and an overall sensitivity of 97.0% [11]. Furthermore, V. B. Semwal et al. placed smartphone MEMS sensors on the abdomen to collect data and applied it to deep learning models to classify the data into fall or non-fall events [12]. H. Choo et al. and S. Hong et al. conducted studies on fall detection and safe behavior monitoring by acquiring data after having workers wear MEMS sensors on safety hooks and equipment to assess the status of workers engaged in scaffolding and high-altitude work [13,14].

Research on developing smart personal protective equipment (PPE) for safety monitoring at construction sites is also actively underway. A. Rashidi et al. conducted a study in which they developed PPE by integrating monitoring systems into gloves and vests, allowing managers to oversee workers [15]. Meanwhile, A. Ojha et al. aimed to measure the overall health of construction workers through wearable biosensors by monitoring three types of physiological signals: PPG, EDA, and ST [16].

However, most of these studies targeted the general public, whose movements often differ from those of construction workers. For example, the general public typically engages in activities close to the ground, such as walking and tripping, whereas construction workers often operate at significant heights using ladders and construction equipment. In addition, when attempting to comprehensively monitor a worker's health and work status, smartphones or commercial IMU sensors can be bulky, expensive, or uncomfortable to wear, causing inconvenience for workers and disrupting their tasks [17]. Moreover, for greater accuracy, commercial sensors often rely on a single connectivity approach at high sampling rates, making integrated management difficult when multiple sensors are worn on different body parts. In particular, limited server connectivity and transmission protocols present significant challenges to implementing a CPS in large-scale construction sites.

Therefore, this study developed an IMU sensor that includes an accelerometer, gyroscope, barometric pressure, PPG, body temperature, and acoustic sensors. By wearing these sensors on six parts of the worker's body (head, body, both hands, and both legs), we developed algorithms capable of classifying not only daily movements such as walking, tripping, jumping, and sitting but also specialized tasks like ladder climbing and high-altitude work. Furthermore, by acquiring health data such as heart rate, oxygen saturation, and body temperature, we enabled the assessment of health conditions like heatstroke and cardiac arrest.

2. Materials and Methods

2.1. *Development of Sensors with Enhanced Field Applicability*

After analyzing worker behavior patterns and workplace environments, we confirmed that incidents such as falls, slips, falls from heights, collisions, and suffocation due to fires occur frequently. We determined that it is necessary to use sensors specifically capable of monitoring these incidents. Therefore, we selected the following six types of sensors for worker safety monitoring in this study. The definitions of these sensors and their respective monitoring items are as follows:

- Accelerometer: by measuring acceleration, the sensor can assess information such as an object's tilt (inclination angle) and vibrations. Sudden changes in acceleration values are considered abnormal signals, used to monitor for events like worker falls.

- Gyroscope: this sensor measures the rotational angle per unit time, allowing for detection of changes in orientation and movement.
- PPG sensor: by measuring a worker's heart rate and oxygen saturation, this sensor aids in identifying critical health risk factors.
- Body temperature sensor: by continuously measuring the worker's body temperature in real time, this sensor detects sudden changes that may indicate illnesses such as heatstroke or hypothermia.
- Barometric pressure sensor: this sensor measures atmospheric pressure, which helps determine the conditions at the worker's job site and identify associated risk factors.
- Acoustic sensor: by detecting changes in sound levels during specialized tasks (e.g., welding, cutting), this sensor monitors the worker's activity duration.

As shown in Figure 1, these six types of sensors were developed and manufactured at a size of 35 × 40 mm to minimize any discomfort workers might experience while wearing them. The prototype IMU sensors were specifically designed to be attachable to a worker's personal protective equipment.

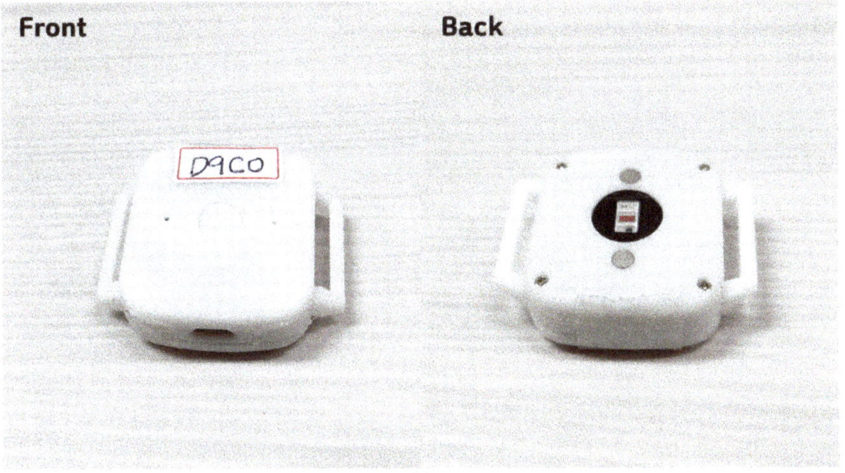

(a)

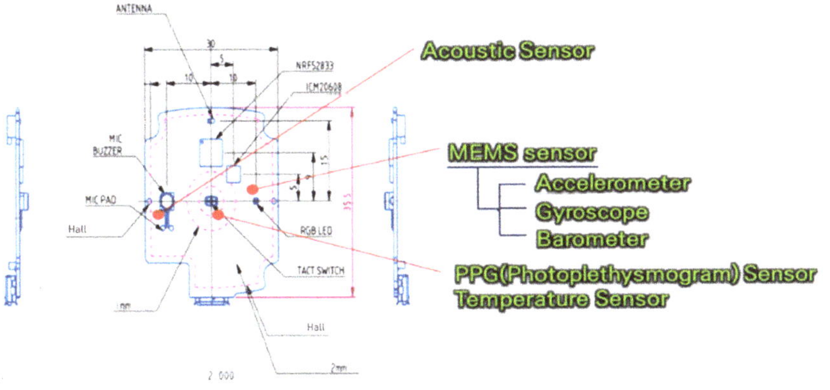

(b)

Figure 1. Fabrication of the prototype IMU sensor: (**a**) appearance of the fabricated IMU sensor; (**b**) diagram of the IMU sensor and the positions of the included sensors.

Each sensor communicates with the main MCU using wired I2C communication. In terms of measurement ranges, the accelerometer operates within ±8 g, the gyroscope within ±1000°/s, and the barometric pressure sensor from 300 to 1200 hPa. The heart rate sensor automatically adjusts its LED current to calibrate for external environmental conditions and skin contact. All sensors are configured to receive data at a rate of 15 times per second, while the heart rate sensor takes measurements after a one-minute interval.

The sensor mainboard is based on a 64 MHz Arm Cortex-M4 and utilizes the IEEE 802.15.4 radio protocol (Bluetooth 5.3). It is powered by a 3.7 V, 500 mAh lithium polymer battery, allowing for approximately 10 h of operation with a charging time of about 3 to 4 h.

2.2. *Worker Behavior Analysis and Algorithm Development*

The IMU sensor used in this study operates at a data collection frequency of 15 times per second, which is relatively low compared to commercial IMU sensors. This limitation makes it challenging to directly apply existing algorithms. Consequently, experiments were conducted that involved data quantification to remove noise, threshold adjustments, and the combination of suitable algorithms. These steps were designed to accurately determine worker status even at low frequencies. In addition, because each worker's body size, stride length, and work patterns vary depending on the individual and the nature of the work, worker types were categorized to configure the algorithms. Highly compatible algorithms were then developed for application to all workers.

For the experiment, the developed prototype IMU sensor was mounted on the head, body, hands, and legs of five workers. Data were collected by repeating actions such as walking, jumping, standing, sitting, working at height, and looking away from the forward direction, each performed 10 times. Based on the sensing data obtained from each mounting location, optimal filters and data processing methods were applied. The data from each location were then combined according to specific scenarios, and a final algorithm was configured to represent the worker's status. As shown in the flowchart in Figure 2, this algorithm enables classification across a variety of situations.

Examining the flowchart, data are first collected from sensors attached to the left and right legs to calculate the stance interval. The stance interval indicates whether the worker is stationary or moving at a given location, based on the number of samples recorded during stationary and moving periods. This information provides a basic assessment of whether the worker is standing, moving, or engaging in other activities.

After calculating the stance interval, if minimal movement is detected in both legs, the state is classified as "Standing". If the worker's body and head height drop below a certain threshold while in the "Standing" state, the state is classified as "Sitting". In this study, the threshold was set at 80 cm. If the stance interval and leg movement are active, the state is classified as "Moving".

In the "Moving" state, the flowchart evaluates whether the worker is looking forward by comparing the directions of the head and body. If these directions are aligned, the state is classified as "Looking Forward". If they do not align, it is recognized as "Not Looking Forward," and a warning message is issued.

Additionally, while in the "Moving" state, activities such as "High-Altitude Work," "Jumping," and "Falling" are classified by measuring both legs' altitude and acceleration energy and comparing them against predefined altitude levels and energy thresholds. The algorithms applied to each body part for classification are as Algorithms 1–4.

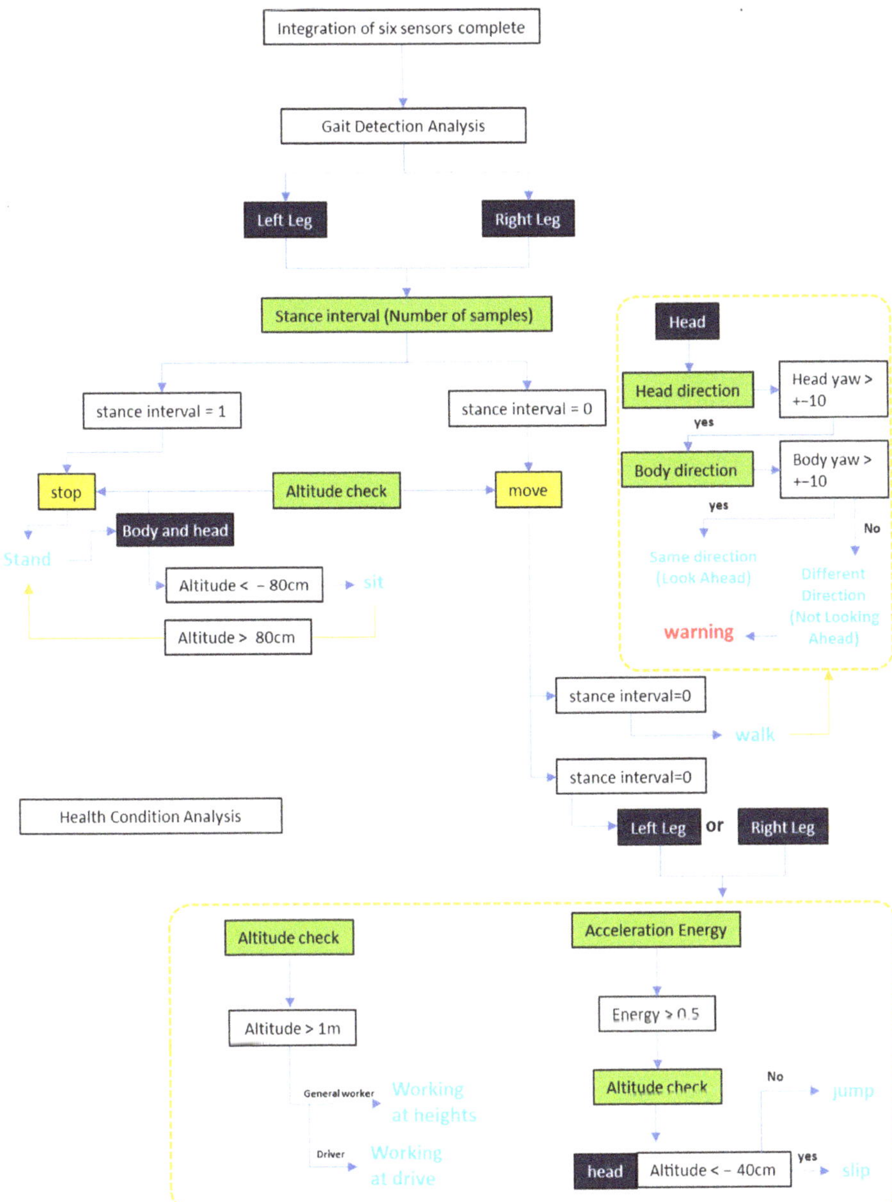

Figure 2. Algorithm flowchart for worker status assessment.

2.2.1. Forward Attention Algorithm

To process the gyroscope data in the Yaw direction for the head and body areas, the NMNI (noise-matched nonlinear inhibition) filter was applied. The NMNI filter removes noise from a specific gyroscope axis to set a threshold for angular velocity, allowing only signals that exceed this threshold [18]. It operates based on an initial window size (window_size = 50) and angular rate sensitivity (ars = 0.13), using the maximum absolute value of the gyroscope axis data within the given window as the threshold for noise removal.

A Kalman filter was subsequently applied to the data produced by the NMNI filter in order to estimate the state (posture angles) of the head and body. In this study, the Roll, Pitch, and Yaw angles were estimated by integrating accelerometer and gyroscope data. The filter's state vector is given by [roll, pitch, yaw, bias_x, bias_y, bias_z], where Roll and Pitch are directly calculated from accelerometer data, and Yaw is derived through the integration of gyroscope data. The prediction and update steps of the Kalman filter are as follows:

- Prediction step: predict the next state based on the current state vector and the error covariance matrix.
- Update step: correct the state vector using the measured Roll and Pitch values, and reduce errors by utilizing the measurement noise covariance (R).

The noise covariance matrices of the Kalman filter are defined as Q and R, where Q represents noise occurring during the state transition process, and R represents noise occurring during the measurement process.

Peak detection is then employed to identify significant events (rotations) in the Yaw data of the body and head devices, enabling the detection of moments when the user rotates in a specific direction. The find_peaks function is used to detect peaks in the Yaw data, with a set threshold (threshold = 10) and a minimum distance (distance = 45). This configuration extracts intervals where changes exceeding a certain angle are detected.

Finally, direction alignment events between the body and head are classified based on the peaks extracted from the Yaw data. As shown in Figure 3, when the worker rotates while walking, and the peak intervals of both devices overlap, the event is classified as "Both Turned". If the worker rotates only the head while walking, and the peak intervals do not overlap, the event is classified as "Head Turned".

Algorithm 1. Detect forward attention events.

```
Input: body_yaw, head_yaw, body_acc, head_acc, timestamps
Output: Forward attention events with timestamps

1. Set parameters
threshold = 10      # Yaw angle threshold for peak detection
distance = 45      # Minimum sample distance between peaks
window_size = 150      # NMNI filter window size
ars = 0.13      # Angular rate sensitivity for NMNI filter

2. Apply NMNI filter to Yaw data
body_yaw_filtered = apply_nmni(body_yaw, window_size, ars)
head_yaw_filtered = apply_nmni(head_yaw, window_size, ars)

3. Initialize Kalman filter for orientation estimation
kf = KalmanFilter(Q_acc=0.001, Q_bias=0.03, R=0.01)

4. Estimate orientation with Kalman filterfor each timestamp t:
roll, pitch, yaw = estimate_orientation(
kf, body_acc[t], head_acc[t], body_yaw_filtered[t], head_yaw_filtered[t], dt)

5. Detect peaks in filtered Yaw data
body_peaks = find_peaks(body_yaw_filtered, height=threshold, distance=distance)
head_peaks = find_peaks(head_yaw_filtered, height=threshold, distance=distance)
```

Algorithm 1. *Cont.*

6. Classify events:
for each peak in body_peaks:
if overlap with head_peaks:
classify as Both Turned
else:
classify as Head Turned

7. Merge overlapping Both Turned events:
for each consecutive Both Turned event:
if overlap:
merge events

8. Output results:
for each event:
record start_time, end_time from timestamps
store event type ("Both Turned" or "Head Turned")

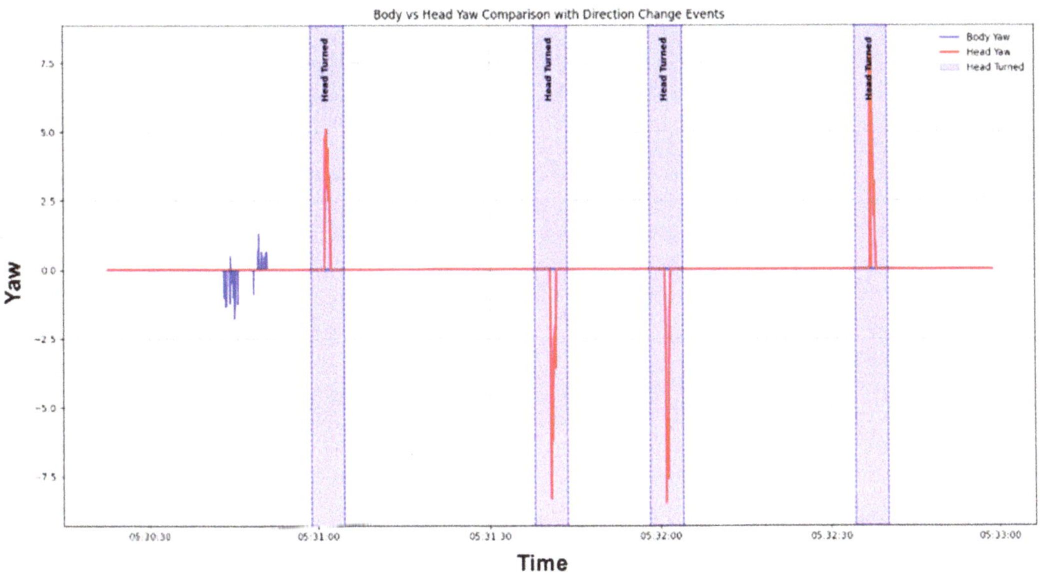

(**a**)

Figure 3. *Cont.*

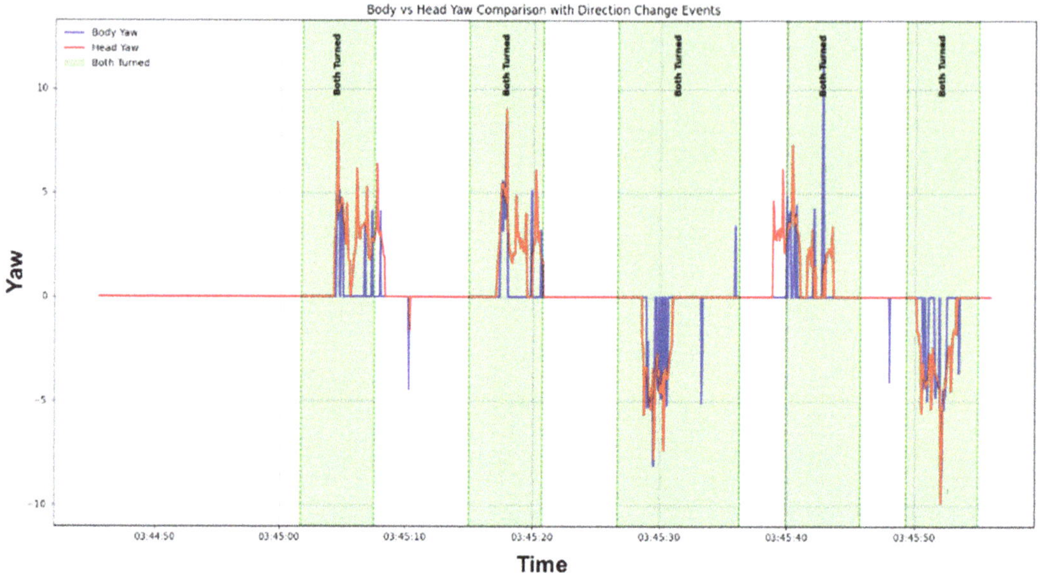

(**b**)

Figure 3. Results of applying the forward gaze algorithm: (**a**) when only the head turns; (**b**) when both body and head turn together (during directional change).

2.2.2. Gait Detection Algorithm

In the walking detection algorithm, the Kalman filter was also utilized to remove noise and correct sensor data. The state vector of the Kalman filter used in this algorithm consisted of [acc_x, acc_y, acc_z, gyro_x, gyro_y, gyro_z], defining acceleration and angular velocity as the state vector, thereby enhancing the stability of the sensor data [19].

Walking states were detected by analyzing the standard deviations of the filtered acceleration and angular velocity data. The Signal Vector Magnitude (SVM) of the acceleration was calculated, and a sliding window (window_size = 30) was applied to compute the standard deviation (σ_a) for each segment. For the Y-axis angular velocity data of the gyroscope (filtered_gyro_y), the same window size was applied to calculate the standard deviation (σ_ω).

Based on these two standard deviations, stance intervals were defined. If, within a specific interval, the acceleration standard deviation is less than 0.1 ($\sigma_a < 0.1$), and the angular velocity standard deviation is less than 20 ($\sigma_\omega < 20$), that interval is classified as a stance state, facilitating effective detection of walking patterns.

As shown in Figure 4, after distinguishing between stance and non-stance intervals, the length of each interval was analyzed to understand the periodicity of the walking state. Intervals identified as stance indicate that the movements of both legs have ceased, which corresponds to a "standing" or "sitting" state. When leg movements occur, non-stance intervals appear, allowing the determination of the leg movement state.

Algorithm 2. Gait detection using Kalman filter and standard deviation.

```
Input: Accelerometer (acc_x, acc_y, acc_z) and gyroscope (gyro_x, gyro_y, gyro_z) data
Output: Stance-phase detection based on filtered acceleration and gyro data

1. Initialize Kalman filter
kalman_filter_left = KalmanFilter()
kalman_filter_right = KalmanFilter()

2. Filter and calibrate data using Kalman filter
for each data point in acc and gyro data:
z = [acc_x, acc_y, acc_z, gyro_x, gyro_y, gyro_z]  # Measurement vector
kalman_filter.predict()  # Prediction step
kalman_filter.update(z)  # Update step
save filtered_acc and filtered_gyro  # Store filtered accelerometer and gyroscope data

3. Calculate standard deviation with sliding window
acc_magnitude = sqrt(filtered_acc_x^2 + filtered_acc_y^2 + filtered_acc_z^2)
sigma_a = rolling_std(acc_magnitude, window=window_size)
sigma_omega = rolling_std(filtered_gyro_y, window=window_size)

4. Detect stance phase
for each sample:
if sigma_a < 0.1 and sigma_omega < 20:
classify as Stance Phase
else:
classify as Non-Stance Phase

5. Analyze stance-phase intervalsfor each classified phase:
if Stance Phase:
count consecutive samples as Stance Interval
else:
count consecutive samples as Non-Stance Interval

6. Output results
- Print Stance Intervals (number of samples in each stance phase)
- Print Non-Stance Intervals (number of samples in each non-stance phase)
```

2.2.3. Energy Detection Algorithm

During the walking state, an energy detection algorithm was applied to analyze the intensity and periodicity of movements, thereby recognizing worker conditions such as "jumping" and "falling". To achieve this, a process was designed to calculate energy by removing the DC component based on the root mean square (RMS). Through this algorithm, the magnitude of acceleration changes within a specific time window was measured to detect the worker's movement patterns [20].

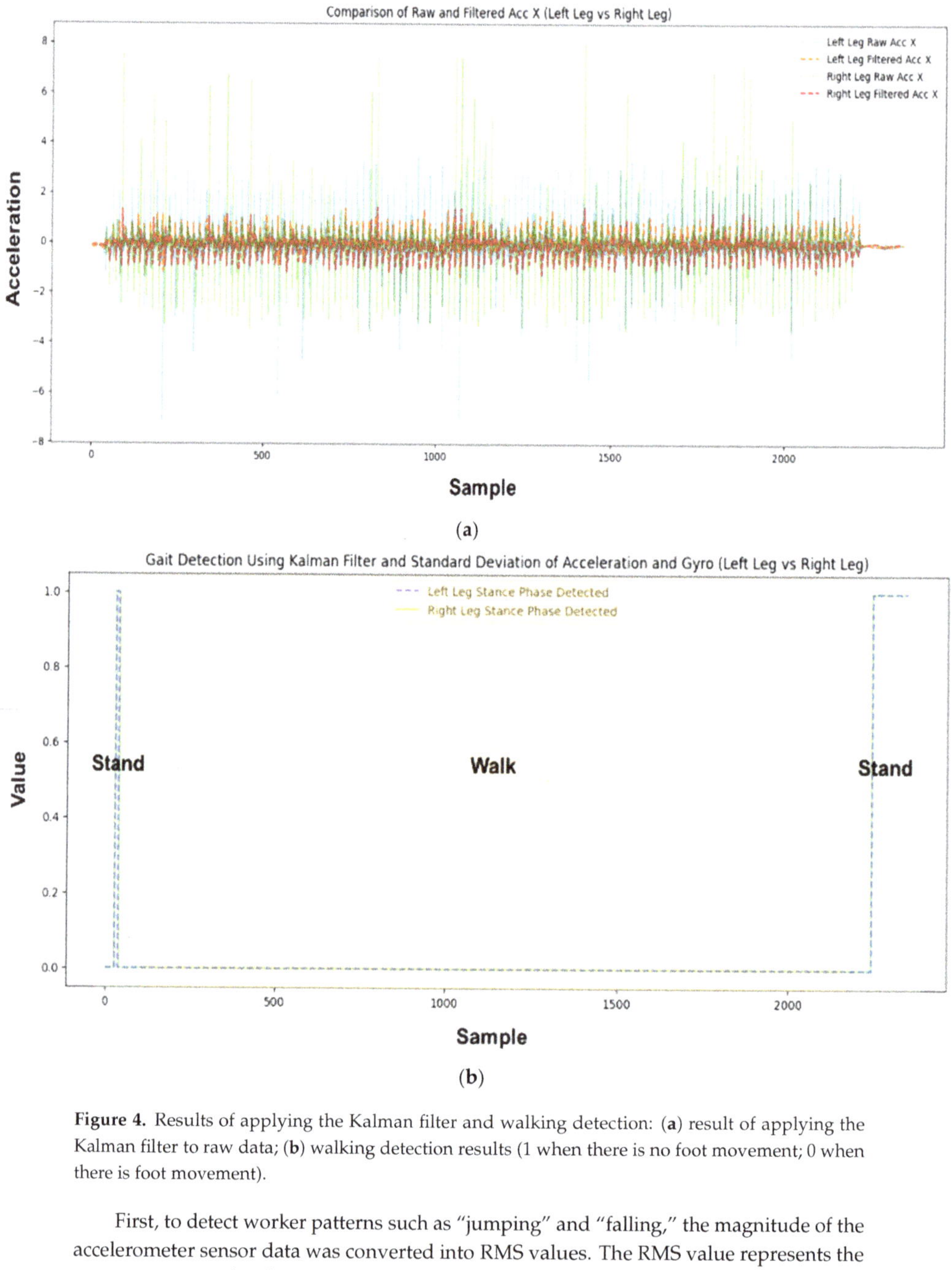

Figure 4. Results of applying the Kalman filter and walking detection: (**a**) result of applying the Kalman filter to raw data; (**b**) walking detection results (1 when there is no foot movement; 0 when there is foot movement).

First, to detect worker patterns such as "jumping" and "falling," the magnitude of the accelerometer sensor data was converted into RMS values. The RMS value represents the average magnitude of the signal, calculated by taking the square root of the sum of the squares of the acceleration vector magnitudes, as defined in Equation (1).

$$RMS_{acc} = \sqrt{acc_x^2 + acc_y^2 + acc_z^2)} \quad (1)$$

By removing the DC component from the RMS data, the fluctuations in the signal are centralized. As shown in Equation (2), the moving average is subtracted from the RMS values using a sliding window (window_size = 30). This process generates a detrended signal, enabling clearer detection of changes in movement.

$$RMS_{acc,\ detrended} = RMS_{acc} - moving\_average(RMS_{acc}) \tag{2}$$

Energy was calculated by quantifying the magnitude changes within a specific window based on the detrended signal. It can be expressed as shown in Equation (3).

$$Energy_{acc} = \frac{1}{N}\sum_{i=1}^{N} RMS^2_{acc,\ detrended} \tag{3}$$

Figure 5 presents a graph showing the results of the algorithm applied based on the above equation.

Algorithm 3. Accelerometer energy detection algorithm.

Input: acc_x, acc_y, acc_z data
Output: Energy values for accelerometer data

1. Calculate RMS
rms_acc = sqrt(acc_x^2 + acc_y^2 + acc_z^2)

2. Remove DC component
rms_acc_detrended = rms_acc–moving_average(rms_acc, window=30)

3. Calculate energy
energy_acc = rolling_mean(rms_acc_detrended^2, window=30)

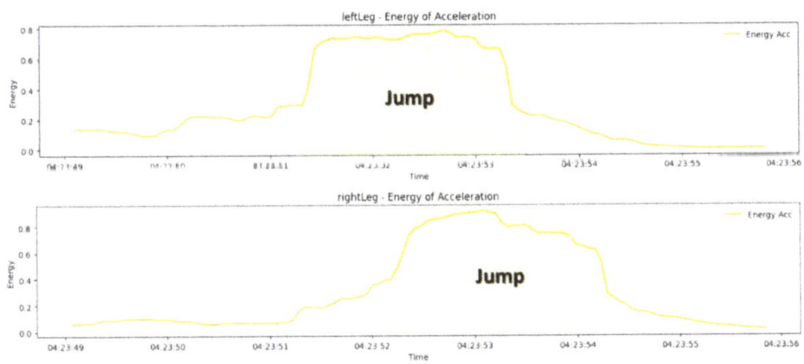

Figure 5. Results of applying the energy detection algorithm during jumping.

2.2.4. Altitude Detection Algorithm

To estimate the worker's altitude changes, an extended Kalman filter (EKF) was applied to the barometric sensor data. The EKF, which facilitates state estimation in nonlinear systems, was used to correct errors in the barometric sensor, thereby detecting patterns in the worker's vertical movement [21].

For altitude estimation, the EKF model's state vector consists solely of altitude data and is therefore expressed as [altitude]. The initial covariance matrix p is assigned large values to account for high uncertainty. The filtering process is as follows. First, the prediction step of the EKF for the state is described by Equations (4) and (5).

$$\hat{x}_{k|k-1} = A\hat{x}_{k-1|k-1} \tag{4}$$

$$P_{k|k-1} = AP_{k-1|k-1}A^T + Q \tag{5}$$

In the above equations, A is the identity matrix A = [1], and Q represents the process noise covariance for altitude prediction. Using the altitude data z obtained from the barometer, the steps for calculating the Kalman gain and updating the state are presented in Equations (6)–(10).

$$y = z - H\hat{x}_{k|k-1} \tag{6}$$

$$S = HP_{k|k-1}H^T + R \tag{7}$$

$$K = P_{k|k-1}H^T S^{-1} \tag{8}$$

$$\hat{x}_{k|k} = \hat{x}_{k|k-1} + Ky \tag{9}$$

$$P_{k|k} = (I - KH)P_{k|k-1} \tag{10}$$

In the above equations, y represents the residual, S is the covariance, K is the Kalman gain, H is the measurement matrix, and R represents the measurement noise covariance of the barometer.

By applying the EKF to filter the altitude data, we estimated the altitude changes. As shown in Figure 6, the altitude change was calculated as the difference between the starting and ending altitudes within a window of 300 samples.

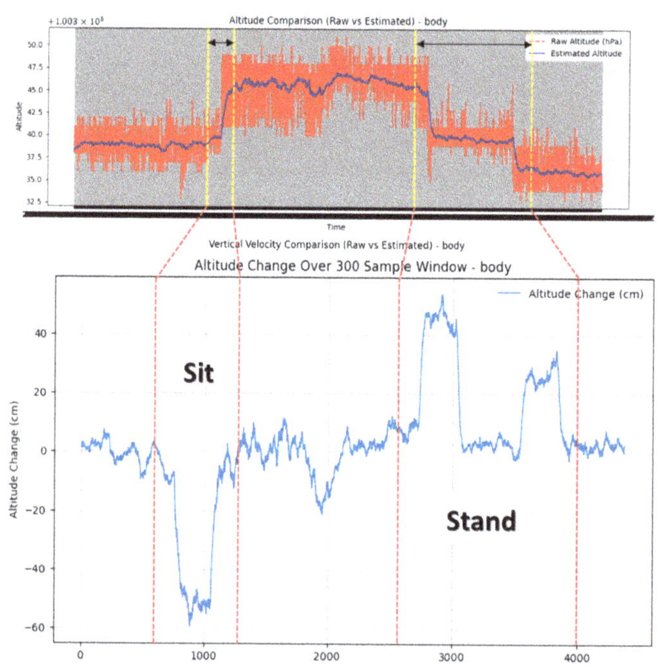

Figure 6. Results of applying the extended Kalman filter to barometric data and estimation of altitude changes.

Algorithm 4. EKF for Altitude Estimation.

Input: Barometer (hPa) data
Output: Altitude estimates over time

1. EKF-based altitude estimation (single state)
Initialize altitude state x and covariance p
For each barometer data point:
- Predict next state: x and p
- Update altitude from barometer: z_barometer = [hPa]
- Compute Kalman Gain K and update x, p

2. Calculate altitude change
Convert pressure to altitude (cm)
Slide a 300-sample window to compute altitude change:
altitude_change = altitude_end–altitude_start

3. Results

The developed IMU sensors were attached to the worker's protective equipment (safety helmet, safety vest, and leg guards), as shown in Figure 7, for experimental purposes. The wrist-mounted IMU sensor was designed in a band form to ensure comfortable use with minimal inconvenience.

Figure 7. IMU sensor placement by body part.

To integrate the developed IMU sensor data into the CPS, an application was created as shown in Figure 8. The application allows users to input the MAC addresses of the IMU sensors for each body part, enabling Bluetooth connectivity. The sensor data transmitted to the mobile device via Bluetooth are then sent to the server using LTE communication. Additionally, the developed algorithms were implemented within the application to analyze the data collected from specific body parts in real time and determine the worker's status.

The worker's status, as assessed by the algorithm, is transmitted to a database through the application, where it is used to update the worker's status in real time within the CPS.

Figure 8. IMU sensor application integration screen and database connection screen.

To evaluate the performance of the developed system, experiments were conducted with five workers. Each worker performed every action ten times, producing a total of fifty trials per action. The classification results from these trials are summarized in Table 1.

Table 1. Classification results for each action.

Action	Total Trials	Correctly Classified	Accuracy (%)
Walking	50	50	100
Jumping	50	47	94
Standing	50	50	100
High-altitude work	50	45	90
Not looking forward	50	43	86
Sitting	50	40	80

The sensor data transmitted to the database include information such as oxygen saturation, heart rate, and body temperature, enabling real-time monitoring of workers' health status. As demonstrated in the experiment, the worker's condition can also be determined based on the algorithm-assessed worker state (e.g., walking, sitting, jumping, performing high-altitude work, not looking forward, etc.).

In addition, if initial measurements of oxygen saturation, heart rate, or body temperature fall below certain thresholds, the worker's health status changes from "normal" to "at risk". This status is displayed on the dashboard, allowing administrators to respond immediately to potential hazards during monitoring.

For the data integration experiment, as shown in Figure 9, a dashboard was developed to monitor the worker's status, and the experimental site was converted into a 3D model using drone imagery. This 3D model was then used to create a CPS environment through the Unity program.

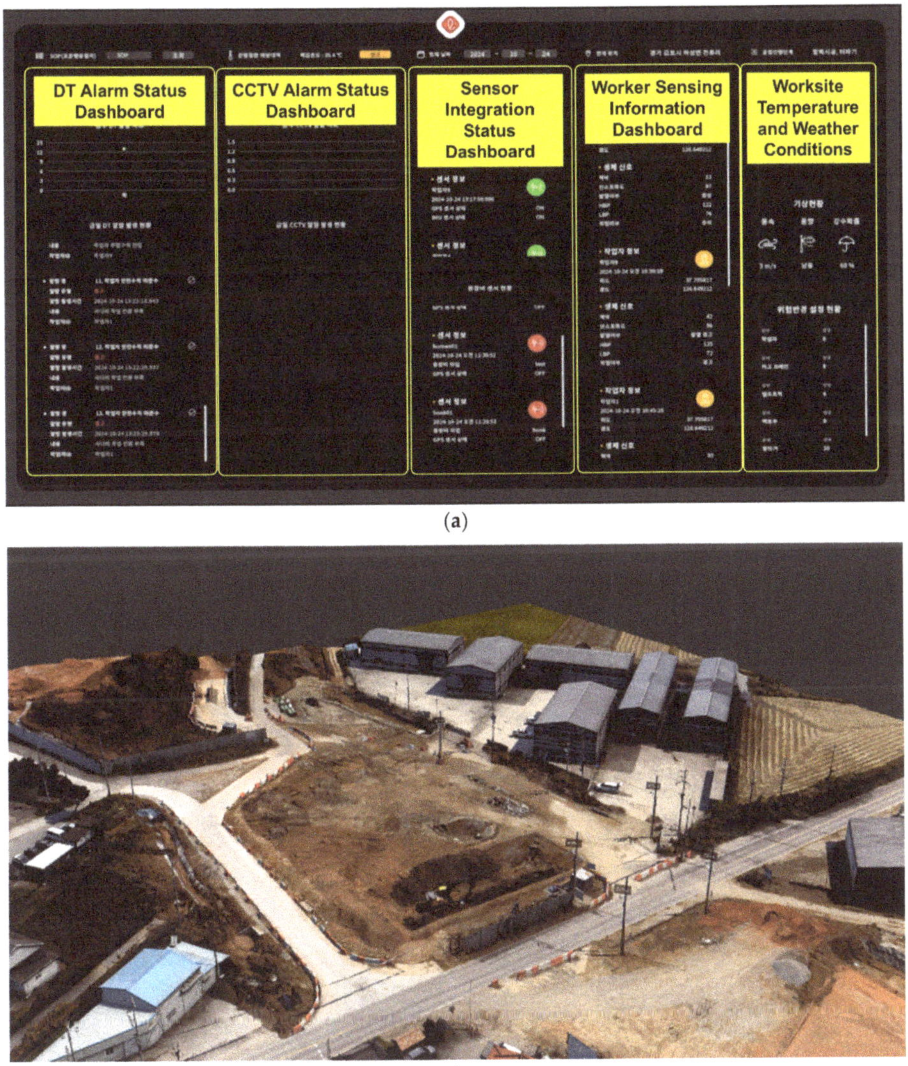

(**a**)

(**b**)

Figure 9. Dashboard and environment setup for CPS implementation: (**a**) CPS dashboard screen layout; (**b**) CPS environment construction scene.

In the CPS, worker monitoring is displayed through icons, and the user interface (UI) presented to the worker is shown in Figure 10. The UI displays the worker's name, date and time, status, and health conditions (such as oxygen saturation, heart rate, and body temperature), which match the data transmitted to the database. These data are updated in real time, enabling managers to monitor and identify any abnormal conditions affecting workers.

The data shown in Figure 10 are also stored on the dashboard, which is further designed to display various types of information such as sensor connection and operation status, worker status, health information, real-time site temperature, and weather conditions. Figure 11 illustrates a screen where multiple workers are monitored simultaneously. In the event of abnormal situations (e.g., irregular conditions), the dashboard not only stores the relevant information for monitoring but also facilitates proactive on-site actions to prevent accidents. For instance, if abnormal conditions (such as falls or jumps) frequently occur at a specific location, the data generated through this study can be used to either prevent accidents or detect them early through on-site interventions.

Figure 10. Worker icons and UI in CPS operation.

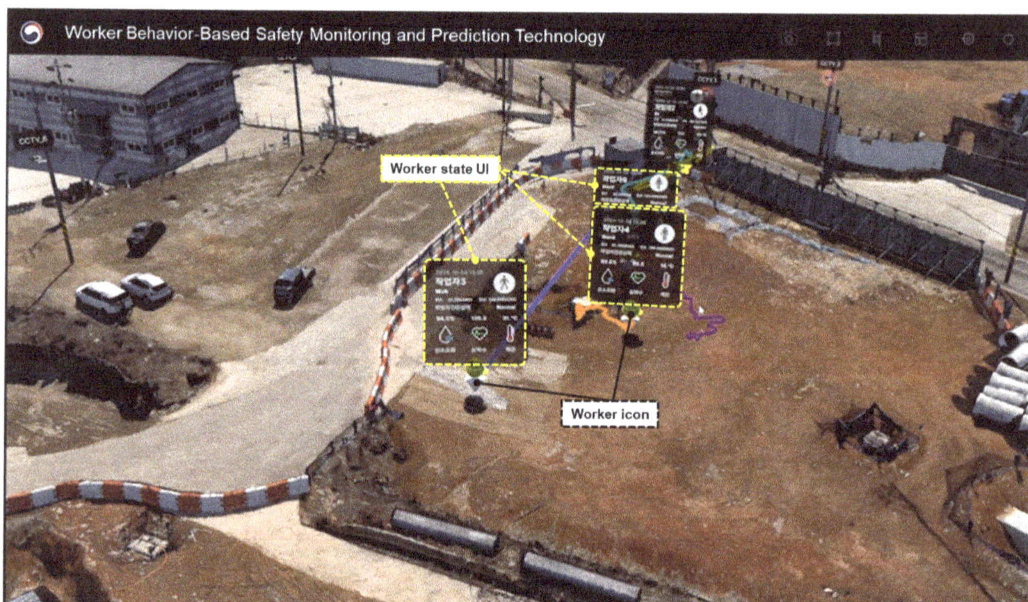

Figure 11. Example of CPS application for multiple workers.

4. Discussion

This study aimed to develop an IMU sensor for construction and industrial environments and to integrate it into a CPS for monitoring worker behavior under real-world conditions that include the use of protective equipment, uneven terrain, and expansive worksites. During this process, the system achieved an overall accuracy of approximately 90% for recognizing worker actions; however, accuracy for the sitting action was relatively lower. This lower performance may stem from the barometric sensor's susceptibility to errors caused by uneven ground conditions and fluctuations in temperature and humidity, despite its need for centimeter-level precision. Nevertheless, real-time monitoring of worker behavior through the CPS proved effective in enhancing safety measures and improving operational management efficiency.

Several limitations were identified in this research. First, a delay of approximately 2–3 s occurs between the sensor's initial detection of movement and its display in the CPS interface. In urgent situations, such as sudden falls, this delay could hinder rapid response. The selected window size for detecting data changes and the latency in transmitting data to the database appear to contribute to this issue. Second, due to the maximum number of Bluetooth devices that can simultaneously connect to an Android system, sensor integration occasionally became unstable. When the IMU sensor's data transmission rate was increased, the intervals between data arrivals became irregular. Although three IMU sensors transmitted data reliably, connecting six sensors sometimes resulted in two or three failing to meet the set data threshold, thereby reducing the accuracy of the algorithms. A slight delay (on the order of milliseconds) was therefore introduced during transmission to ensure all six IMU sensors could still send quantitative data, establishing an optimal transmission rate of 15 Hz (i.e., 15 data points per second).

Lastly, because sensors may be directly exposed to dust, moisture, and other contaminants in harsh field conditions, those with relatively low IP (ingress protection) ratings risk malfunctioning in such environments. These limitations underscore the need for future research aimed at optimizing algorithms for real-time data processing, refining communication and data transmission methods for multi-sensor integration, and improving sensor casing materials and designs to enhance waterproof and dustproof capabilities, thereby increasing practical applicability in the field.

5. Conclusions

This study developed IMU sensors and an application integrated into a CPS to monitor workers' behaviors in construction and industrial environments. The conclusions of this study are as follows:

1. The IMU sensors used in this research address challenges associated with existing commercial sensors—such as large form factors and difficulties in internal filtering, communication, and server integration—when implementing a CPS.
2. To minimize worker discomfort and enable seamless attachment to personal protective equipment, the sensors were miniaturized and designed for placement on the head, body, hands, and legs. This approach allows for more granular measurement of diverse work activities.
3. The IMU sensors were operated at a relatively low sampling rate of 15 times per second to extend their operating time during work hours, while an algorithm was designed to effectively capture workers' movements in on-site conditions. In addition, the algorithm retained the flexibility to operate at higher frequencies (e.g., above 50 Hz) for more detailed motion analysis when needed.
4. By attaching sensors to the head, body, both hands, and both legs, worker behaviors—such as walking, jumping, standing, sitting, working at height, and looking away

from the forward direction—could be detected with approximately 90% accuracy. The IMU sensors also assessed workers' health status (e.g., oxygen saturation, heart rate, and temperature) and transmitted these data to a database, which was then linked to the CPS interface, enabling managers to monitor workers in real time.

In conclusion, by developing IMU sensors and implementing an application and CPS equipped with algorithms to recognize worker behaviors, this study facilitates real-time monitoring, and thereby, contributes to enhanced safety management at construction sites.

Author Contributions: Conceptualization, J.K.; Methodology, J.K.; Software, S.P.; Validation, S.P.; Formal Analysis, S.P.; Data Curation, S.P.; Writing—Original Draft Preparation, S.P.; Writing—Review and Editing, M.Y.; Project Administration, M.Y. All authors have read and agreed to the published version of the manuscript.

Funding: This research was funded by the National Research Foundation of Korea (NRF) grant funded by the Korea government (MSIT) (No. NRF-2020R1C1C1004437) and supported by a grant (2022-MOIS38-002 (RS-2022-ND630021)) of Proactive Technology Development on Safety Accident for Vulnerable Group and Facility funded by the Ministry of Interior and Safety (MOIS, Korea). The APC was funded by the National Research Foundation of Korea (NRF) and the Ministry of Interior and Safety (MOIS, Korea).

Informed Consent Statement: This study was conducted with participants who were part of the same project team, and therefore, no consent form was required. Additionally, it was exempt from review by the Institutional Review Board (IRB) in Korea according to Article 13, Paragraph 2 of the Enforcement Rule, as it involved direct interaction with participants who were unspecified and did not collect or record sensitive information as defined under Article 23 of the Personal Information Protection Act.

Data Availability Statement: The algorithm used in this study is included in the manuscript. The sensing data supporting the findings of this study are available from the corresponding author upon reasonable request.

Conflicts of Interest: The authors declare no conflict of interest.

References

1. Occupational Safety and Health Administration. Commonly Used Statistics. Available online: https://www.osha.gov/data/commonstats (accessed on 21 December 2024).
2. Health and Safety Executive. Work-Related Fatal Injuries in Great Britain. Available online: https://www.hse.gov.uk/statistics/fatals.htm (accessed on 21 December 2024).
3. Zhong, R.; Rau, P.-L.P.; Yan, X. Gait Assessment of Younger and Older Adults with Portable Motion-Sensing Methods: A User Study. *Mob. Inf. Syst.* **2019**, *2019*, 1093514. [CrossRef]
4. Chen, S.; Bangaru, S.S.; Yigit, T.; Trkov, M.; Wang, C.; Yi, J. Real-Time Walking Gait Estimation for Construction Workers Using a Single Wearable Inertial Measurement Unit (IMU). In Proceedings of the 2021 IEEE/ASME International Conference on Advanced Intelligent Mechatronics (AIM), Delft, The Netherlands, 12–16 July 2021. [CrossRef]
5. Yodpijit, N.; Tavichaiyuth, N.; Jongprasithporn, M.; Songwongamarit, C.; Sittiwanchai, T. The use of smartphone for gait analysis. *IEEE Sens. J.* **2017**, *20*, 1191–1201.
6. Awais, M.; Chiari, L.; Ihlen, E.A.F.; Helbostad, J.L.; Palmerini, L. Physical Activity Classification for Elderly People in Free-Living Conditions. *IEEE J. Biomed. Health Inform.* **2018**, *23*, 197–207. [CrossRef] [PubMed]
7. Li, H.; Shrestha, A.; Heidari, H.; Kernec, J.L.; Fioranelli, F. Bi-LSTM Network for Multimodal Continuous Human Activity Recognition and Fall Detection. *IEEE Sens. J.* **2020**, *20*, 1191–1201. [CrossRef]
8. Lee, Y.; Do, W.; Yoon, H.; Heo, J.; Lee, W.; Lee, D. Visual-Inertial Hand Motion Tracking with Robustness Against Occlusion, Interference, and Contact. *Sci. Robot.* **2021**, *6*, eabe1315. [CrossRef] [PubMed]
9. Nia, N.G.; Kaplanoglu, E.; Nasab, A.; Qin, H. Human Activity Recognition Using Machine Learning Algorithms Based on IMU Data. In Proceedings of the 2023 5th International Conference on Bio-Engineering for Smart Technologies, Paris, France, 7–9 June 2023; pp. 7–9.
10. Singh, A.; Rehman, S.U.; Yongcharoen, S.; Chong, P.H.J. Sensor technologies for fall detection systems: A review. *IEEE Sens. J.* **2020**, *20*, 6889–6919. [CrossRef]

11. Shibuya, N.; Nukala, B.T.; Rodriguez, A.I.; Tsay, J.; Nguyen, T.Q.; Zupancic, S. A real-time fall detection system using a wearable gait analysis sensor and a Support Vector Machine (SVM) classifier. In Proceedings of the 2015 Eighth International Conference on Mobile Computing and Ubiquitous Networking (ICMU), Hakodate, Japan, 20–22 January 2015; pp. 66–67.
12. Choi, A.; Kim, T.H.; Yuhai, O.; Jeong, S.; Kim, K.; Kim, H.; Mun, J.W. Deep Learning-Based Near-Fall Detection Algorithm for Fall Risk Monitoring System Using a Single Inertial Measurement Unit. *IEEE Trans. Neural Syst. Rehabil. Eng.* **2022**, *30*, 2385–2394. [CrossRef] [PubMed]
13. Semwal, V.B.; Kumar, A.; Nargesh, P.; Soni, V. Tracking of Fall Detection Using IMU Sensor: An IoHT Application. In *Machine Learning, Image Processing, Network Security and Data Sciences: Select Proceedings of 3rd International Conference on MIND 2021*; Springer: Singapore, 2023.
14. Choo, H.; Lee, B.; Kim, H.; Choi, B. Automated Detection of Construction Work at Heights and Deployment of Safety Hooks Using IMU with a Barometer. *Autom. Constr.* **2023**, *147*, 104714. [CrossRef]
15. Rashidi, A.; Woon, G.L.; Dasandara, M.; Bazghaleh, M.; Pasbakhsh, P. Smart personal protective equipment for intelligent construction safety monitoring. In *Smart and Sustainable Built Environment*; Emerald: Bradford, UK, 2024.
16. Ojha, A.; Shakerian, S.; Habibnezhad, M.; Jebelli, H. Feasibility Verification of Multimodal Wearable Sensing System for Holistic Health Monitoring of Construction Workers. In Proceedings of the Canadian Society of Civil Engineering Annual Conference 2021 (CSCE 2021), Niagara Falls, ON, Canada, 26–29 May 2021; pp. 283–294.
17. Samatas, G.G.; Pachidis, T.P. Inertial Measurement Units (IMUs) in Mobile Robots over the Last Five Years: A Review. *Designs* **2022**, *6*, 17. [CrossRef]
18. Hong, S.; Yoon, J.; Ham, Y.; Lee, B.; Kim, H. Monitoring Safety Behaviors of Scaffolding Workers Using Gramian Angular Field Convolution Neural Network Based on IMU Sensing Data. *Autom. Constr.* **2023**, *148*, 104748. [CrossRef]
19. Hoang, M.L.; Carratù, M.; Paciello, V.; Pietrosanto, A. Fusion Filters between the No Motion No Integration Technique and Kalman Filter in Noise Optimization on a 6DoF Drone for Orientation Tracking. *Sensors* **2023**, *23*, 5603. [CrossRef] [PubMed]
20. Shi, L.-F.; Dong, Y.-J.; Shi, Y. Indoor PDR Method Based on Foot-Mounted Low-Cost IMMU. In Proceedings of the 2022 IEEE International Conference on Networking, Sensing and Control (ICNSC), Shanghai, China, 15–18 December 2022; IEEE: Piscataway, NJ, USA, 2023.
21. Son, Y.; Oh, S. A Barometer-IMU Fusion Method for Vertical Velocity and Height Estimation. In Proceedings of the 2015 IEEE SENSORS, Busan, Republic of Korea, 1–4 November 2015; IEEE: Piscataway, NJ, USA, 2016.

sensors

MDPI

Article

A New Iterative Algorithm for Magnetic Motion Tracking

Tobias Schmidt [1,2], Johannes Hoffmann [1], Moritz Boueke [1], Robert Bergholz [3], Ludger Klinkenbusch [2] and Gerhard Schmidt [1,*]

1 Digital Signal Processing and System Theory, Institute of Electrical Engineering and Information Technology, Faculty of Engineering, Kiel University, Kaiserstr. 2, 24143 Kiel, Germany; tsc@tf.uni-kiel.de (T.S.); jph@tf.uni-kiel.de (J.H.); mobo@tf.uni-kiel.de (M.B.)

2 Computational Electromagnetics, Institute of Electrical Engineering and Information Technology, Faculty of Engineering, Kiel University, Kaiserstr. 2, 24143 Kiel, Germany; lbk@tf.uni-kiel.de

3 Pediatric Surgery, University Hospital Schleswig-Holstein, Kiel University, Arnold-Heller Str. 3, 24105 Kiel, Germany; robert.bergholz@uksh.de

* Correspondence: gus@tf.uni-kiel.de

Abstract: Motion analysis is of great interest to a variety of applications, such as virtual and augmented reality and medical diagnostics. Hand movement tracking systems, in particular, are used as a human–machine interface. In most cases, these systems are based on optical or acceleration/angular speed sensors. These technologies are already well researched and used in commercial systems. In special applications, it can be advantageous to use magnetic sensors to supplement an existing system or even replace the existing sensors. The core of a motion tracking system is a localization unit. The relatively complex localization algorithms present a problem in magnetic systems, leading to a relatively large computational complexity. In this paper, a new approach for pose estimation of a kinematic chain is presented. The new algorithm is based on spatially rotating magnetic dipole sources. A spatial feature is extracted from the sensor signal, the dipole direction in which the maximum magnitude value is detected at the sensor. This is introduced as the "maximum vector". A relationship between this feature, the location vector (pointing from the magnetic source to the sensor position) and the sensor orientation is derived and subsequently exploited. By modelling the hand as a kinematic chain, the posture of the chain can be described in two ways: the knowledge about the magnetic correlations and the structure of the kinematic chain. Both are bundled in an iterative algorithm with very low complexity. The algorithm was implemented in a real-time framework and evaluated in a simulation and first laboratory tests. In tests without movement, it could be shown that there was no significant deviation between the simulated and estimated poses. In tests with periodic movements, an error in the range of 1° was found. Of particular interest here is the required computing power. This was evaluated in terms of the required computing operations and the required computing time. Initial analyses have shown that a computing time of 3 μs per joint is required on a personal computer. Lastly, the first laboratory tests basically prove the functionality of the proposed methodology.

Keywords: magnetic motion tracking; localization; rotating magnetic dipole; iterative algorithms; human–machine interface

1. Introduction

Human motion tracking is of great interest to many applications such as virtual/augmented reality [1] and medical diagnostics [2]. Among the several variants of motion tracking, this contribution focuses on hand-motion tracking as a human–machine interface for robot-assisted surgery. However, the proposed method can also be used for other applications where the movement can be modelled by kinematic chains.

Camera-based (optical motion capture, OMC) systems, which are considered to be the gold standard in motion tracking methods, allow for accuracy in the millimeter or even submillimeter range [3]. However, OMC systems have the disadvantage that direct lines of sight between the objects (usually reflecting markers) and relevant cameras are required.

An alternative method is the use of gloves with attached inertial measurement units (IMU) or flex sensors. Several of the corresponding solutions are shown in [4]. The well-investigated IMU are used in commercial applications such as *XSens' Quantum Metaglove* [5]. However, IMU-based systems do not measure the quantities of interest (i.e., positions and angles) directly but instead measure their time derivatives (i.e., acceleration and angular speed). This leads to drift problems.

Approaches based on magnetic sensors are still in the early phases of research (see [6,7], for examples). Future magnetic methods could be either a stand-alone functional alternative or be used as a supplement to improve the performance of optical or IMU-based systems.

The present work aims to design an input device for robot-assisted surgery based on magnetic sensor technology. For this purpose, a glove will be equipped with magnetic sensors such that each kinematic element can be assigned to at least one sensor. The heart of the proposed motion tracking system is the localization unit. This unit determines the pose of the object with a constant sample rate with a typical duration of the period of 15 ms, which in turn leads to a localization update rate of 67 Hz [8,9]. If the sampling period is longer, it might lead to disruptive handling in human–machine interface applications. In our case, a kinematic chain with up to 20 degrees of freedom has to be estimated every 15 ms. The allowed latency is one of the challenges, as it leads to limited computing time and the algorithms must be designed to work efficiently.

Magnetic localization is usually solved with numerical or analytical approaches. Numerical solutions are used in applications with 1D sensors or flexible setups [10–13]. Analytical methods are used with fixed sensor array configurations, such as 3D sensors [14–16] or gradient sensors [17–20]. On the one hand, numerical methods are generally computationally intensive, which can become a problem if many (>20) sensors are involved, as it may no longer be possible to maintain the latency time. On the other hand, analytical methods usually use defined sensor setups such as 3D sensors. These may already be too large for the structures to be observed, which in case of a finger are only a few centimetres in size. In [6], a magnetic sensor glove with a numerical localization approach is described.

In the approaches mentioned above, while poses are determined by a minimization of a cost function and some kinematic constraints are kept, up to 55 hand reconstructions per second had been achieved thus far. Since about at least 67 hand reconstructions per second are required for surgical interfaces, these algorithms are not fully capable of solving the problem at this time. With the progress in computer hardware, these algorithms could become able to satisfy these conditions in the future. However, we are looking for a solution that can be executed on standard personal computers where further processing beyond motion analysis (e.g., gesture recognition) usually need to be executed.

For the overall system, we use two nested localization methods: The *external* localization is responsible for the absolute localization of a reference point within a defined measurement volume. In our case, this reference point could be the wrist, for example. A 3D coil is attached to this wrist, which can then be localized using conventional algorithms, as shown in [15,16]. Based on this, there is an *internal* localization. This estimates the position and orientation of the sensors attached to the fingers with respect to the reference point mentioned above. To this end, the individual fingers are modelled as kinematic chains. This offers an advantage in that the number of degrees of freedom is reduced. In general, a 1D sensor has five degrees of freedom: three for the position and two for the orientation. By attaching the sensor to the kinematic chain, the number of degrees of freedom per sensor is reduced to two. Here, movement is limited by the rotation of the joints. This will be utilized in an efficient algorithm, which will be explained in the following. An advantage of the presented algorithm is that it combines localization and mapping to a kinematic chain. In this way, prior knowledge about a kinematic chain is integrated into a localization, thus narrowing down the solution space and simplifying the calculation. An overview of this nested localization scheme is shown in Figure 1.

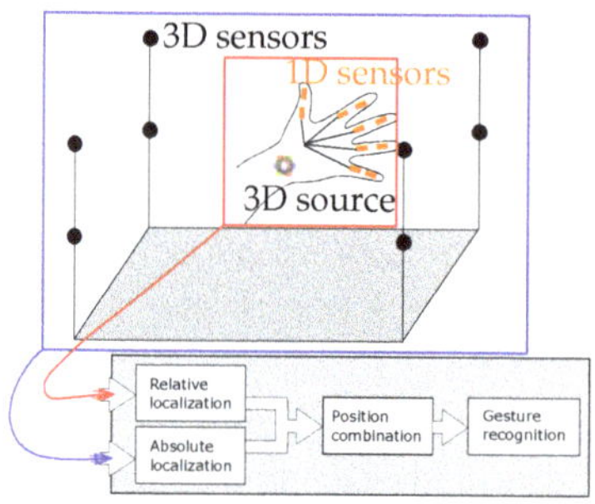

Figure 1. System overview: The illustration includes an external localization (blue) consisting of a defined setup of (here 8) sensors. The inner localization (red) consists of a 3D coil which is attached to the wrist as well as magnetic 1D sensors which are attached to each finger element. Following the localization, gesture recognition or processing of the data for the human–machine interface can be carried out.

First, we will introduce a magnetic signal feature called the "maximum vector". Then, we discuss the relations between this feature, the sensor position, and the sensor orientation. Eventually, these relations are linked to the known anatomy through an iterative algorithm. For validation, the algorithm was implemented in a real-time environment and tested with a simulation and an initial laboratory setup. The paper closes with a discussion about the results and the restrictions of the algorithm. The central idea and a suitable setup is shown in Figure 2.

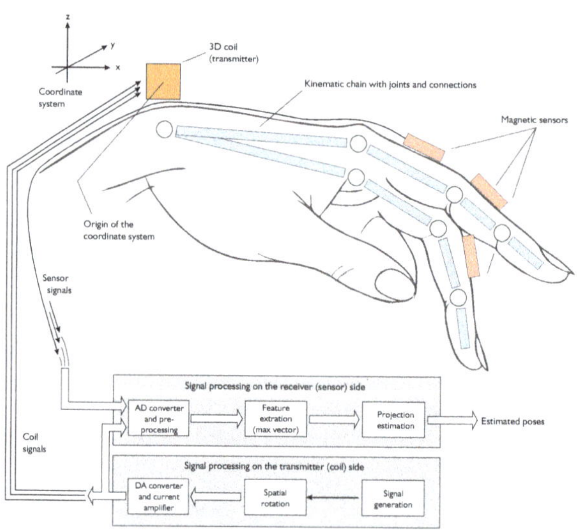

Figure 2. Typical example of use of the presented algorithm: At the origin of the coordinate system a 3D magnetic transmitter is located. A kinematic chain is equipped with 1D magnetic sensors, such as fluxgate magnetometers or magnetoelectric sensors, on every chain element. The kinematic chains are connected through joints with ellipsoidal cross-sections, each providing two degrees of freedom. Any additional information from the kinematic chain about the position is used to increase the speed of the localization algorithm.

2. Spatial Signal Feature

In this section, a magnetic signal feature will be introduced, which we refer to as the "maximum vector", abbreviated as MV in the following. A rotating magnetic dipole at a defined position and a sensor at a defined position and orientation are assumed. The MV describes the dipole orientation for which the maximum signal is detected at the sensor. The spatial relationships between the MV, the sensor location, and the sensor orientation will be derived in the following.

2.1. Field-Theoretical Basics

The magnetic field of a slowly time-varying current density distribution can be approximated by Biot–Savart's law. However, even this simplification of Maxwell's equations can result in a very time-consuming numerical calculation, requiring a spatial integration over each voxel of the current–density distribution. For a localized current–density distribution produced by coils, the magnetic field calculation can be further simplified using a magnetic dipole model. For a good approximation, it is important that the distance between the coil and the sensor is much larger than the typical dimensions of the coil. For a magnetic dipole $\vec{m}$ located at the origin ($r = 0$), the magnetic field $\vec{B}_{\mathrm{dip}}(\vec{r})$ can described by [21]:

$$\vec{B}_{\mathrm{dip}}(\vec{r}) = \frac{1}{4\pi r^2}\frac{3\vec{r}(\vec{m}\cdot\vec{r}) - \vec{m}r^2}{r^3}. \tag{1}$$

In the present work, we assume an ideal sensor at position $\vec{r}$ with known orientation $\vec{e}_s$. "Ideal" means that the sensor is assumed to be located at a single point and that the output of the sensor is an undisturbed projection of the dipole field on the main sensor axis. The output $B_{\mathrm{sensor}}(\vec{r}, \vec{e}_s)$ is then found as follows:

$$B_{\mathrm{sensor}}(\vec{r}, \vec{e}_s) = \vec{B}_{\mathrm{dip}}(\vec{r}) \cdot \vec{e}_s. \tag{2}$$

For the generation of the magnetic field $\vec{B}_{\mathrm{dip}}$, we apply the 3D coil as represented in Figure 3. It consists of a superposition of three orthogonal coils. For the current application, this source can be represented by a superposition of three magnetic dipoles polarized in the x-, y-, and z-directions, respectively. Clearly, by appropriately weighting the amplitudes (i.e., currents) of the orthogonal three coils, an arbitrary single dipole can be created. Eventually, this will be used to form a single dipole that spatially rotates as a function of time. Figure 2 shows the setup. The source is located at the origin and the sensors are aligned with the chain elements.

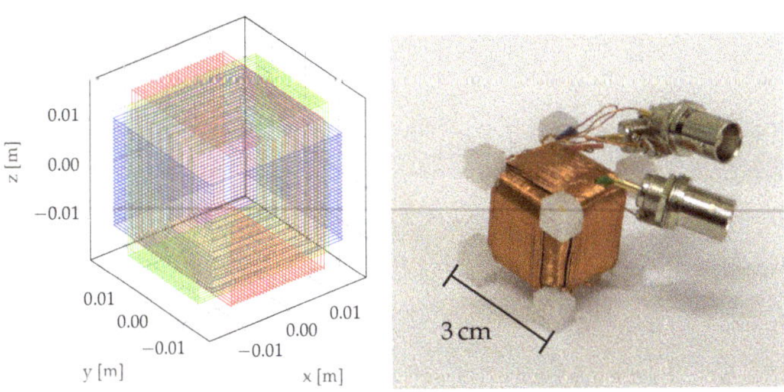

(**a**) Simulation Object (**b**) 3D coil

Figure 3. 3D coil: (**a**) sketches the modelled simulation object. A photograph of the corresponding realization is shown in (**b**). Note that both constructions consist of three orthogonal coils.

2.2. Maximum Vector (MV)

We assume a sensor at an arbitrary position $\vec{r}$ with an arbitrary orientation $\vec{e}_s$ where both values are unknown. A rotating dipole source is located at the origin of the global coordinate system $r = 0$. We define MV $\vec{e}_{max}$ as the orientation of the dipole field $\vec{B}_{dip}$ for which the sensor signal B_{sensor} in Equation (2) becomes a maximum.

We first derive a relationship between the direction of the sensor position $\vec{e}_r$, the sensor orientation $\vec{e}_s$, and the MV $\vec{e}_{max}$. To this end, we first normalize the Equation (1) according to

$$\vec{B}_{norm} = \frac{4\pi r^3}{m}\vec{B}_{dip}(\vec{r}) = 3\vec{e}_r(\vec{e}_m \cdot \vec{e}_r) - \vec{e}_m, \tag{3}$$

where $\vec{m} = m\vec{e}_m$.

Without loss of generality, we next assume that $\vec{e}_r$ and $\vec{e}_s$ lie in the xy-plane. As sketched in Figure 4, for the Cartesian coordinates of $\vec{e}_r$ and $\vec{e}_s$ we have

$$\vec{e}_r = \begin{bmatrix} \cos(\phi) \\ \sin(\phi) \\ 0 \end{bmatrix} \quad \text{and} \quad \vec{e}_s = \begin{bmatrix} \cos(\phi_s) \\ \sin(\phi_s) \\ 0 \end{bmatrix}. \tag{4}$$

The magnetic dipole moment $\vec{m}$ can point in any direction. In spherical coordinates, the Cartesian components of $\vec{e}_m$ read (see Figure 4)

$$\vec{e}_m = \begin{bmatrix} \cos(\phi_m)\sin(\theta_m) \\ \sin(\phi_m)\sin(\theta_m) \\ \cos(\theta_m) \end{bmatrix}. \tag{5}$$

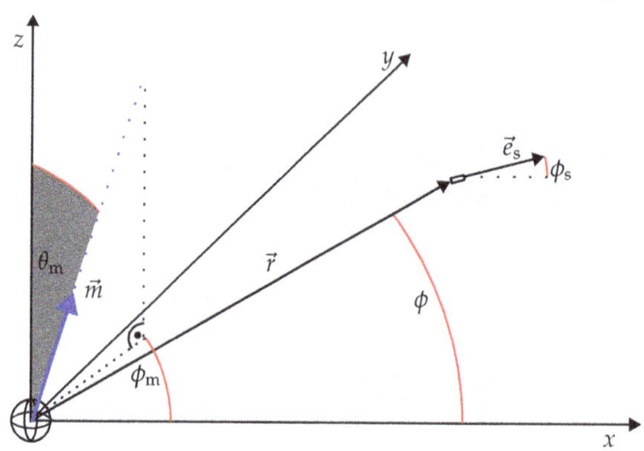

Figure 4. Geometry used for the derivation: $\vec{r}$ and $\vec{e}_s$ both lie in the xy-plane. ϕ_m and θ_m define the orientation of the rotating magnetic dipole $\vec{m}$ in spherical coordinates.

Inserting Equations (4) and (5) into Equation (3) yields the three Cartesian field components of the normalized dipole field:

$$\begin{aligned} B_{norm,x}(\phi, \phi_m, \theta_m) &= \left[3\cos(\phi)^2 - 1\right]\cos(\phi_m)\sin(\theta_m) \\ &+ 3\sin(\phi_m)\sin(\theta_m)\sin(\phi)\cos(\phi), \end{aligned} \tag{6}$$

$$\begin{aligned} B_{norm,y}(\phi, \phi_m, \theta_m) &= \left[3\sin(\phi)^2 - 1\right]\sin(\phi_m)\sin(\theta_m) \\ &+ 3\cos(\phi_m)\sin(\theta_m)\cos(\phi)\sin(\phi), \end{aligned} \tag{7}$$

$$B_{norm,z}(\theta_m) = -\cos(\theta_m). \tag{8}$$

The sensor signal is obtained using Equations (2)–(4) according to

$$B_{\text{sensor}}(\phi, \phi_{\text{s}}, \phi_{\text{m}}, \theta_{\text{m}}, r) = \frac{m}{4\pi r^3}((\cos(\phi_{\text{s}})\, B_{\text{norm,x}}(\phi, \phi_{\text{m}}, \theta_{\text{m}}) + \sin(\phi_{\text{s}})\, B_{\text{norm,y}}(\phi, \phi_{\text{m}}, \theta_{\text{m}})). \quad (9)$$

Obviously, the variation in the distance between the sensor and the rotating dipole affects the measured signal according to $\frac{1}{r^3}$. Regarding the variation in θ_{m}, the measured signal becomes a maximum only if $\theta_m = \pi/2$. Moreover, we remark that the component of the rotating dipole which is perpendicular to the plane spanned by $\vec{e}_{\text{r}}$ and $\vec{e}_{\text{s}}$ has no effect on the measured signal. From these observations we deduce that the MV must also lie in that plane. To find the desired relationship between the three unit vectors, we—without limiting the generality—place the location vector $\vec{r}$ on the x-axis (see the left side of Figure 5). For the Cartesian components of the corresponding unit vectors we thus have:

$$\vec{e}_r = \begin{bmatrix} 1 \\ 0 \end{bmatrix}, \qquad \vec{e}_m = \begin{bmatrix} \cos(\phi_{\text{m}}) \\ \sin(\phi_{\text{m}}) \end{bmatrix}, \qquad \vec{e}_s = \begin{bmatrix} \cos(\phi_{\text{s}}) \\ \sin(\phi_{\text{s}}) \end{bmatrix}. \quad (10)$$

In that case, it holds

$$B_{\text{norm,x}}(\phi) = 2\cos(\phi_{\text{m}}), \quad (11)$$
$$B_{\text{norm,y}}(\phi) = -\sin(\phi_{\text{m}}), \quad (12)$$
$$B_{\text{norm,z}}(\phi) = 0, \quad (13)$$

and Equation (3) simplifies to

$$B_{\text{sensor}}(\phi_{\text{s}}, \phi_{\text{m}}) = \frac{m}{4\pi r^3}(2\cos(\phi_{\text{m}})\cos(\phi_{\text{s}}) - \sin(\phi_{\text{m}})\sin(\phi_{\text{s}})). \quad (14)$$

To derive the angle $\phi_{\text{m}} = \phi_{\text{max}}$ where the right-hand side of Equation (14) becomes a maximum, we calculate

$$\frac{\mathrm{d}B_{\text{sensor}}(\phi_{\text{m}})}{d\phi_{\text{m}}} = \frac{m}{4\pi r^3}(-2\sin(\phi_{\text{m}})\cos(\phi_{\text{s}}) - \sin(\phi_{\text{s}})\cos(\phi_{\text{m}})) \quad (15)$$

$$-2\sin(\phi_{\text{max}})\cos(\phi_{\text{s}}) - \sin(\phi_{\text{s}})\cos(\phi_{\text{max}}) = 0, \quad (16)$$

and finally obtain the relation:

$$-2 \cdot \tan(\phi_{\text{max}}) = \tan(\phi_{\text{s}}). \quad (17)$$

Note that this relation is valid for any ϕ (not just for $\phi = 0$), as sketched in Figure 5.

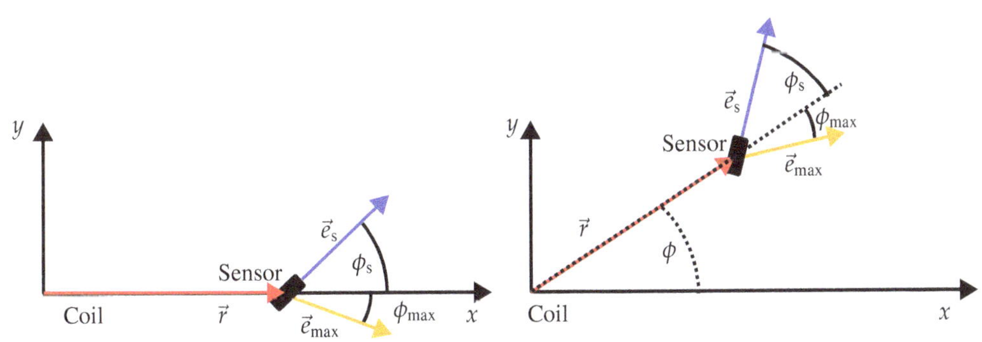

Figure 5. The relation in Equation (17) is independent of the angle ϕ. Moreover, the unique relationship between the three unit vectors $\vec{e}_s, \vec{e}_{max}$, and $\vec{e}_r$ is clarified.

As graphically demonstrated in Figure 5 there is a unique relation between the three unit vectors $\vec{e}_s, \vec{e}_{max}$, and $\vec{e}_r$. This relation will now be used to uniquely derive the sensor orientation $\vec{e}_s$ from a given $\vec{e}_r$ and a measured MV $\vec{e}_{\text{max}}$. As an example, for a systematic procedure we start from a given origin (i.e., the location of the "rotating" 3D coil) and a given sensor location $\vec{r}$.

1. First, we determine the "rotation axis" $\vec{e}_{\text{n}}$:

$$\vec{e}_n = \frac{\vec{e}_{\text{max}} \times \vec{e}_r}{||\vec{e}_{\text{max}} \times \vec{e}_r||}. \tag{18}$$

2. In the second step, the angle between the MV and the location unit vector is calculated:

$$\phi_{\text{max}} = \arccos(\vec{e}_{\text{max}} \cdot \vec{e}_r). \tag{19}$$

3. Subsequently, the angle between the location unit vector and the sensor orientation is determined from Equation (17):

$$\phi_{\text{s}} = \arctan\big(-2\tan(\phi_{\text{max}})\big). \tag{20}$$

4. Finally, for any given $\vec{e}_r$, the sensor orientation $\vec{e}_{\text{s}}$ is calculated by

$$\vec{e}_{\text{s}} = \cos(\phi_{\text{s}})(\vec{e}_n \times \vec{e}_r) \times \vec{e}_n + \sin(\phi_{\text{s}})(\vec{e}_n \times \vec{e}_r). \tag{21}$$

Figure 6 shows the calculated sensor orientations as blue vectors starting at different sensor locations $\vec{r}$ in the xy-plane. The MV is located at the origin and polarized in the y-direction. For the 3D case, i.e., if $\vec{r}$ is an arbitrary vector, we simply have to rotate the blue sensor orientations around the MV.

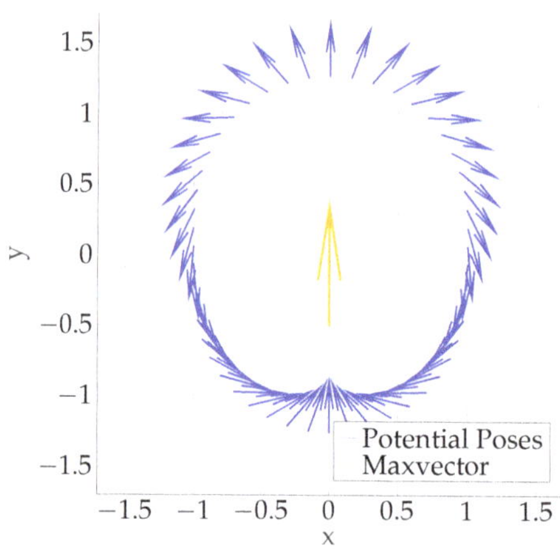

Figure 6. Blue vectors: Calculated sensor orientations $\vec{e}_s$ for different values of the sensor location $\vec{r}$. The starting point of each blue vector represents the corresponding $\vec{r}$. Yellow vector: The maximum vector at the origin, always polarized in the y-direction. Note that the lengths of the blue vectors are not of interest here, as only the directions are relevant.

3. Signal Processing

In this section, it is shown how (temporal) signal processing can be used to extract the required signal feature. Subsequently, an iterative algorithm for pose estimation is presented.

3.1. Feature Extraction

The three orthogonal coils are driven with three different current signals. These currents are chosen such that the absolute value of the dipole moment $|\vec{m}(t)| = m_0$ is constant for all values of t:

$$\vec{m}(t) = m_0 \begin{bmatrix} \cos(\omega_\phi t)\sin(\omega_\theta t) \\ \sin(\omega_\phi t)\sin(\omega_\theta t) \\ \cos(\omega_\theta t) \end{bmatrix}. \tag{22}$$

In particular, for the circle frequencies it holds that $\omega_\theta = N_\omega \omega_\phi$, where N_ω is a positive integer. Thus, the x and y coils are driven by an amplitude-modulated signal while the z coil produces a standard harmonic magnetic signal. Consequently, as a function of time, $\vec{m}$ moves on the surface of a sphere with radius m_0, as exemplary shown for $N_\omega = 10$ in Figure 7.

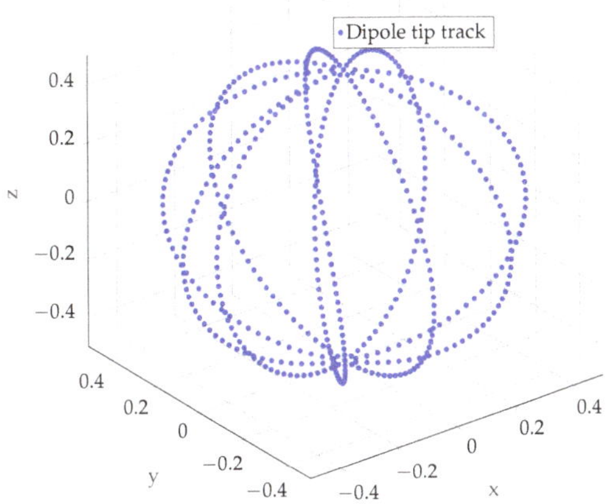

Figure 7. Track of the magnetic dipole $\vec{m}(t)$ with starting point at the origin as a function of time. The tip of $\vec{m}$ moves on the surface a sphere with radius m_0, according to Equation (22) for $N_\omega = \omega_\theta/\omega_\phi = 10$.

While searching for the MV, an obvious method would be to try each direction to detect the maximum field within a given period of time. Instead, we will prove in the following that the directions where no field is measured are orthogonal to the MV. We call such vectors zero-crossing vectors. By detecting two independent zero-crossing vectors, the MV can then be calculated by simply building their ϕ_{max}, we first set Equation (14) (which is valid if $\vec{e}_\text{m}$ and $\vec{e}_\text{s}$ are lying in the xy-plane) for $\phi_\text{m} = \phi_\text{zero}$ to zero:

$$0 = 2\cos(\phi_\text{zero})\cos(\phi_\text{s}) - \sin(\phi_\text{zero})\sin(\phi_\text{s}) \tag{23}$$

$$2\cot(\phi_\text{zero}) = \tan(\phi_\text{s}). \tag{24}$$

With Equation (17) we have

$$\cot(\phi_\text{zero}) = \tan(-\phi_\text{max}) \tag{25}$$

$$\cot\left(\phi_\text{zero}\right) = \cot\left(\frac{\pi}{2} + \phi_\text{max}\right) \tag{26}$$

$$\phi_\text{zero} = \phi_\text{max} \pm \frac{\pi}{2}. \tag{27}$$

Equation (27) proves that the zero-crossing vector and the MV are orthogonal if both are lying in the xy-plane. Since zero-crossing vectors and MVs are orthogonal, we conclude that for the general case the zero-crossing vectors can again be obtained by a rotation around the MV. Figure 8 illustrates an arbitrarily directed MV, the corresponding plane of zero-crossing vectors, and the direction of the sensor.

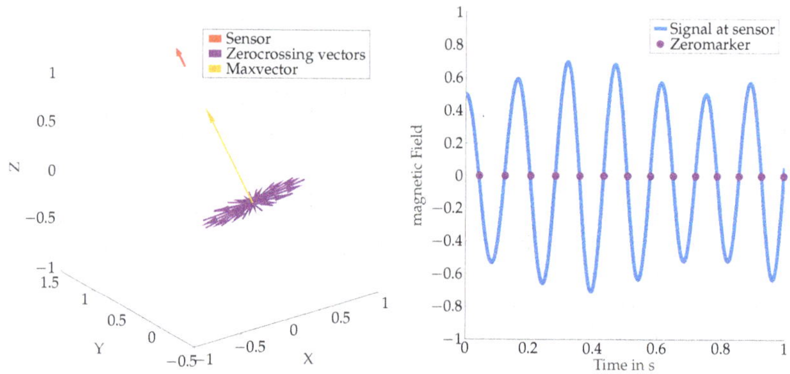

(a) Setup with introduced vectors (b) Simulated signal

Figure 8. The left figure exemplary shows a max vector at the origin (yellow), the position and orientation (orange) of the sensor, and the corresponding plane of zero-crossing vectors (purple). The right side shows the corresponding sensor signal as a function of time. The times when a zero-crossing is achieved are marked with a purple dot. The simulation works with a source which is driven with $N_\omega = \omega_\theta / \omega\phi = 10$. The absolute values/lengths are not relevant, as the relative relationship between the vectors and the zero crossings are both of interest.

3.2. Zero-Crossing Polarity

In the previous section, we showed that the MV is orthogonal to all zero-crossing vectors. Using the cross product, a vector can be determined that is perpendicular to them. There are two solutions to this condition. For example, in the xy-plane the normal vectors are $\vec{e}_z$ and $-\vec{e}_z$. Therefore, it is necessary to observe the polarity here. Each zero-crossing is assigned a polarity that depends on two parameters. The direction of the zero-crossing vector, i.e., from positive to negative (z+) or from negative to positive (z−) and the corresponding z-current I_z. The zero-crossing vectors $\vec{e}_{\text{zero,k}}$ are indexed due to the detection time. Depending on this, the order of the cross product is swapped

$$\vec{e}_{\text{max}} = \begin{cases} \dfrac{\vec{e}_{\text{zero,k}} \times \vec{e}_{\text{zero,k-1}}}{\|\vec{e}_{\text{zero,k}} \times \vec{e}_{\text{zero,k-1}}\|}, & \text{for z+} \wedge \frac{dI_z}{dt} > 0, \text{ or z-} \wedge \frac{dI_z}{dt} < 0 \\ \dfrac{\vec{e}_{\text{zero,k-1}} \times \vec{e}_{\text{zero,k}}}{\|\vec{e}_{\text{zero,k-1}} \times \vec{e}_{\text{zero,k}}\|}, & \text{else.} \end{cases} \quad (28)$$

3.3. Iterative Algorithm

For the proposed algorithm, knowledge of the geometry is required. This includes the relative position of the joint $\vec{r}_\text{j}$ and the distance of the sensor to that joint. The orientation of the sensor is aligned with the second bone. The corresponding setup is sketched in Figure 2. On the condition that the orientation of the sensor is correct, the proposed algorithm is convergent and delivers its position though applying the kinematic chain. Vice versa, the orientation determined for this position again matches the assumed position. To come to an iterative algorithm, we initially assume a random orientation $\vec{e}_{\text{s,i=0}}$, and the kinematic chain model is used to determine a related estimate of the sensor position $\vec{r}_{\text{s,i}}$:

$$\vec{r}_{\text{s},i} = \vec{r}_\text{j} + l_\text{js}\, \vec{e}_{\text{s},i}. \quad (29)$$

From the procedure described in Equations (18)–(21) (Section 2.2), we next determine an update of the sensor orientation $\vec{e}_{s,i+1}$ according to

$$\vec{e}_{s,i+1} = \vec{f}(\hat{r}_{s,i}, \vec{e}_{max}). \tag{30}$$

This process is iteratively repeated until convergence is achieved. The number of iterations needed for this goal depends on the ratio between l_{js} and $|\vec{r}_j|$. The algorithm is represented as a flow chart in Figure 9. Figure 10 shows an example for the corresponding iterative progress. Based on the orientation of the previous chain element, we calculate the position of the next joint. Thus, the true alignment of the kinematic chain is found after a suitable number of repetitions of this systematic procedure.

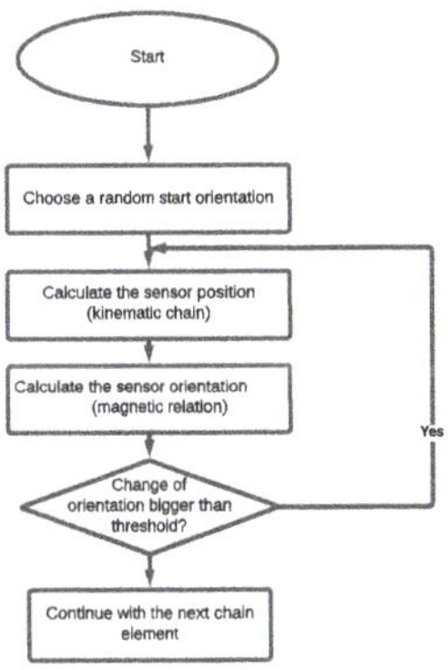

Figure 9. Flow chart of the iterative algorithm: The algorithm starts with a random initial orientation. Then, the sensor position relative to the source is determined. Afterwards, the corresponding orientation is calculated. When there is no relevant change between the data obtained with two subsequent iterations, convergence is reached, and this orientation is the estimated result.

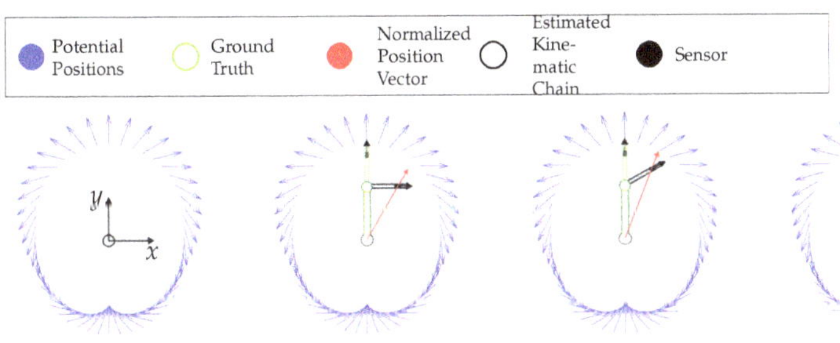

(**a**) Setup (**b**) Iteration 1 (**c**) Iteration 2 (**d**) Iteration 15

Figure 10. Exemplary iterative process: This figure shows the iterations for a simple setup. The first sub-figure shows the used setup with the coordinate system. The origin of this setup is located at the first kinematic chain element, where the source is also located. The source is attached to the first kinematic element in such a way that the relative position of the source to the kinematic chain is always constant. In the following figures, the coordinate system has been omitted. The blue vectors represent the potential poses for the detected MV. The light green construction shows the ground truth. The red vector is a normalized position vector of the sensor which points to the potential pose in this direction. The sensor is mounted on the second bone. It is represented by a black rectangle with a vector in the sensitive direction. Subfigure (**b**) starts with a bone orientation in x-direction. For some iterations, the kinematic chain and the related position vector are shown. After 15 iterations, subfigure (**d**), the sensor pose matches a potential pose (ground truth) and the algorithm converges.

The convergence speed of the algorithm depends on the ratio Q of the length from the actuator point to the joint l_{aj} and the length from this joint to the sensor l_{js}:

$$Q = \frac{l_{js}}{l_{aj}}. \tag{31}$$

Figure 11 shows the amount of the absolute angular error as a function of the number of iterations for each Q. The true sensor orientation is assumed to be in the z-direction. The initial sensor orientation is always assumed to be in the y-direction, i.e., the corresponding angular error starts at 90°.

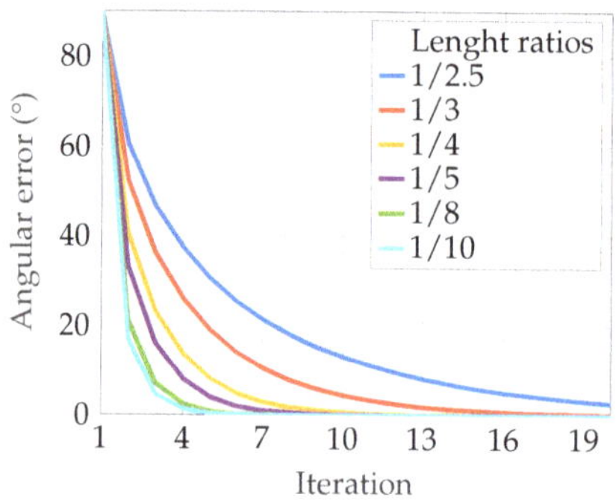

Figure 11. Angular error in dependence of the iteration: The figure shows the behaviour of the angular error in dependence of the number of iteration. Different setups of length ratios are looked at. The legend shows the corresponding Q for each curve. All curves tend closer to zero with each iteration.

3.4. Uniqueness

In this section, we will show that the procedure described above delivers a unique result if the Q as defined in Equation (31) is **not** between 0.5 and 1. For a proof, we refer to Figure 5 and note that the orientation $\vec{e}_s$ has two components, i.e., two scalar degrees of freedom. The input of the algorithm has also two scalar given variables, which leads to a problem with two given variables and two unknowns. To solve this, we first split the two-dimensional solution vector and show that each can be calculated independently. As previously shown, $\vec{e}_{max}$, $\vec{e}_r$, and $\vec{e}_s$ lie in one plane. From the sensor position, the joint position can be obtained by the vector addition of $\vec{e}_s$ scaled by the known length l_{js}. This relationship shows that the joint position must also lie in the plane already shown. This allows the detected $\vec{e}_{max}$ to be used to determine a plane in which the solution vector lies. This reduces the number of unknowns to 1 and the first degree of freedom can thus be determined unambiguously. In the previous derivation, the relative relationship between $\vec{e}_r$, $\vec{e}_s$, and $\vec{e}_{max}$ was shown. In order to show that a unique $\vec{e}_s$ can be assigned to each $\vec{e}_{max}$, a reference point must be selected. The angle ($\phi_{max,j}$) is defined as between $\vec{e}_{max}$ and the position vector of the joint $\vec{r}_j$ and the angle ($\phi_{s,j}$) is defined as being between $\vec{e}_s$ and $\vec{r}_j$. These angles are shown in Figure 12.

We set the coordinate system such that $\vec{e}_r$, $\vec{e}_s$ and $\vec{e}_{max}$ lie in the xy-plane. Furthermore, without limiting the generalization of the solution we assume that $\vec{r}_j$ lies on the y-axis. The position of the joint and the sensor can thus be described as follows:

$$\vec{r}_j = \begin{bmatrix} 0 \\ l_{aj} \end{bmatrix} \tag{32}$$

$$\vec{r}_s = \begin{bmatrix} l_{js}\cos(\phi_{s,j}) \\ l_{aj} + l_{js}\sin(\phi_{s,j}) \end{bmatrix} \tag{33}$$

Now, the angle ϕ_r between $\vec{r}_j$, $\vec{r}_s$ can be determined as

$$\phi_r = \arctan\left(\frac{l_{js}\cos(\phi_{s,j})}{l_{aj} + l_{js}\sin(\phi_{s,j})}\right) \tag{34}$$

These descriptions can now be used to determine ϕ_{max} according to Equation (17):

$$\phi_{max} = -\arctan\left(\frac{1}{2}\tan(\phi_s - \phi_{rs}\right) \tag{35}$$

This angle is now related to the position vector of the sensor. The $\phi_{max,j}$ can be described as follows:

$$\phi_{max,j} = \phi_{max} - \phi_r \tag{36}$$

The obtained formulas reveal the analytical relationship $\phi_{max,j}(\phi_{s,j})$. For the uniqueness of the solution, the inverse function is required. Since this is not a trivial task, a lookup table has been created while the axes are swapped. Figure 13 shows the results obtained for different values of Q.

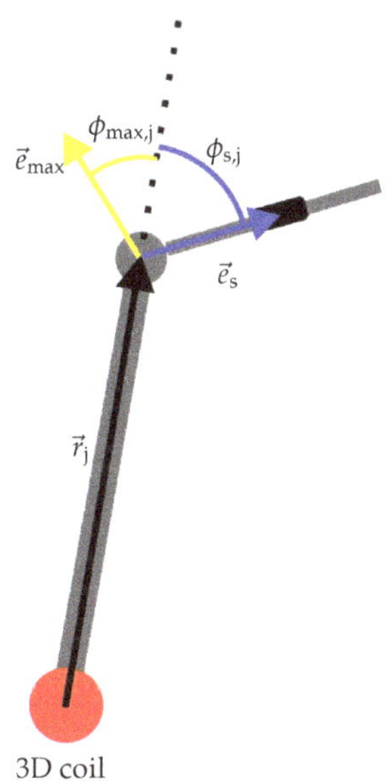

Figure 12. Definition of the angles at a joint between two bones.

Obviously, there is a unique solution only for a certain range of Q. For $Q = 1$, i.e., where the non-uniqueness is most significant, a simulation including a measurement of the convergence speed was carried out, see Figure 14. We observe that the maximum error does not approach zero, but oscillates periodically and is undamped around zero.

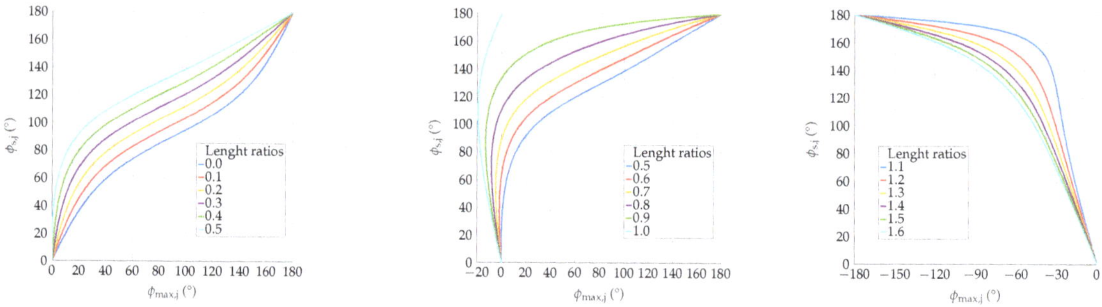

(**a**) $0 < Q <= 0.5$ (**b**) $0.5 < Q <= 1$ (**c**) $1 < Q$

Figure 13. The relation between $\phi_{s,j}$ and $\phi_{max,j}$ is represented for different values of Q. The plots are subdivided for different values of Q. In the ranges $0 < Q < 0.5$ and $Q > 1$ there is a clear assignment, i.e., there is a unique bidirectional relation between $\phi_{max,j}$ and $\phi_{s,j}$. However, between 0.5 and 1 we observe a non-unique relation.

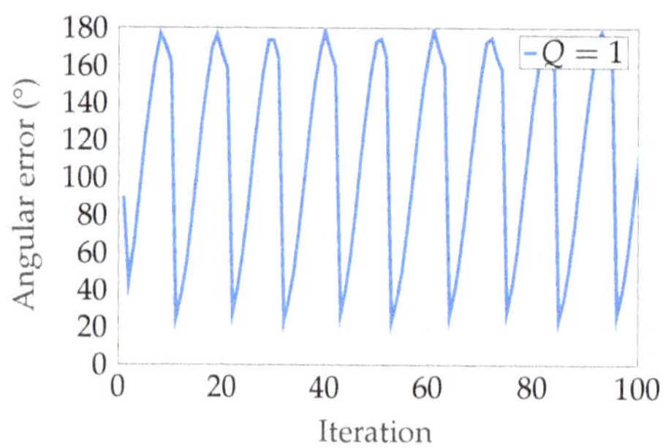

Figure 14. For $Q = 1$, the maximum angular error does not approach zero even after several iterations, i.e., the algorithm is non-convergent.

4. Results

4.1. Simulation Results

For validation, the proposed iterative algorithm was numerically implemented and the motion of a single joint was observed. To that end, an existing real-time framework based on C was applied [22]. An overview of the used modules is shown in Figure 15. A complete description of the implementation can be found in [23].

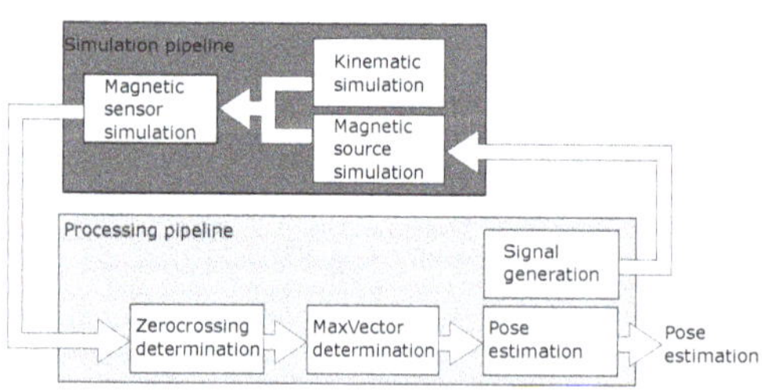

Figure 15. Simulation overview: The simulation is divided in two sections. The upper (dark) part simulates the motion and the resulting field at the sensor. In the lower part (bright), the described algorithm is implemented and the pose is calculated.

As an example, a magnetic source is attached at the beginning of a first bone of 40 cm length. The sensor is attached to the second bone at a distance of 10 cm to the joint. To not repeat the simulation without movement that has already been discussed in Section 3.3, a simple movement in the xz-plane was performed: The second bone rotates in the xz-plane around the y-axis in a range from 90° to -90° with a constant angular frequency 1 Hz. As illustrated in Figure 16, the 3D coil (source) is localized in the origin at the end of the first bone with equivalent magnetic dipoles at frequencies $\omega_\phi = 7\,\text{Hz}$ and $\omega_\theta = 7000\,\text{Hz}$.

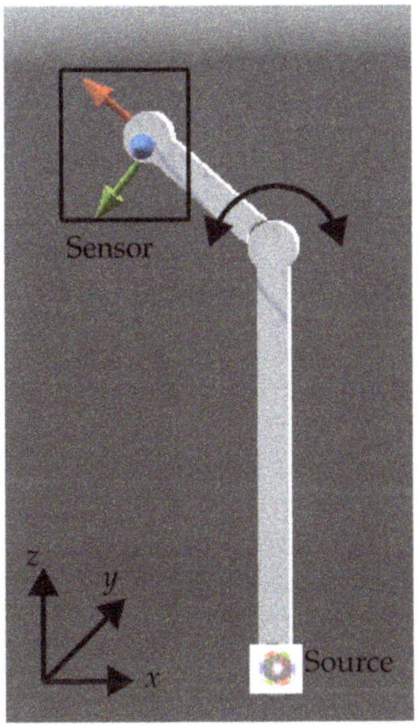

Figure 16. Simulation of a motion: All elements are in the yz-plane. The 3D coil source is located in the origin. The first bone is aligned with the z-axis and its end represents the position of the joint. The second bone moves from 90° to -90° with respect to the axis of the first bone.

The results of the simulations are shown in Figure 17a. The ground-truth angle between the second element and the z-axis is shown for comparison with the estimated angle. For better visibility of both signals, the estimation is shifted by 10°. The absolute error of the amplitude which plotted in Figure 17b, is for most time steps in the range $< 1^\circ$.

(a) Estimated angles vs. simulated angles

(b) Error signal

Figure 17. (**a**) shows both the estimated angle and the simulated one. The dark red line represents the simulation (ground truth) while the light red line is the estimation of the described algorithm. The latter is shifted 10° to enhance the clarity of the visualization. In (**b**), the difference between the simulation and the estimation is plotted. We observe an error signal which follows the angle of the movement.

4.2. Experimental Results

For an initial laboratory test, a prototype consisting of two kinematic elements made of PVC was fabricated (see Figure 18). The two elements are connected by a screw, allowing one degree of freedom. A 3D coil is attached at the beginning of the longer element while a fluxgate magnetometer is attached to the shorter element. Firstly, tests were carried out with a static setup, i.e., the prototype was held in a fixed position using suitable wedges which was attached to the table and the prototype with double-sided adhesive tape.

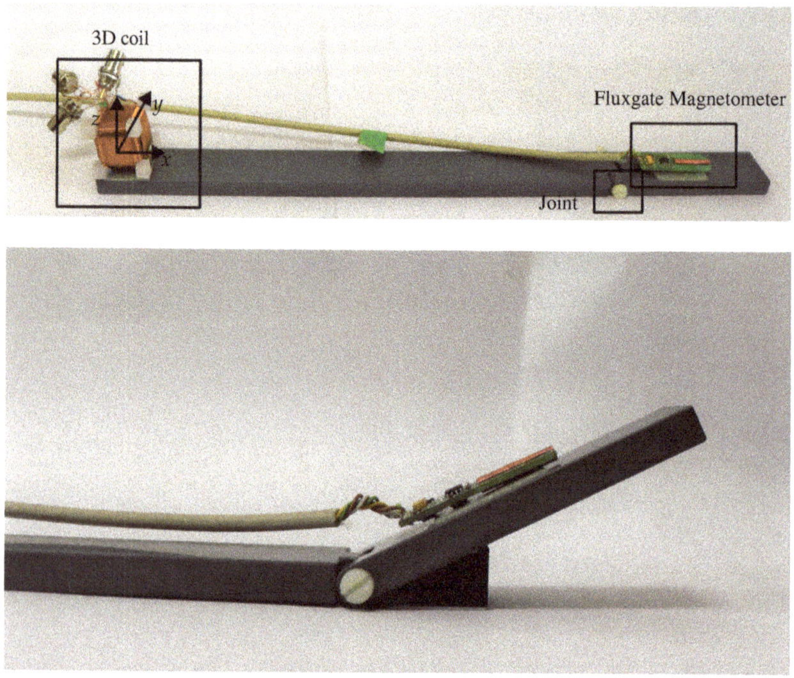

Figure 18. Upper figure: The built prototype consists of two PVC elements, connected to each other with a screw allowing for one degree of freedom. The 3D coil source is located at one end of the longer element. On the shorter element, a fluxgate magnetometer [24] is mounted. The illustration in the lower figure shows the assembly for a 30° position.

We have used seven equidistant angles between 0° and 90° degrees. The same software used for the simulation has been applied for data acquisition and signal processing. A series of 10 s measurements was recorded for each position, and a new angle estimate was calculated every 20 ms. Hence, after 10 s we obtained 500 angle estimations represented in Figure 19.

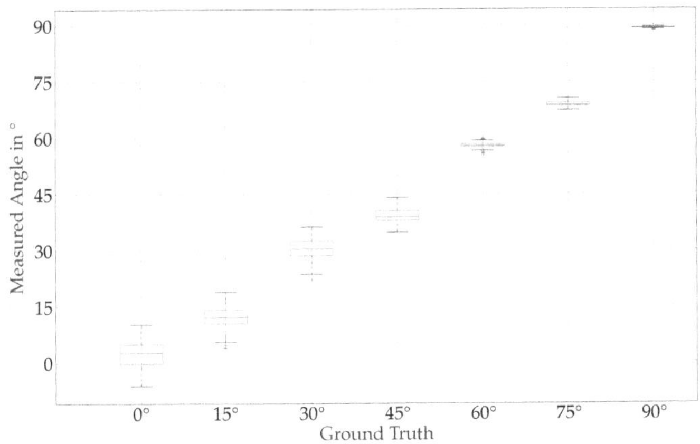

Figure 19. The boxplots show the experimental results of the measured sensor angles for each of the seven given (ground-truth) joint angles. The box plots show the median, the first quartile, the third quartile, the minimum, the maximum, and several outliers for each joint angle.

4.3. Computational Cost

Determining the computational effort of an algorithm is not trivial when using libraries, as the implementation of the functions is not disclosed. Therefore, the mathematical operations used were given a score depending on their complexity. The score was determined by performing the corresponding operation one million times and normalizing it to the ADD operation. This should make it possible to compare the results with other algorithms. All operations are implemented in C with the "math.h" library.

Table 1 shows the calculation effort for the used mathematical operations. One iteration of the presented algorithm has an average equivalent of 212 addition operations. All operations were performed on an AMD Ryzen 5 5600X 6-Core processor.

Table 1. Time consumption of different complex operations for one million executions, normalized to the (basic) addition operation.

Operation	Time Consumption/µs	Score
ADD/SUB	940	1
MULT/DIV	960	1.02
SIN/COS/TAN	4970	5.29
ARCCOS/ARCSIN/ARCTAN	68,000	72.34
SQUARE ROOT	3250	3.46
CROSS PRODUCT	3700	3.94
SCALAR PRODUCT	2200	2.34
Algorithm 1 Iteration	199,280	212.08

5. Discussion

5.1. Convergence and Uniqueness

The convergence of the algorithm depends on the length ratio Q, i.e., the ratio of the distance between the actuator and the joint l_{aj} and the distance between the joint and the sensor location l_{js}. It has been shown that the algorithm uniquely converges unless Q is between 0.5 and 1. Moreover, the number of iterations required for a given error threshold increases as Q increases. As illustrated in Figure 20, such behaviour sounds logical. For a fixed length of the first bone, the permissible angular range δ is limited by the length of the second one.

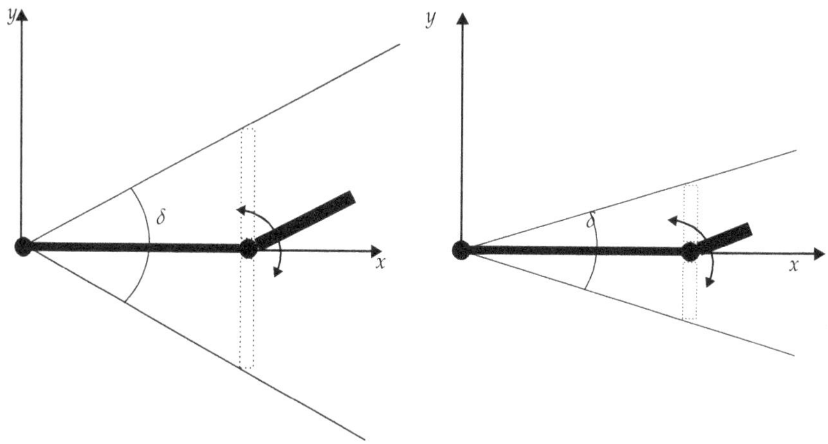

Figure 20. Possible angle ranges δ for two different lengths of the second bone at a fixed length of the first bone (Q is higher for the left realization).

Regarding uniqueness, the role of Q may well lead to problems in a possible subsequent application, where care must be taken when designing and positioning the sensors and sources to ensure that the possible Q is not between 0.5 and 1.

5.2. Results

The algorithm was implemented in an existing real-time framework. A periodic movement was implemented using a simulation pipeline. The simulations have shown that for an unmoved kinematic chain, the estimate agrees with the simulated posture. Subsequently, a periodic movement with a frequency of 1 Hz was performed. The movement showed an error of approximately 1 degree. Outside the simulation, a larger deviation is to be expected. Due to the dipole approximation, small deviations occur in the modelling. In addition, noise was not used in the first investigations. This would not interfere with the algorithm but would worsen the result. Inaccuracies caused by noise may be improved or corrected by averaging the input signal. First experimental results indicate that the algorithm works in practice. It has been observed that the averaged values each have an offset to the true values. These deviations can be explained by the fact that there are model properties that have not yet been taken into account. For example, the algorithm assumes that the sensor is located exactly in the centre of the kinematic element. In this case, the sensor would move on a circular path. However, as the sensor cannot be located in the centre in reality, it tends to move along an elliptical curve. This leads to an error depending on the angle. The dipole approach leads to further errors. The closer the sensor is to the source, the worse the approximation becomes. In [25], it was shown that the deviation from the dipole approximation at a distance of 20 times the radius of the source is only 0.0027%. This is the case in our setup. If the algorithm is used in a setup where the distance cannot be kept large enough, approaches as in [26] can be used. The variance of the measurement series differs greatly. Particularly, it is unclear why the variance becomes smaller and smaller as the sensor angle increases. The signal quality was almost the same in all measurement series, so at first glance a similar variance could actually be assumed for each setup. However, the transfer function from the MV to the sensor projection is non-linear, which would explain a stronger fluctuation in the 0° range.

5.3. Computational Effort and Timings

For a motion capture system, the sample rate at which positions are captured is of particular importance. Therefore, a high sample rate is needed for fast movements. In human–machine interface applications, a low latency in the range of 15 ms is required. If the latency increases, surgery becomes more difficult for the user. To be able to guarantee such a maximum latency, the required computing time must be kept as low as possible. For this analysis, the implemented code was divided into each weighted individual operations. A computing time of 3 μs per joint and 60 μs for a kinematic construct consisting of a hand with up to 20 joints was determined. During the investigation, we have used a number of 15 iterations showing good results for the most setups. In a real application, this number could be even reduced. Because of the limited moving speed of each kinematic chain element, it is possible to use a well-fitting initial orientation. Especially for slow motions, this would reduce the number of needed iterations. Note that the investigation shows only a theoretically possible calculation time. In a real setup, there will be optimizations to the signal processing pipeline, primarily consisting of pre-processing and feature extraction. These additional parts will further increase the computational effort. Such promising results and ideas for finding optimal conditions lead to the outcome that the theoretically maximal latency can also be observed in a real application. Moreover, note that so far the implementation has been performed without any computational parallelization. As an example, the hand consists of several kinematic chains that can move independently of each other. A multi-threading implementation would thus be a further step to increase the efficiency and decrease latencies.

6. Conclusion and Outlook

This work has dealt with a new algorithm for motion tracking. To this end, we have introduced spatially rotating magnetic dipole sources. In this context, the maximum vector (MV) has been introduced as a new signal feature, and the spatial relationship between the MV, the sensor position, and its orientation were investigated. The correlations were linked to the model of a kinematic chain, such that this self-consistency was exploited and a computationally efficient algorithm was developed. The algorithm was implemented and validated in a real-time signal processing code. The performance was evaluated in terms of the accuracy of the results and the required computational effort. It was shown that the presented algorithm is very efficient in determining the posture of a kinematic chain. The theoretical functionality of the algorithm has already been demonstrated by simulation and with the realization of a first demonstrator. These were initially very simple movements with only one degree of freedom. More complex movements of real people are planned for a later stage of research. The behaviour of the algorithm in the presence of magnetic interference or in the event of a sensor failure has not yet been investigated and will be addressed in the future.

The algorithm currently uses a strong simplification of a kinematic chain. In addition, the modelling must take into account further parameters such as the thickness, the precise position of the sensor on the element and a potential tilting of the sensor. A consideration of more details would increase the number of model parameters, and an automatic/semi-automatic calibration procedure should be developed to keep it manageable. Moreover, an additional automated distance measure could be beneficially for the stability of the outcomes. Finally, as a 3D coil generates a signal that provides three independent pieces of information and in the current implementation only two phases of information have been used, from the absolute signal value, more distance information can be obtained. This could be integrated with a Kalman filter approach as in [27] and/or correct a parameter of the model during runtime so that the error can be minimized.

7. Patents

The content of this paper was used for a patent application. It was granted by the German Patent Office with the patent number DE 10 2023 119 167.

Author Contributions: Conceptualization, T.S., L.K. and G.S.; methodology, T.S.; software, T.S.; validation, T.S.; formal analysis, T.S.; investigation, T.S.; resources, T.S., J.H. and M.B.; data curation, T.S.; writing—original draft preparation, T.S.; writing—review and editing, T.S., J.H., M.B., R.B., L.K. and G.S.; visualization, T.S. and G.S.; supervision, R.B., L.K. and G.S.; project administration, L.K. and G.S.; funding acquisition, L.K. and G.S. All authors have read and agreed to the published version of the manuscript.

Funding: This research received no external funding.

Institutional Review Board Statement: Not applicable.

Informed Consent Statement: Not applicable.

Data Availability Statement: The data presented in this study are available on request from the corresponding author.

Conflicts of Interest: The authors declare no conflict of interest.

References

1. Minh, V.T.; Katushin, N.; Pumwa, J. Motion tracking glove for augmented reality andvirtual reality. *J. Behav. Robot.* **2019**, *10*, 160–166. [CrossRef]
2. Mirelman, A.; Bernad-Elazari, H.; Thaler, A.; Giladi-Yacobi, E.; Gurevich, T.; Gana-Weisz, M.; Saunders-Pullman, R.; Raymond, D.; Doan, N.; Bressman, S.B.; et al. Arm swing as a potential new prodromal marker of Parkinson's disease. *Mov. Disord.* **2016**, *31*, 1527–1534. [CrossRef] [PubMed]
3. Qualisys, A.B. Technical Specifications OMC System. Available online: https://www.qualisys.com/cameras/miqus/#tech-specs (accessed on 9 October 2024)
4. Dipietro, L.; Sabatini, A.; Dario, P. A Survey of Glove-Based Systems and Their Applications. *IEEE Trans. Syst. Man. Cybern. Part (Appl. Rev.)* **2008**, *38*, 461–482. [CrossRef]
5. Roetenberg, D.; Luinge, H.; Slycke, P. Xsens MVN: Full 6DOF Human Motion Tracking Using Miniature Inertial Sensors. *Xsens Motion Technol. BV Tech. Rep.* **2009**, *1*, 1–7.
6. Santoni, F.; De Angelis, A.; Moschitta, A.; Carbone, P. MagIK: A Hand-Tracking Magnetic Positioning System Based on a Kinematic Model of the Hand. *IEEE Trans. Instrum. Meas.* **2021**, *70*, 9507313. [CrossRef]
7. Ma, Y.; Mao, Z.; Jia, W.; Li, C.; Yang, J.; Sun, M. Magnetic Hand Tracking for Human-Computer Interface. *IEEE Trans. Magn.* **2011**, *47*, 970–973. [CrossRef]
8. Elbamby, M.S.; Perfecto, C.; Bennis, M.; Doppler, K. Toward low-latency and ultrareliable virtual reality. *IEEE Netw.* **2018**, *32*, 78–84. [CrossRef]
9. Maier, M.; Chowdhury, M.; Rimal, B.P.; Van, D.P. The Tactile Internet: Vision, Recent Progress, and Open Challenges. *IEEE Commun. Mag.* **2016**, *54*, 138–145. [CrossRef]
10. Plotkin, A.; Paperno, E. 3-D Magnetic Tracking of a Single Subminiature Coil with a Large 2-D Array of Uniaxial Transmittes. *IEEE Trans. Magn.* **2003**, *39*, 3295–3297. [CrossRef]
11. Ran, X.; Qiu, W.; Hu, H. Magnetic Dipole Target Localization Using Improved Salp Swarm Algorithm. In Proceedings of the 42nd Chinese Control Conference (CCC), Tianjin, China, 24–26 July 2023 ; pp. 3372–3377.
12. Zeising, S.; Thalmayer, A.; Fischer, G.; Kirchner, J. Toward Magnetic Localization of Capsule Endoscopes during Daily Life Activities. In Proceedings of the 2021 Kleinheubach Conference, Miltengerg, Germany, 28–30 September 2021; pp. 1–4.
13. Shen, H.-M.; Ge, D.; Lian, C.; Yue, Y. Real-Time Passive Magnetic Localization Based on Restricted Kinematic Property for Tongue-Computer-Interface. In Proceedings of the 2019 IEEE/ASME International Conference on Advanced Intelligent Mechatronics Hong Kong, China, 8–12 July 2019.
14. Paperno, E.; Sasada, I.; Leonovich, E. A new method for magnetic position and orientation tracking. *IEEE Trans. Magn.* **2001**, *37*, 1938–1940. [CrossRef]
15. Raab, F.; Blood, E.; Steiner, T.; Jones, H. Magnetic Position and Orientation Tracking System. *IEEE Trans. Aerosp. Electron. Syst.* **1979**, *AES-15*, 709–718. [CrossRef]
16. Paperno, E.; Keisar, P. Three-Dimensional Magnetic Tracking of Biaxial Sensors. *IEEE Trans. Magn.* **2004**, *40*, 1530–1536. [CrossRef]
17. Nara, T.; Suzuki, S.; Ando, S. A closed-form formula for magnetic dipole localization by measurement of its magnetic field and spatial gradients. *IEEE Trans. Magn.* **2006**, *42*, 3291–3293. [CrossRef]
18. Fan, L.; Kang, X.; Zheng, Q.; Zhang, X.; Liu, X.; Chen, C.; Kang, C. A Fast Linear Algorithm for Magnetic Dipole Localization Using Total Magnetic Field Gradient. *IEEE Sensors J.* **2018**, *18*, 1032–1038. [CrossRef]
19. Fischer, C.; Quirin, T.; Chautems, C.; Boehler, Q.; Pascal, J.; Nelson, B.J. Gradiometer-Based Magnetic Localization for Medical Tolls. *IEEE Trans. Magn.* **2023**, *59*, 2. [CrossRef]
20. Sharma, S.; Ding, G.; Aghlmand, F.; Talkhooncheh, A.; Shapiro, M.; Emami, A. Wireless 3D Surgical Navigation and Tracking System with 100 μm Accuracy Using Magnetic-Field Gradient-Based Localization. *IEEE Trans. Med. Imaging* **2021**, *40*, 2066–2079. [CrossRef] [PubMed]

21. Bao, J.; Hu, C.; Lin, W.; Wang, W. On the magnetic field of a current coil and its localization. In Proceedings of the IEEE International Conference on Automation and Logistics, Zhengzhou, China, 15–17 August 2012; pp. 573–577.
22. Chair for Digital Signal Processing and System Theory. Real-Time Framework. Available online: https://dss-kiel.de/index.php/research/realtime-framework (accessed on 9 October 2024).
23. Hoffmann, J.; Bald, C.; Schmidt, T.; Boueke, M.; Engelhardt, E.; Krüger, K.; Elzenheimer, E.; Hansen, C.; Maetzler, W.; Schmidt, G. Designing and Validating Magnetic Motion Sensing Approaches with a Real-time Simulation Pipeline. *Curr. Dir. Biomed. Eng.* **2023**, *9*, 455–458. [CrossRef]
24. Stefan Mayer Instruments GmbH Co. KG. Miniatur Fluxgate FLC100. Available online: https://stefan-mayer.com/de/produkte/magnetometer-und-sensoren/magnetfeldsensor-flc-100.html (accessed on 9 October 2024).
25. Paperno, E.; Plotkin, A. Cylindrical induction coil to accurately imitate the ideal magnetic dipole. *Sens. Actuators Phys.* **2004**, *112*, 248–252. [CrossRef]
26. Ren, Y.; Hu, C.; Xiang, S.; Feng, Z. Magnetic Dipole Model in the Near-field. In Proceedings of the 2015 IEEE International Conference on Information and Automation, Lijiang, China, 8–10 August 2015.
27. Boueke, M.; Hoffmann, J.; Schmidt, T.; Bald, C.; Bergholz, R.; Schmidt, G. Model-based Tracking of Magnetic Sensor Gloves in Real Time. *Curr. Dir. Biomed. Eng.* **2023**, *9*, 85–88. [CrossRef]

MDPI AG
Grosspeteranlage 5
4052 Basel
Switzerland
Tel.: +41 61 683 77 34

Sensors Editorial Office
E-mail: sensors@mdpi.com
www.mdpi.com/journal/sensors

www.ingramcontent.com/pod-product-compliance
Lightning Source LLC
Chambersburg PA
CBHW041018270926
51850CB00024B/1510
9783725870721